THE WORLD ENCYCLOPEDIA OF
SUBMARINES

THE WORLD ENCYCLOPEDIA OF
SUBMARINES

A complete history of over 150 underwater vessels from the
***Hunley* and *Nautilus* to today's nuclear-powered submarines**

JOHN PARKER WITH FRANCIS CROSBY

LORENZ BOOKS

Contents

Introduction

Military forces across the world witnessed some amazing
developments throughout the 20th century, with each turn
of events scaling up the power, death and destruction they
could inflict to previously unimagined levels. Among them,
the men of the Submarine Service must surely stand apart in
that, when all was said and done, through two World Wars
and the deadly brinkmanship of the Cold War that could have
led to Armageddon, they ended that century with the future of
humankind literally in their hands.

TOP AND ABOVE: **The progression of submarine development is perhaps
no better demonstrated by the size comparison of the world's largest
submarine, the Russian Typhoon class** (TOP), **crewed by 160 men and
having a submerged weight of 48,000 tonnes/47,240 tons, and the first
American** *Holland* (ABOVE), **which was a mere 72.83 tonnes/71.7 tons
submerged and was crowded with a full crew of nine.**

This is no overstatement. From virtually a standing start
at the beginning of the 20th century, submarines were rapidly
developed through the patience and ingenuity of a handful of
dedicated engineers and designers who were often financially
challenged, receiving little support from naval chiefs and
governments. Within just a few decades of rapid progress,
the so-called Silent Service became the new Navy and Masters
of the Sea, culminating in an exceedingly volatile head-to-
head nuclear armament. The extent of that progression is
perhaps best illustrated by the size factor. In 1900, America's
first submarine, the Holland, had a submerged weight of 76
tonnes/75 tons, carried two tiny torpedoes and a crew of nine,
whereas the Russian Typhoon SSBN of the 1990s weighed in
at 48,000 tonnes/ 47,240 long tons submerged, was crewed by
160 and carried 20 nation-obliterating ballistic missiles.

As the end of the 20th century came into view, the giant
boats of the opposing forces, collectively carrying more
explosive power than was unleashed in both World Wars up
to and including Hiroshima, were operating in close proximity

along the flashpoint sea lanes of the Cold War. It was fortunate
for humankind that no Hitler or Stalin was around to press
the button to unleash a nuclear holocaust, although the Cuban
missile crisis of October 1962 presented great danger. That
alone did not stop the superpowers in the continuation of their
quest for domination in undersea warfare, and it remains as
high a priority as ever.

Indeed, while the beginning of the 21st century marked a
hundred years of incredible advances in submarine warfare,
it also saw the initiation of a new era of multi-billion-dollar
boats. These carry the mission forward into the next level of
submarine capability, now coupled with a more diverse range
of firepower to provide an effective and flexible response to
the new emerging threats to national interests and the general
population. The newest submarines will include technological
innovations that will further enhance the advent of the true
submarine, realizing the vision of Jules Verne, described in his
novel *Twenty Thousand Leagues under the Sea*, as well as the
ambitions of so many dedicated inventors, past and present.

LEFT: The mighty power of the ballistic missile-carrying submarines at the height of the Cold War is clearly evident from the open tubes of the American Polaris boat, USS *Sam Rayburn*. ABOVE: Despite their post-war pacifist policy, Japan maintained a small fleet of interesting boats, including this Yushio class of teardrop design introduced in 1975, although they steered clear of the nuclear-powered ambitions of other nations. BELOW LEFT: From the same era came the multi-faceted range of America's hunter-killer submarines, predominantly led by USS *Los Angeles*, the first of 67 that carried her class name over the two decades after her arrival in 1976. BELOW: The British contribution to the world power-play of SSNs included the Trafalgar-class boats which became the workhorses of the British fleet, and remained so as late as 2001, when one of the class fired Tomahawk cruise missiles into Afghanistan.

The journey towards unlimited submersibility through the introduction of nuclear propulsion has been just one part – albeit the most vital – of the multi-layered and international saga of the submarine, often spurred by war and the quest for superiority, but generally advanced by building upon the dreams, ideas and inventions of a relatively small number of men of various nationalities.

The range and diversity of boats that emerged during more than a hundred years of submarine development stands as a historical tribute to those who designed, built and served on them. Furthermore, the motives and ambitions of the nations that eventually realized the potential of undersea warfare were equally varied, as demonstrated by the fact that some of the later exponents of submarine warfare, such as Britain, were initially reluctant to participate in the building of a submarine force. It is this story, regardless of the political connotations, that builds into the dramatic narrative presented in the following pages.

There are three sections in this book, the first of which records some of the most important developments, plus major conflicts and incidents, in a complete history of submarines. This is followed by technical examinations in two directory sections, the first of which covers boats built prior to the end of World War II, the second covering submarines from 1945 to the present day. Specifications, performance and armament of each boat is considered in turn.

It is also worth remembering that, although the superpowers have dominated the development of the nuclear submarine, almost all countries with sea borders do have their own submarine force, albeit largely of the diesel variety. They represent what might be viewed as the second level of a voluminous international submarine network, which is as active as ever, if substantially scaled down from the levels of earlier years when great submersible forces were built for two World Wars and, in between, general defensive operations. The past and current stock of most of these nations is also discussed in the book.

The History of Submarines

Submariners will say that, notwithstanding the risks, there is a certain romanticism connected with submarines. After years of trial, error and often fatal attraction, a handful of men emerged in the late 1800s who were clearly making progress towards the realization of the dream, often in the face of adversity and controversy. Traditionalists among the naval hierarchies of several nations – including Britain – fought a bitter struggle to have the submarine banned, but gradually the experimental vessels produced by men such as J.P. Holland and Simon Lake began to show remarkable promise, in spite of the volatile nature and foul conditions inside the boats.

Winston Churchill described submarine development as the most dangerous of all occupations: "Of all the branches of men in the forces there is none which shows more devotion and faces grimmer perils than the submariners." Yet emerging submarine services of nations around the world never lacked volunteers. Indeed, as will be seen, this book tells a very human story, highlighting some of the outstanding events from the very early days to the present, with many tales of courage, drama and quite astounding invention.

LEFT: **In the line of fire: the assassination of Archduke Franz Ferdinand of Austria sent that nation's U-boats, along with those of Germany, into the first major conflict involving submarines, depicted here against a French merchant ship.**

LEFT: **The Confederates'** *Hunley*, **which sank four times during trials, twice killing all her crew. She was raised each time and sent back into commission, and on her fifth voyage torpedoed and sank the Union warship** *Housatonic* **off South Carolina, but in doing so went to the bottom with her victim.** BELOW: **David Bushnell's** *Turtle* **which moved perfectly and with amazing accuracy but failed in its attempts to attach a mine to British ships in New York harbour in 1776. He had more success with his "drifting" mines which harassed the British fleet.**

Trial and error: the pioneers

Through the ages, inventors and sailors alike sought to find the technology that would allow the construction of boats that could travel under water. Since Alexander the Great was lowered to the bottom of the sea in a glass barrel in 337BC, attempts at such endeavour failed to make any progress until the 16th century. Then, in 1578, the principles of creating a truly submersible craft appeared in the writings of Englishman William Bourne and, although he never actually built one, his ideas were pursued by others.

Among them was Dutch scientist Cornelius Drebbel, who was best known at the time for his perpetual-motion machine, a golden globe mounted on pillars which told the time, date and season. By 1620, his work having attracted the interest of dignitaries across Europe, he began work on designs for his submarine. It was a simple construction akin to a rowing boat with raised sides, made water-tight with a greased leather covering and propelled by four oarsmen. A larger model was later demonstrated to King James I, who was reportedly given a submerged trip along the Thames from Westminster to Greenwich.

The fascination with underwater travel gripped the imagination of the inventors, but naval commanders showed little enthusiasm until the American War of Independence (1775–83), when a young Yale graduate named David Bushnell designed a one-man submarine, which he called *Turtle*. Built from wood in the shape of an egg, his machine was powered by a hand-cranked propeller. Its sole purpose was to damage the British fleet during its blockade of New York harbour in 1776.

The next step forward came in 1800, when Robert Fulton, a brilliant American artist and inventor, of quite recent Irish descent, built the *Nautilus*, a copper-covered submersible with a collapsible sail. Born in Little Britain township (now Fulton), Pennsylvania, he went to England as a young man to study

painting. His thoughts quickly turned from art to draughtsmanship, concentrating on canal navigation and, eventually, submersible boats. In 1796 he travelled to France where, in due course, Napoleon commissioned Fulton to build his submarine, 6.4m/21ft long and shaped like a bullet. Fulton and three mechanics descended to a depth of 7.5m/24ft 7in, and later he added a detachable mine to demonstrate his theory of carrying out clandestine attacks on surface ships. The latter part of the equation failed and Napoleon lost interest. Fulton returned to England and managed to bring his invention to the attention of the British government but the Admiralty rejected his plans with a damning condemnation of submarines that was to remain their policy for the remainder of the 19th century. Back in the United States, he enjoyed success with steam-powered navigation, and was still working on a new version of his submarine when he died in 1815.

Other attempts at submarine construction met with modest success, including that of a former Germany artillery sergeant, Wilhelm Bauer. He was sponsored to build a submarine, which he called *Fire Diver*, in 1850, but it sank after only two outings. The German Navy was quietly pleased, although Bauer did eventually build an ambitious 16m/52ft 6in submarine for the Imperial Russian Navy, which was known to have completed at least 120 successful dives.

The historical turning point came during the American Civil War (1861–65) when the Confederacy used the first true submarine to sink an enemy ship in war. It was a massive cigar-shaped boat, 18.25m/59ft 11in in length. Named the *Hunley* after one of the three designers who drew up the blueprint for the Confederates' secret weapon, the boat was powered, when submerged, by a manual crankshaft requiring eight members of the crew to propel it at six knots. During trials, the *Hunley* sank four times, twice killing all her crew. Even so, she was raised and sent back into commission. On her fifth journey in 1864, she carried a torpedo to sink the Union warship *Housatonic* off the coast of South Carolina but, in doing so, went to the bottom with her victim. All aboard perished.

The Union, meanwhile, had less success. What is now officially classed as the American Navy's first submarine, USS *Alligator* was designed and built by French diver and inventor Brutus de Villeroi in 1861. Fabricated from riveted iron plates and originally powered by a system of oars, *Alligator* was constructed and tested at Philadelphia on the Delaware River. Later, a hand-cranked screw propeller was added but while being towed to launch an attack on Charleston Harbour in April 1863, the *Alligator* sank somewhere off Cape Hatteras, North Carolina.

TOP: **CSS *David*, a cigar-shaped 15.2m/50ft steam torpedo boat built at Charleston, South Carolina, in 1863 by David C. Ebaugh, was used by the Confederates in a daring attack on Federal ships in 1863.** ABOVE: **A copy of the original blueprint of H.L. Hunley's submarine, which became the first in history to sink a ship.** BELOW LEFT: **The *Pioneer*, a successful hand-cranked submarine built by two wealthy New Orleans engineers in 1862 for the Confederates, but sunk by them to prevent it falling into enemy hands.** BELOW: **Partially submerged incendiary and gun ships attracted the attention of inventors in the 19th century, and this one, designed by Scottish engineer James Nasmyth in 1853, was described as an anti-invasion floating mortar.**

Closer to the goal

Early setbacks did not deter a worldwide search for a successful design that overcame the most difficult challenge of all, which was to find a workable means of propulsion under water. Another experimental American project involved a boat called the *Intelligent Whale*, a hand-cranked submarine that could stay submerged for ten hours. This was built on the design of Scovel S. Meriam in 1863 by Augustus Price and Cornelius S. Bushnell. The American Submarine Co. was formed to take over production, but this interesting project became bogged down by years of litigation as to who actually owned the rights. When title was established, the *Intelligent Whale* was bought by the US Navy and subsequently abandoned after unreliable trials, eventually being consigned to the Navy Museum, Washington, D.C.

That these difficulties would eventually be overcome was foreshadowed by the appearance in 1870 of the latest novel by Jules Verne, *Twenty Thousand Leagues under the Sea*, the story of Captain Nemo who cruises beneath the oceans in a submarine. It was the inspiration for the Reverend George Garrett, a determined young scholar who had followed his father into the Church but had his heart set on other things. After an education that took him to Trinity College, Cambridge, his interest in mechanical science consumed him. At the age of 26, he produced detailed plans for a bullet-shaped submarine he called *Resurgam* ("rise again"). He raised more than £1,500 and had the submarine built on the banks of the Mersey.

Garrett decided to sail the submarine around the coast to Portsmouth for the ceremonial Spithead Review and set off on December, 10, 1879, with *Resurgam* under tow, crewed by two men while Garrett directed operations from the yacht. The submarine was powered by a coal-fired, single-cylinder steam engine for surface travel, which had to be shut down shortly before the submarine submerged. In theory, residual heat from the engine would keep the vessel under way for about an hour before the need to surface again. It was a dangerous and overpowering contraption, giving off strong carbon monoxide fumes. The crew avoided death from poisoning by wearing a breathing device Garrett himself had invented, although this was not entirely efficient, and lighting was by candles in a craft virtually devoid of instruments.

On February 25, 1880, after a break in the journey at Rhyl, *Resurgam* set off again under tow behind the steam yacht. The weather took a turn for the worse with a heavy swell, and the hawser connecting the yacht to the submarine suddenly went slack. *Resurgam* had gone to the bottom and efforts to find her were unsuccessful. The submarine was to remain undiscovered for more than a century. As for Garrett, he never did get to give the British Navy a demonstration, although a second submarine designed by him and of sleek, revolutionary design did achieve attention.

ABOVE: **The *Intelligent Whale*, a hand-cranked submarine built by Augustus Price and Cornelius S. Bushnell in 1862, was eventually sold to the US Navy, subject to the completion of successful trials. However, the first trial failed to impress naval engineers and the project was abandoned without further payment.** LEFT: ***Resurgam*, the coal-fired and steam-powered submarine built by the Reverend George Garrett in 1879, was originally designed to penetrate the chain netting placed around ships' hulls to defend against attack by torpedo vessels.**

LEFT: **Simon Lake, one of America's first pioneers of submarine development, produced this early boat, *Protector*, in 1901, but it was rejected by the US Navy and sold to Russia in 1904.**

ABOVE RIGHT: **The spacious interior of Simon Lake's first submarine, *Argonaut*, built in 1895 with innovative design features including the ability to stay submerged for 24 hours.** LEFT: **The distinctive wheels of *Argonaut*, added for bottom crawling, and a diver's air-lock hatch, are clearly visible.** BELOW: **Flying the flag, but *Argonaut* was rejected by the US Navy in favour of the *Holland* and Lake began designing submarines for the Austro-Hungarian Navy, although he subsequently built 24 boats for the US Navy during and after World War I.**

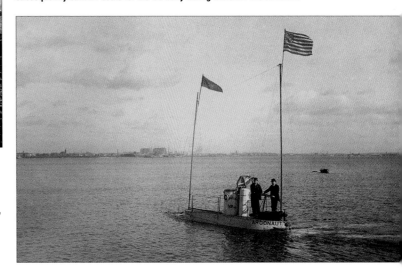

Named the *Nordenfelt*, two were built, one in Stockholm and a second at Barrow-in-Furness. Turkey bought the first and awarded Garrett the title of Pasha Garrett. The second, an incredible 36.75m/120ft 7in long and displacing 230 tonnes/226 tons, sank during the delivery voyage to Russia. Garrett, dismayed at his lack of success, emigrated to America to become a farmer, went bankrupt, and ended up in the US army. In 1995 trawlerman Dennis Hunt was fishing off Rhyl when his nets became snagged. A diver friend, Keith Hurley, came out to free his nets and became the first person to lay eyes on *Resurgam* since February 1880.

Back in America towards the end of the 19th century, Simon Lake, a name now synonymous with submarine development in the US, came to the fore – also carrying a copy of Jules Verne's novel under his arm. Lake was born in Pleasantville, New Jersey in 1866, the son of Christopher J. Lake, whose father was the Honourable Simon Lake, one of the founders of Atlantic City. Simon began work at his father's foundry and machine shop in New Jersey, and the prototype *Argonaut Junior*, constructed in wood, was successfully demonstrated.

The success led to the formation of the Lake Submarine Company of New Jersey in 1895, which built the *Argonaut*, the first submarine to operate successfully in the open sea in 1898, and which subsequently drew a congratulatory telegram from Jules Verne.

Even so, Russia – not America – gave Simon Lake his first contract to built submarines. The US Navy ran a competition for best design for a revolutionary new submarine. Simon Lake came second, and was snapped up by the Tsar's Royal Navy, moving temporarily to St Petersburg to begin production. The Americans – followed soon afterwards by the British – chose to award their contract to Lake's closest rival, the Irish-American inventor J.P. Holland, who became the primary figure in the next stage of the development of the submarine.

Underway in the Hollands

When Irish-American pioneer John Philip Holland (1841–1914) won the American competition for submarine designs, the British Royal Navy at last began to take a real interest, given that France, Germany, Russia and Italy were all entering the field. It was Holland's version that became the model for the first submarines to be built for the fleets of both Britain and America, which was rather ironic. Holland was born in County Clare, Ireland, where he joined a religious order in Cork at the age of 17, but other ideas distracted him from a spiritual calling, and he began to draw sketches of submersible boats. He left the order to join the exodus to America, and in 1873 submitted his drawings to the US Navy, which rejected them. However, the American branch of the Irish patriots, the Fenian Society, heard about Holland's work and gave him $6,000 to build two submarines, which they planned to use against the British Navy.

The Fenian brotherhood was founded in New York by veterans of the 1848 Irish uprising to raise funds for the recruitment and training of exiles to fight the British for Irish independence. Holland, desperate for funds, was not in the least restrained by the possibility that his boats might be turned on British shipping because he, too, harboured strong anti-British feelings.

His first submarine was tested with mixed results in the Passaic River in 1878. She sank on her first outing because of loose-fitting plugs and had to be hauled back from the seabed. Holland himself took the controls on his second trip, and it was a successful run, although still leaky. His second submarine, *Fenian Ram*, was launched in 1881. Powered by one of the earliest internal-combustion engines, the boat was 9.5m/31ft 2in long and displaced 19 tonnes/18.7 tons. She went through a series of successful trials in the lower Hudson River and became the subject of close scrutiny by British spies, aware

TOP: **The Royal Navy's First Submarine Flotilla, commanded by Captain Reginald Bacon arrived in Portsmouth in 1902, consisting of two completed Holland boats. Five were built at a cost of £35,000 each and Bacon reported: "Even these little boats would be a terror to any ship attempting to remain or pass near a harbour holding them."** ABOVE: **J.P. Holland's first submarine, the *Fenian Ram*, built in 1878 and funded by a brotherhood of American Irish patriots with the aim of attacking British shipping. The first Holland boats contained many of the original design features.**

of the Fenian connection. Holland's backers, meanwhile, were becoming impatient and demanded action. When he persisted in continuing his rigorous trials they "stole" the boat, which they said was rightfully theirs anyway, and towed it to New Haven, ready to begin blitzing British shipping. After several attempts to master the controls, however, they gave up and washed their hands of submarines.

Holland came to the attention of a businessman named Isaac Rice, a magazine publisher and industrialist who had already established a monopoly in the American storage battery industry. Rice financed the creation of the Holland Torpedo Boat Company and correctly assessed that this time Holland had come up with a winner. The boat was 17m/55ft 9in long and was powered by a petrol engine on the surface and an electric motor when submerged. The United States

ABOVE: **Drawings for the first of the Holland boats to be bought by the US Navy, the ill-fated *Plunger*, built in 1897 but doomed to failure because US Navy officials insisted on tinkering with Holland's design.**

ABOVE RIGHT: **The famous image of J.P. Holland in his submarine that provided the prototype for the American and British navies.** BELOW: **USS *Holland*, the 65 tonne/64 ton initiator of the US submarine force, successfully completed trials in 1899.** BOTTOM: **The *Fulton* (Holland VII-type design) built by the Electric Boat Company in 1901. The *Fulton* itself was sold to Russia along with another five, and the US Navy also bought five.**

government finally agreed, in April 1900, to purchase the prototype for $165,000 from the renamed Electric Boat Company, and the craft was commissioned as the USS *Holland*.

Rice then travelled to London, armed with the knowledge of highly successful trials in the USA, where the *Holland* had "sunk" a battleship in fleet exercises, and the Admiralty decided that it, too, must finally join the submarine age. The British agreed to buy five improved Hollands, capable of carrying a crew of seven and able to withstand pressure down to 30m/98ft 5in. Each one cost £35,000 to build, although Holland himself saw little profit from his invention. Rice had taken the precaution of including the designs and patents when he established his company, and eventually Holland resigned. Blocked by legal ties from utilizing his designs again, he died in obscurity while his Electric Boat Company went on to become one of the world's foremost manufacturers of submarines, celebrating its centennial in 1999. Therefore, finally, the British were to get a submarine fleet, although the Admiralty stressed to newspapers at the time that the craft were for experimental purposes only. Lord Selborne, First Lord of the Admiralty, would only go as far as to say in his estimates to the Commons, "What future value these boats may have in naval warfare can only be a matter of conjecture".

This negative view at the Admiralty changed virtually overnight. In July 1901, newspaper reports from France brought a graphic account of dramatic developments. A dummy torpedo struck a French battleship as she left Ajaccio harbour during naval manoeuvres. It had been fired from a brand new French submarine, *Gustav Zede*, which had secretly been sent from Toulon for the express purpose of demonstrating to the navies of the world that the French had exceeded every one of them. For Britain, at a time when France, rather than Germany, was considered an "enemy", this was stern news indeed. The race to form submarine fleets was on, across the world.

Towards World War: the dash to build

To many British and American naval chiefs at the start of the 20th century, submarines were a "cursed invention". The very idea of dark, shadowy vessels lurking unseen beneath the waves, waiting to sink their magnificent and beloved capital ships, was simply unthinkable. Sir Arthur Wilson, Third Sea Lord in the British Admiralty, best summed up their view when he described submarines as being "underwater, underhand and damned unEnglish…certainly no occupation for a gentleman. Submarine crews, if captured, should be hanged as pirates".

The Germans, similarly proud of their naval heritage, felt the same. Admiral Alfred von Tirpitz, said "The submarine is, at present, of no great value in war at sea. We have no money to waste on experimental vessels." The Americans were in no hurry to equip either, in spite of their own history of experiments with underwater warfare. However, the new century was barely months old before the great and the good among the naval fraternity were forced to change their tune. The greater urgency emerged after the French – historically Britain's main enemy before *entente cordiale* — launched a competition for the design of a submarine of 200 tonnes/ 197 tons, with a range of 161km/100 miles on the surface, and received some startling new ideas, notably Laubeuf's 1899 double-hulled *Narval*, which used steam propulsion for surface work and batteries when submerged.

In 1900, the Americans bought the Holland prototype, commissioned USS *Holland* for immediate operations and began building more. The British introduced their own class, the A boats, the first of which (*A1*) was put through her paces with the five Hollands for the first-ever fleet exercise involving

TOP: **After utilizing the Holland boats as a starting point and thereafter, principally for experimental and training purposes, the Royal Navy initiated its own A class, British designed and built, 12.2m/40ft longer than the Hollands, and at 193 tonnes/190 tons surface displacement was almost a third heavier. Thirteen boats of the class were completed.** ABOVE: **The US equivalent was the Adder class, also an enlarged production version of the original *Holland*, with a more powerful petrol engine.**

submarines, off the south coast of England in 1904. Although based on the *Holland*, *A1* was 12.2m/40ft longer and 203 tonnes/ 200 tons heavier and was accepted with pride by the Royal Navy. Unfortunately, she did not survive the exhibition. George, Prince of Wales (later King George V), himself a sailor, was aboard for the demonstration, but was called home because of the death of the Duke of Cambridge. Soon after he left, *A1* submerged to continue her trials, and never came back.

The passenger steamer, SS *Berwick Castle*, reported having struck something below the surface. The following day, divers

LEFT: The French were at the forefront of submarine design. The attractive *Anguilla*, in the Naiade class, was a single hull boat with a surface displacement of 71.6 tonnes/70.5 tons, carried a crew of 12 and had a range of 370km/ 200 nautical miles.

ABOVE: **Another French boat that looked well ahead of her time was the *Narval*, built by Laubeuf in 1899. It was the winner of a government-sponsored competition for the best design: a massive 33.8m/111ft long and with a displacement of 170.7 tonnes/168 tons.**

went down at the spot, and found *A1* on her side in 13m/ 42ft 8in of water. All on board were lost. Five more A class vessels were hit by misfortune, resulting in deaths of crew members. Conditions for the dozen crew members in the early models were dire and cramped. There were no toilet facilities in the early boats. Crews used buckets, which were emptied over the side, and when the air – poisoned by the fumes, toilet buckets and mere body odour – became too overpowering, compressed air bottles were tapped to refresh the atmosphere.

In Britain, the A class was followed by new, improved and larger designs: B, C, D and E classes progressively took the experimentation and improvements at a quite exceptional pace, indeed well in time for the early battles of World War I. Despite this, as late as 1912, senior officials were still rejecting the notion that submarines posed a serious threat to the British fleet.

The era of petrol-driven engines was also thankfully coming to an end. For the British, this was signalled with the arrival of the D-class boats, with *D1* becoming the prototype for diesel-driven power, albeit invented by Rudolph Diesel of Germany. She was also the first British submarine with twin propellers, and her ballast tanks were not inside the hull but fitted on the outside as "saddle tanks". The D boats were also the first submarines to have a wireless, and with their greater endurance level, became ocean-going submarines with a range of more than 4,023km/2,500 miles. A two-pounder gun became standard with *D4*. Eight D boats were in commission by the start of World War I, and along with the other classes, Britain could muster 55 submarines as the conflict began.

France, well ahead in terms of numbers, had a creditable total of 62 very decent submarines. The Germans, latecomers to the race for a submarine stock, had fewer boats than Britain and France. In 1914, they could muster just 28 boats, with a further 17 under construction, but their technology was advancing in new directions that others would copy.

ABOVE: **The race towards submarine power was spurred on by another French development, the *Gustav Zede*, which became the first boat to successfully fire a dummy torpedo, aimed at a French battleship in Ajaccio harbour in 1901.**
BELOW: **The D-letter in Britain's fast track to a major submarine fleet was reached in 1907 and the class had far better endurance than any previous boat. The D class was also regarded as the first UK submarine to have a proper patrol capability.**

Birth of the U-boat

ABOVE: *U1* was launched at Keil in 1906 to become a trial and evaluation boat for the German Imperial Navy. She was much larger than the British A class, possessed an exemplary electric motor, and had an endurance of 1,087km/ 587 nautical miles.

Germany's early reluctance to join the race in submarine development was only overcome as other nations around the world – France and Britain in particular – began to take up the challenge. In fact, when Germany's history of submarine building began in 1904, it was inspired, curiously enough, not by the country's own navy. Russia ordered three *Karp*-class vessels, which were duly delivered two years before the arrival of the first German submarine, *U1*, which itself was a full six years behind the first British and French boats. The first U (for *Unterseeboot*) boat, also initially designed for coastal work, was larger than British and American A boats, with a double hull and twin screws, and came with a powerful electric motor for faster speeds submerged. The 298kW/400hp engines used heavy oil rather than petrol, although they did have the drawback of emitting very visible smoke and sparks from the upper deck exhaust system. German designers were therefore encouraged to press ahead with diesel-fuelled engines, which they first produced in 1910.

Even so, *U1* produced impressive trial results, and her first major endurance test from the German port of Wilhelmshaven, passing around Denmark and back to Kiel in northern Germany – a distance of 1,087km/587 nautical miles – was noted with concern by competing nations. There was another major difference in the German boats in that from the outset they possessed real fighting qualities, which were quickly enhanced through the early stages of development. It was a capability that Winston Churchill noted on his appointment as First Lord of the Admiralty in 1910: "The whole character of the German

fleet shows that it is designed for aggressive and offensive action of the largest possible character in the North Sea and the North Atlantic." Armed initially with a single torpedo tube at the bow, *U2* was further enlarged and came with four tubes, two bow and two stern, ahead of the first British D class carrying four tubes.

U1, the pacesetter for fast and capable boats, showed its mettle from the beginning, survived the war, and was eventually moved to a museum in Munich, where she is retained to this day. At the outbreak of war in August 1914, Germany had around 20 operational U-boats assigned to its High Seas Fleet, working from a fortified forward base on the island of Heligoland. When hostilities with Russia began, they combined to form a defensive screen in the North Sea, and when Britain and France declared war on Germany, ten U-boats set out to make a bold surprise move against the British Grand Fleet, at its supposedly secure base at Scapa Flow. This first outing in wartime proved disappointing for the Germans. Two of the boats had to turn back, one was lost en route, and one, *U15*,

BELOW: The results of what became an all too familiar attack on British merchant shipping in the U-boat campaigns of World War I.

LEFT: *U35* was the most successful German submarine in World War I, sinking 224 vessels (excluding warships) during 17 patrols from November 1914 and remaining in action to the very last, when she was surrendered and broken up at Blyth.

was sunk by HMS *Birmingham*. The remainder failed to score any hits, let alone penetrate the British base, although the latter was finally achieved in November 1914, when *U18* under the command of Captain Hans von Hennig gained entry, only to be spotted and sunk. Although this mass attack on the British fleet achieved little, it came as a wake-up call to all opposing nations, and the British in particular. This was reinforced one month later when *U21*, which had taken part in the move on Scapa Flow, became the first submarine since the American *Hunley* to sink a ship in wartime, sending the British cruiser *Pathfinder* to the bottom with a single torpedo hit.

This was indeed a shocking event, analysed with great concern by the seafaring nations of the world, given that the time which elapsed from the launch of the torpedo to the

disappearance of the cruiser was a mere four minutes. Only nine of the 268 crew survived the attack. Undoubtedly the most significant development in submarine warfare to date came on September 22, 1914, when a relatively old boat, *U9*, under the command of Lt Otto Weddigen, sank no fewer than three British cruisers – the *Aboukir*, *Hogue* and *Cressy* – within a 40-minute timeframe, taking down almost 1,400 men. As naval analysts pored over the details, it did not escape anyone's attention that on July 16, 1914, the crew of *U9* had performed the task of reloading torpedoes while submerged, the first time ever that this had been recorded. One further milestone in German submarine history came one month later, when *U17* became the first submarine in history to sink a merchantman. In fact, the boat went on to sink 11 other non-combatant ships.

ABOVE: **The crew of *U9*, then captained by Otto Weddigen, made history by performing the task of reloading torpedoes while submerged. Using this process, Weddigen sank three British cruisers in under an hour in September 1914, with the loss of almost 1,400 men. The captain would himself perish with his *U29* later in the war.** RIGHT: **An interior view of *U9*.**

The head to head of underwater power

The submarines of World War I were engaged in vast arenas of sea warfare, and the crews of these early, technically deprived small boats were relied upon well into the conflict, taking on challenges way beyond the true level of their capabilities and endurance. Furthermore, the sheer numbers of boats in any fleet did not compensate for deficiencies in the infant submarine technology, although the rate of improvement on that score was dramatic. The British Navy was far greater in both experience and numbers, while the newly equipped German fleet was lean, hungry and thoroughly modern.

ABOVE: **In 1915, a new class of efficient German minelayers came into service around coastal waters. Ironically, the class leader *UC1* was sunk by a mine off Nieuport two years later with all 17 hands lost.** BELOW LEFT: **Some of the targets of extensive German minelaying were the new British E-class boats, which began a daring and highly successful campaign in the Baltic and elsewhere as they emerged to fight in the front line of the war at sea.**

On paper, the submarine stock of Britain and France looked healthy as Europe inched towards World War I. However, well over half the boats were of such vintage as to be virtually useless other than for coastal patrols, and to use them – as the British did – on more demanding tasks presented their crews with exceptional challenges that they met with considerable aplomb.

But other developments were already in the pipeline, and by the end of the war the Royal Navy's submarine fleet would extend across a confusing range of 20 different designs and classes. The star of the British submarine fleet was the versatile E class, with boats being launched by the week to match Germany's massively increased production schedule. Additional types F, G and H classes were scheduled to begin rolling out of the production pens from 1915.

In early action, the Heligoland Bight region remained the key to Germany's ability to set forth, so German commanders sealed the route to the Baltic from the North Sea. This area became an early flashpoint as Britain's C, D and E boats made

LEFT: *E1* was the first of 56 E-class boats which came on stream between 1911 and 1917, built in three groups at an average cost of £105,000 each. Sadly, to avoid capture after a successful campaign, *E1* was scuttled off Helsinki in April 1918, along with *E8*, *E9* and *E19*. BELOW LEFT: *E32* was among just 25 E boats that survived World War I, and was sold in 1922.

ABOVE: The famous U-boat poster, one of many produced by Hans Rudi Erdt for the German government in World War I, this one to publicize a film, *U-boats Out!* on submarine warfare. BELOW: Lt Commander Martin Nasmith's *E11*, which began its so-called "career of destruction" against enemy shipping in the Baltic in October 1914. Also in this photograph is Admiral Sir Roger Keyes, who later planned the famous raid on the German submarine base at Zeebrugge.

constant forays into the region. The problems of going to war in craft with, as yet, still unsophisticated communications soon became apparent. Boats went out of wireless range and, in place, intelligence messages were sent back using homing pigeons, which were usually kept in the forward peak of the boats. Usually, important messages were sent in triplicate – using three pigeons.

Britain's first major sortie was led by Lt Commander Max Horton who went on to become an acclaimed hero in British submarine history. His *E9* sank an old German cruiser, the *Hela*, on the approaches to Heligoland and then scored a direct hit on a German destroyer in the North Sea in mid-September 1914. The euphoria of these first submarine successes was to be short-lived, however. A reversal quickly followed, and another "first" in the history of submarine warfare – the first submarine to be sunk by another submarine. The victim was the British *E3*, which was sighted cruising on the surface in the Heligoland Bight by the *U27* captain, Lt Bernhard Wegener. In the weeks and months that followed, the British 8th Flotilla, operating off the east coast, suffered five further losses, although the German fleet was sufficiently harassed to pull back into the comparative safety of the Baltic Sea.

As well as giving trouble to the German fleet in the Baltic, British submarines had the equally important task of interrupting shipments of iron ore from Sweden to Germany. This was eventually achieved, although in terms of attacks on ships, successes were initially few, partly because the British submarines had been placed under inefficient Russian control. The German propaganda machine complained bitterly of the "underhand and criminal methods of the British pirate submarines" in the Baltic.

LEFT: **The sinking of the passenger liner** *Lusitania* **by** *U20* **in February 1915, with the loss of 1,195 lives, brought allegations that the boat laid in wait for the ship as part of a policy of unrestricted warfare, although Lt Commander Walther Schweiger denied it.**
BELOW: **The sinking of the great ship undoubtedly inspired what a German newspaper described as "national pride", and a special medal was cast for the submariners involved.**

The sinking of the Lusitania

Battle for control of the high seas intensified by the day, eventually resorting to what many described as "sheer bloody murder" on February 4, 1915. On that day, Germany declared that the international waters around the coasts of Great Britain and Ireland would henceforth become a war zone. Ships sailing under the British flag would be sunk on sight, and the Germans said they could not guarantee the safety of ships from neutral countries because of the difficulty of identifying flags at a distance or in fog.

On May 7, the threat became a reality. *U20*, under Lt Commander Walther Schweiger, was – according to the German version of events – heading home at the end of a week-long patrol off the south coast of Ireland, having sunk two small steamers and one sailing boat. Schweiger was travelling west from Waterford at 13:20 hours when he saw a very large passenger liner steaming into view, sailing eastwards. It was the *Lusitania*, a magnificent vessel of 31,500 tonnes/31,003 tons, carrying 1,257 passengers and 702 crew. As the liner came closer and closer, she was an unmissable target. Schweiger ordered his crew to battle stations, took aim and at 14:09 hours gave the order to fire.

From a range of less than 730m/798yds, there was no chance of avoidance, no chance of a miss and no chance of escape for the hundreds of men, women and children on board. The torpedo struck amidships. Within 20 minutes, the great liner lurched beneath the waves in a great mass of white foam. Schweiger had sunk the pride of the Cunard Line,

and in doing so, 1,195 passengers perished. He watched them as hundreds scrambled to save themselves, and made the following note in his war diary:

> *An unusually heavy explosion takes place with a very strong explosion cloud (cloud reaches far beyond front funnel). The explosion of the torpedo must have been followed by a second one (boiler or coal or powder?). The superstructure right above the point of impact and the bridge are torn asunder, fire breaks out, and smoke envelops the high bridge. The ship stops immediately and heels over to starboard very quickly, immersing simultaneously at the bow. It appears as if the ship were going to capsize very shortly. Great confusion ensues on board; the boats are made clear and some of them are lowered to the water with either stem or stern first and founder immediately. On the port side fewer boats are made clear than on the starboard side on account of the ship's list. The ship blows off [steam]; on the bow the name* Lusitania *becomes visible in golden letters. The funnels were painted black, no flag was set astern. Ship was running twenty knots. Since it seems as if the steamer will keep above*

LEFT: **Although America had not yet entered the war, the sinking of the *Lusitania* finally brought home to Atlantic travellers the potential of the German U-boat campaign against shipping, given that there were many US passengers among the casualties, whose bodies were carried ashore covered in the national flag.** BELOW: **The famous ship depicted on a postcard of the day.**

water only a short time, we dived to a depth of twenty-four meters and ran out to sea. It would have been impossible for me, anyhow, to fire a second torpedo into this crowd of people struggling to save their lives.

Many claimed that Schwieger added the last sentence after the voyage, after the world became shocked by the sinking. Indeed, the reaction was one of stunned disbelief, but not in Germany. Naval chief Admiral von Tirpitz received hundreds of telegrams congratulating him. An article in an influential German newspaper summed up the "national pride" with the comment that "the news will be received by the German people with unanimous satisfaction since it proves to England and the whole of the world that Germany is quite in earnest in regard to her submarine warfare". Despite the fact that 124 Americans were among the passengers who died, "riotous scenes" were reported in New York's German clubs and restaurants. Elsewhere, of course, the monstrous crime was universally condemned, and few believed that it was a coincidence that Schwieger just happened upon the *Lusitania* but, more likely, had been lying in wait. That view was reinforced when it became known that the German ambassador to the United States had published a warning to those intending to embark on the *Lusitania*, days before she sailed.

Meanwhile, the deadlocked war of attrition in the trenches and Germany's home-front crisis of shortages of food and supplies through the blockade being waged by the British fleet turned the Germans towards a merciless campaign on the high seas in which submarines were to spearhead a blockade of the British Isles. In spite of the international protests in the wake of the *Lusitania* calamity, Germany began to focus U-boat attention on unarmed merchant shipping in addition, of course, to any British fleet ships they might come upon. In spite of the assurances given to America, in August 1915 *U24* torpedoed and sank the small White Star liner *Arabic* and in early 1916 the French steamer *Sussex*, with the loss of American lives.

ABOVE: **A steamer is torpedoed when, convinced they could starve Britain into submission, the Germans began an all-out U-boat war against merchant shipping. By the autumn of 1916, British and Allied vessels sunk by the Germans reached a staggering 300,000 tonnes/295,262 tons a month, double the totals reached in the summer months.** BELOW: **Nor were attacks limited to below the surface, as demonstrated here, when a U-boat crew launches a surface assault using their powerful deck guns.**

The famous naval confrontation, the Battle of Jutland, waged on May 31 and June 1, 1916, between the British Grand Fleet and the German High Seas Fleet, resolved nothing. British losses in both ships and human lives were greater than Germany's. Even so, Germany's capital ships returned to home ports and did not venture to give battle again during the war. The battle on the high seas was handed over to the U-boat commanders, convinced that they could starve the British into submission.

Forcing the Dardanelles

Apart from the war in the main European waters, there were battles elsewhere that brought praise and tragedy in equal measure for the British and Allied submariners. The most famous of all came in the Gallipoli campaign against Turkey, as the Royal Navy was tasked with forcing the Dardanelles straits. From the outset, this was to become a life or death mission for many submarine crews when the waterway became bitterly contested as soon as Turkey sided with Germany in the autumn of 1914. In return, the Turks received German military advisers, military hardware and two brand-new ships, the *Breslau*, a light cruiser, and the *Goeben,* a battlecruiser. The two ships were stabled at Constantinople (Istanbul), on the northern coast of the Sea of Marmara, from where the Turks unleashed them to bombard Russian Black Sea ports. In December 1914, Britain's War Council decided to attack Turkey to neutralize the attacks on Russia. Among the advance party in this mission was the submarine service.

For centuries, the Dardanelles had provided the Turks with a natural defence to their capital city. Running south out of the Sea of Marmara past the Gallipoli Peninsula into the Aegean and on to the Mediterranean, the straits are 45km/28 miles long and contained many hazards. Although 6.4km/4 miles from shore to shore at its widest points, there was a rat-run 19.3km/12 miles upstream, known as the Narrows, reducing to just over 1.6km/1 mile in width, and notorious for unpredictable currents. The rocky banks of the straits bristled with forts, guns, torpedo launchers and mobile howitzers, while below the water there were floating and fixed minefields and anti-submarine nets. In December 1914, well before the infamous invasion of the Gallipoli Peninsula began, the French and the British sent a large flotilla of ships of all kinds to settle in the wide harbour of Moudros on the Greek island of Limnos. Among them were

TOP: **The British and French sent many submarines into the costly attempt to take control of the Dardanelles, in conjunction with the ill-fated Gallipoli campaign. These submarines included some of the earliest and most basic boats, such as the *B11*, which undertook heroic efforts to force a path through the deadly minefields.** ABOVE: **The crew of *B11*, with their skipper, Lt Commander Norman Holbrook – early heroes in the battle for control of the Dardanelle straits.**

six submarines, including three small and very basic British B-class boats, *B9*, *B10* and *B11*, all hankering to have a shot at forcing the straits. Lt Norman Holbrook in *B11* was the first to try. On the morning of December 13, 1914, having warned his crew of the dangers, they set off and covered 19.3km/12 miles before the boat reached minefields at Sari Siglar Bay. There, the Turkish battleship *Messudieh* was spotted at anchor. Holbrook dived his vessel under five rows of mines and torpedoed the battleship. He then managed to turn around and bring the *B11* safely back, although assailed by gunfire and torpedo boats, having been submerged on one occasion for nine hours.

The operation brought great acclaim in Britain, and Holbrook was awarded the Victoria Cross, thus becoming the first submariner to be so honoured. The dangers were re-emphasized on January 14, 1915, when the French submarine *Saphir* attempted to get through but was lost with all hands just beyond the Narrows. Naval commanders called for help from the larger E boats, which were promptly despatched from England.

The E boats began arriving in March, ahead of the planned invasion of Allied ground forces scheduled for April 25. The first to try to run the gauntlet of the Dardanelles was *E15*, under the command of Lt Commander Theodore Brodie. In dodging the minefields, his boat was caught by the infamous current and ran aground directly below heavy guns that opened fire immediately. The boat was hit twice, killing Brodie himself, and the crew had no alternative but to surrender.

The next boat to make the attempt was Australia's *AE2*, which began the journey through the straits in the early hours of April 25, the same day that ANZAC troops landed on the beaches at Gallipoli. Lt Commander Hew Stoker, the Irish-born captain of *AE2*, set off steadily on the surface under a moonless sky until searchlights suddenly swept his boat. The shellfire that quickly followed forced him to dive, and as he did so, he ran straight into a minefield. Stoker was forced to keep his boat on the bottom for 13 hours, with barely enough air to sustain life. Finally, he was able to move forward, and at 07:30 hours on April 26, the jubilant skipper signalled that *AE2* had entered the Sea of Marmara. In spite of the somewhat fragile state of his boat, and without a gun, Hew Stoker and his crew immediately began to wreak havoc. Virtually overnight, enemy shipping was curtailed substantially.

Lt Commander Edward Courtney Boyle was dispatched in *E14* to join Stoker. He, too, successfully negotiated the Dardanelles, to enter the Marmara on April 29, and rendezvous with Stoker in Atarki Bay to discuss a plan of action. The following day, *AE2* was shelled by a Turkish torpedo boat and went down, although all hands escaped before the boat sank, and became prisoners of war. Boyle, in *E14*, carried on as planned, carrying out a series of remarkable and daring raids, dodging the Turks hunting for him and sinking several ships before returning to base on May 15, to discover that he too had been awarded the Victoria Cross for his "conspicuous bravery".

ABOVE: **A depiction of one of the most acclaimed events of the Gallipoli campaign, when *B11* negotiated a treacherous minefield five rows deep to torpedo and sink the Turkish battleship *Messudieh*, for which Holbrook was subsequently awarded the Victoria Cross.** BELOW: **The French Navy had numerous submarines in the Allied assault on the Dardanelles, including the *Saphir*, which was lost with all hands in January 1915.**

ABOVE: **Another French casualty was the hefty and very visible *Mariotte*, sunk by murderous Turkish shoreline gunfire after being trapped in anti-submarine nets in the Dardanelles on July 27, 1915.** LEFT: **One of the hero boats of World War I was the Austrialian *AE2*, here in the Suez Canal en route to the Dardanelles, where, after a successful opening sortie, she was sunk by Turkish torpedo boats. All hands escaped, only to be taken prisoner.**

Stealth and style of the Victoria Cross winners

There were yet other VCs to be won in the dramatic sequence of events that set in stone the stealth, style and drama of British submariners operating in the Dardanelles, and in particular the adventures of *E11*, captained by Lt Commander Martin Nasmith. The exploits of this boat, and others of the period, were to become the stuff of legend, winning worldwide acclaim. Nasmith began his journey through the Dardanelles on the night of May 18, 1915, emerging 16 hours later into the Sea of Marmara. There he and his crew began a remarkable run of success. First, they seized a Turkish vessel and strapped her to the landward side of the submarine to serve as a disguise as she passed shore observers, and using this disguise, *E11* torpedoed a Turkish gunboat and sank several smaller craft. On May 23, a Turkish transport ship, the *Nagara*, which was heading for the Dardanelles, came into view.

E11 surfaced close by and Nasmith appeared in the conning tower and warned that he was going to sink the ship. When all crew and passengers were safely aboard lifeboats, an *E11* boarding party carried explosives to the Turkish ship. As *E11* sailed away, the *Nagara* blew up in a sheet of flame. She had been carrying ammunition. *E11* now headed for Constantinople itself, where another audacious scheme was hatched. Nasmith planned to deliver an assault on the harbour that supposedly could never be attacked from the sea: his first torpedo smashed into the sea wall and the second sank a moored Turkish gunboat.

The city flew into panic, convinced that a group of British enemy submarines were in the Marmara. Nasmith continued on, diving and surfacing around the approaches to Constantinople, replenishing his own supplies of food, fuel and water from craft his men boarded, and in this way kept on the move for an incredible three weeks before arriving back on June 6, 1915, to the news that he too had been awarded the Victoria Cross. This ongoing campaign was handed over to Edward Courtney Boyle in *E14*, which returned to the Marmara to keep up the pressure, and was joined eight days later by Lt Commander Ken Bruce in *E12*. Nasmith also returned to the fray in July, and literally within minutes of entering the Marmara he had sunk a transport. The next day he sank another transport and then while on the surface shot up a column of Turkish troops, passing along a coast road with his brand new 12-pounder gun. His greatest triumph came just before dawn on August 8, when Nasmith found the Turkish battleship *Hayreddin Barbarossa* in his sights. He stalked the ship for 20 minutes before firing a single torpedo. It scored a direct hit, followed soon afterwards by a massive explosion when the magazine went up. The battleship sank within minutes.

Nasmith and Boyle continued their patrols, sinking ships and bombarding troops on the coast road well into the autumn. They were joined in September 1915 by Lt Commander Archie Cochrane, 33-year-old captain of *E7*, making his second tour of the Marmara. But bad luck dogged Cochrane from the outset. First, he discovered that a second anti-submarine net had been positioned in the Narrows and, as he tried to break through, part of the metal entwined around his propeller. Repeated attempts to free the boat failed, and the Turks, spotting the commotion, began dropping depth mines. When the boat had been submerged for almost 13 hours he decided to surrender to ensure his men's safety. He asked for full astern and managed to surface promptly in the midst of an array of enemy craft waiting to shell him. Amid a hail of gunfire, Lt John Scaife scrambled on deck to surrender the crew. Two motorboats manned by German submarine crews came alongside and took the men off. Cochrane himself

ABOVE: **Light cruiser *Breslau*, one of two warships supplied to the Turks by Germany for the Dardanelles campaign, ran straight into a minefield in the Aegean in January 1918, and was sunk.**
RIGHT: **The wreck of hero boat *E15*, which ran aground en route to the sea of Mamara directly under the fire of defensive batteries, which killed Lt Commander T.S. Brodie and six crew. The remainder were captured and five more died in prison camps.**

ABOVE: *E11* 1st/Lt Guy D'Oyley-Hughes swam ashore pushing a platform packed with explosives to blow up a railway line that was out of reach of shells. RIGHT: Returning safely home, VC winner Lt Commander Martin Nasmith, aged 32, and his crew of *E11* following their action-packed campaign in the Dardanelles, sinking a record 122 enemy vessels, mostly in the harbour of Constantinople, a tally achieved by no other submarine.

was the last to leave, and as the rescue boats cleared the stricken submarine a time-fuse explosive set by Cochrane before he left was detonated, returning *E7* quickly to the bottom. Cochrane joined Hew Stoker in the prisoner-of-war camp at Yozgat.

Back in the Marmara, Nasmith continued his operations which he now extended to include a number of onshore sabotage missions. He remained operational for an incredible 47 days, a record equalled by no other commander in World War I. During that time, the crew of *E11* sank 11 steamers, 5 large sailing vessels and 30 small sailing vessels. By then, the need for such daring assaults was diminishing rapidly as the land battles around Gallipoli were firmly entrenched in a hopeless stalemate from which there seemed no respite from the daily sacrifice of human life. That one battle zone had engaged more than a million men from the two sides, half of whom became casualties. Early in December 1915, the Allies finally decided to call a halt and to withdraw. In the final days of the campaign, *E14*, now under the command of Lt Commander Geoffrey White, was severely damaged. White gave the order to surface in the hope of making a final dash to safety but immediately came under heavy fire from the shore batteries. With no hope of escape, White altered course towards the shore to give his crew a chance of safety, but was

ABOVE: Through the guile and daring of their skippers, the British E class became one of the most successful boats in early British submarine history, with a significant tally that included seven U-boats. They were fast, versatile and safe and much loved by their crews, but the cost was high, with almost half of the 56 E boats built being lost to enemy action. RIGHT: Hovering, to keep a low profile.

himself killed shortly before *E14* sank. Geoffrey White, who had two sons and a daughter he had never seen, was posthumously awarded the Victoria Cross, received by his widow at Buckingham Palace on July 2, her late husband's birthday. Nonetheless, the statistics for the Dardanelles campaign told their own story: 13 Allied submarines completed 27 successful passages through the straits. Seven were sunk, but the scorecard was somewhat uneven. The Turks lost 2 battleships, 1 destroyer, 5 gunboats, 11 transports, 44 steamers and 148 sailing boats.

A U-boat in Baltimore

Of all the major seafaring nations of the Western world, the United States Navy was slow in equipping itself with a submarine force, for which it would later become renowned. America did not enter World War I until April 6, 1917, at which time her navy possessed a mere 24 diesel-powered submarines that had been used to patrol the waters off the east coast. Until that date, U-boats had been visiting the US since mid-1916 for trading purposes, as well as operating unhindered in the western Atlantic. In July that year, *Deutschland,* a large German cargo-carrying submarine, broke through the British Atlantic blockade by submerging to avoid British patrols. She arrived in the American port of Baltimore with a shipment of chemicals and dyestuffs, which were traded for a quantity of strategic war materials to be carried back to Germany. The boat, capable of carrying 711 tonnes/700 tons of cargo, made another round trip in November, although the next time the boat travelled the Atlantic, she had been converted to a combatant role.

When America entered the war, US submarines were deployed overseas to the British territory of the Azores and also around the coast of Ireland. Their primary mission was to assist in countering the U-boat threat to Allied shipping, although there were to be no confirmed sinkings of U-boats by American submarines. Back in the territorial waters of the United States, the US Navy began dispatching its submarines as far afield as the Panama Canal Zone and the Philippines, as well as mounting numerous defensive patrols along the

TOP: **A depiction of one of the epic escapes of World War I, when the passenger line USS *President Lincoln,* which transported 23,000 American troops across the Atlantic, was torpedoed by the German submarine *U90* on May 29, 1918, and sank with the loss of only 26 of the more than 700 personnel on board.** ABOVE: **An interior view of *Deutschland* at the end of the war, when she was in French hands.**

east coast, where there was significant concern about U-boat attacks on American shipping.

The threat was very real. Germany had by then created the ultimate World War I U-boat – a true long-range submarine cruiser. These boats were 70.1m/230ft long, with a speed of 15.3 knots on the surface, and an incredible range of 20,326km/12,630 miles at eight knots. They were heavily armed, with twin 15cm/5.9in deck guns for which 1,600 rounds of ammunition were carried along with 19 torpedoes, manned by a crew of 56 with room for 20 more if needed for special missions. Although 47 boats were ordered, only nine were in service before the war ended, six of them deploying to the east coast of the United States, where they laid mines and sank 174 ships, mostly smaller vessels without radios which could

ABOVE: The compartmentalized *Deutschland*, one of the first of the UA-class boats. These appeared in 1916 and were considered to be the ultimate long-range submarine cruisers. They were 70m/230ft long, 1,524 tonnes/1500 tons, had a speed of 15.3 knots on the surface, a range of 20,326km/12,630 miles at 8 knots, and carried a crew of 56. *Deutschland*, specifically built as a blockade-breaking civilian cargo submarine, with a carrying capacity of 711 tonnes/

700 tons, caused an uproar among the Allied nations in Europe when the US government allowed her access to US ports, carrying dyestuff and gemstones to America and returning with a cargo of nickel, tin and rubber. She made two trips in civilian mode before being converted for hostilities. BELOW: Fully flagged and impressively majestic, the largest of the German submarines of that era, pictured in civilian mode, was clearly a model for future developments.

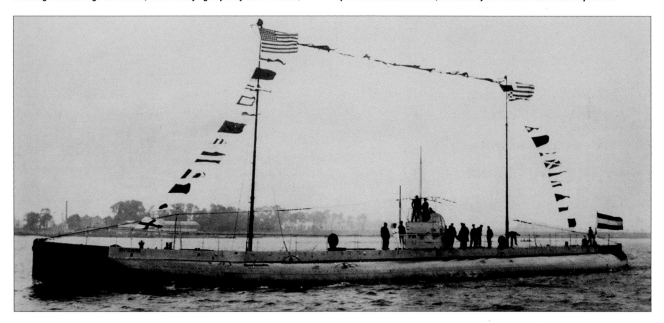

neither be warned or give warning. They proved emphatically that submarines could operate with ease 6,437km/4,000 miles from their home base.

By comparison, the dozen submarines that America sent to the Azores and Ireland had little or no effect on the outcome of the war, in that they existed mainly to provide an anti-submarine patrol for the trans-Atlantic convoys, using L-class boats that were no match for German submarines. One statistic alone proved the point: the L boats took almost two-and-a-half-minutes to dive, whereas the U-boats were out of sight in less than half a minute.

One of the most successful boats in the cruiser flotilla was *U151*, which left Kiel in mid-April 1918 and mined the entrances to Chesapeake and Delaware Bays and severed several telegraph cables near New York. During a career of four major patrols, the boat sank 51 ships totalling 140,503 tonnes/138,284 tons – excluding warships. Of these, 23 totalling 61,979 tonnes/61,000 tons were sunk off New Jersey and North Carolina in a seven week onslaught in the summer of 1918. The most notorious became known locally

as Black Sunday – June 2, 1918. On that day, *U151* destroyed six American vessels, including the passenger liner SS *Carolina* en route to New York from San Juan with 217 passengers and 113 crew aboard. Although the U-boat captain observed the rules, and allowed all aboard to take to the lifeboats before sinking her, 13 passengers were drowned.

These seemingly fearless German long-range boats also sank or damaged several major American warships. It was a stark lesson for the Americans, as the Germans had convincingly demonstrated that modern submarines could operate with ease over transoceanic distances.

When the war ended, the US Navy had 74 submarines in commission, with another 59 under construction. Except for two submarines sunk in accidents, the US Navy lost no submarines to enemy action, and by early February 1919, all the boats that had served in the Azores and Ireland had returned to the United States. America knew by then that her submarine resources were insufficient compared to those of Europe, and set about developing a world-class force that began to emerge in the late 1920s and beyond.

Labels on the aerial photograph: N, W, E, S (compass); Lighthouse; Daffodil; Vindictive; Iris; Armed Barges; Net Defence; German Destroyer; German Submarines; Thetis; Seaplane Station; S.S. Brussels; Iphigenia; Intrepid; Viaduct Destroyed by Submarine C3; ZEEBRUGGE; To Bruges; Scale in Feet 0 500 1000

LEFT: **An aerial view of the waterway to be attacked and blocked.**

The last vital, courageous act

Many of the U-boats that caused so much damage in the Atlantic had been based at Bruges, in Belgium, following its capture by German land forces. It was because of this forward position from which the U-boats were able to operate that the system of convoying fleets of merchant ships was introduced. Warships stood guard, seaplanes spotted the submarines and depth bombs or charges were available for destroying them. By the beginning of 1918, the convoy system allowed the Allies to begin to regain the momentum, but the U-boat base remained a major thorn in their side. Finally, in the spring of that year, one major, daring operation was planned to directly attack the U-boat campaign at its source.

The U-boats' safe haven was strongly defended, allowing boats to come and go with comparative ease. Their hideaway was 13km/8 miles from the open sea and accessed through two canals, one via Ostend and the other through Zeebrugge. A joint operation was planned utilizing air, land and sea units to block the canals and force the U-boats to use the more dangerous northerly route, where the British could attack them. It was proposed that old ships could be sailed to the canal entrances and then sunk, a task that the Royal Navy undertook with relish with the Royal Marines in a large military operation involving 1,760 men and numerous vessels.

A crucial element of the main operation was handed to the 6th Submarine Flotilla. It entailed blowing up a viaduct connecting the Zeebrugge mole to the mainland to stop troop

ABOVE: **The vintage submarine *C3*, one of the two boats packed with explosives to be rammed into the viaduct while the block ships were being put into position. Unfortunately, the second boat, *C1*, broke down and it was left to some heroic work by the five-man crew of *C3* to ensure her deadly cargo was positioned and time-fuses set before they made their escape.**

reinforcements being brought to the scene at the time of the raid. Two older-type submarines, *C1* and *C3*, were nominated for duty. Six tonnes/5.9 tons of explosives were packed into the bows, and it was planned to ram the submarines under the viaduct using an automatic pilot. In theory, the crew would make a quick getaway in a motor skiff 1.6km/1 mile from the target, and they would hopefully be well clear when the time-fuse blew everything up.

Only unmarried volunteers were accepted, and the crew was stripped to a bare minimum of two officers and four ratings. Lt Aubrey Newbold was already captain of *C1*, while Lt Richard Sandford, who had just reached his 26th birthday, took

LEFT: **The ancient cruiser HMS *Vindictive* was one of the principal ships carrying the diversionary raiding parties of Royal Marines who swarmed ashore at Zeebrugge to engage the German defenders until the block ships had been manoeuvred into position and scuttled (ABOVE). These were to block the entrance to the harbour used by U-boats for their forays into the Atlantic. While the Marines dashed ashore, the ship's gunners bombarded the German emplacements on the mole. Even so, she remained an easy target for the incoming shells and took a number of severe hits. *Vindictive* managed to get away when the task was complete, albeit with heavy casualties.**

command of *C3*. The task force moved out after dark on April 22, with the two submarines towed by destroyers towards a rendezvous point 8km/5 miles from the viaduct. *C1* never made it, having been delayed by mechanical trouble en route, and Sandford took *C3* into attack alone, but made a significant deviation from the original plan. He was to have set the submarine on automatic pilot for the final stages of the journey, thus allowing him and his crew to abandon the submarine at a safe distance. However, having lost his companion boat, he decided to manually steer right to the last. German gun emplacements were firing all around, while star shells bursting directly overhead brought fake daylight for the gunners to take a range and fire. Sandford held course and made it to the target, ramming the bow of the submarine into the side of the masonry. Overhead, there were howls of laughter as German troops mistakenly believed a British submarine had become stuck.

Even so, as Sandford led his five crew members out after setting the time-fuse, the Germans opened fire. Their little motor skiff was badly shot up and the engine was useless, so they had to row. As they pushed off, two of them were hit, then Sandford himself took two bullets. Four of the six were wounded, but they managed to keep rowing until they were rescued by a picket boat, driven by Sandford's brother, from their destroyer. As they climbed aboard, the sound of a terrific explosion from the place they had just vacated confirmed that the job was done – and, indeed the viaduct was missing a very large chunk in the middle of the run. All who took part in the operation received medals, and Sandford was among eight officers involved who were awarded Victoria Crosses. His citation read:

ABOVE: **The results of the explosion can be clearly seen – a gaping stretch of broken masonry after the submarine exploded.**

"He eagerly undertook this hazardous enterprise, although well aware (as were all his crew) that if the means of rescue failed and he or any of his crew were in the water at the moment of the explosion, they could be killed outright by the force of such explosion. Yet Lieutenant Sandford disdained to use the gyro steering, which would have enabled him and his crew to abandon the submarine at a safe distance, and preferred to make sure, as far as humanly possible, of the accomplishment of his duty."

This was represented at the time as a tremendous British victory by Allied propaganda with the consequence that its devisor, the Navy's youngest admiral Sir Roger Keyes, was ennobled. Conversely, the Germans cited it as a demonstration of their success by holding the two ports. In reality, the Zeebrugge raid did not hinder German operations from either port for more than a few days. Some 500 British casualties were incurred during the operation, of which approximately 200 were fatalities.

The final reckoning

The threat of what could have been a massive U-boat offensive against the Allies was only revealed at the end of the war. While talk of mutiny and rebellion among the German Navy matched the mood of many of the nation's citizens, the submarine service remained loyal to the last, with 176 U-boats still in operation and another 200 or so still under construction. However, there was no role for them, at least not in the foreseeable future. Under the Treaty of Versailles, Germany was hammered into straitjacket surrender terms, and in addition was to have her fleet confiscated and her government was barred from keeping, buying or building any submarines whatsoever.

The Germans were forced to hand over the bulk of their ships to the Allies, comprising 10 battleships, 17 cruisers, 50 torpedo boats and 176 submarines. Most of the fleet, with the exception of the submarines, was interned at Scapa Flow in November 1918, where many were scuttled by their own crews under the very noses of their British guards. All operational U-boats were delivered into the hands of the Royal Navy initially at the port of Harwich, temporarily giving the British the largest submarine fleet in the world. In fact, the spoils were shared among the Allies and some even ended up in Japan, allowing naval architects and scientists to copy the technology.

Most were eventually scrapped, and 250 damaged or unfinished U-boats were also destroyed where they lay in the German shipyards. It seemed an appalling waste, but in reality this was trifling when set against the cost of the war itself to all the belligerents, amounting in total to about $186 billion. Casualties in the land forces amounted to more than 37 million men, with almost 10 million deaths among the civilian populations caused indirectly by the war. Famously talked of as

TOP: **The image that came to signify the horror of the mounting U-boat attacks among the Allied fleets, a fate that befell 6,596 merchant ships totalling 13,006,146 tonnes/12,800,733 tons during the war years.** ABOVE: **To the Germans, their submariners were heroes, and there are numerous memorials to them, such as this one, which mentions the U-boat flotillas in the Aegean and Mediterranean seas.**

"the war to end all wars", which would bring permanent world peace, quite the reverse would result.

From the British standpoint, the only salvation was that the nation had not fallen to defeat at sea at the hands of the U-boat commanders, although it had been a very close contest. Even so, the nation's near bankruptcy as the war ended more or less forced the British government to embark on a major culling programme of its own, scrapping and selling dozens of submarines, many of which had seen little service and some not even commissioned. At the end of the war, Britain's submarine stock included 10 out of the original 13 A boats, 9 of 11 Bs, 27 of 38 Cs and 3 of the 9 Ds remaining in service. All were scrapped, as were the following:

E class: These boats had seen terrific service during the war years but were all destined for the breaker's yard. Twenty-seven had been sunk in enemy action, mined, scuttled or lost for reasons unknown. The remaining 30 were all scrapped by 1924.

F class: Only three were built; all were used for training and then scrapped.

G class: Designed initially as an overseas patrol boat, with powerful engines and long endurance submerged, the G class also had the distinction of being the first to carry a 533mm/21in torpedo as well as two 457mm/18in tubes on both bow and beam. Fourteen were built, and four were lost during the war, including *G67*, the last submarine lost to enemy action, sunk in the North Sea on November 1, 1918. The remaining ten were to be sold or scrapped.

H class: Forty-three were built between 1914 and 1918; this was another workhorse of the period. Eight were lost, 18 were scrapped or sold in the 1920s and the remainder were kept in service for several years hence; some still active in World War II.

J class: Seven were launched, one lost and the remainder transferred to Australia in 1919.

L class: Another major production schedule produced this class from midway through the war. The design was based on an elongated E class; 34 were ordered, although only 27 were commissioned. They were of variable designs to provide boats for basic torpedo armament, as minelayers, and later all carried a 102mm/4in gun mounted on the superstructure; three were lost (two accidentally) during the war and another sank with all 40 hands in 1924. The rest remained in service until the 1930s, when most were sold, although a handful was still in service at the beginning of World War II.

R class: Ten were launched in 1918, but few were commissioned before the war's end. They were notable for their very attractive streamlined hull design, which produced a fast underwater speed capability. They were designed specifically as attack boats and had a huge firepower of six 457mm/18in torpedo tubes. Since most of them were launched when the need for attack boats had virtually passed, they saw little in the way of active service and were all scrapped in 1923. Two more, known as the second R class, with various amendments, were built in 1930.

ABOVE LEFT: **Under the terms of the Armistice at the end of World War I, Germany was required to surrender her submarines to the Allied nations. Britain received a large number at the east coast port of Harwich and these two, *U124* and *U164*, were almost brand new.** ABOVE: ***U117* was among the boats surrendered to the USA and was subsequently used for naval exhibitions along the Atlantic coast before she sank in June 1921 off Virginia during tests.**

ABOVE: ***U120* had been operational for only two months prior to the end of the war and was one of the boats surrendered to Italy for inspection by their own designers and engineers before being broken up at La Spezia in April 1919.**
BELOW: **The continuing stream of forlorn U-boat commanders and skeleton crews who surrendered vessels allotted to Britain at the end the war, coming ashore at Harwich in 1919.**

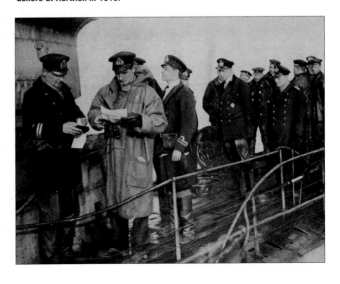

The "jinx" on the K boats

Among the boats retained for post-war service by the Royal Navy were those in the experimental K class, a steam-driven fleet submarine, hugely impressive in appearance and, at the time of their first commissioning in 1916, the largest and fastest submarines in the world, bar none. Unfortunately, their performance and stability did not live up to the great expectations surrounding them, and after a succession of disasters, the tag of "jinxed" was soon assigned.

Their design called for steam engines, which had never been completely successful in submarines, not least because they required funnels. They were 103m/337ft 11in in length, with a surface displacement of 1,850 tonnes/1,821 tons and 2,450 tonnes/2,411 tons submerged, driven by a pair of massive steam turbines powered by oil-fired boilers which could produce a speed of 23 knots on the surface and 10 knots dived from four electric motors. There were eight 457mm/18in torpedo tubes on the bow and beam and a crew of 55.

However, steam power had a number of drawbacks. The boilers had to be shut down on the command of "Dive!" a process that took up to five minutes. The funnels had to be retracted into their housings and covered by watertight shutters. Four mushroom-shaped ventilators that took heat from the boiler room were also retracted and sealed. It was perhaps a prophetic omen that the first of the class to be accepted into service almost changed the course of history in a serious way. The future King George VI, then a youthful naval officer in the Grand Fleet, was having a personal demonstration run in the vessel when the boat went into an uncontrolled dive, and ended up bow down on the muddy bottom in 40m/131ft 3in of water off Portsmouth. It took 20 minutes of delicate manoeuvres before Commander Leir managed to extricate his boat from the mud and return the future king to safety.

K6 also hit problems during her diving trials. Having submerged during tests at Devonport, the boat simply refused to return to the surface after the ballast tanks had been blown. The 50 men on board were trapped for two hours before the trouble was traced to a fault in the compressed-air system. Next, K4 ran aground at Walney Island during surface trials, and then K11 suffered generator failure when she too shipped water through the funnel intakes during trials in heavy seas.

On January 29, 1917, K13 set off from the Clyde heading for Gare Loch with a crew of 53 complemented on this day by civilian passengers, mostly VIPs from the shipbuilders, 82 people in all. Barely had the boat reached the dive depth when the boiler room began to flood. K13 dropped to the bottom with a bump. As the captain picked up the voice-pipe to give the order to stop engines, water spurted out, which meant the engine room was totally flooded. Then flames erupted on the

ABOVE: **K22 (ex-K13)** lowering her steam-turbine funnels prior to diving, a procedure that took up to five minutes. She sank on her maiden voyage with 82 crew and civilians aboard. Only 47 survived. BELOW: **K6** also sank on her diving trials, and went to the bottom where she stubbornly remained for two hours until a fault was traced.

control switchboard, which the men beat out with their bare hands. The boat was immovable, the flooding was becoming more serious by the second and there was no means of contacting the surface. Two men courageously went out through the conning tower to raise the alarm, one of whom died in the attempt. Several hours passed before a rescue operation could be mounted. A head-count of survivors on the boat revealed that 31 on board were already dead.

Further deaths occurred before air pipes were fed into the boat from the surface after 35 hours, but it was another 22 hours before wire ropes had been looped under the bows to raise the boat and holes were cut through the hulls with oxyacetylene equipment to free the remaining 47 still alive on board. A subsequent court of inquiry heard that an inspection had revealed that the ventilator doors were open and that the instruments showed it. The boat was salvaged and was quickly recommissioned as K22.

Further dramas were soon to follow, including one of the most horrific accidents in naval history. On February 1, 1918, two submarine flotillas, the 12th and 13th, made up entirely of K-class boats, nine in all, were assigned for exercises with the fleet in the Firth of Forth. As they approached the estuary, the 13th Flotilla had to take avoiding action when a flotilla of

ABOVE LEFT: *K2* suffered an explosion in the engine room just after she submerged and only the quick thinking of skipper Lt Commander Noel Laurence in surfacing immediately saved her from disaster. ABOVE: K-class ratings were confronted with endless problems and dangers in these boats. Many of their colleagues did not survive.

destroyers crossed their path. K14 was rammed by K22 (the salvaged K13). Both submarines were damaged, and as she battled to stay afloat with flooding problems K22 was hit squarely by the battlecruiser *Inflexible* and had to be taken under tow.

In the chaos that developed, K17 was rammed and it vanished within seven minutes. Miraculously, all 57 crew managed to escape and were splashing about in the water waiting to be rescued when three destroyers steamed directly towards them unaware of their presence and ran over them. Only eight survived. In the continuing confusion, K6 rammed K4, which sank instantly, and her entire crew of 55 went down with her. The misfortunes of these magnificent boats continued and, in all, 16 were involved in major accidents, and eight finished up on the bottom of the sea before the class was scrapped in 1932. Over 300 men lost their lives in K-class or converted K-class boats – not one of them to enemy action.

BELOW: **The K class was in fact an imposing looking vessel, but designed in haste during World War I, when naval intelligence learned that the Germans had launched a U-boat capable of 20 knots on the surface. The K boats were capable of 23 knots.**
RIGHT: **The familiar bulbous nose of *K12*, one of the lucky ones of the class, surviving a near-miss during exercises with the fleet.**

Big guns and aircraft carriers

Innovation in the design and use of submarines has been constant over the years, and none more so than in the early days when experimentation and high-risk projects were quickly coming off the ideas boards. Two in particular dominated the thoughts of many design enthusiasts in the British Naval hierarchy, especially during the war years in Europe, when competitive military might became the mother of invention.

The first aircraft to be used as bombers, for example, instantly caught the imagination of many. Apart from the obvious notion of surface carriers, the prospect of aircraft launched from submarines became an immediate prospect, as indeed did the use of big guns in the style of surface warships. In August 1915, Admiral Sir John "Jackie" Fisher, the instigator of the Dreadnought class of battleship, voiced his theory of having a submarine equivalent with a big gun that could surface amid flotillas of enemy vessels, perform untold damage and vanish again.

Four boats from the K class, *18*, *19*, *20* and *21* were selected for conversion into M class to be reconfigured with revolutionary features that were to make them more like submersible battleships. They were to be armed with a 60-tonne/59.1 tons, 305mm/12in gun, which had a much greater range than any torpedo but could be fired only from a depth of 6m/19ft 8in, hardly a concealed position, and reloading had to be carried out on the surface. Although approval was given for the conversion in 1916, delays and Navy red tape meant none was ready in time for war service and only three were completed. They became *M1*, *M2* and *M3* and looked exceedingly menacing but never fired a shot in anger. They were rendered obsolete by the 1921 Washington Disarmament Treaty, which limited the size of submarine-mounted guns to 216mm/8.5in.

Nor did the change of prefix rid the boats of the jinx of the K class. While submerged, *M1* sank after a collision with a Swedish coaster, SS *Vidar*, off Start Point on November 12,

TOP: **A famous image of *M2*, the first British boat to be turned into an aircraft carrier, although ambition proved more hopeful than reality in their use, and the jinx of the K class, from which they were converted, continued. She was lost with all hands.** ABOVE: **The speed of take-off had to be brisk with the engine racing, as demonstrated here, to achieve lift to avoid dumping into the sea, as often happened.**

1925, with the loss of her crew of 68. The wreck was found in 1999 by a sport diver 35 miles south-east of Plymouth.

M2, meanwhile, had a hangar fitted with a gantry to lift a light seaplane, the Parnell Peto, with an endurance of two hours, aboard to become Britain's first submarine aircraft carrier. She too suffered the K-fate. On January 26, 1932, the boat was seen to nose-dive at an angle of about 45 degrees by a passing cargo steamer whose captain did not know anything about submarines and did not realize the significance of such a dive. Only when newspapers carried the reports of a missing submarines did he come forward, but by then the 67 crew and two RAF airmen had already perished. Before long, the submariners who knew of the K-class stories were pointing out that *M2* was commissioned exactly 13 years earlier.

Only *M3* saved the reputation of the class, operating as an experimental minelayer stowing 100 mines on rails inside a free-flooding casing. The mines were laid out over her stern by means of a chain conveyor belt.

The death of *M2* finally brought an end to British attempts to launch an effective submarine aircraft carrier, the Royal

ABOVE: **The Americans' *S1* submarine became the experimental platform for their hull-mounted collapsible seaplane, here the XS-2 all-metal version. After surfacing, the aircraft could be rolled out of its pod, quickly assembled, and launched by balancing the submarine until the deck was awash.**
LEFT: **The Japanese produced some of the best examples of submarine aircraft carriers, notably the *I400* with a hangar carrying three catapult-launched Aichi M6A seaplanes.** BELOW: **The Japanese submarine-launched plane E14Y, the only aircraft to drop bombs on the United States mainland in World War II.**
BOTTOM: **Britain's *M3* which was converted to carry a 305mm/12in gun, and later became a minesweeper.**

Navy constructors having failed in earlier attempts using Sopwith Schneider floatplanes attached to a modified *E22*. This submarine was converted in 1916, with the intention of intercepting German airships over the North Sea. The distinct disadvantage of this first carrier was the boat could not submerge with the aircraft aboard. Only one successful trial was carried out before the submarine sank.

Other navies continued with the carrier experiments. France, Italy and America all produced submarine carriers but none matched the extensive work in this area carried out by the Japanese who began building aircraft-carrying submarines in 1925. Most of their early boats were classified as scouting submarines, *B1* Type, of the I15 class, displacing 2,626 tonnes/2,584 tons submerged and 108.5m/356ft in length. Powered by twin diesel engines and electric motors driving two propeller shafts, the *B1* type boats had a cruising range of more than 22,530km/14,000 miles. They were also heavily armed, and thus doubled as attack boats, carrying 17 torpedoes and sporting a 140mm/5.5in deck gun. The crews were comprised of 97 officers and enlisted men.

The floatplane carried by the *B1* model was collapsed into a water-tight hangar installed forward of the conning tower. Two launching rails extended from the hangar to the bow, from which the reassembled aircraft would be catapulted into the air by compressed air. The returning aircraft had to land on the sea and was recovered using a retractable crane. The Uokosuka E14Y aircraft had an operating range of about 322km/200 miles.

The United States Navy, like the Royal Navy, had no such success with their attempts to launch a submarine aircraft carrier. Their experiments began in 1923, using an S-class submarine with an MS-1 seaplane on deck. The aircraft was to be stowed, disassembled, in a cylinder on deck while the

submarine was submerged. It proved to be a totally impractical idea and was abandoned in 1926. Meanwhile, the Japanese proceeded to enhance and advance their own technology in this area, and by World War II they had 47 boats capable of carrying seaplanes. *I14*, for example, was fitted with a hangar capable of housing two aircraft, and the gigantic I400-class boats could carry three. All were at sea preparing for an attack on the US fleet anchorage at Ulithi Atoll, when the Japanese surrendered.

Giants of the deep

By the mid-1920s, it was clear that Britain had made a rod for her own back with rapid developments of submarine technology matched and copied by other nations, now sharing the benefits of the technology gleaned from captured U-boats. Having come through the devastating experience of having so much of the nation's merchant fleet wiped out, the British naval chiefs went through a reappraisal of their own and many reverted to the original thoughts of the traditionalists – that submarines were a cursed invention. In attending the 1921 post-war Washington conference of the five naval powers – the others being France, the United States, Italy and Japan – the British representatives shocked everyone by proposing an international ban on submarines.

The idea was rejected out of hand by the other nations, understandably since most – especially America and Japan – were already embarking on a massive submarine development programme. What the British and the Germans had produced during the war years, however, amounted to a catalogue of designs and ideas that would provide base plans for the construction of bigger, faster, more potent vessels.

The designs of the two senior combatant nations set the standard for progressive and bold experiments that resulted in the production of the world's largest ever submarine, X1. The road to that development emerged directly from the fear of what Germany possessed, and vice versa. The British move towards "bigger and better" began first with the production of the V class, which was noted for its increased hull strength,

TOP: **The giant, USS *Nautilus*, one of the *Narwhal*-class submarines, the fifth ship of the US Navy to bear that name, although she was designated *V-6*. Commissioned in 1930, she won a presidential citation for aggressive patrolling and 14 battle stars in World War II.**
ABOVE: ***Nautilus* under construction.**

achieved by external framing between the inner and outer hulls. This allowed the submarine to dive to 45m/147ft 8in, as opposed to the norm of 30m/98ft 5in. Next in the pursuit of the ultimate diving machine came the *Nautilus*, later renamed *N1*, which was built over a four-year period at Vickers shipyards, went through various changes of design and cost £203,850. She was a sleek, fine-looking boat which, at 79m/259ft 2in in length, was at the time of her original design work almost twice the size of any existing submarine. The boat was regarded by many as a failure and never saw service of any description other than for training purposes and as a depot ship. However, that was indeed a short-sighted view. It was first and foremost an experimental boat, an early footprint on the road to the giants of the deep that were to follow. The next major development – outside of Germany's own fast and deep cruiser submarines, already discussed – came the one and only *X1*, which was another milestone in every way. She was a cruiser submarine of 3,600 tonnes/3,543 tons submerged – in no uncertain terms a true submersible cruiser, she could travel at 18.5 knots on the surface, was 110m/360ft 11in in length, and carried four 132mm/5.2in guns in twin turrets. Although conceived in 1915 – when Germany was already producing her cruiser boats – *X1* was not completed until 1925 and successfully passed a rigorous trials procedure. The trouble was, now there was no role for her in the British fleet, and the colossus was finally scrapped in 1937.

Other nations began to pursue the theme of giants of the deep. America produced its own *Nautilus* in 1930, following on from *Narwhal*, first introduced in 1927. Both were still effective and well used in World War II. They were massive boats – 113m/370ft 9in long, sleek in design and excellent to handle.

Elsewhere, other giants had emerged. The Japanese hired German technicians and began a programme of building submarines that went to the extremes of range and size, from midget subs to the largest cruisers, some capable of travelling 31,187km/20,000 miles and with an endurance of more than 100 days. The French also appreciated that size mattered and introduced the *Surcouf*, 110m/360ft 11in in length and 3,357 tonnes/3,304 tons, armed with two 203mm/8in guns and a light aircraft. Such was the fear and loathing of submarine warfare – loathing by the politicians because of the cost – that in 1930, Britain, America and Japan agreed to limit tonnage and impose armament limitations for all future cruisers, destroyers and submarines, with no new capital ships to be laid down until 1937. Neither France nor Italy agreed to sign, and in any event, the whole deal collapsed within three years because of developments in Germany.

ABOVE: **USS *Narwhal* (originally designated *V5*) was the lead ship in her class, commissioned in 1930, and was one of five submarines docked in Pearl Harbor when the Japanese attacked. Her gunners were quickly in action and shot down two of the torpedo bombers.** BELOW: **The one and only *X1*, the British cruiser submarine that led the field in the development of these underwater giants when built in 1925.**

LEFT: **USS *Barracuda*, (originally *V1*) was the first of the American V boats, commissioned in 1925, but at 2,032 tonnes/2,000 tons was considerably smaller than the giants that followed in the V-designation. She was recommissioned for service in 1942 to patrol the American Pacific coast.** ABOVE: **The pride of France, *Surcouf*, with a surface displacement of 3,302 tonnes/3,250 tons, was the largest submarine in the world when launched in 1929. She was lost with all 130 crew, supposedly sunk in the Gulf of Mexico in November 1942 amid accusations that she was spying for Hitler.**

The inter-war years

While the maritime nations experimented with the *Nautilus* and similar boats, the main area of development in the 1930s was concentrated on building new workhorses for the various national submarine fleets. Britain had particular difficulty in achieving the aspirations of her admirals because of the country's parlous financial state, which was one of the reasons the government was so keen on maintaining international agreements curbing the arms race. However, in this regard, she was in danger of being left behind.

While Japan, Italy, France and Russia were now all focusing heavily on submarine manufacture, Britain had to rely on old stock well into the third decade of the century for the bulk of the service's work. The only new models apart from the experimental classes to appear beyond those ordered up during World War I were eight 1,524 tonne/1,500 ton O class and six slightly larger P class. They were excellent boats, designed for overseas patrols around the far-flung Empire, and especially the Far East. Nevertheless, they had a limited capability and also, by then, America, Japan, France and even Russia all possessed more submarines than Britain. Added to this was soon to be a new fear that would change the complexion of everything.

Adolf Hitler came to power in Germany, and secretly began to re-equip his military. Plans for the rebirth of the U-boat were already underway by 1934 when the Nazis issued bold statements repudiating the Treaty of Versailles, and in March 1935 demanded renegotiation of the permitted level of their armed forces. Britain's appeasement of Hitler in these times through the creation of the Anglo-German Naval Agreement allowed him to begin rebuilding the German Navy, supposedly to be kept within 35 per cent of the tonnage of the Royal Navy.

The single exception to this was in the dispensation for a new U-boat force, under the command of Admiral Karl Dönitz, which was allowed a tonnage 45 per cent of Britain's. The figures were both meaningless and unenforceable. Hitler made it clear that he would no longer be bound by a 20-year-old treaty and was already on the way to creating a new navy, although his plans for it were still far from complete when World War II began. Indeed, Dönitz himself had proclaimed in 1938 that it would take six years to rebuild Germany's U-boat force. In fact, as history now shows, the power house of the new Nazi machine achieved remarkable output and very soon the U-boats were back in business.

ABOVE: **Salute to the U-boats. These were Hitler's greatest sea-borne asset at the onset of World War II and throughout the conflict, given that Germany had been prevented from rebuilding the naval fleet that the nation was forced to surrender in 1918.** LEFT: **An early casualty in the undersea war: the British *Starfish*, commissioned as the third boat in the new S class in 1933, was depth-charged by German minesweeper *M7* in Heligoland Bight in January 1940. She was forced to surface and her crew went into captivity.**

ABOVE: **USS *Cachalot*, lead ship in the class bearing her name and another version of the V boats, lay in Pearl Harbor when the Japanese attacked. One of her men was wounded, but the submarine suffered no damage. Work on her was completed at a furious pace, and just one month later she sailed on her first war patrol and eight weeks later returned with vital intelligence of Japanese bases.**

Coincidence or not – but certainly by good fortune – the Royal Navy had begun its own modernization programme for the submarine service by ordering the building of a smaller boat specifically designed for operating in the North Sea and other confined theatres such as the Mediterranean. The boat to fill this role was another brilliant model, the S class, just 66m/216ft 6in long and displacing 886 tonnes/872 tons. In the fullness of time – and especially during World War II – the S class would prove to be one of the most important of all the Royal Navy submarines, with a total of 62 constructed over a 15-year period from 1935. This was to be quickly followed by the introduction of the T class, another exceptional boat particularly noted for the simplicity of its design. Approval for the build was given in 1935, and the first, *Triton*, came out for trials in 1938 to become the first of the 21 boats of this class built between 1937 and 1941. They were the largest class of ocean-going submarines to have been built by the Royal Navy, displacing 1,348 tonnes/1,327 tons surfaced and 83m/272ft in length, but only a handful were anywhere near ready by the outbreak of World War II.

The Americans, meanwhile, continued to be slow in their construction of new submarines. They were held back to some extent by their own financial depression, and also the fact that some in the US administration were of the same view of many naval traditionalists in Britain who still questioned the morality of submarine warfare and would have preferred the 1930 curtailment to have held.

However, with Hitler casting off the shackles of Versailles, Japan setting her sights across the Pacific and Mussolini already on a mission to build the New Roman Empire, the US Navy was forced to begin a rapid building programme, principally to meet the Japanese threat. By 1940, the American submarine force had answered its fundamental strategic questions and was rapidly enhancing its capability.

ABOVE: **The gathering storm. Hitler's submarine force was presented with a new flag when the swastika became the official emblem of the German nation in 1934.** BELOW: **An early workhorse of the US submarine fleet on America's entry into the war, USS *Sturgeon*, a 1,472-tonne/1,449-ton *Salmon*-class boat, was commissioned in 1938. She was operating in Hawaiian waters until December 1941 when she switched to war patrols in the Far East. One of the most notable events in her log occurred after her attack on a nine-ship Japanese convoy in 1943, when, in response, she was dived under a barrage of 196 depth charges and aerial bombs and survived to return safely home.**

The Japanese story

Japan, more than any other nation, benefited from the era when Germany was prevented from reviving the U-boat force. Under the terms of international treaties to which the Japanese were signatories, their engineers – like those of Britain, American and France – were able to take apart surrendered U-boats and copy German technology. However, they went one better. They shrewdly hired more than 1,000 German technicians and designers who had built the U-boats in the first place – a move that no other nation had felt inclined to do. The Japanese government approved massive bounty payments to encourage the employment of German expertise, which even included former naval officers who had themselves commanded U-boats. They were offered five-year contracts, some with an annual salary of $12,000 plus bonuses, which was a huge amount of money at the time.

Armed with this double dose of technological know-how, Japan set about building a massive new submarine fleet. As early as 1928, American Intelligence reports noted with some alarm that Japanese efforts, based upon this German input was reaching worrying proportions. "Furthermore," one report stated, "as various submarines were completed, Japanese engineers gradually took over the entire production, from design to completion until finally a distinctly Japanese type of submarine gradually emerged." Indeed, by the mid-1930s Japan was in the final stages of creating the most versatile submarine fleet of any nation in World War II.

Even so, similarities to the U-boats were very evident in three main classes of submarine. The I class, for example, was the Japanese version of the fast and potent German

TOP: **Japanese enthusiasm for submarine construction was already evident in the early 1920s, with *RO60*, which was one of nine L4 type medium series submarines, commissioned in 1923, with a surface displacement of 1,012 tonnes/ 996 tons.** ABOVE: **Early Japanese boats had many of the characteristics of U-boats, not unnaturally perhaps, since they took apart surrendered World War I German submarines and then hired many U-boat engineers and designers.**

cruiser submarine. It was the ultimate fleet boat, which Britain and America had also tried to perfect. It was also produced in several versions, including aircraft carriers and submarines that could carry multiple bombers; seaplane tenders; cargo ships; and some as submarine support vessels for the military. Next came the RO class, similar to but not as capable as the German coastal boats, and finally the HA class, which were smaller and intended for local defence and special missions, again sometimes attached to support ground forces. The most notable of the HA class, however, included midget submarines, one of the number of purpose-built boats developed in utmost secrecy by the Japanese in the late 1930s. They also built submarines large enough to transport the midget boats into

LEFT: **Another useful Japanese boat, the *HA101*, lead ship of the 376 tonne/370 ton SS type of small transport submarines, entered service late in the war but was well thought of, and closely examined when surrendered with the Japanese Navy's other surviving warships.** ABOVE: **Torpedo technology was also well advanced: these tubes housed the Type 95 torpedo that was based on the formidable Long Lance design, air launched and, some experts have claimed, was the best torpedo of the war.**

combat or enemy coastal areas where they would be released in swarms to attack – as it transpired – American warships. In fact, every aspect of Japanese technology throughout these years – obviously with an eye on the massive journeys involved in any future action in the boundless space of the Pacific – was geared to extremes in endurance and capability. They had the largest submarines in the world, the only boats with more than 5,080 tonnes/5,000 tons submerged displacement, or submarines over 121.9m/400ft in length – an achievement that was not matched until the arrival of nuclear-powered boats. They were said to have a range of 60,350km/37,500 miles at 14 knots, an achievement unmatched by any other diesel-electric submarine. These giants could carry three floatplane bombers, the only submarines ever built with such a capability.

Of the 56 submarines greater than 3,048 tonnes/3,000 tons built for action by the nations engaged in World War II, at least 50 were Japanese. They also led the field in diesel-electric submarines with 7457kW/10,000hp, and also in diesel-electric submarines capable of more than 23 knots surface speed – unmatched by any other nation.

Japanese boats also came equipped with some of the best torpedoes available. One significant development in this field was a torpedo known as the Long Lance, a submarine version of which, Mk95, was built with a 408kg/900lb warhead driven by an oxygen-fuelled turbine that left no wake, and was capable of travelling a full five miles at 40 knots. It was operative at the start of World War II and was well ahead of anything comparable built by the Allies at the time.

The Mk95 also carried the largest warhead of any submarine torpedo, initially 405kg/893lb, which was increased to 549kg/1,210lb in the final stages of the war. Another vital innovation in the Mk95 was the use of a simple contact

ABOVE: **The *I52* was a Type C-3 cargo boat, known as Japan's Golden Submarine because she was carrying £25 million in gold to Germany as payment for war material when she was sunk by a US Task Force. In 2006, attempts were made to raise the treasure by diver Paul Tidwell.** BELOW: **The sleek lines of the *I21*, a member of the elite Japanese Sixth Fleet, and the boat that famously shelled Australian cities in 1942, presumed lost with all hands in December 1943 while tracking an American convoy in the Pacific.**

exploder, which was far more reliable than the American counterpart, the Mark 14, although the latter was improved early in 1944. Although there was no denying the sheer fire-power and versatility of the Japanese submarine fleet developed between the wars, and during the conflict itself, it has to be said that overall, Japan's submarine warfare – as will be seen – was not as effective as her masters expected.

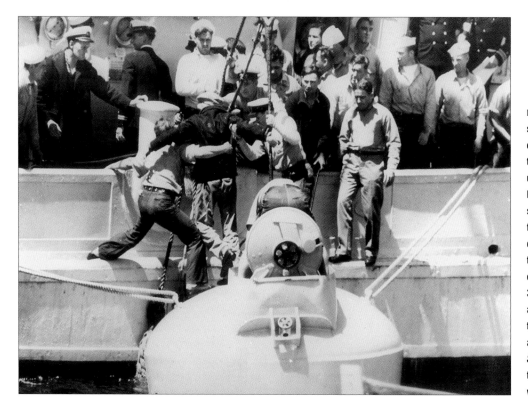

LEFT: **A defining moment in submarine history, the arrival on the surface of the first men to be saved from a stricken boat using the experimental McCann Rescue Chamber, following the sinking of USS *Squalus*, which failed to surface after the final crash dive test in her last sea trials. She sank in 73.2m/240ft of water, and the surviving 33 crew waited in total darkness and without power for more than 24 hours before the rescue attempt began.** BELOW: **The *Squalus* badge, although when the boat was recovered, she was given a new name.**

The sinking and recovery of USS Squalus

In the months leading up to World War II, two notable and tragic events occurred, both of which highlighted the perils faced by submariners of the participant navies in the coming months and years, and drew attention to the rescue possibilities from stricken boats. The two events, involving the US submarine *Squalus* and, across the Atlantic, the British boat *Thetis*, were remarkably similar in detail, but the outcomes were drastically different.

The *Squalus* left the Portsmouth Navy Yard, New Hampshire at 07:30 hours on May 23, 1939, for its 19th test dive under the command of Lt Oliver Naquin with 59 men on board — five officers, 51 enlisted men and three civilian inspectors. The exercise, part of a rigorous series of performance tests to which all boats were subjected, was to perform an emergency dive while cruising at 16 knots, diving to 15.24m/50ft within 60 seconds in order to avoid enemy attack. The dive was to be carried out just south-east of the Isles of Shoals where there was an average depth of 76.2m/250ft. When the order to dive was given at about 08:45 hours, the boat initially refused to respond, but within just a few minutes had settled gently on the bottom at 74.06m/243ft with the bow raised by 11 degrees.

The catastrophe had been caused by flooding of the aft section, and immediate action was taken to isolate the individual compartments to prevent total flooding, a procedure largely completed during the sinking. However, lighting had failed and only a few hand lanterns were available to relieve the darkness as the commander began the process of checking his situation. Of the 59 people who sailed that morning, 23

were in the control room and 10 in the forward torpedo room. It was likely that everyone in the after battery room and both engine rooms had died. No contact was made with the after torpedo room. The possibility of survivors there remained, but communications with the control room had failed.

Saltwater was leaking into the forward battery and if it infiltrated the battery acid, chlorine gas might be released, or it could short-circuit the cells and cause a fire. This meant that the forward battery compartment, which was located between the two occupied spaces, would have to be left vacant. Meanwhile, a communications buoy attached to *Squalus* was released and surfaced soon after the sinking. Rockets were also fired from time to time and the sixth launched after four hours on the bottom was by chance spotted by a lookout on the sister submarine USS *Sculpin*, which rushed immediately to the scene and located the communications buoy to establish contact. Just two minutes later, however, the connecting cable snapped. By mid-afternoon, two ships had arrived at the scene, one with an oscillator that enabled Morse code transmissions. As wives and families awaited news, a part-read message from *Squalus* transcribed as "condition satisfactory but cold" was taken to offer more hope than was the case.

In fact, by that time there were only 33 survivors, and their lives were at risk as the atmosphere in the boat reached twice the normal pressure. The US Navy's attempts to rescue the survivors went through various stages of discussion. The first, to pump out the flooded compartments to bring the *Squalus* to the surface was dismissed as too risky, because the reasons for the sinking were unknown.

Finally, on the morning of May 24, the submarine rescue vessel USS *Falcon* arrived above the submarine with a team of divers and a McCann Rescue Chamber to begin a dramatic rescue attempt that was to last a full ten hours. The divers were commanded by Lt Commander Charles Momsen, who had invented both the Momsen Lung and the diving bell. The latter would be attached to an escape hatch over the forward torpedo room allowing survivors to be drawn to the surface by cable. The theory was fine, and well rehearsed in training conditions, but in practice this was to be an historic, drama-filled mission. By 10:07 hours, divers had managed to get the diving bell over the escape hatch and the crew inside the *Squalus* banged out a welcome on the hull. However, this was merely the beginning of a long and exhausting process, as the bell with its two operators for the motors, ballast, air pressure and communications sought to make the connection to begin the first evacuation, a task that overall would take two hours or more from leaving the mother ship to returning with survivors, with a maximum of eight men at a time. All went smoothly until the last trip, the one carrying Commander Naquin and the last seven of his crew. They were safely aboard the diving bell by 19:50 hours to begin the ascent when the cable attached to the *Falcon* fouled and frayed. It took four and a half hours to bring the chamber to the surface. Nevertheless, all 33 survivors of the original accident were safe.

The boat was salvaged in the summer of 1939, and after repair was recommissioned as USS *Sailfish*. She went on to survive World War II, sinking 40,642 tonnes/40,000 tons of enemy shipping.

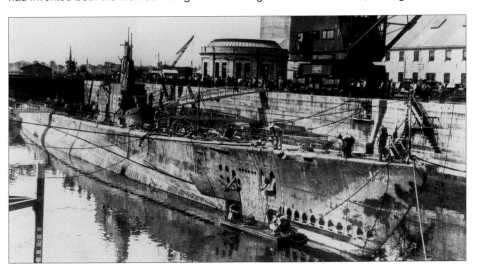

ABOVE LEFT: **The internal lay-out of the McCann diving bell, which could extract crew through the escape hatch and return to the surface carrying up to eight passengers on each trip.** ABOVE: **During a three-month salvage effort by the US Navy using air tanks on the surface, the bodies of those who died were removed and the *Squalus* finally returned to the surface.** LEFT: **The salvaged submarine in a sorry state. She was immediately sent to the shipyards for repairs and was recommissioned to serve for the duration of World War II under her new name, USS *Sailfish*.**

The tragic loss of the Thetis

Barely a week after the *Squalus* tragedy, an accidental sinking bearing incredible similarities occurred off the coast of Wales where a brand-new British submarine went to the bottom, with totally catastrophic results. It was indeed a disastrous event for the Royal Navy with so much riding on the new T-class submarines just weeks before the outbreak of World War II. HMS *Thetis* was the third of the T boats scheduled for commissioning, and after months of rigorous tests since her launch in 1938, she was to begin final acceptance trials in late May 1939. Her captain, Lt Commander Guy Bolus, had stood by her during her fitting out and, with a crew of five other officers and 48 ratings, left the yard at Merseyside for trial runs in the Clyde estuary during May. There were a few problems to be ironed out, which was not unusual with a new boat, and *Thetis* returned to Cammell Laird yards for adjustments. The final diving trial was postponed until June 1, in Liverpool Bay.

Thetis sailed from Birkenhead soon after 09:00 hours that day with an unusually large number of people on board. In addition to the crew, there were officers from the flotilla *Thetis* was to join when she was fully commissioned, civilian observers from the Admiralty, 26 employees of shipbuilders Cammell Laird, five from other shipbuilding firms who would be building T-class boats, two members of staff from City Caterers of Liverpool, who were supplying the luncheon, and a Mersey pilot: 103 men in all. The weather was fine, the sea was calm with only a touch of an easterly wind. Everyone on

board was looking forward to an interesting trip, and for the non-sailors it was an adventure to be enjoyed with perhaps a touch of apprehension. Accompanying *Thetis* during the initial stages of the trial was the *Grebecock*, a two-year-old steam tug manned by a crew of seven and laid on by Cammell Laird as part of their contract with the navy. On board was a navy observer and submariner, Lt Dick Coltart, whose task it was to keep a general watch and to warn any ships that might sail into the diving area. The *Grebecock* was also to stand by to take off any civilian passengers from *Thetis* who might wish to disembark after lunch, but none chose to do so. Then came a signal from *Thetis* that she would be diving for three hours. Coltart watched as Lt Commander Bolus left the bridge and the conning tower hatch was closed. At precisely 14:00 hours, Bolus gave the order to dive. But *Thetis* stubbornly refused to budge. Minutes later, she disappeared beneath the waves very quickly, and it was assumed that all was now going to plan.

Unfortunately it was not. The 533mm/21in wide No. 5 torpedo tube was open to the sea and the internal rear door of No. 5 tube had also been opened because a faulty test drain pipe showed empty when, in fact, the tube was full. Therefore, the door was open and *Thetis* sank. The situation was critical. As time passed, Coltart became convinced the submarine was in trouble and sent a carefully worded signal to the submarine base at Fort Blockhouse. Unfortunately, the telegraph delivery boy's bike got a puncture en route and the message was

LEFT: **HMS *Thetis*, one of the new British T boats, launched into her acceptance trials in May 1939 in the Clyde estuary before finally beginning diving trials in Liverpool Bay on June 1. On that day, she had a full crew of 54 officers and ratings aboard, along with shipbuilders, civilian observers and other guests, 103 men in all, when disaster struck.** ABOVE: **The *Thetis* badge that was never operationally used.**

ABOVE LEFT: **Pristine again after the dramas below, the *Thetis* was recovered and recommissioned as *Thunderbolt* to enter service in World War II.**
ABOVE RIGHT: **As *Thetis*, she went upside down and stuck firm in the mud when on her pre-acceptance trails. Although rescue ships reached her after some delay, they could not gain access before she finally sank to the bottom with great loss of life.** LEFT: **The salvage boats hover as the recovery begins.**
BELOW: **The *Thetis* is brought to the surface and dragged ashore for repairs and renewal.**

delayed. When it did arrive, fast destroyers were ordered to the scene and the RAF sent a flight of four Ansons, conducting low-level fly-bys until dusk closed in. A salvage vessel, *Valiant* sailed from Liverpool but by then it was almost eight hours since any word had been heard from *Thetis*.

Three hours later, searching over a wider arc, a crewman on the destroyer *Brazen* spotted something in the distance, and as the ship headed towards it, an incredible sight became visible – 5.5m/18ft of the stern of the 83.5m/274ft-long *Thetis* was protruding from the sea. She lay at an angle, nose down in 45m/147ft 8in of water 24km/15 miles off the North Wales coast. Inside the boat, conditions were desperate. The air was foul and rapidly running out. Bolus decided that the only solution was to make an attempt to leave the boat, using the David Submerged Escape Apparatus (DSEA), although few men were fully trained in the procedure. Volunteers stepped forward. Captain Joe Oram, officer commanding the 5th Flotilla, and Lt Woods were selected and successfully made their escape, popping to the surface within seconds. They were picked up by *Brazen* and proceeded to give details of the situation below.

Four more men escaped later, but after that, no further exit attempts were made, for unknown reasons. By then, *Brazen* had been joined by six destroyers, five tugs, the Llandudno

lifeboat and the salvage vessel *Vigilant*, all strewn in an arc around the stricken submarine.

One final hope remained: to cut a hole in the side of *Thetis* with oxyacetylene gear, for which that section of the boat had to be raised above the surface. At 15:10 hours on June 2, as efforts were being made to achieve this, the wire rope snapped and *Thetis* plunged back to the bottom, taken all remaining 99 personnel with her. After further attempts to reach the boat failed, the rescue efforts were abandoned the following day amid a critical uproar from relatives. An inquiry did nothing to satisfy the relatives and trade unions, and a long and bitter legal action ended six and a half years later in the House of Lords, where claims for negligence were finally rejected on the grounds that there was no proof of liability.

Thetis was raised three months after she sank. Human remains still on board were retrieved for burial. The boat was repaired and went back to sea under the name of *Thunderbolt*, and had a successful campaign in the Mediterranean before being depth-charged north of Sicily on March 14, 1943, sinking for the second and last time.

The action begins, and Athenia goes down

Just after 11:15 hours on September 3, 1939, Royal Navy ships and submarines received the signal: "Commence hostilities with German forthwith." Four minutes later, the submarine *Spearfish* commanded by Lt J.H. Eden delivered a torpedo towards a German U-boat in the North Sea. It missed the target but established the first confrontation with the enemy. The Nazi High Command gave similar instructions to its U-boats that afternoon and before the day was out, Germany had launched into a controversy that matched its World War I attack on the passenger liner, *Lusitania*. This time, the victim was the 13,717 tonne/13,500-ton passenger liner, *Athenia* carrying 1,103 civilians, including more than 300 Americans attempting to escape the war in Europe. She became the first British ship sunk by a German U-boat in World War II.

The *Athenia* had already sailed from Glasgow en route to Montreal when war was official declared, and that afternoon as she steamed 402km/250 miles north-west of Inishtrahull, Northern Ireland, she was spotted by *U30* under the command of Lt Fritz-Julius Lemp. Regardless of the fact that German U-boats were supposed to be operating under prize regulations that obliged them to stop and search any potential targets, Lemp ordered his crew to open fire without giving any prior warning.

In the controversy that followed, and which remained an issue to be considered in the Nuremberg War Crimes trials, it was passed off as a case of mistaken identity. Lemp stated that he believed the *Athenia* was an armed merchant cruiser, and fired two torpedoes. The ship sank quickly with the loss of 112 passengers and crew, including 28 Americans, although that

TOP: **A photograph of the *Athenia* in the final throes of her sinking, apparently taken from the one of the rescue boats that rushed to the scene after the alert of the attack upon her by the *U30*. Three British destroyers and three merchant ships aided the rescue, which saved 90 per cent of the 1,103 civilians aboard.** ABOVE: **The majestic liner in all her glory, a ship that the U-boat commander who ordered the sinking claimed he mistook for an armed merchant cruiser. Few believed him.**

did not prevent President Franklin D. Roosevelt continuing with his plans to declare America's neutrality in the war. Some of the passengers claimed they were attacked again when they were at sea, escaping in lifeboats.

Lemp later offered an explanation. He stated that having received three radio messages sent to all Kriegsmarine vessels stating that war existed between Britain and Germany, he spotted the ship heading away from Britain in a north-westerly direction. Having ordered his boat to dive to periscope depth, he

FAR LEFT: **Fritz-Julius Lemp,** captain of *U30* in the controversial sinking of the *Athenia.* He later sank a total of 17 ships in the same submarine, becoming the seventh U-boat commander to be awarded the Knights Cross at the age of 26. He met his match in May 1941: he was killed in action when the British captured his new submarine, *U110,* with its vital Enigma machine.

ABOVE: **The killer blow to the *Athenia* may well have been struck by this torpedo, one of 11 that the Type VIIA *U30* could stow on each mission, a task made easier on July 7, 1940, when the boat became the first German submarine to make use of the newly captured French bases, docking in Lorient.**

BELOW: ***U30,* one of the busiest in early exchanges of the war and, as the front boat in Germany's 2nd Flotilla, completed eight patrols before she became a training submarine.** BOTTOM: **The British submarine *Oxley* lost off the coast of Norway after being mistaken for a U-boat and torpedoed by companion submarine *Triton* in September 1939.**

saw that the ship was blacked out and came to the conclusion that she was an armed merchant cruiser, and therefore a legitimate target. He fired two torpedoes, the first striking the ship squarely, and the other missing. He claimed he dived to avoid the possibility of being hit by the second torpedo and, returning to periscope depth, fired a third because the ship did not seem to be sinking. This too missed, but undoubtedly ran towards the escaping passengers. At this point, Lemp checked his Lloyd's Register and discovered his mistake.

Soon afterwards, *U30* intercepted a plain-language transmission from the stricken ship identifying itself as the *Athenia,* but even then he did not attempt to aid survivors, as Prize Rules required, and maintained radio silence throughout. Thus, in an instant the memories of Germany's U-boat campaign of unrestricted warfare in World War I were revived.

In fact, the effect worldwide was such that Hitler himself decreed that all such accusations would be dealt with by categorical denial and Goebels even put out a statement accusing Britain of deliberately sinking the *Athenia* to stop Roosevelt declaring neutrality. The Nazis even went to the extent of falsifying records to show that *U30* was at least 322km/200 miles from the *Athenia* at the time. The truth, however, was confirmed at Nuremberg by Adolf Schmidt, a member of Lemp's crew who had been wounded in a later action and was left in Iceland, where he became a prisoner of war. Even so, the international outcry did have immediate repercussions when Hitler signed an order to prevent further attacks on passenger ships, regardless of the nation of origin.

The British, meanwhile, also proved that accidents could happen in this electrifying turmoil at the start of the war. On September 10, an old O-class submarine, *Oxley,* set off on her

first major patrol off the coast of Norway. In heavy seas, at night and in poor visibility, she was spotted in the distance by one of her companion submarines, *Triton.* She failed to make the correct recognition signal. As a result, she was mistaken for a U-boat and torpedoed, and became the first submarine loss of World War II. Of the 54 crew, only her captain, Lt Commander H.G. Bowerman, and one other survived.

LEFT: The explosion caused by depth charges is violent and dramatic, and Lt Sheldon H. Kinney, Commander, USS *Bronstein* described them as "having a magnificent laxative effect on a submariner". They were used by ships or aircraft to attack submerged submarines and were first developed by the British for use against German submarines in World War I but were substantially improved by 1939. BELOW: Firing depth charges from the deck of a ship.

Mines, depth charges and leaky boats

Heligoland Bight and Skagerrak once again became the early scene of battles between British submarines and their German opponents, and Sir Max Horton, hero of great actions in World War I and whom the Germans had called a "pirate", was now directing operations under the personal eye of his good friend and First Lord of the Admiralty, Winston Churchill. As the battles began in earnest, they identified a particular target for the submarines in the unhindered supply of iron ore, which was being turned into ships and aircraft, coming down into Germany from northern Sweden – exactly the same problem that first emerged in 1914. The ore was being trans-shipped through the ice-free port of Narvik in northern Norway, still a neutral country.

On the same day, the British War Cabinet pronounced that British submarines could and would henceforth sink transport ships in the region on sight, and two days later it extended that order to cover any ship sighted within 16km/10 miles of the Norwegian coast. Max Horton had committed virtually his entire force to the Norwegian campaign a week earlier and although the British force would stay well away from the Baltic, where Horton had made his name, he dispatched every available submarine to join those already on patrol to cover all the German exits from Heligoland Bight, Skagerrak and the Kattegat.

The Skagerrak strait, between the southern coast of Norway and the Jutland peninsula of Denmark, was a vital seaway. Together with the Kattegat strait, it connects the North Sea with the Baltic Sea. About 214km/150 miles long and from 121km/75 to 145km/90 miles wide, the Skagerrak is shallow

near Jutland but deepens near the Norwegian coast. It was in these treacherous waters that Max Horton placed an arc of submarines at the beginning of 1940. These were supplemented by others laying 50 mines apiece on each trip, and in the first half of the year there was probably not a single home-based submarine commander who did not see service there. Several would never return.

The extent of their activity is demonstrated by the amount of shipping sunk by the submarine service in the month between April 8 and May 4: close on 35 assorted vessels, of almost 90,000 tonnes/88,579 tons, with the loss of four British submarines. It was a dangerous time, particularly for the less experienced submariners, because it was the first time in history that efficient depth charges were used in abundance, in addition to the normal hazard of mines.

ABOVE LEFT: **Destroyer Escorts accompanying shipping movements routinely carried a heavy load of 100 or more depth charges to ward off enemy submarines or preferably kill them off completely. To be fully effective, they had to be fired with extreme accuracy.** ABOVE RIGHT: **An even greater threat to both surface ships and submarines alike was the greatly improved technology for creating minefields. The toll was heavy on both sides.** LEFT: **The British submarine minelayer,** *Porpoise*, **who made her name helping to break the blockade of Malta with food and fuel stacked on her mine deck. She subsequently fell victim to either mines or depth charges while on minelaying patrols in the Far East.** BELOW: **The jubilant crew of the British boat** *Truant*, **which was forced to remain on the bottom for a long period to escape the retribution of depth charges after torpedoing the German cruiser** *Karlsruhe*.

Depth charges first came into use during World War I. The early forms of the weapon consisted of large cylinders containing TNT, which were rolled or catapulted from the stern of a ship. In the intervening years, depth charges and machinery for launching them had improved dramatically, and experimental work on new designs was ongoing and came into use in the early stages of World War II. The use of a new and more powerful explosive called Torpex, a mixture of RDX, TNT and aluminium, substantially reduced the size of depth charges. The casings were also streamlined to make them sink faster and thus more difficult to avoid. To have literally dozens of these sinking towards your boat and exploding all around as the commander looked worryingly at his depth gauge was one of the most frightening experiences imaginable.

The T boat *Tetrarch*, under the command of Captain Roland Mills, took the record for staying submerged for the longest known period to date of 43 hours while under heavy counter-attack by depth charges. When he finally came up for air, his crew were literally falling as if drunk. He confessed in a memoir: "The effects of successive long spells under water, accompanied by depth-charge attacks, could have untoward effects, especially when the charges were poured into the sea by a posse of marauding destroyers, angry because the submarine had just fatally damaged one of Germany's brand-new cruisers."

That is exactly what happened to Admiral C.H. Hutchinson, then a Lt Commander of another of the early T boats, *Truant*. He had carried out a number of successful patrols in the North Sea during the Norwegian campaign, when in April 1940 he,

along with other boats, was to provide protection and diversion for what proved to be the ill-fated Allied landings of troops at Narvik to counter the German invasion. One evening his attention was drawn to propeller noises, very faint, to the north. The sounds gradually got louder, and eventually he saw through the periscope a German cruiser dead ahead, screened by an escort of four small destroyers. He fired a large salvo of torpedoes and raised his periscope to take a look. He could see nothing but a very enlarged after-part of a destroyer which was right on top of him.

Unbeknown to Hutchinson at the time, he had torpedoed the famous German cruiser *Karlsruhe*, which was homeward bound from Oslo. The Germans were naturally furious. The cruiser was abandoned and was so badly damaged that Berlin ordered that she should be scuttled immediately.

Heroic work in the Mediterranean

The Norwegian campaign was followed quickly by the Battle of Britain, and the Royal Navy and the submarine force played its own part defending the potentially vulnerable eastern sea board as the threat of invasion mounted in the summer of 1940. It also provided cover for the massive operation to rescue the British Expeditionary force from France, while at the same time confronting the rising tide of U-boat activity in the Atlantic, soon to be facilitated by the use of France's Atlantic ports. But even as the demands of this new menace grew, a fresh area of conflict at sea opened up in the Mediterranean when Mussolini joined forces with Hitler and decided to rebuild the Roman Empire out of British possessions in North Africa and the Suez Canal in particular. One of the keys to this operation was his intention to capture the island of Malta, where defences were woefully meagre.

From the beginning, British resources were stretched to the limit, especially for the submarine flotillas, such as they were. Overnight, traditional British supply routes to its eastern outposts were closed down. The British had to send their ships on the long journey, lasting two or three months, around the Cape of Good Hope for all supplies, other than those borne by special convoys with major fleet escort operations, which the Royal Navy could ill afford. With the lack of very serious competition, the Italian Navy put up a very worthwhile case for supremacy in the Mediterranean, fielding five capital ships, 25 cruisers, 90 destroyers and 90 excellent submarines under

a very capable command structure. They had back-up from 2,000 front-line aircraft and were undoubtedly leading the West in the diversity of experiments with mini-subs, human torpedoes, underwater chariots for frogmen and exploding motorboats. When Mussolini entered the war, the British had no real naval force between Gibraltar and the Italian fleet ports. The British base at Malta possessed a puny collection of just six submarines. Three of them, the minelayer *Grampus* and *Odin* and *Orpheus*, were lost in the first week after Mussolini signed

ABOVE: **British submarine *Upholder* sank or damaged 22 enemy ships, which earned her skipper, Lt Commander Malcolm Wanklyn, the award of a Victoria Cross, though sadly he and his boat did not survive the war.** INSET: **The badge of HMS *Upholder* linked by the crest as a tribute to the original Wanklyn boat when a new British diesel electric submarine was launched in 1987.** BELOW: **Submarines of the 10th Flotilla based at Lazaretto, Malta, went into maritime history for their exploits. They included *Upright* (second from right) which sank Mussolini's cruiser *Armando Diaz*.**

his pact with Hitler. It was believed that they were all sunk with no survivors by deeply laid Italian mines.

Very soon, however, the British submariners began to show their mettle. Substantial totals of enemy shipping were sunk, and none better than that achieved by the brand new *Upholder,* under the command of Lt Commander Malcolm Wanklyn. He became the most successful submarine commander in World War II in spite of what would prove to be a relatively short career. *Upholder* arrived for duty in the Mediterranean on January 12, 1941. On her first patrol, she sank a 5,000-tonne/ 4,921-ton cargo vessel in one of the Axis convoys just off Tripoli, and in almost the same spot two days later sank an 8,000-tonne/ 7,874-ton supply ship. This time, *Upholder* was counter-attacked and took the brunt of 32 depth charges before escaping. After a brief lay-off, *Upholder* returned to the fray and in April sank three separate targets in a single convoy: a destroyer, a 4,000-tonne/3,937-ton supply ship and a 10,000-tonne/9.842-ton supply ship. On May 24, Wanklyn sighted a troopship, the Italian liner *Conte Rosso* of 17,800 tonnes/17,519 tons, carrying 4,000 troops, with an escort of three cruisers and several destroyers. He launched two torpedoes, which both scored direct hits amidships. The liner sank rapidly, killing 1,500 of the men on board. Wanklyn was awarded the DSO for this attack.

However, it was not all good news. During those vital months, the British submarine force in the Mediterranean lost four of its own boats in quick succession. *Usk* struck a mine at Cape Bon, *Undaunted* and *Union* were both depth-charged off Tripoli and the minelaying submarine *Cachalot* was rammed by an Italian torpedo boat. Malcolm Wanklyn and his fellow commanders began to take greater risks and shorter breaks. In September 1941, as Wanklyn set out on his fourteenth patrol, he joined up with *Unbeaten, Upright* and *Ursula* for a prearranged joint-assault to intercept a troop-carrying convoy leaving the southern Italian port of Taranto bound for Tunisia.

ABOVE: **The minelayer *Grampus*, lead boat of her class, built in 1935, was deployed off the coast of Sicily in June 1940, when she was spotted by a group of Italian torpedo boats and torpedoed. There were no survivors.** BELOW: **The *Undine*-class submarine *Ursula*, also in the Mediterranean flotilla, was noted earlier in action near the *Elbe*, when her captain, Lt Commander G.C. Phillips, courageously dived beneath a screen of six destroyers to sink the German cruiser *Leipzig* at a range so close that the *Ursula* herself was badly shaken by the explosion.**

Two torpedoes from *Upholder* hit the transport *Neptunia,* which sank in eight minutes. Wanklyn's third torpedo hit *Oceania* and ripped away her stern. The third transport, *Vulcania,* was hit by *Ursula* from long range, and *Utmost* finished her off as she tried to limp away. Meanwhile, *Utmost* now sighted three Italian cruisers and several destroyers and promptly sank one of the cruisers. As a result of his latest exploits, Malcolm Wanklyn was awarded the Victoria Cross in December 1941. On April 6, 1942, *Upholder* sailed out of the base for her twenty-fifth and last patrol before heading home for a refit, but she never made it back. On April 14, *Upholder* was depth-charged and sunk by the Italian torpedo boat *Pegaso* north-east of Tripoli. Wanklyn's was a remarkable record. In 16 months, *Upholder* had sunk or damaged 22 enemy ships, including three U-boats, two destroyers and one cruiser as well as 120,910 tonnes/119,000 tons of supply ships.

"Finest work" by British submarines

Much action remained, and more VCs were to be won in the continuing saga of the battle for the Mediterranean. Among them was an incident involving *Thrasher*. She had been in the Mediterranean only a couple of months and in February 1942 was operating off northern Crete. There, on February 16, she penetrated an escort screen of five destroyers in broad daylight and torpedoed and sank a large Axis supply ship off Suda Bay. The destroyers gave chase, and as she crash-dived they remained overhead for an hour or more, sending down more than 30 depth charges. She surfaced after dark and headed off towards the Gulf of Taranto, but very soon banging noises were heard on the casing. Two unexploded bombs had become lodged on the submarine.

Lt Peter Roberts and Petty Officer Tommy Gould volunteered to go out and recover the bombs. The first bomb was located and gently removed, wrapped in sacking and dropped over the stern. The second was lodged in a narrow space and they had to lay full length in complete darkness, pushing and dragging the bomb for a distance of some 6.1m/20ft until it could be lowered over the side, a task which took more than half and hour. There was a very great chance that the submarine might have to crash-dive while they were under the casing. Had this happened, they would have been drowned. Robert and Gould deservedly won the VC for their heroic action.

Throughout this period, there were many acts of great gallantry and daring among the submarine flotillas in the

ABOVE: **A classic shot of the periscope in operation in the control room, and without which the submarine would be useless. The skills of the operators in judging the distance, heading and speed of the target were imperative when firing a torpedo.**

Mediterranean, many of which resulted in their final demise. In March 1942, the *Torbay* won particular attention and a Victoria Cross for her captain, Lt Commander Anthony Miers. He sighted a north-bound convoy of four ships too far distant for him to attack initially, and he decided to follow in the hope of catching them in Corfu harbour. During the night, *Torbay* approached undetected up the channel and remained on the surface charging her battery. Unfortunately, the convoy passed straight through the channel, but on the morning of March 5, in glassy sea conditions, Miers successfully attacked two store ships and then brought *Torbay* safely back to the open sea. The submarine endured 40 depth charges and had been in closely patrolled enemy waters for 17 hours.

Turbulent also had numerous successes recorded against her name and represented a remarkable achievement which eventually brought the award of a Victoria Cross for the "great valour" of her captain, Commander John Wallace "Tubby" Linton, at the end of what was ultimately a tragic journey. In March 1943, Linton had already been hailed as one of the greats in the submarine hall of fame, but his was not simply a story of "big hits" in the Mediterranean. It went well beyond that, in terms of courage, daring and dedication to duty in the face of great adversity, as recorded in the citation for the VC he was awarded: "From the outbreak of war until *Turbulent's* last patrol, Commander Linton was constantly in command of submarines, and during that time inflicted great damage on the enemy."

The journey for Linton and his crew was drawing to a close in February 1943, when they sailed from Algiers for a patrol in the Tyrrhenian Sea. On March 1, she attacked and sank the Italian steamship *Vincenz*. On March 11, she torpedoed the mail and supply ship *Mafalda.* She was herself attacked the following morning by the anti-submarine trawler *Teti II* but escaped, only to hit a mine off Maddalena, Sardinia, on March 23. The discovery of her wreck many years later confirmed the irony of her last voyage.

The part played by the submarines of the 1st and 10th flotillas has not always been fully recognized by historians, although Commander F.W. Lipscomb was moved to record: "There is no doubt that the whole Mediterranean offensive can be regarded as the finest work ever accomplished by British submarines." In the crucial two years between January 1941 and December 1942, the Italians lost 171 ships in the Mediterranean, totalling well over half a million tonnes/492,103 tons, a large proportion of which were sunk by the submarine flotillas. On the debit side at that time, Britain lost 14 submarines in the Mediterranean, with 70 officers and 720 ratings.

TOP LEFT: **HMS *Thunderbolt*, the salvaged and recommissioned *Thetis* which re-emerged in October 1940, later adapted to carry Britain's "human torpedoes", known as Chariots, before she was lost again, this time sunk by an Italian corvette in March 1943**. TOP RIGHT: ***Sokol*, of the Polish Navy, in Malta Harbour, flying the Jolly Roger to denote her successes. She was previously HMS *Urchin*, loaned to the Poles after the loss of their own submarines.**
ABOVE LEFT: **Survivors of a U-boat rescued by Allied vessels in 1943, the year in which the Germans saw their highest number of losses, with 242 boats sunk.**
ABOVE RIGHT: **The uncommon sight of a U-boat in the Mediterranean: only 62 German boats passed through the Straits of Gibraltar throughout the war and none of them returned: all being sunk, severely damaged or scuttled.**
BELOW: **A memorial tribute in Valetta to the British and Allied submarine forces for their efforts during the war.**

TO COMMEMORATE THE CLOSE TIES FORGED BETWEEN THE PEOPLE OF MALTA G.C. AND THE OFFICERS AND MEN OF THE BRITISH AND ALLIED SUBMARINES BASED IN MALTA IN H.M.S. TALBOT, LAZARETTO MANOEL ISLAND IN TIME OF WAR, 1939-1945

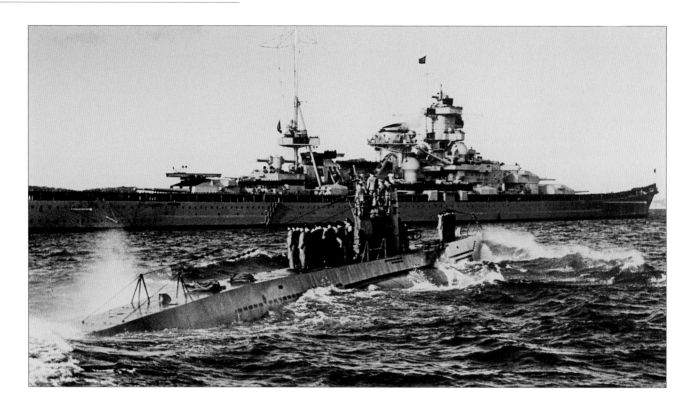

U-boat war in the Atlantic

In World War I, U-boats operating in the Atlantic almost brought Britain to her knees. The same procedure was attempted by Admiral Karl Dönitz, head of the German submarine service, by attacking Allied shipping at its weakest point – merchant vessels – with what was, at the time, a comparatively small fleet of U-boats. The aim was to harass the movement of essential British troop convoys to the Mediterranean and beyond, and cut Britain's vital seaborne supply routes. This developed into what Churchill christened the Battle of the Atlantic.

Restrictions placed on Germany's re-armament during the inter-war years meant that Hitler began his war with just 46 operational vessels, of which just over half were submarines. Dönitz ensured this state of affairs was quickly rectified as German shipyards began turning out the new-era U-boats at an incredible rate. Notwithstanding the *Athenia* debacle, the U-boats opened their account against the British with spectacular results very early in the war.

U29, under the command of Kapitän-Leutnant Otto Schuhart, sank HMS *Courageous*, one of Britain's four aircraft carriers, off the coast of Ireland on September 17, 1939. The ship went down in 20 minutes, taking with her 518 of her 1,200 crew. On October 13, a U-boat adventurer, Kapitän-Leutnant Günther Prien, commanding *U47*, set course for Scapa Flow, the Royal Navy's northern anchorage, hoping to do some damage. The fleet was out, but the fine old battleship *Royal Oak* was standing guard and Prien promptly dispatched her to the deep with his torpedoes. In all, 833 men lost their lives, and many of the 396 survivors suffered severe burns and life-threatening injuries.

TOP: **A rare shot of battlecruiser *Gneisenau* and *U47* together. The latter, having entered the supposedly impregnable Royal Navy base at Scapa Flow in October 1939, sank the battleship *Royal Oak*, with the loss of 833 men. *Gneisenau*, operating with her sister ship *Scharnhorst*, infamously sank the carrier *Glorious* and two escort destroyers, leaving 3,000 men floundering in the ice-cold waters of the North Atlantic. Only 36 survived.** ABOVE: **A view of an Atlantic convoy of merchantmen from one of the many destroyers that screened their journeys across the Atlantic carrying vital supplies.**

By repeating their tactics of World War I, the Germans – having failed to invade – hoped to subdue the British by starving the nation of food and equipment. Germany's main naval weapon was to be the U-boat, and control of the French Biscay ports provided bases from which they could sally forth into the Atlantic without having to pass either through the Channel or around the north of the British Isles at the end of every patrol. The convoy system of bringing in supplies was operated from the outset and in the first full two years of the

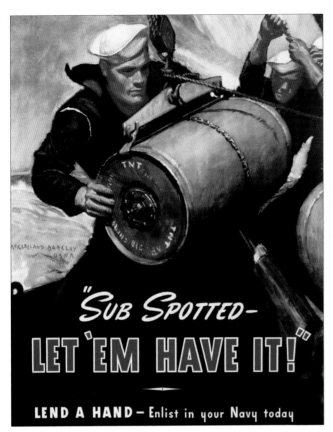

"SUB SPOTTED —
LET 'EM HAVE IT!"

LEND A HAND — Enlist in your Navy today

FAR LEFT: **The popular wartime poster expressing the heartfelt feelings of many: "Let 'em have it!" Similar poster art was also rife in Germany.** LEFT: **Admiral Karl Dönitz, naval strategist, was a mastermind of the U-boat campaign and briefly Hitler's successor after the Führer committed suicide.** ABOVE: **The Kriegsmarine U-boat golden badge of honour.**

BELOW: **U-boat wolf-packs made a direct course for the American Liberty ships in the Atlantic convoys. More than 2,750 such ships were built in the US to mass-produced design, each in about 70 days at a cost of less than $2 million per vessel. They could cross the Atlantic at an average speed of 11 knots, carrying over 9,144 tonnes/9,000 tons of cargo in the five holds, plus airplanes, tanks and locomotives lashed to the deck. A Liberty could carry 2,840 jeeps, 440 tanks, or 230 million rounds of rifle ammunition.**

war, 12,057 ships arrived at British ports in 900 convoys. The convoys grew in size: eventually between 40 and 60 ships would steam in columns with 3.2km/2 miles between each column and 0.53km/0.33 miles between each ship. A 12-column convoy would extend almost 11.1km/6 nautical miles in length and almost two miles deep. They needed massive protection: escorts of surface ships, destroyers, submarines and aircraft, when in range, would accompany convoys at various stages en route.

However, the U-boats gradually built their devastating campaign against Allied ships, supplemented by mines, aircraft and surface ships, and by the end of 1940 alone, 3,048,141 tonnes/3,000,000 tons of Allied shipping were lost, and the tonnage escalated dramatically when Dönitz introduced the infamous wolf-pack tactics and night surface attacks. The admiral often directed wolf-pack operations himself. A group of U-boats would patrol in lines scouting for convoys and once spotted, one boat would act as the shadow, reporting its heading and speed to U-boat headquarters. Other boats would be directed to form around the convoy, and at a given time, when all were gathered and in position, launch a combined attack, usually on the surface at night, thus greatly reducing the effectiveness of ASDIC.

A number of German U-boat commanders made their name as wolf-pack specialists, notably Günther Prien, whose *U47* sank 31 ships and damaged eight others before he and his crew were lost when their boat went down in battle on March 7, 1941. Prien, then just 33 years old, was one of the most highly decorated U-boat commanders, and the first

to be awarded the Knight's Cross – a feat mentioned in the post-war writings of Winston Churchill. Another famous wolf-pack expert was Otto Kretschmer, who was 28 years old in 1940 and in command of *U99*. He sank almost 304,814 tonnes/300,000 tons of shipping and, like Prien, was awarded the Knight's Cross with Oak Leaves, and later the Knight's Cross with Oak Leaves and Swords. He survived the war and lived to the age of 86.

Almost 140 U-boat wolf-packs were assembled during 1940–43. Their operations were meticulously recorded, some fast and effective, others lasting ten days or more. The number of U-boats in each pack ranged from a minimum of three to around 20 in the biggest groups. This phase of the war became known among the Germans as the "happy time", a constant wearing down of merchant shipping that, in fact, became a far greater threat than the possibility of invasion. Eventually, however, brilliant work by scientists and all branches of the armed forces combined to bring an end to this devastating instrument of attrition.

LEFT: **USS** *Pompano*, one of the *Perch*-class of American submarines, built in the mid-1930s, which saw great service against the Japanese. She was also one of the many losses, having left Midway in August 1943 bound for the coasts of Hokkaido and Honshu. She sank two ships in early September, but was never heard from again, presumed lost to a mine. ABOVE: Poster art in America, blunt and to the point.

Pacific encounters of America and Japan

American naval experts are the first to admit that prior to their nation's entry into World War II in December 1941, their submarine capability was faulty and neglected. This was due in part to the numerous international treaties that the US had supported on the banning of unrestricted submarine warfare, and due also to the general malaise about getting involved in the war. There were other vital flaws in America's somewhat archaic peacetime submarine strategy in that many considered it to be an unduly hazardous occupation, and suicidal if operating within range of an enemy air base. Thus, the Silent Service amounted to little more than one per cent of the total resources of the US Navy at the beginning of the 1940s. Also on the debit side was the fact that American torpedoes were not always effective, a fact which was not fully corrected until well into the war.

The U-boat campaigns in the Atlantic changed many minds: suicidal or not, an effective submarine force was a necessary evil to be embraced by the US, a fact which was finally confirmed by the Japanese attack on Pearl Harbor on December 7, 1941. The Japanese had been powering ahead: from the late 1920s, submarine development had become an intrinsic element of their growing front-line naval capability.

While the Navy struggled to recover from the Pearl Harbor attack, the submarine force took the war to the enemy. Operating from Pearl Harbor, and Australian bases at Fremantle and Brisbane, and eventually employing the reliable new Gato, Balao and Tench classes, the submariners began to fight back in some style. By the late summer

ABOVE: **USS** *Plunger*, sister submarine of *Pompano*, survived the war and members of the crew display her battle-flag, while the sailor seated in the centre is wearing a Japanese sailor's hat. The photograph was dated June 21, 1943, following *Plunger's* sixth war patrol.

of 1942, the scorecard was beginning to show signs of improvement but the Japanese still held the upper hand by far, and were inflicting heavy losses on the US Navy. In August, the aircraft carrier *Saratoga* was torpedoed and knocked out of the war for months. Three weeks later, the Japanese submarine *I-19* sank the aircraft carrier *Wasp* and seriously damaged *North Carolina*, America's newest and most powerful battleship. *Wasp's* sister carrier *Hornet* was hit in October, a crippling blow at the time when the Battle of Guadalcanal hung in the balance.

Apart from the hasty building programme, the Americans also had to make considerable readjustments to methods of attack, given that most training and operational work had been planned around the principal role of coastal defence. Across America, too, scientists and mathematicians were working around the clock to produce new technology for submarine detection.

One of the leaders in new methods of tactical warfare that became common practice emerged among submarines operating from the Brisbane base, under the command of Admiral James Fife. He suggested a trial of a new command and control system in USS *Wahoo* under Lt Commander Dudley W. Morton. Executive Officer, Lt Richard O'Kane, manned the periscope leaving Morton free to evaluate the entire combat situation. On her next patrol, *Wahoo* sank 32,402 tonnes/31,890 tons of Japanese shipping. Morton received the first of four Navy Crosses and his ship took home a Presidential Unit Citation. Later in the war, as commanding officer of USS *Tang*, O'Kane received the Congressional Medal of Honour and became the Submarine Force's leading ace of the war, credited with destroying 31 ships totalling 227,800 tonnes/224,202 tons.

Similar initiatives were introduced at the Fremantle base under Admiral Charles Lockwood. He totally revamped tactics employed by the newer submarines and towards the year's end, America's submariners slowly began to turn the tide, and ended 1942 with 180 Japanese ships sunk, totalling 725,000 tonnes/713,550 tons. In fact, it was a meagre tonnage compared to the U-boat tally for the same year – 1,160 Allied ships of more than 6 million tonnes/5,905,239 tons sunk.

The impetus continued apace as the new American submarines piled into the region, and after the recapture of Guam in August 1944, boats based there and at Saipan succeeded in imposing a virtual blockade against Japan, causing massive shortages in oil, raw materials and food. By the autumn of 1944, Japan's remaining five fleet carriers had been sunk, and the sea war in the region was as good as settled.

TOP: **A typical scene in the control area of a US submarine before the action gets hot, but the apparent calmness belies the fact that at any moment chaos and confusion may ensue. This was especially so when the US submarine chiefs raised the stakes early in 1943 by totally overhauling tactics, and continued to do so as the war progressed. They employed more aggressive daytime submerged and night-time surface attacks, partly enabled by improving technology, which resulted in considerable damage to the Japanese fleet.** ABOVE: **A periscope view of the carnage on the surface after a successful attack upon enemy shipping, indicating whether it was safe to surface.** LEFT: **The crews of all American boats kept track of progress with their battle flags, this one from USS *Besugo*, a *Balao*-class submarine, circa early 1944.**

Clandestine travellers aboard

Submarines in all theatres of World War II were used by all sides for many special operations. The Germans landed agents in Britain, America and elsewhere. The British did the same across Europe and the Far East, and to the last, submarines were in continuous use for clandestine operations. Indeed, some of the most famous exploits of particular heroism, which resulted in many a post-war movie, were launched from submarines, including sabotage operations by the Special Boat Service, assault operations by Commando units, the famed but ill-fated Cockleshell heroes and members of the Special Operation Executive. Submariners were also the carriers of a top secret organization whose very existence was denied for 15 years after the war because of ongoing operations on sensitive coastlines – that of the Combined Operations Pilotage Parties (COPPS). This was formed in great secrecy in September 1942 for harbour and beach reconnaissance prior to landings of Allied forces in virtually every theatre of war, operations which still exist today in the shape of Special Forces the world over.

More than 40 Royal Navy submarines were involved in clandestine operations in World War II, and several of them, including the T boats in the Mediterranean and the brand new S-class boat of Lt Norman "Bill" Jewell, commissioned in 1942, were used repeatedly for the service. The British submarine service was a forerunner of these operations and gained early practice in 1940, carrying Commandos to the German-held Norwegian coastline, bristling with all kinds of anti-submarine vessels, mines and air attacks. Lt Commander A.C. Hutchinson and the crew of *Truant* experienced the fiercest and most sustained attacks by depth charges ever known by a British submarine up to that point of the war while carrying his Commando passengers.

Next, the early exploits of the fledgling SBS began in the Mediterranean, when teams were carried around by submarines to be landed clandestinely on Italian shores to

blow up railway lines, viaducts, water supplies and bridges. The most famous duo of Lt Robert "Tug" Wilson, an architect from Leamington Spa, and his partner, Marine Wally Hughes, led the way, hitching rides in *Urge* with Lt Commander Tommy Tomkinson. They would be floated off the casing of the boat in their canoe, perhaps 4.8km/3 miles offshore. They would then paddle their little craft ashore, loaded with explosives, where the two men would carry their load to the designated target, set the charges and make a hasty exit. They would lay up until the appointed time, when their host submarine would (hopefully) reappear to pick them up, mission completed.

There were many, many dangerous moments when these operations were interrupted by German and Italian aircraft or surface ships. In one ill-fated operation in November 1941, two T boats, *Talisman* and *Torbay*, were put at great risk to insert 56 Commandos on to a beach 322km/200 miles inside enemy lines on a most dangerous mission. Shortly before British forces launched an all-out attack to gain control of the North African coast from German and Italian forces, they were assigned to assassinate Field Marshal Erwin Rommel, then

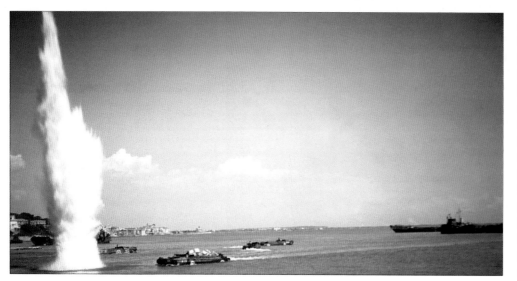

ABOVE: **The control room of HMS *Tuna*, with Lt Norman at the periscope of the boat that launched "The Cockleshell Heroes", 12 Royal Marines who made their famed canoe-borne attempt to blow up German ships in the Gironde estuary.**
LEFT: **The Anzio landings, part of the Allied invasion of Italy. The beaches had been presurveyed by members of the top-secret Royal Navy Combined Operations Pilotage Parties in their canoes, and clandestinely delivered by submarine.**

FAR LEFT: **The T-class submarine *Triumph* that delivered many of the secret operatives of organizations such as the Special Boat Squadron or the Special Operations Executive to their destinations on dangerous missions behind enemy lines.** LEFT: **Folboats or canoes used by the SBS and Navy frogmen were stowed aboard the submarines and unloaded near the target coastline.** BELOW: **The canoeists would then paddle their way into shore, and then, in most cases, the submarine would return at a pre-determined time to collect the saboteurs.**

commander in chief of Axis forces, who was supposed to be at his inland villa. In very rough seas, *Torbay* and *Talisman* were heaving as the inflatable boats were launched towards the shore. It was so choppy that only 45 made it off the submarines. It was a heroic but ultimately unsuccessful mission. Rommel, it turned out, was not at the villa but in Rome. The Commando force met heavy resistance, and the submarine commanders risked their own safety in waiting around at the rendezvous to pick up the men who, in fact, never returned. Only four Commandos survived the mission and only evaded capture by walking back to their base across a hostile landscape, a journey that took 40 days.

One of them was Bombadier Brittlebank of the Royal Artillery, who subsequently replaced Marine Hughes, who was ill, as Tug Wilson's partner for further missions off the Italian coastline. Their exploits were, however, to be curtailed. The danger of these operations to the submarines was demonstrated by the fate of *Triumph*, under Lt Commander W.J.W. Woods. She carried out a number of special operations, landing commando teams all around the Italian coastline until she was assigned to land a unit near Athens, sailing from Alexandria on December 26, 1941. Four days later

ABOVE: **The American Navy paid particular interest to early British successes in clandestine operations and set up their own units. Although hardly invisible, the USS *Nautilus* was used on early missions, and sailing with submarine *Argonaut*, carried Marines of the 2nd Raider Battalion to stage diversionary attacks on Japanese-held territory.**

Lt Commander Woods sent a signal confirming the landing of the party, and *Triumph* was due to return to pick up the commandos two weeks later, but failed to make the rendezvous. Nothing further was heard of the submarine.

Another of the famous submarine-launched sabotage groups were the canoeists of Operation Frankton, more commonly known as The Cockleshell Heroes, the brainchild of Lt Colonel H.G. "Blondie" Hasler. Pairs of men were carried by the submarine *Tuna* to the mouth of the river Gironde, on the west coast of France. Five pairs then paddled 113km/70 miles upstream by night to attack 12 German ships lying in the supposed safe haven in the Bassens-Bordeaux area. However, only one pair, Hasler and his colleague Ned Sparks, survived the mission. Of the remaining eight men involved, six were captured and shot as saboteurs by the Germans and the remaining two were lost, presumed drowned.

"The most important capture of the war"

TOP: **HMS *Bulldog*, the most famous of the seven Royal Navy ships to bear the name, was a Class B destroyer launched in 1930, and she remained in service until 1946 when she was scrapped. The heroic actions of her crew in capturing the first Enigma machine undoubtedly helped change the course of the war.**
ABOVE: **The submarine from which the Enigma machine was extracted, *U110* was captained by Fritz-Julius Lemp, a commander of some notoriety, notably for sinking the liner *Athenia*.**

Kapitänleutnant Fritz-Julius Lemp, the U-boat captain who sank the *Athenia* on the first day of the war, had been a busy man, commanding *U30*, the lead boat in the 2nd U-boat Flotilla. By May 1941, he was a holder of the Knight's Cross and commander of *U110* in the wolf-packs scouring the Atlantic for their prey, operating in partnership with *U201*.

On May 9, Lemp sank two ships totalling 10,000 tonnes/9,842 tons, but when he came up to confirm his final "kill", he left his periscope aloft too long and was spotted by the convoy escort, the corvette HMS *Aubretia*. The escort gave the alert to other ships while she herself unloaded a massive bombardment of depth charges.

Aubretia was joined by the destroyers *Bulldog* and *Broadway*, and their attack was delivered with such force that Lemp was forced to surface. As he came up, a dozen men on *U110* rushed to man the guns but were themselves shot by the waiting British ships. Lemp also discovered that *Bulldog* was already lined up for a ramming operation, which her commander Commander Joe Baker-Creswell had no intention of carrying out, having already considered the possibility of a capture. Lemp, expecting the ramming to arrive any time soon, ordered his men to abandon ship, apparently assuming that once his boat was sunk, her secrets would go to the bottom with her. This boat did, indeed, contain secrets – none other than one of the famous Enigma cipher machines, as well as a vital codebook on how to use it.

So, over the side went the surviving members of the crew, Lemp with them, but he never made it to the British ships which picked up the survivors. Many said after the war that he was shot in the water by a British officer who led the boarding party from *Bulldog* to take possession of *U110*. David Balme, the man accused of this act by a German author after the war, denies this categorically in his memoir held in the Imperial War Museum's Sound Archive, and said Lemp died in some other way. The speculation was that realizing his boat, a IXB class, was not going to sink, he either tried to swim back to save the secrets aboard and drowned, or committed suicide, realizing his cardinal sin of failing to scuttle his boat.

Bulldog's crew, meanwhile, had pulled alongside the U-boat and began stripping her of everything they could carry. David Balme recalled: "I was in the control room when our telegraphist called me over and said '*Look* at this, sir,' pointing to what appeared to be an old typewriter. We both thought it looked interesting, and that we'd better take it over. And that is how we discovered the Enigma cipher on board *U110*."

ABOVE LEFT: **Another Enigma-carrying boat,** *U505* **was captured by the Americans exactly three years after** *U110* **was taken by the crew of HMS** *Bulldog***, but because the British government had ordered a clampdown, which remained in force for 30 years, it was widely believed that** *U505* **was the first to be captured – a belief wrongly portrayed in a Hollywood movie.** ABOVE: **U-boat pens provided a safe haven for the German submarine fleet around the French coast as well as in Germany. These were especially vital at the time of the Battle for the Atlantic.** LEFT: **A typical interior of the boats operating during that era.** BELOW: **The Enigma machine, whose mysteries were unlocked at Bletchley Park, thus providing the British with an incredible insight into forthcoming Nazi operations.**

Along with it were masses of charts, maps and codebooks – the whole shooting match that revealed the Enigma code, as well as charts of German minefields. David Balme also discovered what became known in the Royal Navy as the grid map – a remarkable map of the Atlantic, divided into squares with lists of U-boats assigned to certain areas.

It took hours to ferry the material back to *Bulldog* and then Baker-Creswell took the boat under tow. However, as soon as the Admiralty received a description of what had been found, they ordered the boat to be scuttled at once, and all the prisoners taken to Iceland, where they would be interned. The whole operation was now very cloak and dagger to ensure that no one – especially not the German High Command – should know the U-boat and her secrets were in British hands.

An expert from Bletchley Park met *Bulldog* when she arrived in Scapa Flow and took the Enigma machine and the books away. Every man on board the ship was sworn to secrecy. The find was enormously significant and helped the Ultra code-breakers to read top secret communications between Hitler and the German High Command for months ahead, a fact that Churchill did not reveal even to Roosevelt until the end of 1942.

The capture of *U110* was one to become one of the best kept secrets of the war, and indeed was not publicly revealed until 30 years later. That is why the American Navy put into printed history the claim that it captured the first U-boat

containing dramatic secrets. How were they to know the British had already done it! Their capture came in May 1944 when US Navy Task Group 22.3 sailed from Norfolk, Virginia, for an anti-submarine patrol near the Canary Islands. On June 4, USS *Chatelain* reported a sonar contact with a submerged submarine. Two fighter planes from the USS *Guadalcanal* were called down to fire their guns into the water to help mark the location of the submerged *U505*. The USS *Chatelain* then fired a pattern of 14 depth charges, forcing *U505* to surface. While the USS *Chatelain* and the USS *Jenks* picked up survivors, the USS *Pillsbury* sent its whaleboat to the *U505*, where Lt Albert L. David led a nine-man boarding party to capture the submarine.

Issued in lieu of N° 09650 lost.
Page 3
Navy Form S.1511

Surname MARTIN

NAVAL
IDENTITY CARD No. 148228

Other Names WILLIAM

Rank (at time of issue) CAPTAIN, R.M.
(ACTING MAJOR)

Ship (at time of issue) H Q
COMBINED OPERATIONS

Place of Birth CARDIFF
Year of Birth 1907

Issued by [signature]

At ADMIRALTY

Date 2nd February 1943.

Signature of Bearer
W. Martin

Visible distinguishing marks
NIL.

LEFT: **The fake identity documents secreted in the pockets of "Major Martin", which helped persuade German intelligence into accepting that he carried genuine details of plans for an Allied invasion of the southern coastline of Greece when, in fact, they were to descend upon Sicily.** BELOW: **US Paratroops join the Allied invasion of Sicily, a task greatly facilitated by the fake documents found on the body launched from HMS *Seraph*.**

Operation Mincemeat (or "The Man Who Never Was")

L t Commander Norman Jewell had already carried out numerous special operations along the coast of North Africa since taking delivery of the new S-class submarine *Seraph,* including the covert delivery of US General Mark Clark to Algeria in October 1942 to try to persuade the Vichy French to support the planned North African landings. A month later, Jewell and his crew provided the transport for the rescue of French General Henri Giraud off the south coast of France after he had escaped from a German prison camp. It was a dangerous episode because the general's arrival was delayed for almost a week, but *Seraph* had to remain on station, diving and surfacing in hostile waters, ready to pick up her passenger.

The most famous of *Seraph's* secret exploits subsequently became popularly known as "The Man Who Never Was": a cunning scheme codenamed Operation Mincement, aimed at fooling the Axis powers into thinking that the Allied landings in Sicily would, in fact, take place elsewhere. Norman Jewell tells the story personally, in his memoir for the Imperial War Museum sound archive:

"I was told to report to naval intelligence and there met up with a team concocting an incredible scheme…A body was to be washed up on the coast of Spain which would carry in an attaché case secret papers, a letter for Eisenhower, the Commander-in-Chief in North Africa, saying that rather than going for Sicily the invasion would be on the south coast of Greece.

"My knowledge was limited exactly to that which I needed to know in order to carry out my part of the plan. However, we spent a good deal of time building up a background for this body, who was to be called Major Martin, providing him with a life, a girlfriend, and in his pockets theatre tickets, restaurant receipts, a letter and so on. They knew it would be checked out by German spies in London. Then (when the time came), the body of Major Martin was placed in a canister about the size of a torpedo.

"The body was packed in ice so that it would be the right age when washed up. We were given clear passage down to

LEFT: **The fictitious Major William Martin – "The Man Who Never Was" – being cast into the sea off the coast of Spain.**

LEFT: **HMS *Seraph* was one of the improved British S-class boats, commissioned in 1942.** BELOW LEFT: **One of the restaurant bills found in the pockets of the dead man that also helped convince the Germans as to his authenticity.** BELOW: **On their way to the true target, the massive task force of British and American troops join the invasion of Sicily by sea and air.**

the coast of Spain, which meant that the RAF was aware of our presence. We were also told that we would not be required to attack anything en route because our mission was too important. However, we were taken out of our safe passage line to attack some shipping going to Bordeaux. We never saw them, but thanks to that instruction we were then bombed three times by the RAF. We eventually arrived off the coast of Spain at the point where Spain joins Portugal. Until that point, no one on board – apart from myself – knew that the canister contained a body.

"The cover story was that it was carrying meteorological equipment to fill in the reporting gap for the Meteorological Office in London. But now, the body was to be retrieved from the canister to be put over the side. I had to tell the officers because I could not do the whole thing on my own. I did not give details of the plan, but in any event I had to swear them to secrecy. They were surprised; some were shocked…dispatching the body of an unknown man into the sea in this manner. We took off the end of the canister and brought the body out. It was the first time I had seen it. We made a final check to make sure that his papers and attaché case containing the secret 'invasion' plans were intact and attached to his wrist, and then slid him over the side. We went full astern on the motor so that he would be pushed on his way. We said a few words as a funeral service over him and then secured the canister on the casing and dived. At daybreak we surfaced to try to get rid of the canister

and we had a hell of a time. It had been so designed to keep the ice from melting that it had air pockets all the way around it, and even though we had put about 200 bullet holes through it from a machine-gun nothing happened at all. We then had to go alongside it again and put some plastic explosives inside and outside and then withdrew while it blew up. It then disappeared finally. We then went on to Gibraltar, arriving the next evening. As we arrived, someone came over the gangway carrying a telegram for me, which said the parcel had been received: so the body had arrived safely.

"As would be discovered later, the Germans went to great lengths to discover the background of Major Martin through their spies in London and could not discredit the information that we had placed about him. In due course, the Germans withdrew an armoured division and sent it through Italy and down the other side towards Greece. They were at least a division less in Sicily when the landings eventually took place."

In fact, the ploy was so successful that the Germans thought Sardinia and Greece were the intended objectives until well after the landings in Sicily had begun. As for the "body" that became Major Martin, it was reported in 1997 that it was that of a homeless alcoholic from Wales named Glyndwr Michael, although even that claim has since been challenged. Whoever it was, the body was buried in Heluva, Spain, with a gravestone in the name of Martin.

LEFT: **The Italians were masters of the human torpedoes and Chariots and had produced a working prototype, which was tested at La Spezia in 1936. This ultimately led to the construction of submarine-borne containers to deliver them to the target area.** BELOW: **The British quickly caught on and introduced their own charioteers, here in rehearsal for the invasion of Sicily.**

The chariots of stealth

The Japanese, Italians and latterly the British all had specialist teams working on the development of underwater guerrilla warfare. The Axis navies were well ahead of the field when war came as a result of experimental work in the 1930s. After the exploits of the SBS and the Cockleshell Heroes, Lord Mountbatten, as head of Combined Operations, sent a memo to the Chiefs of Staff, pointing out that the men's determination and courage demonstrated a good example of the successful use of limpeteers.

He already had a report which indicated that Italian underwater activity was "filled with ideas involving gadgetry and motorisation and experimentation". In fact, the Italians were well ahead of everyone in their perfection of a number of devices and submarine attack apparatus that would become the model for the future. These included effective breathing apparatus for underwater swimmers, double limpets, human torpedoes, piloted torpedoes, miniature torpedoes and exploding attack boats. Teams of dedicated and highly trained men were inspired by the famous Commander Belloni and the infamous Prince Julio Valerie Borghese from the 10th Light Flotilla of the Italian Navy.

This particular skill of the Italians really began to worry the Allies in 1941, at a time when the British fleet was reduced to two battleships in the Mediterranean, HMS *Valiant* and the brand new HMS *Queen Elizabeth*, which lay sheltered behind torpedo nets at Alexandria. At 03:30 hours on December 19, two Italians were discovered clinging to the anchor buoy of *Valiant*. They surrendered immediately and were taken ashore for interrogation and then, to their dismay, back to *Valiant*, where they confessed that the battleship was about to blow up.

The crew was mustered on deck and the watertight doors were closed, but shortly after 06:00 hours the ship rocked and shuddered as the charge set by the two Italians blasted a large hole in her stern. Soon afterwards, *Queen Elizabeth* reared up from two explosions from charges attached below the water line, and both ships were temporarily out of the war.

It soon emerged that they had been attacked by three human torpedoes known as Maiali (sea pigs) driven by a team of six men from the 10th Light Flotilla, trained to remain under water for miles wearing flexible rubber suits, breathing gear and fins. They had been launched from Prince Borghese's submarine *Sciré* off Alexandria, two astride each of the human torpedoes. The operation even drew praise from Churchill as an example of "extraordinary courage and ingenuity".

Mountbatten drew together a number of eminent military and scientific experts to look at new weapons and methods for his men to "study, coordinate and develop all forms of stealthy seaborne attack by small parties and pay particular attention to attacking ships in harbour". Among the projects launched immediately was the Chariot, a hefty torpedo-shaped submersible which was a copy of the two-man Maiali used by the Italians (one had been captured off Crete). Its crew, equipped with breathing sets that would allow six hours of diving, sat in the open astride the Chariot, which could travel at about 16 knots and carried one 272kg/600lb charge. They were hazardous and slow. The first torpedo force came into operation in September 1942, under the auspices of the submarine service, in a plan to attack *Tirpitz*, the largest and strongest warship ever built in Germany, at 53,000 tonnes/ 52,163 tons.

She was even more powerful than her elder sister, *Bismarck*, and was based in occupied Norway from January 1942. From there, she and her supporting ships would sally forth to attack Allied shipping.

The British began to consider every scheme to destroy the German monster, and in October 1942, an audacious plan was launched to sink her using the Chariots. Two of the Chariots were hidden in a double bulkhead of a Norwegian fishing trawler which would then proceed to Trondheim; there, they would be released with crews to attack *Tirpitz* in her berth behind anti-submarine nets in a fjord north of Trondheim. Although the trawler managed to get through three German checkpoints, the expedition was hit by a sudden change in the weather as the Chariots were being launched. They had to be abandoned, and the crews swam ashore and escaped into Sweden. No further attempts could be launched because of the low temperatures that year.

More than 50 Chariots were built, and their crews experienced mixed fortunes. Their best results were in the

Mediterranean, although they were never really considered a success. Operation Principal, for example, was an attack on Palermo harbour on January 3, 1943. Five Chariots were used. Each, with a crew of two, was embarked on the deck in watertight containers in the submarines *Trooper* and *Thunderbolt* (ex-*Thetis*). *Unruffled* took part as the recovery boat after the operation was complete. One Chariot sank the Italian cruiser *Ulpio Traiano*, and another damaged the liner *Viminale*, which sank later in the year. Of the remaining three, one broke down en route and was picked up by *Unruffled* six hours later, a second sank through unknown causes, and on the third, the driver ripped his diving suit negotiating harbour defences and drowned.

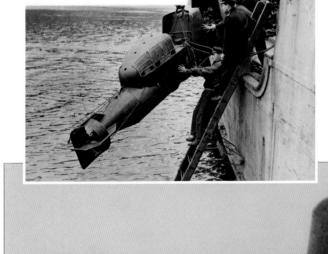

ABOVE LEFT: **Luigi de la Penne, one of the pioneers of Italian charioteers, was one of a team of six that attacked British ships in Alexandria harbour in December 1941, causing damage to two British battleships, Queen Elizabeth and Valiant. He was captured but he refused to inform the ship's captain of the mines attached to the ships' hull until a few minutes before detonation, thus allowing the British to evacuate. Although imprisoned, he worked for the British as a frogman after the Italian surrender.** ABOVE RIGHT: **The British version of the charioteers, whose operations came to the fore at the time of the Allied invasion of Sicily and elsewhere in the Mediterranean.** LEFT: **A British Chariot being unloaded for operations.** BELOW: **The altogether more successful Italian version of charioteering.**

Giant tasks for midget submarines

W hile Chariots were something of a haphazard affair, midget submarines were a different story altogether. Various nations had experimented with the small boats that could be transported and utilized in situations that their giant sisters would have little chance of even approaching, let alone manoeuvring into position for an operation. The Japanese and the Italians were well ahead of the field in design and numbers, the former producing several dozen in different classes and sizes. By the beginning of the war, the Japanese were already well advanced in their use, also with several dozen in operation, beginning with the A class, 23.9m/78ft 6in long and displacing 46.7 tonnes/46 tons submerged, and capable of a tidy 23 knots on the surface and an incredible 19 knots submerged.

They were originally intended to be carried by larger submarines or surface vessels and deployed to attack an enemy fleet, but they discovered that the midgets were particularly useful for special operations against ships in enemy harbours, where they could be transported and released in packs. Five of the A-class boats took part in the attack on Pearl Harbor and were evident again in May 1942 in raids on Sydney, Australia, and Diego Suarez in the Indian Ocean. Notably, however, they were well used against American ships at Guadalcanal in 1942–43. Japanese midgets in the A, B and C classes were in continual production, ending with the Type D

boat, *HA-77*, completed in January 1945. Some 115 units had been completed when Japan capitulated in August 1945, and nearly 500 more were under construction.

Japan also produced some special attack midget submarines which were actually manned torpedoes. The highly successful Type 93 Long Lance torpedo was lengthened and adapted by inserting a central cockpit for the pilot. They became the Kaiten midget submarine that could reach speeds of up to 35.4kph/22mph, and up to six could be piggy-backed on conventional submarines for delivery to the attack area.

Meanwhile, the Italians were in production with a stylish-looking craft in their CB class as the war began, and it was this model that provided additional tips for both the British and the Germans, who took possession of a couple of their boats operating in the Mediterranean. In fact, the British,

ABOVE: **The Japanese Navy was first in action with midget submarines, launching five Type A models in the Pearl Harbor raid of December 7, 1941, transporting them piggy-back on larger submarines and launching the night before the attack, and thereafter throughout the war.** LEFT: **The British X-craft, which had a varied, terrifying but VC-winning history of high-profile operations, including an attack on the German battleship *Tirpitz*.**

LEFT: **In mid-1944, the Japanese Navy developed the Koryu Type D midget coastal defence submarine for a five-man crew, two more than in the Type C.** ABOVE: **Although classed as a human torpedo, this version of a Japanese *Kaiten* was more of a mini-submarine, with a large conning station attached.**

the Americans and the Germans both came late to this field of development, the latter eventually launching a massive programme of midget development, building six different classes, ranging from one-man torpedoes to seven-man midgets. In all, the Germans had planned to produce over 1,700 of such craft, the first appearing early in 1944, but the war ended before many of that number were actually commissioned.

The Royal Navy's own prototype X-craft was laid down in 1939, when intelligence reports gave inspiring accounts of foreign developments, but the British and the Americans had already experienced attacks from midget craft at Pearl Harbor and in the Mediterranean before the British version was commissioned in October 1942. It was classed as *X3* (the first two Xs were already taken: *X1* was an experimental boat built in 1925, and *X2* was a captured Italian submarine which had given the British a few extra pointers). A second prototype vessel, *X4*, was constructed and based on the first British boat and the Italian version. Thereafter, rapid production began with six X-craft (*X5* to *X10*) being built by Vickers, initially for deployment in European waters. The British midgets made their name in some spectacular special missions and, later in the war, when they were used for risky surveillance and mapping of landing sites on hostile coastlines.

Their most famous mission was the attack on the German battleship *Tirpitz*, with which Churchill had an obsession. This magnificent and powerful vessel represented a major threat to British shipping and he wanted it out of the war. The Germans, well aware of British intentions, kept the ship Altenfjord, Norway, out of harm's way, which was also the berth of the Germans' other heavy weapons, the battleship *Scharnhorst* and the pocket battleship *Lützow*. They were the targets in September 1943 when six X5-class submarines, each crewed by four highly trained operatives, set out on a mission that is today a classic point in submarine warfare.

The X-craft, unlike the high-speed Japanese models, had electric motors that generated just 30hp and a 12-knot top

ABOVE: **The German *Neger* consisted of two linked G7e torpedoes, the upper with the warhead removed and a transparent driver cockpit installed; the bottom torpedo would be released.** BELOW: **The 11.2 tonne/11 ton one-man German Molch midgets were all electric, designed for submerged coastal operations, with a range of 64.4km/40 miles, carrying two torpedoes. Around 390 were built.**

speed when submerged. So they had to be towed towards their quarry by regular-sized submarines. Even so, the outward journey to Norway of 1,770km/1,100 miles took eight days in often heavy seas. En route, *X9* (which had been detailed to attack *Scharnhorst*) sank and *X8* (heading for *Lützow*) had to be scuttled, leaving the four remaining X-craft to cover the last 80.5km/50 miles under their own power through the treacherous fjords, mine fields and anti-submarine nets that were in place on the approach to the *Tirpitz*.

On September 22, 1943, *X6* (under the command of Lt Donald Cameron) and *X7* (under Lt Basil Place) followed an old freighter through this obstacle course and reached their target. *X6* was spotted, and was under heavy fire from the surface. When Cameron attempted to make his escape, he became caught in the nets but still did not give up. As he surfaced, he dropped two explosive charges and then managed to scuttle the boat before leading his crew to surrender. *X7* also released two charges beneath *Tirpitz* but ironically was damaged when the explosives left by *X6* detonated, and Basil Place also had to surrender. Two of his crew did not survive.

Meanwhile, *X10* under the command of Lt K.R. Hudspeth also managed to sneak into the inner fjord, only to be hit by mechanical trouble. Rather than give up and possibly alert the Germans to the presence of a larger force, he remained hidden

ABOVE: **The aft portion of the Kaiten (Return to Heaven) Type 1, of which 300 were produced. It became the first Japanese Special Attack weapon whose operational use involved the certain death of the crew and preceded the Kamikaze aircraft.** BELOW LEFT: **The Biber (Beaver), the smallest German submarine built to attack coastal shipping ahead of the Allied invasion of Europe.**

for five days before he could return to the towing ship. The boat had to be scuttled on the return journey to England. A third submarine, probably *X5*, was sighted by Cameron close to its target but came under heavy fire and was never seen again.

In spite of this set-back, the raid on *Tirpitz* herself was successful, and that was the key object of the exercise. Although the explosive charges left by the midget did not have the power to sink her, they did sufficient damage for the vessel to be put out of the war temporarily, and had to be towed south for repairs. Apart from an actual sinking, this could not have been a better result because *Tirpitz* was now in the range of RAF and Fleet Air Arm bombers and over the coming months, after several attempts, she was finally blown apart when her own ammunition store was hit by British bombers. Fewer than 90 of her 1,000 crew survived. The role played by the midget submarines in crippling *Tirpitz* was recognized in 1944, when Basil Place and Donald Cameron were awarded the Victoria Cross.

Meanwhile, new versions of the British midgets were coming off the production line, beginning with the XE class which carried out a number of successful raids around Europe, including that of *XE3* under the command of Lt Ian Fraser, which put a large floating dock at Bergen out of action for the rest of the war. As targets began to become fewer, six of the *XE*-class boats were shipped for operations in the Far East for what turned out to be the final months of the war. They were earmarked to carry out raids against the Japanese at a number of locations, including Singapore and Hong Kong. Again, a

LEFT: An aerial view of the German battleship *Tirpitz*, which was damaged in an attack by the British X-craft midget submarines. This allowed British bombers to sink her. ABOVE: One of the most successful German miniature submarines was the Seehund Type 127, of which the Kriegsmarine had planned to build over 1,000 from 1944. They had a crew of two, carried two under-slung G7e torpedoes and had a range of 300km/186 miles at 7 knots.

number of successes were chalked up, including that of *XE4* under the command of Lt M.H. Shean, of the Royal Australian Navy Volunteer Reserve, whose team managed to cut the Hong Kong to Saigon cable and the Saigon to Singapore cable.

The most famous of the missions, however, was reserved for Ian Fraser's *XE3*. His mission was a *Tirpitz*-style raid on the Japanese heavy cruiser *Takao*, moored in the Johore Strait, Singapore. Once again, the X-craft was towed towards its target location, and then continued on under her own steam. They reached the *Takao* without incident and settled beneath her to get to work. Leading seaman James Magennis, the diver, went out and attached six limpet mines to the hull of the ship, a task which took forty minutes because he had to scrape each position free of mud and barnacles. He returned aboard exhausted. A further problem occurred as Fraser attempted to turn away and escape before the explosion. To his horror, the boat would not budge because, while working

on the explosives, the tide had gone down and the boat had become stuck in a very narrow hole. Only by going ahead and then full astern for several minutes did he manage to escape, only to encounter a further problem: an empty limpet container had jammed, preventing the side cargoes of explosives from being jettisoned, which gave the submarine an uncontrollable list. Magennis volunteered to go back outside, and spent 15 minutes freeing the load. *XE3* eventually made her escape and, while returning to base unscathed, the charges detonated to put the 11,177-tonne/11,000-ton cruiser on the bottom. Lt Fraser and Leading Seaman Magennis were both awarded the Victoria Cross for their bravery in performing this operation.

Although disliked by some, the X-craft had performed a number of exceedingly useful tasks, including their use by the top-secret group Combined Operations Pilotage Parties (Copps) in preliminary surveys ahead of troop landings and, notably, to mark the invasion beaches for the D-Day invasions.

ABOVE: The Kairyu (Sea Dragon) was another Kamikaze midget submarine for a two-man crew and was fitted with an internal warhead for suicide missions. Designed at the beginning of 1945 to meet the anticipated approach of invading American naval forces, 200 had been built by the time of Japan's surrender. RIGHT: Various methods were tried to disguise the tell-tale periscope of midget boats; this was the Beaver camouflage.

The cost and the legacy

For the second time in the 20th century, the final reckoning of submarine warfare produced a devastating catalogue of destruction of hardware and human life, as well as a record of many thousands of incidents of great heroism and skill, regardless of the flag under which the men were fighting. The U-boat force was undoubtedly the greatest in the world in terms of quality and innovation. It also suffered the highest proportion of casualties. A total of 1,154 diverse and versatile U-boats were commissioned prior to or during World War II, not counting the 135 still under construction at the end of the war and excluding the midget submarines. However, the toll had been relentless: 727 U-boats manned by crews totalling 26,918 were lost, the majority sunk by Allied surface ships and shore-based aircraft. The progression of those U-boat losses paints a mini-portrait of the way the fortune of war proceeded: 1939: 9 lost with 204 crew. 1940: 24 lost; 643 crew. 1941: 34 lost; 887 crew. 1942: 85 lost; 3,277 crew. 1943: 235 lost; 10,081 crew. 1944: 219 lost; 8,020 crew. 1945: 121 lost; 3,806 crew. The human cost was enormous, and the final figures showed that Germany lost an astonishing two-thirds of the men who served in the submarine force.

The British, with far fewer submarines, lost 74 boats during the war years, manned by crews totalling 341 officers and 2,801 ratings. In addition, 50 officers and 309 ratings became prisoners of war. America lost 52 submarines and of the 16,000 men serving in the US submarine force, 375 officers and 3,332 men did not survive. For all her productive pre-war promise, Japan's submarine service did not perform as well as her enemies'. Excluding midgets, Japan started the war with

63 ocean-going submarines and completed 111 during the war, giving a total of 174, of which 128 were lost during the conflict. Japan's emphasis on size proved to be a disadvantage, in that the huge boats were easy to sight and target. They were slow to dive, hard to manoeuvre underwater, easy to track, and easy to hit, especially by the US Air Force. Japanese submarines also had no radar until the first sets were installed in June 1944. Russia had 272 submarines in operation during the war and lost 108. Details of their operations are scant because Soviet submarines were rarely on patrol. However, it is known that one of their boats caused the greatest disaster in maritime history, in sinking the German liner *Wilhelm Gustloff* on March 30, 1945. The liner was moving more than 6,000 German troops and up to 2,000 civilians from Poland ahead of advancing Russian forces. She was sunk soon after leaving the port of Gotenhafen (Gdynia), and fewer than 1,000 people were rescued.

LEFT: Surrendered VIIC boats, the mainstay of the German force from 1941 and still in production at the end of the war. They bore the brunt of the Allied anti-submarine onslaught from late 1943 onwards. One of them, *U96*, was featured in the film *Das Boot*.
BELOW: The revolutionary snorkel fitted to the XXI types that could have won the war, had they been in production earlier.

At the end of it all, as in World War I, the victors picked over the spoils. There had been a resurgence of successful U-boat activity towards the autumn of 1944, when freshly launched German submarines were fitted with an important new invention: the snorkel ventilating tube. First tested by the Dutch Navy and picked up by German scientists, the retractable device contained air-intake and exhaust pipes for the engines and general ventilation. The telescopic tube fed air into the diesel engine and carried off exhaust gases. A U-boat equipped with the snorkel could run submerged on her diesel engine while also charging her batteries; while the boat could do so only at a slow speed and at shallow depth, the chances of being picked up by radar were greatly reduced. When they heard of it, Allied naval commanders breathed a sigh of relief that its development had not arrived earlier in the war.

It was one of a number of significant developments in German U-boat technology which were about to come on stream as the war reached the final stages. By then, it was already clear that submarine technology was on the threshold of dramatic developments. The Allies made a dash for the German U-boats and their accompanying manuals, which were to provide some inspiration for a new breed of submarines built on both sides of the Iron Curtain after it had slammed down at the start of the Cold War.

The Walther engine, used in four U-boats built before the war ended, was put under the microscope. It was a steam-generating power plant of a kind that had eluded British and American submarine engineers for years. It worked on the principle that hydrogen peroxide, when passed over a catalyst, produced oxygen and water. The oxygen and water were fed into a combustion chamber, sprayed with fuel, and the resulting mixture generated steam that powered a turbine. Walther had

been working on the engine for four years, but because of its revolutionary principles there was little chance of proving it at the time of increasing pressure on the U-boat command.

One of the Walther boats commissioned in March 1945 was scuttled at the German port of Cuxhaven on 5 May 1945. The British had already learned of its existence and raised the boat by the end of the month. It was recovered, towed back to England, rebuilt and commissioned as *Meteorite* for evaluation. By then, the two big powers – picking over the bones of German technology – were on the threshold of a new era. Nuclear power was in sight.

BELOW: Sections of the Type XXI, the first real combat submarines whose technology the Allies could not wait to get their hands on. Perhaps this type could have won the Battle for the Atlantic, had she arrived earlier.

Unfinished business: surviving a sinking

With so much loss of life due to submarines lost during the war, a special committee formed in 1939 after the *Thetis* disaster was reactivated under the chairmanship of Rear-Admiral P. Ruck-Keene, and was able to draw on a vast wealth of experience. He was given a large team of experts to assist him, and they began by taking detailed statements from survivors of 32 submarine incidents involving British, American, Norwegian and German vessels. All past methods of escape were examined, and new ideas were brought forward, extended training programmes drawn up and a better system for rescue response recommended and acted upon.

The immediate outcome of the early testimony was to improve escape training for crews. For this a 30m/98ft 5in water-filled tower, 5.5m/18ft in diameter, was built at the submarine school at Fort Blockhouse, although it was not completed until 1952. The rescue alerts for submarines in distress, with particular attention to reaction times, were also overhauled as part of the two systems called Subsmash and Subsunk. Some of the modifications to submarine safety and rescue procedures were thus to be tested sooner than anyone could possibly imagine. Less than five years after the end of the war, Britain suffered two major submarine disasters.

On January 12, 1950, the World War II submarine *Truculent* spent the day at sea off the Thames Estuary carrying out trials, following a long refit in Chatham dockyard. On board was her crew of 59, plus 18 civilian dockyard technicians who were to check the final performance before officially handing her back to the Royal Navy. As *Truculent* made her way back to Sheerness, she was in collision with a tanker with ice-breaking bows, *Dvina,* on passage from Purfleet bound for Sweden with a cargo of paraffin. Sixty-seven men made a near-perfect escape from the sunken submarine and, apart from one or two problems with untrained technicians, the Davis gate saw everyone get to the surface alive. However, in the end, only 11 men were picked up alive. The remainder died of the cold or were swept away by the tide.

At the subsequent inquiry, it was observed that had the men remained inside the submarine for 20 or 30 minutes longer, the rescue ships sent under the Subsunk alert would have arrived over *Truculent* to save them. By the same token, it was also pointed out that because of the flooding and the closure of all but the after-compartments of the submarine, the 67 men on board were already beginning to feel the effects of carbon dioxide poisoning when the first officer made the decision to get them to the surface. He had little choice. If he had delayed, they might have been in no state to make the attempt, as had been the case in so many previous incidents examined in recent times. *Truculent* was salvaged on March 14, 1950, and

ABOVE LEFT: **The salvage operation to raise HMS** *Truculent*, **which sank after a collision. Even though almost all aboard escaped, only 11 survived on the surface.** ABOVE: **U-boat crews were well advanced in their training to escape a catastrophe.** LEFT: **HMS** *Affray*, **which was lost on a patrol exercise in 1951. The search for her kept the British nation agonizingly enthralled for days.**

beached at Cheney Spit. The wreck was moved inshore the following day, where ten bodies were recovered. She was refloated on March 23, 1950, and towed into Sheerness Dockyard. A subsequent inquiry attributed blame both to *Truculent* and to a lesser extent *Dvina*. The loss led to the introduction of the "Truculent light", an extra steaming all-round white light on the bow of British submarines.

The *Truculent* disaster was comparatively fresh in the memories of submariners when a second post-war tragedy struck, with further implications. At 16:30 hours on the afternoon of Monday, April 16, 1951, the six-year-old A-class submarine *Affray* left Portsmouth for a war patrol exercise with an unusually large number of men on board. Under the command of Lt John Blackburn, she carried his team of four officers and 55 ratings. There were also 23 young sub-lieutenants in training, who came along to observe a simulated war patrol, and a party of four marines. Blackburn's orders were to proceed down the Channel to the Western Approaches, carry out dummy attacks for three days to give experience to the junior officers and then land the marines at a bay on the Cornish coast.

At 20:56 hours, Blackburn signalled from the Isle of Wight that he intended to dive and proceed westwards up the Channel. He would surface at 08:00 hours the next morning. No surfacing signal was received, and at 09:00 hours on the 17th a Subsunk operation was launched. By midday, forty ships, eight submarines, various aircraft from the RAF and Fleet Air Arm and a flotilla of US destroyers visiting Plymouth were all engaged in the search for *Affray*.

But after 46 hours, the massive search operation was stood down. The task of locating her was handed over to a smaller team, consisting of four frigates and three minesweepers equipped with all the special electronics available for underwater location. It was an epic search lasting 59 days, covering 37,013km/23,000 miles and involving the investigation of 161 shipwrecks in the search area before the submarine was found. Navy divers discovered the snort mast had broken off, but that probably occurred when the sub hit the bottom. Suggestions of a battery explosion were also evaluated, but in truth the cause of the sinking could not be ascertained. What was brought home once again, however, was that dramatic new escape systems were needed. The *Affray* was the last British submarine to be lost with all hands.

ABOVE: **Immediately after the war, when so many recent experiences could be recalled, the safety issues for the escape and rescue of personnel from a stricken submarine were the subject of numerous studies and experiments, including a large tank for training purposes with breathing apparatus.** LEFT: **Other training methods and equipment were tried, but survival remained something of a haphazard affair.** ABOVE: **Immersion suits and life jackets were also tested, although their suitability for escaping from a submarine – as opposed to surviving an accident or the sinking of a surface ship – proved to require many more years of trial and error before satisfactory solutions to catastrophe beneath the waves were found. Meanwhile, the accidents and tragedies continued to occur.**

The Cold War: teardrops and Guppies

After World War II, the beginning of an undersea warfare revolution brought the United States and the Soviet Union into a confrontation in which they were the only two serious players – and it was the submarine forces of the two nations on which the naval developments were stridently focused. Building on the advanced German XXI submarines – the United States, Russia and Britain took possession of one apiece – the US Navy anticipated submarines of the future going deeper, staying there longer, and moving much faster. However, they weren't alone in these endeavours, of course, and naval and civilian advisers warned that in exploiting the XXI type, the Soviet Union presented "the most potent post-war naval threat to the United States".

It was known that the Soviets, still repairing the devastating effects of the war, lagged behind the Americans. They publicly boasted a potential force of 300 Soviet Type XXI equivalents by 1950, but it was not until 1949 that the first post-war Soviet submarine designs went to sea. Two classes were deployed: the Whiskey and the Zulu. The Zulu was a true Type XXI, equipped with a snorkel, capable of 16 knots submerged. But only 21 Zulus were commissioned between 1949 and 1958. During the same period, 236 Whiskeys were commissioned. They were smaller, shorter range boats, designed more for European littoral operations.

Technology was still in its infancy and intelligence gathering tended to be of the manual kind. US submariners were on round-the-clock front-line positions to gather clues as to Russian advances. In August 1949, for instance, submarines *Cochino* and *Tusk* were deployed to the waters off Norway 161km/100 miles from the Soviet Northern Fleet's bases at Murmansk and Polyarnyy to learn what they could about Soviet missile testing. Without warning, batteries in *Cochino* exploded and badly burned one officer. Fire and noxious gases

TOP: **Initially, the Soviet Union lagged behind the West. Their largest class of new boats was the Whiskey class, of which 236 were built between 1949 and 1958, all of conventional shape.** ABOVE: **USS *Albacore* changed everything. Her design became the model for the teardrop hull adopted in all modern submarines across the world, and was critical in the race for the development of superior submarines.**

released by this and subsequent blasts spread throughout the submarine, endangering the entire crew. Two *Cochino* men, trying to bring help from nearby *Tusk* while maintaining radio silence, were pitched into the bitterly cold water when their rubber boat overturned. Without hesitation, men from *Tusk* jumped in to help rescue their fellow sailors. Several men drowned in the attempt and their bodies drifted silently off into the northern waters. Finally, after heroic efforts by everyone, the surviving crewmen of both submarines gathered safely on board *Tusk*, and as they prepared to set sail for home, the *Cochino*, gutted by fire and explosion, vanished beneath the waves.

This was one of the last occasions that such primitive cloak and dagger work was undertaken. The Guppies made sure of that. This was the name given to the boats produced for the sole purpose of "Greater Underwater Propulsive Power". They were developed in the United States, and followed by the

ABOVE: **USS** *Cochino*, a Balao-class submarine, commissioned in 1946, was transformed into one of the world's most modern submarines with the Guppy conversion. She sank after a severe battery explosion in stormy seas off northern Norway, though the crew was rescued by USS *Tusk*. ABOVE RIGHT: **USS** *Pickerel*, a Tench-class submarine, was another boat converted to Guppy, and in 1950 she made a record 8,369km/5,200 miles submerged trans-Pacific voyage. RIGHT: **USS** *Blueback,* commissioned in 1959, was the first US submarine built specifically to the Guppy configuration (as opposed to a conversion) and was also the last non-nuclear boat to take her place in the US Navy. Key features included removing the deck guns, streamlining the outer hull, replacing the conning tower with a sail, installing more air conditioning and a snorkel, and doubling the battery capacity. She can be seen in the Sean Connery movie *The Hunt for Red October* in the role of USS *Dallas*.

Soviets both using features borrowed from the XXI. The star elements of the Guppy design consisted of the removal of the deck guns, streamlining of the outer hull, installing new propellers for submerged operations and – most distinctively of all – replacing the conning tower with a sail. Initially, existing boats were converted to take the new developments, and instantly underwater speeds were almost doubled. The first Guppy sent to the Far East, *Pickerel* made the entire trip back from Hong Kong to Pearl Harbor on snorkel – 8,359km/ 5,194 miles in 21 days submerged, a record that was held until 1958. In the new boats that were to get these innovations as standard, the Tang class first commissioned in 1951 led the field in this development. The *Tang* was the first truly new post-war construction that represented the first step towards greater speed and endurance below the surface.

There was one other innovation that was to change the look of submarines forever. American researchers and designers

had been drawing new shapes on their board since 1944. In 1950, the one that grabbed the eye of everyone was an attractive hydrodynamic hull shape that became known as the teardrop.

A prototype was built and extensively tested in wind tunnels, subsequently leading to a $20 million development budget out of which came the *Albacore*: the first teardrop submarine, fast and whale-like with a sail distinctively positioned a third of the overall length from the bow.

She was commissioned in December 1953, and initial trials showed that she was faster submerged than the designers had anticipated. The attractive design set the standard, and was adopted in due course by most navies of the world.

BELOW: **USS** *Tang* was the first of the American new breed to be designed post-war and as such was the first of six that incorporated the Guppy (snorkel) configuration into the design, as well as being test platforms for the first nuclear submarines.

LEFT: **USS** *Nautilus*, **the sixth American ship to carry that name, was the world's first operational nuclear-powered submarine. Heading south for her** shakedown cruise, she travelled 2,100km/1,300 miles from New London to San Juan, Puerto Rico, in less than 90 hours, which was the longest ever submerged cruise by a submarine and at the highest sustained speed ever recorded. Later, she became the first vessel to complete a submerged transit across the North Pole. By February 4, 1957, *Nautilus* had logged 111,120km/ 60,000 nautical miles, matching the endurance of the fictional *Nautilus* in Jules Verne's *Twenty Thousand Leagues under the Sea*. INSET: **The badge of SSN-571, the first nuclear-powered attack submarine.**

Nautilus, the first true submarine

And so to the vessel that Jules Verne predicted in his 1870 novel, *Twenty Thousand Leagues under the Sea*: a true submarine that could travel the globe without ever surfacing, a fictional construction that bore many similarities to the reality that finally emerged in 1955. Even the name was the same: *Nautilus*. It all began in the mid-1940s, when Captain Hyman Rickover, a brilliant naval engineer and experienced submariner, was burning the midnight oil, working on his own theories for such a boat. Without any great enthusiasm from more senior naval figures, Dr Ross Gunn of the US Naval Research Laboratory and Dr Philip Abelson of the Carnegie Institute joined Hyman in 1948. Both had been working on similar themes that would bring about a revolution in submarine propulsion on similar lines to the Walther boat, and indeed their eventual product bore a number of similarities. The difference was that unlike Walther who used highly concentrated hydrogen peroxide, Gunn proposed the use of nuclear fission.

In the simplest terms, a reactor would generate steam, which would drive the turbine. For the next two years they struggled with the theory of a nuclear-powered submarine while at the same time fighting a relentless rearguard action against formidable opponents. Early in 1950, Rickover's team produced designs for a land-based nuclear reactor as a prototype for one that could power a substantial submarine. They demonstrated how a single power plant could provide the propulsion for unlimited surface and submerged travel. A small quantity of enriched uranium would produce enough power to run for years, and the nuclear submarine would be able to

ABOVE: **All eyes on the monitors as** *Nautilus* **travels under the North Pole. The main Control Room was located directly below the Attack Centre, accommodating the instruments and controls for diving, surfacing and steering the ship. The Diving Officer of the Watch was in charge of this space and received orders for depth, course and speed from the Officer of the Deck in the Attack Centre.**

operate at high speed, completely and indefinitely submerged and restricted only by human endurance.

Rickover drew the comparison against even the most modern conventional diesel-electric submarines, in which the submerged approach to a target had to be made at a very low speed of no more than three knots, to avoid wasting battery power, and whose ability to stay submerged was limited to the state of on-board batteries. As every submarine commander well knew, this was critical in any attack situation because sufficient power always had to be husbanded in case of counter-attack and the possibility of having to sit on the bottom

After Crews Quarters — Engine Room — Reactor — Attack Centre — Bridge — Periscope Room — Captain's Stateroom — Officers' Wardroom — Galley — Crews Quarters — Forward Torpedo Room

Control Room — Crews Mess — Batteries — Stores

ABOVE: **Apart from the historic nature of the submarine's development, great emphasis was placed on interior design, as is evident from this compartmentalized view of the various operational stations.** LEFT: **A fine starboard view of SSN-571 *Nautilus* at sea.** BELOW: **A view of the Torpedo Room, which held six tubes, initially for Mk 14 torpedoes as displayed above, as well as stowage racks for 24 torpedoes. Directly aft of the Torpedo Room was a small berthing area with 10 bunks, toilets, shower and sinks for the weapons crew.**

until the danger had passed. The need to conserve battery power had always meant that submarines had to be cautious about engaging fast surface warships. Nuclear submarines, said Rickover, would end all those problems overnight. They would be fast, they could travel at top speed without ever having to surface and they could remain submerged for great distances. The size of the nuclear reactor and its shielding meant that the submarine had to be 97m/318ft 3in long and displace 3,539 tonnes/3,483 tons on the surface, which was more or less the size of a modern cruiser.

Many were unconvinced by these claims; some were even scared by them. Even so, the US Congress approved a $30 million budget to build the world's first nuclear-powered submarine, and her keel was laid down by President Harry Truman at the Electric Boat Company shipyard – the same company that had produced the first Hollands at the turn of the century – in Groton, Connecticut, on June 14, 1952. On

the morning of January 17, 1955, the first commanding officer, Commander Eugene P. Wilkinson, ordered all lines cast off and signalled the historic message: "Under way on nuclear power."

Very soon, *Nautilus* began to shatter all speed and distance records, and in August 1958, then under Commander Bill Anderson and with 116 men on board, she left Pearl Harbor under top secret orders to commence Operation Sunshine – the first crossing of the North Pole by a ship, a mission that many said was impossible. The achievement became known to the world when, on August 3, *Nautilus* reached the geographic North Pole 90 degrees north and Anderson signalled a message that would be echoed by the moon landing team a few years later, he said: "For the world, our country and the navy – the North Pole."

These developments came at a time of mounting East-West tension and, we now know, were to have a profound effect on the race for nuclear domination by the superpowers.

Skipjack sets the standard

Now the Americans had nuclear power in a relatively conventionally shaped boat, *Nautilus*, and the teardrop design of *Albacore*, which had proved exceptionally fast, even with conventional power. Next, the two technologies were merged to create the *Skipjack* class, combining the endurance of nuclear propulsion with the streamlined hull that at a stroke would produce the world's fastest submarine, said to be capable of an incredible 30 knots dived. The American team had also created the design base for all future US submarines.

In 1955, five *Skipjacks* were ordered, and were subsequently commissioned between 1959 and 1961. They were essentially attack submarines in support of the American anti-submarine warfare programme, codenamed SOS-US, which came into effect after US intelligence surmised that any atom-bomb attack on the United States would most likely be carried by submarines.

This was extrapolated from the fact that both sides were already working on the development of ballistic missiles, again based initially on the German technology of the V1 and V2 rockets that had caused so much devastation in wartime London. From that one assessment, the whole development of attack submarines subsequently began to take on a new complexion, as indeed did America's own anti-submarine protection. From the late 1950s, a detection system revealing the advance of any submarine towards the American east coast was installed along the entire coastline, from north to south, and later extended to cover the west coast and Hawaii.

Skipjack was also unique in that it was the first nuclear submarine with a single shaft. Placement of the bow planes on the sail greatly reduced flow noise at the bow-mounted sonar. The deep-diving and high speed capabilities of the class were the result a new reactor design, the S5Ws, that became the US Navy's standard until the Los Angeles class joined the fleet in the mid-1970s.

Further developments focused on reducing the noise levels of the Skipjacks, which were easy to detect even at extreme range. For this, the designers turned to the smaller *Tullibee*, which had been designed specifically as an Anti-Submarine Warfare (ASW) weapon. These boats were noted in US submarine history as the quietest nuclear submarine with turbo-electric drive, the first with a sonar suite that included a low-frequency passive array for long-range detection and

LEFT: **USS *Shark*, a Skipjack-class submarine commissioned in 1961, later joined the Sixth Fleet in the Mediterranean, the first such deployment for a nuclear submarine. In 1964, she was awarded a commendation for "achieving results of great importance in the field of anti-submarine warfare". She was decommissioned in 1986.**
ABOVE: **The Soviet Hotel-class ballistic missile submarine was put into service in 1959, designed to carry the D-2 launch system. This version, from the 1969 era, with a NATO reporting name of Hotel III, had been lengthened to test R-29 missiles.**

LEFT: **USS** *Tullibee*, commissioned in 1960, was something of a test platform, with innovative designs. She was nicknamed the "boat of firsts" – the first designed for anti-submarine warfare, the first to be equipped with a new series of sonar equipment, the first with torpedo tubes amidships and the first to use turbo-electric propulsion.

ABOVE: The Russian November class was also a boat of firsts – the first Soviet nuclear-powered submarine in 1958, the first to traverse the North Pole (four years after the Americans) and the first to carry ballistic weapons when the class was modified.

LEFT: **USS** *George Washington* was already under construction when the nuclear arms race opened up, and was cut in two for the installation of a ballistic missile compartment, to become America's first ballistic boomer.

ABOVE: **USS** *Scamp*, a *Skipjack*-class submarine, was among the early nuclear boats later converted to receive SubSafe, whereby every component and every action is intensively managed. The system added significant cost, but no submarine certified by SubSafe has ever been lost.

a spherical array for approach and attack, and the first submarine with torpedo tubes amidships. This step was a further milestone in the history of nuclear boats, which signalled the development of the multipurpose SSN that combined the speed of *Skipjack* and the ASW capability of *Tullibee* into one boat. This became the *Thresher* from which all future US submarine classes derived. The acoustic advantages were hailed as dramatic, and the new boats were in a class of their own when compared with the fleet that the Russians were in the process of building. These were colloquially known as the Soviet HENS, standing for the initials of the Red Navy's principal classes, Hotel (SSBN), Echo (SSGN) and November (SSN), which began deploying alongside the Threshers in the early 1960s as these great monsters jostled for position and supremacy.

However, there was yet to be one more crucial development based on the *Skipjack* model. Since the end of the war, both nations had been experimenting with submarine-launched ballistic missiles, and *Skipjack* proved

to be an ideal platform for that purpose. It was the beginning of the true era of potential nuclear annihilation launched from beneath the waves. Unlike easily targeted land-based missiles, submarines carrying strategic ballistic missiles (SSBNs) were constantly on the move, lurking deep in the ocean, with almost unlimited staying power. They were regarded as being capable of reaching almost any target in the world, and after the successful trials of the Polaris A1, *Scorpion*, an SSN of the *Skipjack* class, was sliced in two for a 39.6m/130ft missile section to be inserted to create the first nuclear-powered ballistic missile carrier. *Scorpion* was renamed *George Washington*, thereby establishing a new class of submarine. This giant weighed in at 5,900 tonnes/5,807 tons, was 116.4m/382ft long and carried 16 Polaris missiles with a range of 2,222km/1,200 nautical miles. They were to be matched and bettered, at least in terms of size, by the Soviet Union's 8,128-tonne/8,000-ton Yankee class, which eventually packed in an armoury of 16 SS-N-6 missiles with a range of 2,408km/1,300 nautical miles.

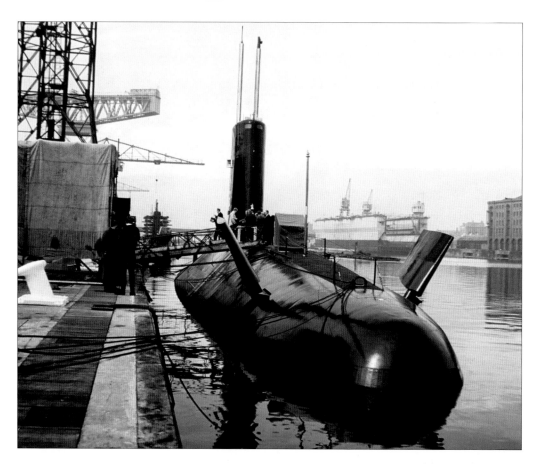

Life aboard the Dreadnought

Britain, once the greatest sea power in the world, could not even begin to contemplate anything more than a tag-along role to the United States in the two-horse race for supremacy in submarine warfare. Her shipyards were still very capable of producing world-class boats, of course, but the nation's submarine capability at the start of the 1960s would barely raise a blip on the radar screen. Her only nuclear deterrents were the RAF's V-bomber force and land-based missiles strung down the east coast pointing towards the Soviet Union. However, Lord Louis Mountbatten, as First Sea Lord and later as Chief of Defence Staff, was an ardent campaigner for Britain's own nuclear submarines and eventually persuaded the British government to provide the finance to begin the process of turning the nation's submarine force into an all-nuclear complement, a process that would take several years.

It began with the building of Britain's first nuclear powered submarine with a power plant bought from the Americans. She was to be christened *Dreadnought,* the ninth ship in British naval history to carry that most famous name and in a subliminal way this perhaps demonstrated that the Admiralty had finally acknowledged that the submarine had graduated to capital ship. She was launched by the Queen at Barrow-in-Furness on Trafalgar Day, October 21, 1960, by which time, incidentally, the United States had stopped building conventional submarines altogether.

Dreadnought was a proud bearer of a bit of British face-saving in a world where submarine power was assuming astronomical proportions. She had a surface displacement of 3,500 tonnes/3,445 tons and 4,000 tonnes/3,937 tons submerged. She was 78m/256ft long, had a beam of 10m/32ft 10in, could travel effortlessly at 28 knots submerged and had a crew of 88. She was classed as a hunter-killer fleet submarine, armed with six conventional bow torpedoes. She was to be the prototype for the creation of Britain's nuclear submarine force, which from now on would be built entirely by British scientists, engineers and shipbuilders, with more planned for the immediate future, to form the Valiant class. The price the First

ABOVE: **Nuclear propulsion also presented other considerations, given the greater length of time spent submerged. The medics on the 1969-built USS *Andrew* had to perform an emergency operation on a makeshift table in the mess room, although by then newer ships were already being fitted with full medical suites.** BELOW: **An image demonstrating the sleek lines of HMS *Dreadnought*, which rightly instilled pride among the British submarine community.**

ABOVE: **Catering was also to become a major new consideration for submarines of the nuclear age with enough chefs to prepare meals for several sittings in pleasant, clean and hygienic surroundings, carrying enough stores for extended journeys at sea, and with a varied and healthy diet of fine quality fruit, vegetables and meat.** BELOW: **The mess halls on the nuclear submarines also took on the air of a relaxing, spacious restaurant with modern accoutrements.**

Sea Lord had to pay for that agreement from the government was a halt on the building of further diesel-electric submarines, which in turn left Britain very short of boats a decade later.

Dreadnought delivered the long-awaited revolution to the British submarine force. She was new in every regard, handled by telemotor controls using a joystick and a dazzling array of dials that made up the elaborate instrument panel. For the crew going aboard for the first time, it was a jaw-dropping experience, with accommodation to a standard they had never seen before, even in surface vessels. Apart from an efficient air-conditioning and purification system, there were numerous luxuries, such as showers, washing facilities, a laundry, and a large galley equipped for serving decent meals. There were also separate messes for junior and senior ratings, well-furnished recreational spaces and a range of leisure facilities, such as a cinema, a library and other features to relieve the monotony of long periods submerged.

By then, the British government had approved the building of Valiant-class boats, for which *Dreadnought* was the prototype. Five were to be laid down for construction between 1962 and 1970, and with that approval came a major operation in recruitment and retraining to prepare the crews and shore bases to take control of these revolutionary boats. Nor was it simply a question of training. As had been discovered in the United States, the unique qualities of life aboard a nuclear submarine required commanders of outstanding leadership skills and crews capable of withstanding the particular pressures that came with long periods of life beneath the waves. There was no precedent to the experience. The whole

point of nuclear boats was that they would submerge as soon as they left their base and, if necessary, remain submerged for the duration of their patrol. From the very beginning, crews might go for weeks without seeing daylight or having any contact whatsoever with the outside world. Most on board would not have the slightest inclination of their whereabouts, the time zone they were in or even whether it was night or day.

Two, three or four month patrols submerged became commonplace, and the aspects of crew welfare necessarily became a priority in both selection and training. The fact of life that had faced all submariners since the beginning – the confined and restricted nature of travelling in a boat tight for space and packed with dangerous gear – was no less pronounced in the comparatively palatial surroundings of the nuclear boats. If anything, they were heightened by the longer periods of time spent submerged in what was still a confining, if not confined, space. Greater studies would follow, but from the early American experience, repeated in Britain, it was immediately evident that prospective crews needed careful screening for temperament, intelligence and fitness. Selection and training of commanders, officers and senior ratings in turn became perhaps the most crucial elements of all. In their hands rested the responsibility for all elements, human and mechanical, in these highly sophisticated war machines.

Two lost submarines jolt the US nuclear team

American leaders had called USS *Thresher* the most advanced submarine in the world in the new era of hunter-killer submarines. She was in fact a star, capable of speeds and depths never before achieved, and early in 1963 her manoeuvres off Charleston had been watched and applauded by the US Naval Antisubmarine Warfare Council. However, during her return to port she was accidentally struck by a tug, sustaining slight damage to one of her ballast tanks, and she went off to Groton, Connecticut for repairs at the Electric Boat Company. On completion, she underwent further trials with dockyard technicians aboard before her final release, 322km/200 miles off the coast of New England.

There, on April 10, she put to sea for deep-diving exercises with 16 officers, 96 enlisted men and 17 civilian technicians aboard. She had an escort vessel, *Skylark*, on the surface equipped with monitoring and underwater telephonic equipment, maintaining contact throughout the dive. Then, the submarine reported she was in difficulties. Transmissions became unclear and garbled.

Subsequently, investigators concluded that a seawater pipe in the aft engine spaces had broken, spraying water into the engine room and shorting one of the main electrical bus boards. The sub lost electrical power and couldn't operate the reactor. Darkness, a sea mist and sheer terror inhibited the crew from manually actuating the valves. The aft part of the sub filled up with water and tilted down. With no power to get back on line, the sub drifted down below 1,676m/5,500ft, to crush depth and

ABOVE: **When the USS *Thresher* went down with all hands, the US Navy vowed that such a tragedy should never occur again. A Presidential Deep Submergence Review Group initiated a study and initiated the Deep Submergence Rescue System: the *Mystic* (DSRV 1) and *Avalon* (DSRV 2), pictured here, became the genesis of that programme.** RIGHT: **The newly honed emblem of the Deep Submergence Unit.**

imploded. A ghastly death for an entire crew, and one whose impact on the whole submarine community, as well as the nation, brought the US Navy to declare that it would never happen again.

Lessons learned from the *Thresher* tragedy led to the formation of the American SubSafe Programme, which called for checks on every submarine in the US fleet and every pressure-related part within their systems. In future, they could not move without certification that the systems were completely safe. The Deep Submergence Rescue System was developed from a special Presidential Deep Submergence Review Group in the mid-1960s. The deep submergence rescue vehicles *Mystic* (DSRV 1) and *Avalon* (DSRV 2) were constructed, and over the years they progressively improved.

Despite these measures, America lost a second nuclear submarine five years later. *Scorpion*, which had assumed the

ABOVE: **The USS** *Scorpion*, **lost in May 1968, is reported to be resting on a sandy seabed 3,048m/10,000ft down in the Atlantic, approximately 644km/400 miles south-west of the Azores. The US Navy acknowledged that it periodically visited the site to conduct testing for the release of nuclear materials from the nuclear reactor or the two nuclear weapons aboard her.**

ABOVE: **The loss of USS** *Thresher* **with military and civilian technicians aboard stunned the nation: the boat was the best of the newest, built at the Portsmouth Naval Shipyard and was the first of a new class of submarine, designed for optimum performance of sonar and weapons systems.** LEFT: **The high-tech sail of USS** *Scorpion*.

name from the earlier boat which was converted to the SSBN *George Washington*, was reported missing. Although overdue for a major overhaul because of budget concerns and tight operational schedules, in April 1968 she was operating with the Sixth Fleet on anti-submarine warfare exercises in the Mediterranean, until she was suddenly pulled out and ordered to the Canaries. It was reported later that her mission was to check on some curious activity involving large balloons by Soviet ships and submarines. Crew on the *Scorpion* spent two or three days monitoring the situation and photographing activity among the Soviet group but in fact reported nothing unusual, and she was ordered back to her home port on May 21. Six days later, it was reported that she was overdue at Norfolk and that all contact had been lost. A massive search was mounted, but on June 5 it was conceded that *Scorpion* and her crew of 99 officers and men were presumed lost.

Various causes were surmised, not least rumours of a clash with the Soviets. However, the search continued using the same techniques employed to find a missing H-Bomb that had fallen out of a B-52 off the coast of Spain after the aircraft had collided with its fuel tanker. At the end of October, a Navy oceanographic research ship located the hull of *Scorpion* in more than 3,048m/10,000ft of water 644km/400 miles south-west of the Azores. Deep submergence vehicles were sent down to record the scene, and found that the boat had made a huge gash in the ocean floor, her back was broken and the two portions of the hull were held together by mere slivers of metal. A Court of Inquiry concluded that her loss could not be determined with any certainty but conjectured that the most probable cause was the accidental activation of the battery of

a Mark 37 torpedo during an inspection, causing a live "hot run" within the tube. If it had been released from the tube, the torpedo, fully armed, would have engaged its nearest target, *Scorpion*. Alternative theories suggested that the torpedo may have exploded in the tube or that there was an explosion in the battery well. Monitoring stations did record a "loud acoustic event" coinciding with the loss of the boat.

In 1969, when the Court of Inquiry resumed to consider its final verdict, it found that there was no "incontrovertible proof" of the exact cause, and that the loss of *Scorpion* remained a mystery. Further investigations using the deep submergence vehicles showed that the battery well had been destroyed, the torpedo room remained intact and there was no external evidence of being hit by a torpedo. No further inquiry was initiated, but the media did reveal that one of the crew had written to his parents complaining that internally the submarine was in constant need of running repairs, and that another had written to demand his transfer from "USS *Scrap Iron*". Meanwhile, as with any nuclear accident, the navy had to monitor the area of the sinking for any possible effects on the environment.

The ballistic boomers

One fact underlines the great race between the superpowers to equip themselves with submarines packed with ballistic missiles: In any one of their boats, the total nuclear armoury was more powerful than all the bombs dropped in World War II by all sides put together. Such a situation began when the need for a hidden second-strike nuclear force arose in the contemplation of a nuclear conflict – this at a time when the two superpowers already had their H-bombers constantly in the air. Then came MAD – Mutually Assured Destruction – which was promised by Eisenhower in the event of an attack by the Soviet Union. This "madness" was pursued year upon year with bigger and more powerful nuclear ballistic submarines, some military advisers concluding that when an optimum level of destructive capability was reached by both sides, an effective stalemate would be achieved and further weapons, as Winston Churchill laconically put it, would merely "make the rubble bounce".

However, the Americans, shocked by the event of Sputnik 1 being delivered into the earth's orbit, decided to maintain the principle of being able to strike or retaliate with hugely destructive power. Thus, as already noted, USS *George Washington* conducted the world's first submarine launch of a strategic ballistic missile on June 28, 1960, and the floodgates opened for the great "boomers", as ballistic missile submarines became known. The boomers moved out into the areas of potential confrontation, often surrounded by "minders", the new breed of nuclear hunter-killer submarines.

ABOVE: **USS *James K. Polk*, of the Benjamin Franklin class, was originally completed with the Polaris A3, but was refitted with the Poseidon missile in the 1970s. In 1994, as the Cold War began to scale down, she converted from missile carrier to an attack-mission submarine to operate with US special forces.**
BELOW: **The badge of the USS-645 *James K. Polk*.**

ABOVE: **Poseidon was the second US Navy ballistic missile system and had improved accuracy compared with the Polaris A3, along with 14 W68 multiple independently targetable re-entry vehicles.**

The Soviet Union was never far behind in the race, and indeed aimed to outnumber the US boat for boat, promising a fleet of at least 300. Their Yankee-class submarines were

FAR LEFT: **The *Ohio*, lead ship of the class that bore her name, led the American modernization programme to replace the ageing ballistic missile submarines of the 1960s, and was far more capable. These submarines could carry 24 ballistic missiles which could be accurately delivered to selected targets from almost anywhere in the world's oceans. In 2005, *Ohio* was converted to an SSGN – a guided missile carrier.** ABOVE: **The corridors are long and spooky in the ballistic boats, especially in the huge missile compartment, as here aboard the USS *Ohio*.** INSET: **The missile tubes of an SSBN.**

the first Soviet ballistic missile carriers with firepower comparable to that of their US counterparts, and their arrival signalled the first step in the Soviet leadership's avowed intention to defend the homeland.

The Yankees were significantly quieter than any other previous Russian boats, due to their smoother hull shape, propeller design, exterior sound-deadening coatings and other modifications. They were also the base model for the Delta class of Russian SSBNs, which became the mainstay of the Soviet sea-launched deterrent, having been laid down in 1969 and maintaining a presence in the fleet until the beginning of the 21st century.

The Delta-class submarines could deploy on alert patrols in the Soviet arctic and the Norwegian and Barents seas. Consequently, unlike their predecessors, they no longer needed to pass through Western SOSUS sonar sound detection barriers to come within range of their targets. Deployed close to home, they could be protected in "bastions" by the rest of the Soviet Navy.

The submerged firing of the missiles could be conducted in a single salvo while the submarine moved at a speed of 5 knots. A high degree of automation allowed a significant reduction in the time required for pre-launch preparations in comparison with the Yankee class.

LEFT: **There is great ceremony for the christening of submarines and the names often have poignancy too, even if somewhat obscure. The *Mariano G. Vallejo* was named after a 19th century Mexican who helped bring about the annexation of California by the United States. The boat that bore his name began the routine of all ballistic boomers in 1965 and continued for the next 30 years before being decommissioned to join the growing graveyard of old nuclear boats in the recycling programme.** ABOVE: **A pre-launch photograph of the *Lafayette*-class ballistic missile submarine *Thomas A. Edison*.**

The Soviets also began building the world's biggest ballistic submarine, the massive *Typhoon*, 175.3m/575ft in length and 22.9m/75ft wide (compared to *George Washington*, 116m/382ft and 10m/33ft respectively). The design was based on a multi-hulled construction that bore a resemblance to a catamaran. The submarine had two separate pressure hulls with a diameter of 7.3m/24ft each, five inner habitable hulls and 19 compartments.

The *Typhoon* was introduced with a specific role in mind when she was laid down in 1977, a much feared vehicle capable of carrying 20 long-range ballistic missiles with up to 200 nuclear warheads that were once aimed at the United States. Like the Americans, the Soviet leadership determined that they must have the capability to maintain a massive and ever-ready retaliatory position by putting the Typhoons on

permanent patrol beneath the Arctic Ocean, only to come out of hiding if and when a strike back became necessary. With hulls of ultra-strength, they would supposedly then crash their way to the surface through an ice-cap up to 3.7m/12ft thick and make their attack.

The six boats of the class were the ultimate in largesse, with a crew of 150. They were also expensive to operate and proved less than satisfactory in service. However, the last of the breed remained in service until 1994 when the Americans promised cash and technical aid to decommission them, which in itself was also a problem of gigantic proportions.

Next in this progression to annihilation, if it ever came to the crunch, came the American's Lafayette and Benjamin Franklin classes, which were a prelude to the *Ohio*, laid down

RIGHT: **The distinctive look of a Soviet nuclear submarine, always with a slightly dishevelled appearance and perhaps all the more menacing for it, like the rough kid on the block. The Yankee-class boats were the first Soviet boomers with firepower comparable to that of their US counterparts. In 1986, a missile fuel leak on** *K219* **caused an explosion, and the resulting fire killed four people. The ship sank off the east coast of America. By 2005, all but two had been taken out of service.**

LEFT: **The dramatic spectacle of a Trident 1 C4 missile MIRV warhead re-entry. Every line represents the path of a warhead which, were it live, would detonate with an explosive power 25 times greater than the atom bomb dropped on Hiroshima in 1945.**
RIGHT: **The** *Trident II D-5* **missile is the sixth generation member of the US Navy's Fleet Ballistic Missile programme. It is a three-stage inertia-guided FBM with a range of more than 7,408km/ 4,000 nautical miles and has a significantly greater payload than its predecessor.**

in 1976, and which came with the tag of possessing the "world's most powerful weapons platform". The Ohio class became the principal workhorse of the US boomer fleet, with 18 of the boats launched between 1979 and 1996, eventually with the Trident strategic ballistic missile system. The US Navy gives the range of the Trident II missile as "greater than 7,360km" and it could be up to 12,000km/7,456 miles. Trident II was capable of carrying up to 12 MIRVs (multiple independent re-entry vehicles), each with a yield of 100 kilotons, although the SALT treaty between the superpowers limited this number to eight per missile.

Lower down the scale of possible contributors to a nuclear Armageddon came the British SSBN fleet, for which Prime Minister Harold Macmillan persuaded President John F. Kennedy to supply the latest Polaris A3P ballistic missiles at a historic meeting in the Bahamas. This decision, which aroused great controversy in Britain at the time, enabled the Royal Navy to build its own Resolution class, four submarines built in pairs at the Vickers Armstrong yard in Barrow-in Furness. These were later to be replaced with the Vanguard class, to carry the Trident missile in the 1990s. China, France and Australia were the only other nations to operate SSBNs, albeit on a limited scale.

LEFT: **The 1980s British Trafalgar-class boats were designed as hunter-killers for Cold War operations in the North Atlantic, and were on constant patrols with dual crews. But cracks were discovered in one of them in August 2000, and it was found that only one of the seven boats could remain operational until repairs had been carried out. They were also fitted with Tomahawk land attack cruise missiles and used them in the 2001 attack on Afghanistan in the action to oust the Taliban.** BELOW: **Control room action.**

Fast and versatile: the hunter-killers

While the boomers of both sides played out their role of maintaining a "hidden and survivable retaliatory strike capability", fully loaded for a nuclear strike, the fast attack submarines (SSNs), commonly known as "hunter-killers", were established from the outset as multi-functional boats, in the "do anything, go anywhere" mode. They are, of course, also widely used by nations of the world who do not possess SSBNs, although there principally were and still are only two major nuclear submarine forces, with the United Kingdom in third place following the arrival of her Resolution-class SSBN fleet and the supporting Trafalgar-class SSNs.

They are designed to operate in the truer role of the submarine, so often demonstrated in World War II: operating alone in anti-submarine or anti-surface missions, surveillance and intelligence-gathering or with submarine battle groups or Joint Task Force operations with surface vessels. Most Cold War operations remain classified, but the very few that have been revealed demonstrate how it all works. In the 1970s, USS *Guardfish* was tracking a Soviet cruise missile submarine (SSGN), which, in turn, was following US aircraft carriers off Vietnam, ready to pounce should the Soviet sub launch her missile. In 1978, USS *Batfish* (SSN) tracked a Soviet ballistic missile submarine sailing off the east coast of America, thus learning Soviet SSBN patrol areas and operating patterns, to provide early indications of any potential attack on the US.

In modern times, their stealth and virtually unlimited endurance allowed the SSNs to operate in the most sensitive of regions, or as one US commander put it "up close and

personal with the Russians", who were doing exactly the same thing. The SSNs can reach their target or areas of operations at a high rate of knots, independently and undetected.

Now bristling with a highly efficient torpedo armoury (SSN) and/or cruise missiles (SSGN), they are lethal against enemy submarines, surface ships and targets ashore. The latter has been spectacularly demonstrated by launches against land targets during the conflicts of Kosovo, Afghanistan and the two Gulf Wars. Nevertheless, at the height of the Cold War, the principal role of the attack boats was in anti-submarine warfare, and in that regard, the scientists and designers strove to produce the fastest, quietest and generally most capable fast attack vessel, and each class that arrived significantly improved upon its predecessor.

LEFT: The French submarine *Rubis*, an Amethyste-class hunter-killer nuclear boat, serves with the Toulon-based *Escadrille des Sous-marins Nucléaires d'Attaque* (ESNA) or nuclear submarine attack squadron. Modern upgrades provided additional firepower when she was re-equipped to carry both anti-surface and anti-submarine weaponry, with a mixed load of 14 missiles and torpedoes. The record of long patrols by *Rubis* included operations with the coalition forces during the first Gulf War and Operation Trident, the 1999 NATO bombing campaign over Yugoslavia. ABOVE: In 2002, *Rubis* took part in the naval bombardment of Afghanistan, using Exocet SM39 missiles.

The key element for both sides during that period, however, was the survivability of strategic assets – the SSBNs. This became a key role in the work of the SSNs of both sides, who each had around 80 operational boats of various classes. Eleven of the American SSNs were specially equipped to perform the sole task of locating and following Soviet submarines without the enemy counter-detecting their presence, day and night, 365 days a year. Soviet missions matched that capability. The anti-submarine missions of the SSNs, therefore had two major roles: to get into a position to sink the opposing SSBNs before they could launch a pre-emptive attack, and second, to destroy the opposition's SSNs or cruise missile submarines (SSGNs) to protect carrier battle groups. Therefore, for almost four decades, opposing teams roamed the oceans looking for each other. Quietness and stealth became the absolute keynote of all progressive technology surrounding the building of fast attack boats.

Overall, the SSNs operated under a much wider brief, as part a complete naval battle scenario involving the capital ships of the national sides, the US Carrier Battle Groups and the Soviet Surface Action Groups fighting it out for control of the sea. By the 1980s, however, the emphasis shifted heavily towards submarines as the attackers, being assigned to "take out" the heavy surface vessels. The days of a head-to-head Battle of Jutland-style surface shooting match between capital ships were finally put to rest. From that point on, the two sides concentrated heavily on improving their SSNs and SSGNs, and that situation continues in the post-Cold War environment. Indeed, far-ahead projections from both sides see the retention of a strong force of fast attack submarines.

ABOVE: Inside the control room of the US hunter-killer submarine *Los Angeles*, a key element in the American SSN fleet for more than thirty-six years.

The boats of both sides were designed for a life span of 20 or 30 years, but technology rapidly caught up with them. The American Thresher class of 14 boats was quickly overtaken by the Sturgeon class, of which 38 were built from the mid-1960s. However, the Los Angeles class, which arrived in the mid-1970s and was built through to 1996, was the absolute workhorse of the US SSN fleet. Initially designed as an escort for the carrier battle groups and for attacks on Soviet surface battle groups, the class went through over 20 years in production with continual updates and improvement. They were fast, quiet, and could launch Mk48 and Advanced Capability (ADCAP) torpedoes, Harpoon anti-ship missiles, and both land attack and anti-ship Tomahawk cruise missiles. The newer submarines in the class showed another step improvement in quieting, perhaps the most competitive element between the main protagonists, and an increase in operating speed.

Escort duties regularly included conducting ASW sweeps of hundreds of miles ahead of the carrier group and conducting surveillance and attacks against the Soviet surface actions groups, the Kirov-class Soviet cruiser being a particular target. It was fitted with state-of-the art surface-to-air missiles, surface-to-surface missiles and anti-cruise missile defences. While operating in concert with a surface group, the *Kirov* was reckoned to be an almost unreachable target, but in fact particular studies carried out by the Americans showed that, with the exception of the helicopters she carried, her ASW defences were minimal. Therefore, each time the *Kirov* was encountered, particular boats were assigned the sole task of preparing to sink her if it became necessary.

Another SSN in the American repertoire is the *Seawolf,* a magnificent advanced but hugely expensive vessel when

TOP: **The US Navy has long collected its formations into battle groups, each one deployed as a unique combination of ships or submarines. Naturally, whenever these groups were on the move, Soviet submarines would be close at hand, keeping watch, and vice versa.** ABOVE: **The fast Akula SSNs of the Soviet fleet were spy boats, introduced in 1986 and constantly upgraded since.**

commissioned in 1997. It has been claimed to be the fastest, quietest and most heavily armed submarine in existence, carrying 50 torpedoes or 100 mines. Two others exist in the class – Connecticut, commissioned in 1998, and Jimmy Carter, commissioned in 2005. They were followed into US Navy servie, from 204, by the Virginia class incorporating the very lagtest design and technology innovations to improve stealth, intelligence gathering capability, and weapons effectiveness.

Against this, the Soviets lined up a greater range of SSNs, if less technologically sound boats. The range began with the November class, introduced in 1959, which provided *K3*, the first Soviet submarine to reach the North Pole in 1962. Twelve boats were built for patrols in the North Atlantic, Pacific and Mediterranean, primarily targeted at surface battle groups, although their greatest disadvantage was that of noise. The Russians' principal anti-submarine warfare boats arrived with the long-running *Victor* class, which was produced in three versions from 1967 to 1984, operating in the classic role of hunters for enemy SSBNs, while protecting the Red Navy's own SSBNs and surface groups from the Americans. During the Cold War, Victors were operational around the globe. Far less successful was the Alfa class, which initially promised much as a highly automated, high speed submarine noted for its high acceleration rate. The hull was constructed from titanium alloy to achieve greater diving depth, with the intention of negating some of the acoustic advantages of Western submarines. Sadly for the Soviets, however, it was an expensive boat to build and maintain, and ultimately unreliable. The first of the class, *K64*, had so many problems it was decommissioned after only two years of service. A dozen were eventually built to a new design standard and remained in service throughout the Cold War. Another of the long serving classes in the Soviet fleet was the *Akula* class, designed as multipurpose attack submarines to take over from the Viktors in ASW operations and shadowing American battle groups. The class became a workhorse of the Russian fleet and went through three major developments, adding an improved version and the Akula II, remaining in production until the late 1990s.

Most of the Russian SSNs were larger than their US counterparts, and it took years for their designers to come close to matching the Americans in terms of noise and acoustics. Surprisingly to Western observers, it was achieved with the *Oscar* class, a massive boat, 154m/505ft in length with a 18.3m/60ft beam, with a dived displacement of 18,594 tonnes/18,300 tons. The *Oscar II* version was hugely armed, with 24 Shipwreck surface-to-surface missiles with nuclear warheads or 40 torpedoes and 200 depth charges. Eleven *Oscar IIs* were built, with four apiece being constantly deployed with the Pacific and Northern fleets. Among them was the ill-fated *Kursk*, which sank in the Barents Sea with the loss of all hands.

ABOVE: **HMS *Talent*, one of the Trafalgar-class submarines, which in spite of problems with cracks in one of their systems in 2000, remained the Royal Navy's most advanced SSN until the arrival of the Astute class.**

SECOND FROM TOP: **Soviet Victor-class SSNs were designed to protect Soviet surface fleets and attack American ballistic missile boats, should the need arise. When the Soviet spy network discovered that the Americans could easily track Victor II-class submarines, production was halted to design *Victor III* (pictured).** ABOVE: **The US trackers might well have been this crew, in the control room of the US *Los Angeles* SSN.** LEFT: ***Los Angeles*, lead boat in her class, undergoing trials. Sixty-two were built.**

Sink the Belgrano!

The invasion of the Falkland Islands by Argentina in 1982 brought the British submarine service into immediate action, and it was the first to get the alert, presenting the real possibility that they would fire their first shots in anger since World War II. The SSN *Splendid,* from the UK's Swiftsure class, was chasing a Russian submarine, when she was called off by Northwood and ordered to go quickly to Faslane and fill the boat with stores and torpedoes. The order came on March 30, 1982, two days before the invasion. It was a top-secret move and no telephone calls could be made to relatives by the crew, in spite of the fact that *Splendid* had already been at sea for ten weeks. At that point, the crew had no idea of the plan of action, and the politicians probably didn't either.

For years, submarines had been used for a spot of old-fashioned gunboat diplomacy in British-linked hot spots, but this time it was altogether more serious. Sure enough, on April 1, Argentine troops began pouring into the Falklands, and the token British force of Royal Marines was taken prisoner. Argentinian photographers flashed around the world a photograph of them being marched away with their hands over their heads. British Prime Minister Margaret Thatcher was furious, and immediately announced she was sending a task force of 40 warships and a very large contingent of her finest soldiers, including Commandos, Gurkhas, Paras and a large special forces contingent from the SBS and SAS, to take the islands back.

She also announced a 322km/200-mile Maritime Exclusion Zone around the Falklands and that any ships entering that zone did so at their peril. The fast nuclear boats were dispatched immediately to enforce the order. *Spartan* completed the 10,461km/6,500-mile journey to her designated patrol area in less than ten days, a speed of advance of around 26 knots, which, allowing for navigational checks and going to shallow depth to receive messages, was virtually flat out. *Splendid* and *Conqueror* were not far behind, although a long way back came the diesel-engined Oberon boat, *Onyx,* which had a submerged speed of just eight knots. She arrived three weeks after the nuclear boats. Information on Argentina for the submarine commander was sparse, to say the least. *Jane's* provided the best intelligence. Whitehall and the Ministry of Defence had little to offer in the way of up-to-date information about the Argentine fleet and what kind of opposition or anti-submarine operations the British boats might expect.

Splendid, commanded by Commander Roger Lane-Nott, arrived on station 11 days after leaving Faslane, her journey down utilized for a heavy training programme that involved a great deal of effort on the part of every member of the crew. Commander Jim Taylor in *Spartan* had already begun his

TOP RIGHT: **HMS *Splendid*, a hunter-killer SSN of the Swiftsure class, was one of the British submarines on patrol at the time of the Falklands war, providing vital reconnaissance for the Royal Navy Task Force.** ABOVE: **The ill-fated Argentine ship *General Belgrano*, sunk by conventional torpedoes fired from the submarine HMS *Conqueror*, which had tracked her for 30 hours.** RIGHT: **HMS *Sheffield* sank after being hit by Exocet missiles fired by a French-made Dassault Super Etendard aircraft belonging to the Argentine Navy.**

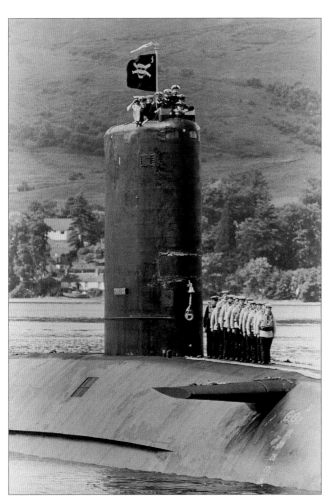

LEFT: Coming home to controversy and flying the Jolly Roger, a customary act of Royal Navy submarines after a "kill", HMS *Conqueror*, the Churchill-class boat that went into the history books as the only British nuclear-powered

submarine to sink an enemy ship with torpedoes since World War II. NEAR LEFT: Survivors come ashore after the Falklands bombing of British troop-landing ship, *Sir Galahad*, which had been hit by a 453.6kg/1,000lb bomb that did not detonate. She was later hit again by two or three bombs while unloading soldiers from the 1st Welsh Guards, of whom 48 were killed in the explosions and subsequent fire. BELOW: The image that made the front pages: the *Belgrano* going down, with the loss of 368 lives.

patrol, but both commanders were short of information. They were eventually tasked by submarine HQ to locate and observe a suspected movement of Argentine ships towards the Falkland Islands, including the aircraft carrier *25 de Mayo* and the cruiser *General Belgrano.* It was a slow process because they had no idea where they were. They did know, however, that the Argentinians had a US-built Guppy-class diesel submarine transmitting somewhere around the Falklands.

Splendid was then moved to patrol the northern end of the Falkland Sound, since there was a great fear that the *25 de Mayo* would get into that area before the British task force arrived so that she could extend the range of her aircraft armed with Exocet missiles. Diplomatic efforts were still proceeding, and the rules of engagement were still changing from "sink" to "do not sink Argentinian ships".

On April 26, *Splendid* reported to Northwood that she had sighted an Argentine task group composed of two Type 42 destroyers together with Exocet-armed frigates moving south along the coast. However, although *Splendid*'s commander had had the destroyers in his periscope sights, he did not have rules of engagement and could not fire. Instead, he was ordered to break off and join the hunt elsewhere when concern now switched to the activities of the cruiser *General Belgrano,* thought to be moving towards the exclusion zone. *Splendid* went north with *Spartan* between Argentina and the

task force, while *Conqueror* searched to the south. The rules of engagement had started to become specific, and the British made known their intention to order the sinking of anything within the 322km/200-mile exclusion zone.

On May 1, however, *Conqueror*'s CO, Chris Wreford-Brown, found *General Belgrano* in his sights. His submarine's nuclear power allowed him to track the cruiser for 30 hours and choose the moment for attack when authorized to do so. The "sink her" command came from London, and he fired a salvo of three ancient Mark VIII torpedoes from 1,100m/1,203yd. They were straight-running, non-homing torpedoes of 1940s vintage, travelling at 45 knots, and two of them struck on a right-angle track. The cruiser sank fast, with the loss of 368 lives. The question arose immediately as to whether the ship was inside or outside the exclusion zone. As it transpired, it was outside and had been for six hours. However this question, as far as the three submarine commanders were concerned, was immaterial. Orders came from on high. If the cruiser had been allowed to get through, the submariners would have been castigated because the ship would have posed an immediate threat to the British ships.

The question of the location and intentions of the *Belgrano* did not go away, and the submariners became caught up in the politics of the affair, although the sinking and the loss of life did bear heavily on some members of the crew.

Submarine TLAMs rain on Iraq, Belgrade and Afghanistan

The commissioning of *Seawolf*, when it was the latest in America's long line of hunter-killer submarines, was notable for a specific inclusion: whereas all US SSNs carry Tomahawk land attack missiles (TLAMs), *Seawolf* can carry 50 torpedo tube-launched TLAMs, the very latest in subsonic, all-weather cruise missiles with a range of 1,111km/600 nautical miles. The TLAMs were also very evident in the war in Iraq to oust Saddam Hussein and indeed have featured in all of the major areas of conflict of modern times. Another feature of their use is that they have, without exception, been used in joint operations with the British, with Royal Navy submarines also firing the missiles. This somewhat new feature to American foreign policy caused some observers to ponder the motives behind the two-handed firing of such weapons, given that almost all were originally created with the annihilation of the Soviet Union in mind.

The submarine programmes the missile flight profile from the launch point to landfall, and thereafter a pre-stored flight plan is followed. According to the Americans who manufacture the TLAMs, high accuracy in hitting the target was assured by the use of a Global Positioning System receiver, inertial and terrain contour matching guidance, and a Digital Scene

TOP: **USS *Minneapolis–Saint Paul*, the 26th member of the Los Angeles class, became the first submarine to carry Tomahawk land attack missiles, specifically designated for use in strikes against Iraq during the Gulf War.** ABOVE: **General Tommy Franks, commander of the US forces in the Gulf, inspects TLAM damage in Baghdad after the 2003 bombardment.**

Matching Area Correlation system. However, there was considerable comment in the media about the number of TLAMs that appeared to miss their targets in the first Gulf War. However, the systems have been updated and improved, particularly those in the brand new *Seawolf* class, which was launched under the tag of "the most advanced and most capable submarine fleet in the world". There is, however, no doubt that competition with the Soviet Union in the final stages of the Cold War played its part in forging continued improvements to the systems and boats of both sides.

The Tomahawk missile was long ago judged by the American scenario planners to be an integral part of future submarine operations, and so it was to be proved. Tomahawk was used extensively during Operation Desert Storm in 1991 and again in Iraq in January and June 1993 during air

RIGHT: **The Regulus guided cruise missile was successfully developed into America's sea-going deterrent, first deployed on the heavy cruiser USS *Los Angeles* in 1955 – and after successful trials five submarines were also fitted to carry and launch the missile, thus to become America's principal deterrent force of that era.**
MIDDLE RIGHT: **The Tomahawk cruise missile became the much-used and most feared arm of the British and US land attack suite: 600 were fired by the US in the first six days of the 2003 attack on Iraqi targets.** BELOW: **HMS *Triumph* which launched Tomahawk missiles during Operation Veritas on targets inside Afghanistan and returned home after operations had ended flying the Jolly Roger to indicate "kills" during a successful patrol.** BELOW RIGHT: **Another of the targets, an alleged terrorist training camp inside Iraq.**

operations against Saddam Hussein. They were used again in Bosnia (Deliberate Force) in 1995 and in Iraq (Desert Strike) in 1996. Four hundred Block II and Block III missiles were fired on five separate occasions.

This and improvements in subsequent operations was taken as fair evidence that long-range missiles fired from hidden submarines could carry out some of the missions of strike aircraft and reduce the risk of pilot and aircraft losses. It was following these operations that British submarines were also equipped with Tomahawks, and they were first introduced in 1998 and used operationally the following year during the Kosovo crisis. During the 78-day NATO bombing campaign, the British submarine *Splendid* was among the launchers of TLAMs that slammed into Belgrade. According to a summary of the cruise attacks published in *Jane's Defence Weekly*, *Splendid* fired 20 Tomahawk cruise missiles during the war, 17 of which hit their targets. US ships and submarines fired 218 cruise missiles at 66 targets, and 181 reached their "intended aim-points" according to US naval officers. The attack on a television building, in which 16 civilians were killed, was strongly criticized by US human rights groups and

Amnesty International. However, NATO's supreme commander at the time, General Wesley Clark, and his British counterparts insisted that the building was a legitimate military target because it was used to pass information to Serbian military units in Kosovo and to promote Serbian propaganda.

The use of *Splendid* in the bombing campaign was a significant departure from the established pattern of patrols and surveillance. It also gave a pointer to the future and the kind of situations that might engage the British submarine service in its more global approach. Warning signs of possible future trouble spots were already evident at the dawn of the new millennium and after 9/11 when the Americans, with British support, decided to unseat the Taliban regime in Afghanistan.

A Royal Navy surface fleet, along with the SSNs *Superb*, *Trafalgar* and *Triumph*, were in the Indian Ocean in support of air operations against the land-locked nation. The two T boats carried out the cruise missile attacks. British submarines kept up the vigil all year long, and another T boat, *Turbulent*, had just finished her tour of duty at Christmas 2002, having been at sea for a full six months without a break, when she was placed on alert to go to the Gulf. Before she was done, *Turbulent* played a full part in the "shock and awe" bombing campaign over Baghdad. When she was finally released from this duty, she had travelled 85,295km/53,000m during a single deployment lasting ten months.

LEFT: **The wreck of the *Kursk* is discovered, and spotlights reveal catastrophic damage to the submarine of a nature and extent that would have rapidly enveloped the whole structure.** BELOW: **A memorial plaque to the lost submarine and her crew.**

The tragedy of the Kursk

On August 12, 2000, scientists at the Norwegian Seismic Institute recorded two explosions, the second registering 3.4 on the Richter scale, which would have required the massive power of 2,032kg/2 tons of explosives to create such a reaction. A "thundering boom" was also picked up by an American spy ship, USS *Loyal* which, at the time, was listening into transmissions from one of the giant Russian submarines of the Oscar II class, *Kursk*, as she participated in a major naval exercise 322km/200 miles away. The Americans knew that the sound could only mean one thing. The submarine had suffered

a major catastrophe. As word got out that one of the most technically advanced boats in the Russian fleet was in trouble, the official word from Moscow was initially quite different.

First, they admitted there was a problem and the vessel had been allowed to drift to the bottom in about 103.6m/340ft of water until technicians had resolved the issue. They could not bring themselves to admit – or perhaps believe – that the showpiece of the Russian submarine fleet displacing 18,594 tonnes/18,300 tons submerged was in dire straits. Therefore, in the style of the Soviet Union of old, they tried to pass it off as a minor incident and rejected offers of help from the West.

However, there was more to it than that. The boat was packed with technology the West knew little about, including her brand new armoury pack – 24 SS-N-19 Shipwreck missiles with either a 500-kilotonne nuclear warhead or 350kg/772lb of high explosives – which in total added up to the equivalent of about two Hiroshima bombs. Also, fitted to the bulbous bow of the 153.9m/505ft long boat was a top-secret target detection sonar which up to that point had never been outside a Russian naval base. It was no wonder, then, that the Russians stalled when the other side offered to send in their deep sea rescue craft.

Thus began what developed into a horrendous saga that gripped the world for days as the Russians tried unsuccessfully to retrieve the 118 men aboard the stricken sub. As relatives began their vigil on the dockside, those who had followed the Russian catalogue of costly mishaps with their submarines, dating back through the decades, feared the worst, regardless of the spin and contradictory stories. As the Russians alone pressed on with their rescue attempt, conflicting stories came out of Moscow suggesting the damage resulted from

ABOVE: **USS *Loyal*, an American intelligence ship, was among those in the area monitoring the Russian exercises, along with submarines USS *Memphis*, USS *Toledo* and HMS *Splendid*.**

LEFT: **The massive surface profile of the stricken submarine *Kursk*, which was on "routine exercises" in the Barents Sea, a region that had seen no fewer than 25 reported accidents or collisions between opposing submarines in the previous three decades of the Cold War. The theory that the *Kursk* had been bumped by an opposing submarine monitoring her movements was propagated in Russia, but proved to be false.**
BELOW: **Damaged: the aft escape hatch of the *Kursk*, photographed by rescuers.**

a collision with another submarine. The deputy prime minister told the media that it had been hit by a "very large tonnage". It was also pointed out that British and American submarines were in the area at the time, monitoring Russian exercises. Some websites to this day still support such allegations, though long ago disproved.

Analysts in the West worked out a probable scenario. The Russians' use of cheap but dangerous liquid hydrogen peroxide fuel to power their torpedoes had triggered an explosion so powerful that it ripped through the first four or five compartments of the boat. Day after day, Russian attempts to get into the boat failed, despite assurances from the government that no foreign help was needed. By Day 7 of the crisis a multi-national team aboard a Norwegian rescue ship was finally invited in. On August 20, they wrenched the after escape hatch free, only to discover the boat was totally besieged.

It took another two months before the Russians were able to set up a mission to retrieve the bodies, during which notes written by members of the crew were found. They poignantly demonstrated the hell they had experienced in the pitch black of the boat before they were eventually overwhelmed by the water. The task of raising the *Kursk* took many months and she was finally brought to the surface by a Dutch contractor in 2001, when it was discovered that the whole of the forward section of the boat had been blown apart. It took another two years for the Russian authorities to admit that there was no collision, that no other boat was involved, and that the cause was, just as Western analysts had surmised, some sort of malfunction in the torpedo room that caused the hydrogen peroxide to ignite while the *Kursk* was practising torpedo firings.

ABOVE: **A Russian photograph showing two submarine personnel in training for underwater escape and rescue missions.**

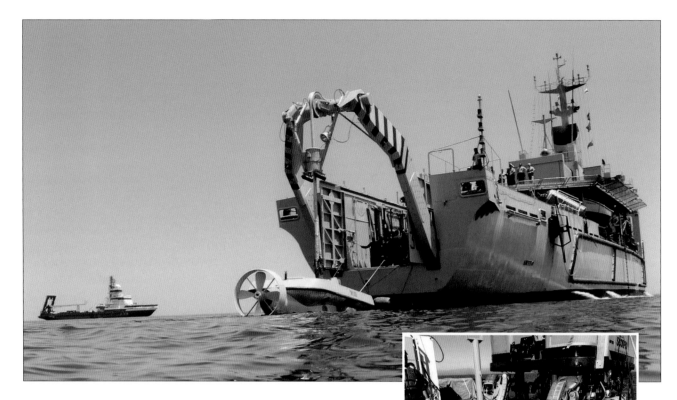

International rescue: deep sea survival teams

Although submarine accidents of a life-threatening nature are becoming less frequent, the development of more sophisticated tools for the deep sea rescue of stranded crews is ongoing. In June 2004, Britain, France and Norway funded the development of a totally new rescue platform, the NATO Submarine Rescue System (NSRS) to replace the LR5 crewed submersible, used by the Royal Navy until 2009 when it was leased to the Royal Australian Navy. NSRS is an international submarine rescue system not just for partner nations but for NATO as a whole, allied nations, and any submarine equipped with a suitable hatch-mating surface. NSRS is available to be deployed anywhere in the world – it is a fast response, highly mobile, distressed submarine (DISSUB) rescue platform.

All equipment is fully road and air transportable to the necessary port, where it will be embarked upon the selected mothership (MOSHIP) before being deployed. Different aircraft and ships may be available at any particular time and location, thus the equipment is designed to maximize the use of any potential aircraft and MOSHIPs. The NSRS system can be launched and recovered in challenging conditions, with wave heights of up to 5m/16.5ft – approximately Sea State 6 – and can reach any distressed submarine (DISSUB) in 72–96 hours from the alert, depending on the location of the incident.

NSRS consists of two sub-systems that can be independently mobilized. When a "SUBSUNK" alert is received, "Intervention", a smaller sub-system focused around the

TOP: **International submarine rescue efforts are co-ordinated by NATO. In one of the largest-ever rescue exercises in the wake of** *Kursk*, **the Italian SRV-300 vehicle was deployed from the mother ship** *Anteo* **and successfully rehearsed docking procedures with the Italian submarine** *Prini*. **Two sailors from** *Prini* **were evacuated to a Turkish ship, using a McCann rescue bell.**
ABOVE: **The** *Scorpio* **ROV (remotely operated deep submergence vehicle) which was used in an attempt to save** *Kursk*'s **crew, shown here recovering the flight recorder. It is commonly used in the offshore oil industry.**

Intervention Remotely Operated Vehicle (IROV) is rapidly mobilized to a distressed submarine in order to prepare the site for the Rescue System. The IROV is supported with a dedicated A-Frame Launch and Recovery system, winch and umbilical, control cabin, navigation, tracking and power generation equipment. The 100 tonne/97.4 tons A-frame has a safe working load of 30 tonnes/29.5 tons and is equipped with a range of heavy compensated winches and motion dampers to allow safe operations in the most demanding and dangerous sea conditions.

The IROV performs DISSUB location, checks for signs of life, establishes communications, begins rescue site preparation (including debris removal and radiation detection) and provides Emergency Life Saving Stores (ELSS) to the DISSUB, such as food, water, atmosphere control equipment and medical supplies if required. All of this activity ensures the DISSUB is ready for rescue operations.

The main Rescue System is used to recover the crew from the stricken submarine. This component of the NSRS system arrives approximately 24 hours after the IROV element, via air and sea. The Rescue System is larger and consists of a free-swimming Submarine Rescue Vehicle (SRV), a Portable Launch and Recovery System (PLARS), a Transfer Under Pressure (TUP) decompression system and other associated support equipment. The SRV is able to dive as deep as 610m/2,001ft, locate, and mate with the distressed submarine. Following pressure equalization, up to 15 rescuees can be transferred into the rescue vehicle, including patients on stretchers, before the SRV returns to the surface. The PLARS has also been designed to recover the rescue vehicle without the need for swimmers to attach lift ropes in high sea states. This unique capability uses guide ropes, sub-sea operations and a latching catcher unit to maximize the safety of all personnel involved.

The SRV is approximately 9m/29.5ft long and weighs 30 tonnes/29.5 tons. The 3-man crew consists of a pilot, co-pilot and rescue chamber operator. The SRV rescue chamber can be pressurized to 6 bar to allow the complete transfer, under pressure, of rescuees from the submarine through to the decompression facility. Communications are achieved using an advanced array of equipment including an underwater telephone, underwater modem and a lightweight fibre-optic umbilical. Using ZEBRA batteries, the vehicle is able to sustain continuous dive cycles with only minimal charging between missions. The aim is to always achieve a time-to-first-rescue of 72 hours.

Once recovered to the ship, the SRV deck-cradle then manoeuvres the vehicle to mate with the Transfer Under Pressure decompression facility, allowing the transfer and safe decompression of pressurised rescuees. While this goes on, the SRV can then perform further recovery dives.

The 120 tonne/118 ton Transfer Under Pressure system has two identical decompression chambers capable of holding a total of 72 rescuees, along with a combination of adjoining

ABOVE: **DSRV-1 (*Mystic*) deep-submergence rescue vehicle docked to a Los Angeles-class attack submarine, 2002. DSRV-1 *Mystic* was rated to dive up to 1,500m/5,000ft and was in US Navy service from 1977 until 2008. The submarine is preserved by the US Naval Undersea Museum.**

ABOVE: **The *Scorpio* ROV was called to assist the Russians again, on August 4, 2005, to join an international effort to free the AS-28 mini-sub *Priz* – itself a rescue vehicle – which had become trapped deep in the Pacific, near the Kamchatka peninsula, with seven submariners trapped on board and oxygen supplies dwindling. The *Scorpio* craft had to cut the vessel free from the debris pinning it to the seabed.** LEFT: **The Russian SS-750 rescue vehicle, with a 66-tonne/65-ton heavy lift gantry at the stern, was built as a very large mooring tender and reclassified in 1995 to serve as a submersible support and transport submarine. A similar craft was unsuccessful in the effort to reach the *Kursk* crew.** BELOW: **An underwater photograph of attempts to drag the *Priz* free.**

chambers allowing rescued crew members to be transferred from the SRV to the compartments whilst under pressure up to 6 bar. The complex facility has oxygen transport modules, workshop, control cabin and environmental control. There are also two portable 2-man decompression chambers to allow removal and treatment of individual patients.

Rescue operations are directed from the Portable Navigation, Tracking and Communication System (PNTCS) housed in a standard 2.44 x 3.05m/8 x 10ft ISO shipping container. This contains all the equipment needed for tracking NSRS underwater assets and for underwater communications with the SRV and the DISSUB. Using a portable acoustic positioning system and deployment system, the rescue team can locate and navigate between the primary assets, including the Rescue Vehicle, ROV, DISSUB and the MOSHIP. The container is also equipped with SATCOM, VHF, UHF, underwater telephone, underwater modems, and interfaces directly with the SRV via a lightweight fibre-optic umbilical.

The NSRS is based at HM Naval Base Clyde in Scotland, UK. British, Norwegian and French navies provide overall command and control personnel for deployments, as well as medical staff, TUP operators, divers and swimmers. Civilian specialists support and complement the military personnel. The NSRS system is expected to be in service into the mid-2030s.

The US Navy is equipped with the Deep Submergence Rescue Vehicle (DSRV), designed to rescue up to 24 people at a time from depths of up to 600m/1,969ft. The DSRV can be transported by US Air Force C-5 anywhere in the world within 24 hours. The DSRV would then be loaded onto a mother submarine (MOSUB) which then transports the DSRV to the location where several trips are made to rescue all personnel,

ABOVE AND BELOW: **The NATO Submarine Rescue System (NSRS) – the most advanced and strongest rescue system when it entered service. Weighing in at 30 tonnes/29.5 tons, with a maximum speed of 4.5 knots, it can dive to a depth of 610m/2,001ft pressurized to 5 bar, and has a rescue angle of up to 60 degrees.**

who are returned to the MOSUB or a suitably equipped surface ship. The DSRV's maximum operating depth is 1,500m/4,921ft. The DSRV can match any angle up to 45 degrees in both pitch and roll, and mate to a stricken submarine that may be lying at an awkward angle on the sea floor.

Over 40 nations operate military submarines and most navies have a rescue system in place, but most are committed to cooperating with each other when submariners' lives are in jeopardy. To this end, and following the *Kursk* disaster in 2000, the International Submarine Escape and Rescue Liaison Organisation (ISMERLO) was formed to assist with the coordination of future submarine rescue missions.

RIGHT: **The 40 tonne/39.3 ton Japanese Maritime Self Defense Force (JMSDF) Deep Submergence Rescue Vehicle (DSRV) *Angler Fish 2*, is lowered through the middle of the JMSDF submarine rescue ship, JDS *Chihaya* during exercises in 2002. The DSRV deployed 50m/164ft below and mated with a simulated disabled Republic of Korea Navy submarine on the ocean floor. International cooperation like this increases the odds for a successful rescue.** BELOW: **The US Submarine Rescue Diving Recompression System (SRDRS) is a remotely operated underwater vehicle and its associated systems developed to replace the *Mystic*-class deep submergence rescue vehicle. Based on the Royal Australian Navy Submarine rescue vehicle *Remora*, the system can be rapidly deployed to a given location, mounted on a mothership, then detect a downed submarine and submerge to depths of up to 610m/2,000ft to retrieve crew members who can then decompress onboard the SRDRS.**

Shaping the future

Submarine warfare is always evolving, introducing new boats, new technology, new concepts and an overall leaning towards the demands of diversity in modern operational requirements. Brand new nuclear-powered attack boats, such as the Columbia class produced in the United States and the Dreadnought class for the UK, heralded the entry into service of fast, powerful attack submarines designed to serve well into the 21st century.

Boats designed with the Cold War in mind continue to serve but are gradually being replaced in the major navies by more capable submarines designed to flexibly meet the varied needs of 21st century conflict. This move towards flexibility began with the repurposing of older boats.

It will be recalled that the very first SSBN carrier in the US submarine service was quickly constructed by cutting the attack submarine *Scorpion* in two and inserting the missile section. The boat re-emerged two years later as *George Washington*, America's first "boomer" carrying a very large pod of doomsday weaponry.

The reverse situation emerged in the early 2000s, and in the process transformed submarine warfare. *Ohio*-class ballistic missile submarines were converted to bring forward a totally new concept, although in many ways one which harked back to the heyday of British submarines in World War II, when they undertook many varied tasks, such as clandestine insertion of special forces, in addition to their main role as attack boats.

The concept emerged in discussions following the end

TOP: *Astute* Class HMS *Audacious* under construction at Barrow in Furness shipyard in Cumbria, UK, 2013. Commissioned in April 2020, this submarine is now on active service with the Royal Navy. The class is equipped with the very sophisticated BAE Systems Sonar 2076 integrated passive/active search and attack sonar suite with bow, intercept, flank and towed arrays. ABOVE: The *Astute*, Britain's 21st-century entry into the multi-functional world of SSN boats, carrying a weapon load 50 per cent greater than the Trafalgar class, which includes Spearfish torpedoes and Tomahawk cruise missiles.

of the Cold War, which subsequently became conjoined with the events of 9/11 and all that came in its wake. Urgent studies were initiated by governments and military study groups around the globe on how future threats could be faced effectively. Initially, the role of submarines in this scenario was not immediately clear, but the pointers were already there, in history and in fact, the US Navy had the model ready to bring forward. Their plan was to introduce a new class of SSGN boats: nuclear-powered submarines carrying guided missiles based on the boomers, whose numbers were already being culled as the Cold War faded into history. The converted boats would carry an armoury of missiles with tremendous firepower, but also include operational possibilities that would revolutionize submarine activity.

Other requirements identified included:
• Stealth, power, reliability and versatility of the converted boats, with more than 20 years of service life remaining for

each SSGN, plus the operation of two crews so that each boat would be available for continuous operations.

• Large-volume precision strike, with up to 154 Tomahawk and Tactical Tomahawk cruise missiles aboard, 20 times larger than the payload of the SSNs.

• Sustained special forces operations capability, including insertion, extraction and continued support while in action. Also planned were the use of unmanned vehicles that could deliver weapons and communications equipment to the surface from a submerged submarine, for a "dry" landing with the troops. It was the US Navy's ambition for it to become "the most advanced covert special forces platform ever".

Conversion designs were produced for the insertion of vertical launch systems to provide the SSGNs with the massive firepower of 154 Tomahawk cruise missiles – more than the total complement of a normal US Navy battle group at the time. As the concept developed, new additions further transformed submarine operations as the boats were equipped with large manned and unmanned undersea vehicles for special operations, unmanned aerial vehicles and off-board sensors, all capable of submerged operations.

ABOVE LEFT: **A cutaway of USS** *Ohio*, **one of the US strategic missile carriers converted to carry Tomahawk cruise missiles.** *Ohio* **also allowed the installation of lockin-lockout chambers for up to 100 Special Forces personnel and equipment. This was achieved by utilizing 22 of the 24 tubes for the Vertical Launch System canisters, which could stow six conventional land attack missiles per tube.**

ABOVE RIGHT: **USS** *Florida* **launches a Tomahawk cruise missile on the firing range off the coast of the Bahamas as part of the trials for the conversion work.**

These developments were heralded by submarine warfare analysts as the most innovative since the arrival of nuclear-powered, nuclear-armed boats. Project delivery began when the oldest US Trident ballistic missile submarine, *Ohio*, arrived at the Electric Boat Company's Puget Sound Naval Shipyard in Bremerton, Washington, in 2003, where the conversion work took place at the same time as her mid-life refuelling. She was to be followed in the conversion at other shipyards by three other Trident boats, *Florida*, *Michigan* and *Georgia* – all were back in operation by 2008.

Notably, the transformation work included the installation of advanced equipment such as sensors and surveillance systems. Specifically, the new boats brought a rapid precision

RIGHT: **USS** *Ohio* **returning to Puget Sound Naval Shipyard in December 2005 after sea trials to test the functions of the conversion, which was completed in less than three years. Three other Ohio class Trident boats –** *Michigan*, *Florida* **and** *Georgia* **– had similar surgery at a total cost of $1.4 billion, and the four also tested new weapons systems, sensors and littoral operational concepts that transformed naval warfare by carrying large unmanned undersea vehicles.**

strike capability against land-based targets and assured access to hostile or denied areas.

As already noted, these developments came alongside the much-anticipated arrival of two spectacular new boats in the international inventory, the Virginia class in the US and the *Astute* in Britain. Indeed, some of the technology of the Virginia class was included in the SSGN conversions, inasmuch as the *Virginia* – the newest of the US Navy's fast attack boats – was fully loaded with the latest in stealth, intelligence gathering, and weapons systems technology to keep it viable for as long as possible. The Virginia-class boats will be acquired (34 boats in all) through to 2043, and are expected to remain in service until at least 2060, with later submarines expected to remain in front-line use into the 2070s. Again, the emphasis in the creation of the class has been to extend the capability of the SSN into multi-purpose functions. The whole concept of submarine warfare is rolled into a massive package of what the Americans claim "will surpass the performance of any current projected threat

BELOW: **As littoral operations become more vital, so does the training, as shown here with two US SEALs on a rigorous Combat Swim.**

TOP LEFT: **Special Forces and submarines go together, as proved here by a SEAL Delivery Vehicle (SDV) team fast-roping from a Seahawk helicopter to the deck of USS *Toledo* of the Improved Los Angeles attack class.** ABOVE LEFT: **A SEAL Delivery Vehicle (SDV) is loaded aboard the Los Angeles-class fast attack submarine USS *Dallas* (SSN 700). A Dry Deck Shelter (DDS) equipped submarine is attached to the submarine's forward escape trunk to provide a dry environment for Navy Seals to prepare for special warfare exercises or operations.** TOP: **The dexterity of submarine-based forces is demonstrated here by an SDV team being launched in their vehicle from the back of another Los Angeles-class boat, USS *Philadelphia*, sending them underwater and undetected towards enemy targets ashore. Royal Navy Astute-class boats can also be fitted with a dry deck shelter for special forces ops.** ABOVE: **The US Navy Special Warfare Trident insignia worn by qualified SEALs, whose expansion in terms of numbers and ability is being matched by most major seafaring nations.**

submarine, ensuring US dominance well into the 21st century."

The Royal Navy has, however, also laid claim to a share of that dominance with the launch of their *Astute*, along with the extravagant description of it as the "biggest and most powerful attack submarine to be built for the Royal Navy", yet it has a much smaller ship's company. HMS *Astute*, launched in 2007 and commissioned in 2010, displaces 7,800 tonnes/7,700 tons dived and is 97m/318ft long and fully equipped for cruise missiles. The bridge fin of these boats, in keeping with earlier Royal Navy submarines, is reinforced to allow surfacing through ice caps, and these boats can also be fitted with a dry deck shelter to enable special forces to deploy whilst the boat remains submerged. Fifth in the Astute class, *Anson*, was commissioned in 2022, and a further two boats, the last of the class, are expected to be commissioned by 2026.

LEFT: **HMS *Ambush*, 2012.** Over 39,000 acoustic tiles mask the Astute class boats' sonar signature, bestowing the class with much improved acoustic qualities over any Royal Navy submarines. Continued advances in materials science, design, and acoustic signature reduction technologies have led to significant improvements in submarine stealth over recent decades and make them increasingly difficult to detect.
BELOW LEFT: **A Tactical Tomahawk cruise missile,** photographed during a controlled test flight from a vertical submerged launch in 2002, hitting its target 1,255km/780 miles away. BELOW: Members of a SEAL Delivery Vehicle team inside a flooded Dry Deck shelter aboard USS *Philadelphia*, from which they are launched on missions while the submarine remains submerged.

Meanwhile, the Royal Navy also recognizes that the needs of the modern navy are changing rapidly, particularly in submarine operations. As a result, the RN set in motion what it described as a decisive break away from the Cold War emphasis on anti-submarine warfare, to embrace an operational concept aligned to Joint Operations, meeting a range of tasks in direct support of surface forces. The transformation of submarine operations across the board is underway.

The Royal Navy is of course also looking forward to its new Dreadnought class, which will replace the RN's Vanguard class of ballistic missile submarines, necessary if the Royal Navy is to maintain a continuous at-sea deterrent.

In terms of submarine design, perhaps the most significant development in propulsion technology in recent years has been the introduction of air-independent propulsion (AIP). These systems can augment or replace the diesel-electric propulsion system of non-nuclear vessels and enable a non-nuclear submarine to operate without access to atmospheric oxygen by surfacing or via snorkel. AIP allows non-nuclear submarines (e.g. Germany's Dolphin class or Type 212) to stay submerged for longer periods of time without needing to surface or use their diesel engines. This capability makes modern non-nuclear submarines potentially stealthier than nuclear submarines, which can still generate some detectable noise. Although nuclear-powered designs excel in terms of submergence times, speed and range, small, very quiet non-nuclear attack submarines can be highly effective in littoral operations and pose a real and significant threat to less-stealthy and less-manoeuvrable nuclear-powered boats.

ABOVE: **The versatile USS *Seawolf* fast attack submarine** was built to achieve the lowest noise levels while achieving the highest tactical speed.

Directory of Submarines

1900–45

In 1900, the Royal Navy did not possess a single submarine. In fact, Britain was the only major maritime power not to have even the beginnings of a submarine flotilla. The United States Navy was trialling her own *Holland I*, and the Royal Navy followed the US lead in 1901. Thereafter it became a race to produce boats of ever-increasing endurance and sophistication.

By the outbreak of World War I, the unimaginable was already happening: submarines could actually take on the mighty surface ships – and win. Between the wars, design emphasis switched to diesel-electric boats, and considerable advances had been made by the onset of World War II. With the outbreak of hostilities, Germany turned to her submarines to take the war to the Allies at sea, using their boats as submersible destroyers.

Britain relied on her new O, S, T and U-class boats, but was forced to begin with older stock. The Japanese had begun producing giant boats, while the Americans went into mass production with a number of major classes, such as Gato, Balao and Tench, that were to become the workhorses of the US submarine fleet.

LEFT: **British submarines of the 10th Flotilla based at Lazaretto, Malta, included *Upright* (second from right), which sank Mussolini's cruiser *Armando Diaz* on February 25, 1941.**

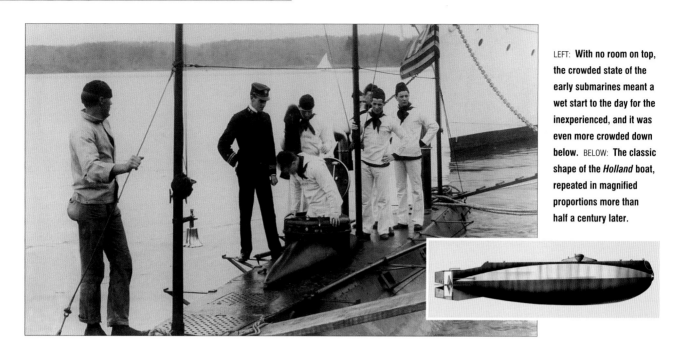

LEFT: **With no room on top, the crowded state of the early submarines meant a wet start to the day for the inexperienced, and it was even more crowded down below.** BELOW: **The classic shape of the *Holland* boat, repeated in magnified proportions more than half a century later.**

The Holland

After much deliberation, submarines formally became part of the US Navy's inventory in 1899 when a series of trials of the *Holland* convinced the Navy Board that they should go ahead.
It had been a long and difficult journey for her creator, J.P. Holland, who had won a competition staged by the Navy 11 years earlier to build a torpedo-firing submarine that could "travel submerged for two hours at eight knots at depths up to 150 feet".

Although he won the competition, Holland did not receive a contract to build his boat, and it took several more unsuccessful attempts that saw him slide into near bankruptcy before the US Navy finally came up with a $165,000 contract for *Holland VI*.

Launched on May 17, 1897, at Elizabethport, New Jersey, it was equipped with a 37.3kW/50hp petrol

engine for surface propulsion, for which a range of 1,609km/1,000 miles was claimed. The US Navy was impressed during trials when the boat managed to get within 91.4m/100 yards of the US battleship *Kearsage*, whereupon a light was flashed to demonstrate that the ship could have been sunk with the submarine's 450mm/17.7in Whitehead torpedoes.

The *Holland* was built under her designer's supervision at the Crescent Shipyard at Elizabethport, New Jersey, and was noted for her sleek lines in the likeness of a porpoise. In reality, however, she travelled low in the water when on the surface, making it precarious for her crew to work on deck, especially when operating the Zalinski dynamite gun mounted on the bow, which was subsequently removed. The Navy contracted for the building of five boats, although there were serious doubts as

to their viability among those who still had to be convinced of the usefulness of submarines. Not least among these were some of the sailors who were destined to man the new contraptions. The boat's stability on the surface left much to be desired and the internal arrangements were spartan and dangerous.

Inside the boat, the slightest malfunction of the exhaust system from the petrol-driven engine could kill the entire crew by carbon monoxide poisoning. Even a minor fuel leak might cause an explosion, as could battery problems, which plagued submarines for years hence. The *Holland* did not see any serious service, and was used mainly for training as the first new boats of an improved Holland design came on stream.

LEFT: **The original *Holland* drawings for his boat, more or less adhered to by the US Navy designers.**

Holland

Displacement: 62.98 tonnes/62 tons (surfaced); 72.83 tonnes/71.7 tons (submerged)
Length: 16.18m/53ft
Beam: 3.13m/10ft 3in
Armament: 1 x 457mm/18in bow tube, 2 x torpedoes
Propulsion: 33.6kW/45hp petrol; 41kW/55hp electric
Speed: 8.0 knots (surfaced); 5.0 knots (dived)
Complement: 9 crew

A class

The seven boats of this class entered service in the first three years of the new century, all based upon an enlarged version of the *Holland I*, although confusingly the first boat in the class, originally named *Plunger*, was classified as *A1* on the creation of the class. However when all US submarines were given the SS classification in 1920, she became *SS2*, the first Holland to enter service becoming *SS1*.

The *Plunger* and the rest of the A class saw considerable service in those early years, and despite all problems concerning human habitation inside the boats, remained in service well into the second decade of the century. Three were reconditioned for coastal work and training in the early years of World War I. *Plunger* also went into history as being the first submarine to have a President of the United States aboard. She was conducting trials at Oyster Bay, close to the home of Theodore Roosevelt, in the summer of 1905. The crew had been

given advance warning, giving them time to paint the outside of the boat before the president stepped aboard on August 22, 1905.

He spent almost three hours on board, and was given a full demonstration and experienced a number of dives, an event that of course captured the interest of the media and public, many of whom were still somewhat sceptical about the safety of these underwater creatures. Roosevelt took note of the reaction, and later wrote, "I went down in it chiefly because I did not like to have the officers and enlisted men think I wanted them to try things I was reluctant to try myself. I believe a good deal can be done with these submarines, although there is always the danger of people getting carried away with the idea and thinking that they can be of more use than they possibly could be".

Later, *Plunger* hosted another figure of subsequent fame: Chester W. Nimitz became her skipper in May 1909, the first

command of the man who would rise to become Fleet Admiral. Although at the time Nimitz said he considered submarines "a cross between a Jules Verne fantasy and a humpbacked whale", he later became one of America's most distinguished naval figures. The experience on board *Plunger* and others of the early classes, however, was unforgettable. A Navy Medical Officer's report at the time was scathing about conditions on the boats, with the crew sleeping, cooking, eating, and answering the calls of nature in such a confined space. He said even in moderate seas, the boat rolled and pitched so that practically the whole crew was seasick. Food had to be packed in crates and the cooked meats soon spoiled and, coupled with the use of the open toilet, the air was foul.

RIGHT: **Assigned to the Naval Torpedo Station at Newport, Rhode Island, *Plunger* operated locally for the first two years.**

A class

Displacement: 105.30 tonnes/103.6 tons (surfaced); 121 tonnes/119.1 tons (submerged)
Length: 19.24m/63ft 1in
Beam: 3.6m/11ft 10in
Armament: 1 x 457mm/18in tube, 5 x torpedoes
Propulsion: 119kW/160hp petrol; 111.9kW/150hp electric
Speed: 8.0 knots (surfaced); 7.0 knots (dived)
Complement: 7 crew

B class

Three boats of this class, *Viper*, *Cuttlefish* and *Tarantula* (*B1*, *B2* and *B3*), commissioned in 1907, saw the final stage of development in the Holland single-screw design and introduced a more extensive superstructure for sea keeping. On the original plans, *Viper* had only the single periscope let into the conning tower; however a second periscope was added later. Air compressors and the main bilge pumps were driven from the main shaft via noisy clutches and gears. The boats were altogether more substantial in appearance, and length, stability and conditions aboard were better, but still very cramped. A reload torpedo in the B class, for example, left little space in the hull. Even so, this class saw considerable service in the Atlantic Torpedo Boat Fleet and in April 1914 was posted for an assignment in distant waters.

B1 was towed to Norfolk to be loaded on board USS *Hector* to be carried to the Philippine Islands, arriving at Luzon in March 1915 to be recommissioned into the Submarine Division 1, Torpedo Flotilla, Asiatic Fleet. She remained in the Philippines throughout the rest of her working life before being decommissioned in 1921. *B2* and *B3* had a similar history to the first-born of the class.

B3, for example, operated along the Atlantic coast with the 1st and 2nd Submarine Flotillas on training and experimental exercises until going into reserve at Charleston Navy Yard on November 6, 1909.

She came back into service when she was recommissioned on April 15, 1910, and served with the Atlantic Torpedo Fleet until assigned to the Reserve Torpedo Group on May 9, 1911, and placed out of commission again in December 1912. Two days later, she was towed to Norfolk and loaded on board *Ajax* for transfer to the Asiatic Station. Arriving at Cavite, Philippine Islands on April 30, 1913, *B3* was launched

TOP: **Beginning to look like a workable boat, the B class was a considerable improvement in terms of stability but conditions inside were still primitive.**
ABOVE: **The shape and accoutrements to the deck along with additional length gave the B class a more definitive shape.**

from *Ajax* on May 12. She remained in the Philippines, where she served with Submarine Division 4, Torpedo Flotilla, Asiatic Fleet until she was decommissioned in July 1921, and subsequently used as a target.

LEFT: **For the first decade, US submarines were attached to the Torpedo Fleet, until finally they were accepted as permanent, and the name was changed to Submarine Flotillas.**

B class	
Displacement: 142 tonnes/140 tons (surfaced); 170 tonnes/167 tons (submerged)	
Length: 25.15m/82ft 6in	
Beam: 3.85m/12ft 8in	
Armament: 2 x 457mm/18in tube, 4 x torpedoes	
Propulsion: 186.4kW/250hp petrol; 44.7kW/60hp electric	
Speed: 9.0 knots (surfaced); 8.0 knots (dived)	
Complement: 10 crew	

LEFT AND ABOVE: **Although subs had been around for a decade or more, there were still many doubters in the hierarchy of the US Navy, but these boats of the C class,** *Octopus* **(***C1***)** (LEFT) **and** *Tarpon* **(***C3***)** (ABOVE) **at last turned a few heads.**

C class

With the entry of *C1*, originally christened *Octopus*, US submarines were beginning to be taken seriously by naval aficionados. Even so, the boats of the equivalent British class were already much larger – almost one third longer and with 447kW/600hp engines, compared with the 373kW/500hp for the US C class. The debate in the United States over the true value of submarines in warfare was probably still weighted towards the doubters, but the new designs were beginning to change minds.

In that regard, *Octopus* had the distinction of introducing what was to become the recognizable stern design of the Electric Boat Company, and was the first boat designed by L.Y. Spear following the departure of J.P. Holland from the company. It was also the first of the US boats that came with an air-operated bell for underwater signalling, which was then fitted to all earlier submarines. By the time *C5* (*Snapper*) was commissioned in 1911, further improvements were under way and this boat was also used for experiments with radio, signalling apparatus, alternative batteries types and a number of other innovations which eventually became standard. With war clouds gathering in Europe, the C class was also used in the first major trials in operations with warships, and later with aircraft with the advent of naval aviation. Lt Chester Nimitz wrote an interesting observation about *C5*:

"Her Craig gasoline engines were built in Jersey City by James Craig an extraordinarily wise and capable builder. Craig was a self-taught engineer who began as a draftsman in the Machinery Division of the New York Navy Yard and who started his Machine & Engine Works in Jersey City at a later date. C5's engines were excellent as were the Craig diesel engines he built for a subsequent submarine. These engines were designed and built by Craig and I have never forgotten his Foreword to the pamphlet of Operating Instructions which read briefly somewhat like this: 'No matter what the designer and the builder may have planned for these engines and no matter what the operator may try to do with them the Laws of Nature will prevail in the End'. How True!" Five C class were built.

ABOVE: **C-class submarines in the Gatun Locks, Panama Canal, just prior to World War I. The submarines in the line-up were** *C1*, *C2*, *C3*, *C4* **and** *C5*.

C class

Displacement: 234.25 tonnes/230.6 tons (surfaced); 270 tonnes/265.7 tons (submerged)
Length: 32.12m/105ft 5in
Beam: 4.25m/14ft
Armament: 1 x 457mm/18in forward tube, 5 x torpedoes
Propulsion: 372.8kW/500hp petrol; 111.9kW/150hp electric
Speed: 10.5 knots (surfaced); 9.0 knots (dived)
Complement: 15 crew

LEFT: **Getting visibly larger, a starboard-side view of** *Grayling (D2)*, **circa 1914, thought to be in the harbour of Newport, Rhode Island.**
ABOVE: **The somewhat spartan control panel.**

D class

The experiences among all submariner nations gradually drew the emphasis in design and development towards greater safety for crew members in the event of a catastrophe. In conjunction with US Navy engineers, designers at the Electric Boat Company came up with some ingenious techniques first tried with *D1*, originally launched in 1908. She became the first US boat to be compartmentally divided specifically for survivability. Each compartment was defined by closely positioned bulkheads so that the submarine (surfaced) could survive flooding.

In fact, the layout proved to be difficult in terms of the complicated internal access because of the closeness of the bulkheads. The US Navy ordered a hasty re-design for *D3* that actually reversed the overall safety ideal that had been the original aim. As a result she had only two bulkheads, one at the after end of the torpedo room and one at the fore-end of the engine room. By pushing out the bulkheads, space in the control room was greatly increased, but the resulting compartments were so large that the boat was unlikely to survive if one of them was flooded.

This re-adjustment was considered by some analysts to be the cause of a number of US submarine losses in the 1920s, especially after collisions.

There were other experimental features with *D3* that led to further development, including placing the two periscopes very close to each other, which made it possible to brace both against vibration, a very serious problem with these boats. The object of the forward periscope was to act as a ventilator. The original drawings for *D3* also showed an improved temporary bridge, with a portable canopy frame and external ladder, protected by a trunk. Three D-class submarines were built.

LEFT: *Grayling*, **moored prior to a Presidential Review of the fleet in North River, New York.**

D class

Displacement: 234.23 tonnes/230.5 tons (surfaced); 270 tonnes/265.7 tons (submerged)
Length: 32.10m/105ft 4in
Beam: 4.26m/14ft
Armament: 2 x 457mm/18in tubes, 4 x torpedoes
Propulsion: 186.4kW/250hp petrol; 111.9kW/150hp electric
Speed: 10.5 knots (surfaced); 9 knots (dived)
Complement: 15 crew

E and F classes

These boats represented a substantial step forward in looks, style and design over their predecessors and were also the carriers of a number of US innovations. *E1* (laid down under the name of *Skipjack*) was commissioned in February 1912 under Lt Chester Nimitz, who also took command of the US Atlantic Submarine Flotilla before coming ashore in 1913 to continue his outstanding career in the big ships. *E1* was used to pioneer a number of major innovations, including the first ballistic gyro compass, invented by Elmer A. Sperry.

E1 was also used to trial submerged radio transmission and other major experiments initially under Nimitz. During his time with the boat, he was awarded a Silver Medal for his heroic action in saving W.J. Walsh, fireman second class, from drowning. A strong tide was running and Walsh was rapidly being swept away from his ship. Nimitz dived into the water and kept Walsh afloat until both were picked up by a small boat.

In December 1917, *E1* left Newport for the Azores to begin patrols against U-boats, and at the end of the war, *E1* resumed

her role in experimental work, conducting trials with undersea listening equipment.

The F-class boats were launched around the same time as the E class. The first, *F1*, was commissioned in June 1912 and was assigned to the 1st Submarine Group, Pacific Torpedo Flotilla, operating along the US west coast between San Diego and San Pedro until 1915, when the Flotilla moved to Honolulu for development operations in the Hawaiian Islands. Later, she returned to San Pedro to begin surface and submerged trials in the development of submarine tactics. On December 17, 1917, while manoeuvring in exercises at sea, *F1* and *F3* collided, the former sinking in

TOP AND ABOVE: **Commissioned in 1912,** ***Skipjack (E1)*** **had the distinction of being fitted with the first Sperry gyro compass in submarines, for which she became a pioneer underwater test ship.**

10 seconds, her port side torn forward of the engine room. Nineteen of her men were lost, while the others were rescued by the submarines with whom they were operating. Two E-class and four F-class submarines were built.

E1	

Displacement: 282 tonnes/277.5 tons (surfaced); 336 tonnes/330.7 tons (submerged)
Length: 41.24m/135ft 4in
Beam: 4.5m/14ft 9in
Armament: 4 x 457mm/18in tubes; 4 x torpedoes
Propulsion: 522kW/700hp diesel; 447.4kW/600hp electric
Speed: 13.5 knots (surfaced); 11.5 knots (dived)
Complement: 20 crew

F1	

Displacement: 324 tonnes/318.9 tons (surfaced); 394 tonnes/387.8 tons (submerged)
Length: 43.50m/142ft 9in
Beam: 4.70m/15ft 5in
Armament: 4 x 457mm/18in tubes, 4 x torpedoes
Propulsion: 581.6kW/780hp diesel; 462.3kW/620hp electric
Speed: 13.5 knots (surfaced); 11.5 knots (dived)
Complement: 22 crew

LEFT: **Simon Lake's** *Seal (F1)* **saw major advances in submarine technology in many ways, with innovations to improve comfort and safety.** ABOVE: **The launching of** *Turbot (G3)* **on December 27, 1913.**

G class

G1 has the distinction of being the first submarine designed for the US Navy by Simon Lake, the brilliant engineer from Pleasantville, New Jersey, whose submarine *Argonaut* had lost out to John Holland in the competition to build America's first boat. Rejected by his own country, he was poached by the Russians, then at war with Japan. He went on to build boats for several other nations. The American Navy chiefs thereafter shut him out of the competition for contracts until 1908 when, realizing the error of their ways, they finally approached him to build USS *Seal*, the first boat in G class.

It proved to be one of the most important developments in American naval history. Given virtually a free hand, Lake produced a revolutionary design for *Seal (G1)* in that it was the first-ever even keel submarine to be built by the United States Navy, and it was particularly noted

for its sleek lines. However, it was only the beginning. Lake went on to initiate the introduction of many innovations in a long career producing boats for the United States, and his designs would influence submarine development well into the atomic age. It was only a pity that his enormous contribution was not formally recognized until after his death, in 1945.

G1 joined the Atlantic Torpedo Flotilla and made a record dive of 78m/256ft in Long Island Sound. In October 1915, she began a new career as a submarine designated for experimental tests and instructional purposes. The G class thus became established in the important role of school ships for the newly established Submarine Base and Submarine School at New London. This was much needed as the submarine service expanded to meet the demands of World War I.

G1 was also used to test new detector devices for the US Navy Experiment Board, off Provincetown, and played a similar role in the development and use of sound detection. Notably, she spent two four-day periscope and listening patrols against U-boats thought to be operating in the vicinity of Nantucket.

After the war, she resumed her role as a schooling boat for student submariners of the Listener and Hydrophone School, at New London, until January 13, 1920, when *G1* was towed to the Philadelphia Navy Yard. It was decommissioned on March 6, 1920.

She ended her days as a target for depth charge experiments by the Bureau of Ordnance before finally sinking on June 21, 1921 following a bombardment of eight attacks using experimental bombs.

LEFT: **A starboard side view of** *Turbot (G3),* **looking aft at the Lake Torpedo Boat Company shipyard, Bridgeport, Connecticut, 1915. Four G class were built.**

G class	
Displacement: 393 tonnes/387.8 tons (surfaced); 507 tonnes/499 tons (submerged)	
Length: 49m/160ft 9in	
Beam: 3.9m/12ft 10in	
Armament: 6 x 457mm/18in tubes, (including two deck firing tubes), 6 x torpedoes	
Propulsion: 894.8kW/1,200hp petrol; 387.8kW/520hp electric	
Speed: 14 knots (surfaced); 10 knots (dived)	
Complement: 24 crew	

H class

*H*1, commissioned as *Seawolf*, was attached to the 2nd Torpedo Flotilla, Pacific Fleet, principally used for patrols along the west coast of America, as were other members of the class, operating out of San Pedro. When America entered World War I, the H boats were shifted to the east coast. *H1* completed the journey to New London 22 days later via Acapulco, Balboa, Key West, Charleston and Philadelphia. She remained on the east coast, patrolling Long Island Sound for the duration, often with officer students from the submarine school on board. *H1* and *H2* (originally named *Nautilus*) returned to San Pedro in 1920 via the Panama Canal but on March 12, *H1* ran aground on a sandbank off Santa Margarita Island, California. *H2* stood by and sent rescue and search parties for survivors, helping to save all but four of her sister ship's crew. Those killed included the commanding officer, Lt Commander James R. Webb. A salvage ship dragged her clear only to see her sink in 18.3m/60ft of water.

A similar misfortune hit *H3*. While engaged in patrolling the Californian coast, near Eureka, she ran aground in heavy fog on December 16, 1916. The crew was rescued by Coast Guard breeches buoy, but the cruiser *Milwaukee* was also stranded trying to pull the submarine off the beach, and the Navy was forced to call in a commercial salvage firm. Their job was made all the more difficult because *H3* was marooned on a high sandbank surrounded by quicksand,

ABOVE: **USS *Garfish* (*H3*) in dry dock at the Mare Island Navy Yard, California, in 1915, to repair damage following a recent grounding, evident on the bilge keel.**
LEFT: ***H2*, the first US submarine to bear the name *Nautilus*.**

and at low tide she was 22.9m/75ft from the water, but at high tide the ocean reached almost 76.2m/250ft beyond her. Eventually, after a month of trying, she was pulled on to giant log rollers and taken overland to the sea.

Six other H-class submarines originally built by the Electric Boat Company for the Imperial Russian Government also came into the US inventory under the H4 class title. Their shipment was held up pending the

outcome of the Russian Revolution, and the boats were stored in knockdown condition at Vancouver, B.C. All six were eventually purchased by the Navy on May 20, 1918, and assembled at Puget Sound Navy Yard. The first went into service in November 1918, and were engaged in extensive battle and training exercises out of San Pedro, varying this routine with patrols off Santa Catalina Island, but by then, of course, the Armistice had been signed. They were decommissioned in the early 1920s and eventually sold for scrap.

LEFT: **USS *Sea Wolf* (*H1*) was the prototype for a class that attracted considerable orders from overseas, yet only three were built for the US Navy. Most were destined for Britain in the latter stages of World War I.**

H class

Displacement: 352 tonnes/346.4 tons (surfaced); 459 tonnes/451.8 tons (submerged)
Length: 45.82m/150ft 4in
Beam: 4.84m/15ft 11in
Armament: 4 x 457mm/18in tubes, 8 x torpedoes
Propulsion: kW/950hp diesel; kW/600hp electric
Speed: 14 knots (surfaced); 10.5 knots (dived)
Complement: 25 crew

K class

$K1$, commissioned as *Haddock*, and her sister ships continued the emerging theme in US submarine design: to increase and improve space, conditions and safety inside the boats without a massively increased overall displacement or length. This class was no exception, increasing the complement to 28 men with the addition of little more than 30 tonnes/29.5 tons surface displacement. The K boats were deployed on both the east and west coasts of America, mostly in almost continual trials in underwater manoeuvres, diving and torpedo-firing practice. The techniques learned from these experiments were soon to prove useful when U-boats began their attacks on Allied shipping bound for Europe.

Five of the K boats were among the first US submarines assigned to duties in World War I and saw service off the Azores, conducting patrol cruises and protecting shipping from surface attack. Some boats were modified for these operations, including the introduction of passive sound gear forward, a permanent chariot bridge and housing periscopes. These vital patrols continued almost to Armistice Day, by which time they returned to North America to resume coastal operations. They were then assigned to naval exercises and trials of new technology that contributed much to the improvements that lay ahead.

The K-class boats were especially engaged in experimental work, notably in the areas of listening devices, storage

TOP: **The US Navy dropped the practice of naming their boats in the K class, retaining the class number and boat number, in this case *K8* and *SS39*, here dry-docked at Honolulu.**
ABOVE: **K5 underway on a 1919 cruise down the Mississippi River.**

batteries and torpedoes, and the *Dictionary of American Naval Fighting Ships* states that this work "greatly accelerated" the technology learned from these experiments. The boats were gradually decommissioned in the early 1920s. Eight K-class boats were built.

LEFT: ***K2* off Pensacola, Florida, in April, 1916, in a new "zebra" camouflage.**

K class	🇺🇸
Displacement: 385 tonnes/378.9 tons (surfaced); 512 tonnes/503.9 tons (submerged)	
Length: 46.8m/153ft 6in	
Beam: 5.07m/16ft 8in	
Armament: 4 x 457mm/18in torpedo tubes, 8 x torpedoes	
Propulsion: 708.4kW/950hp diesel; 507.1kW/680hp electric	
Speed: 14 knots (surfaced); 10.5 knots (dived)	
Complement: 28 crew	

L class

L 1 was christened as *SS40* when the new numbering classification replaced the tradition of naming the boats came into effect with the last three of the K boats. This was to last until names, as well as numbers, were introduced with the Barracuda class in the early 1920s. Again, displacement and length were further extended, and wartime modifications to the class included the installation of a retractable mount for the 76mm/3in gun, and sound gear as well as a permanent sheltered bridge. The retractable gun mount was an idea inspired by a version seen on board a pre-war U-boat.

The L boats were also the first to use independent torpedo tube shutters, which replaced a single-rotating bow cap. A further interesting aspect of the Ls was the difference between those designed and built by the Electric Boat Company and those developed by Simon Lake. The latter's boats were more compartmentalized in terms of the mechanics of the boat than the Electric Boat Company vessels, providing separate engine and motor rooms aft, and concentrating pumps and other auxiliary tools into the large space beneath the control room.

For their war service, L boats crossed the Atlantic after brief service around the Azores and operated from Bantry Bay,

ABOVE: **A profile of the L class, the first of which began operations in the US in 1916. It became the largest class of American submarines to date, with 11 being built for service in World War I.**

Ireland, where they began patrols in support of Allied shipping and hunting U-boats. In July 1918, a large explosion rocked *L2* while patrolling in the Irish Sea. A periscope was sighted and the *L2* submerged and tried to ram the submarine, but the U-boat had superior underwater speed. Later, it was suspected that a U-boat had fired on the *L2*, but another U-boat, the *U65*, was in the way and was badly damaged and sank. Some time later, when the *L2* was dry-docked, her hull plating was noted to be heavily dented from the proximity of the explosion. The *U65* never returned to port.

Meanwhile, in the US, one of the Lake boats, *L8*, was seconded to a top secret mission initiated in 1918 to lure U-boats into a trap. The boat joined forces with the schooner USS *Charles Whittemore*, which was to act as a decoy in the hope of prompting an attack from a pair of enemy submarines menacing the Atlantic coast. The *Whittemore* towed the submerged *L8* to avoid the submarine's detection, while at the same time acting

as mother ship, carrying supplies, fuel and torpedoes. In the event, the war ended while the pair was on patrol without firing a shot. Eleven L boats were built and they were decommissioned progressively in the mid-1920s.

ABOVE: **Submarine bridges of the day were small to limit underwater drag. *L3* had an enlarged chariot bridge, in contrast to the more streamlined *L9*.**
LEFT: ***L10* arrived in the British Isles in January 1918 with other submarines of the Atlantic Division to take part in operations hampering U-boat activity.**

L class	
Displacement: 443 tonnes/436 tons (surfaced); 539 tonnes/530.5 tons (submerged)	
Length: 51m/167ft 4in	
Beam: 5.3m/17ft 5in	
Armament: 4 x 457mm/18in tubes, 8 x torpedoes, 1 x 76mm/3in (23 calibres) deck gun	
Propulsion: 671.1kW/900hp diesel; 507.1kW/680hp electric	
Speed: 14 knots (surfaced); 10.5 knots (dived)	
Complement: 28 crew	

M class

M1 was something of an experimental boat, and as only one of the class was built, it was generally assumed that there were flaws that prevented further orders. Doubtless there were flaws, but she was rightly in a class of her own. *M1* was the longest boat built to that point in time (1918) and was the Electric Boat Company's first US double-hull submarine. The company had already designed larger double-hull boats for Russia, which were a match for the cruiser-style boats coming out of Germany. In her trials, she was promoted as being the embodiment of all the newest technology in submarine construction and design. Her battery was to have solved some of the past difficulties in submarine battery design and operation.

With a stern described as being honed to a vertical chisel shape, much like contemporary cruiser sterns, she

LEFT: *M1* was the Electric Boat Company's first US double-hull submarine, although the company had already designed a larger double-hull boat for Russia. This submarine also had a number of internal innovations, including an efficient heating system and an ice box/refrigerator.

was an impressive sight. Inside, there was decent – if somewhat crowded – accommodation for the crew. Indeed, a Royal Navy observer, Stanley Goodall, later knighted as head of British naval construction, noted that facilities were very presentable, with bunks stacked three high that were light and easily stowed. An additional luxury was that the boat was heated and had an ice tank for food storage.

Even so, *M1* had a short life of barely four years' active service post-war, before being decommissioned and scrapped.

M class

Displacement: 480 tonnes/472.4 tons (surfaced); 665 tonnes/654.5 tons (submerged)
Length: 58.75m/192ft 9in
Beam: 4.49m/14ft 9in
Armament: 4 x 457mm/18in tubes, 8 x torpedoes, 1 x 76mm/3in (23 calibres) deck gun
Propulsion: 626.4kW/840hp diesel; 507.1kW/680hp electric
Speed: 14 knots (surfaced); 10.5 knots (dived)
Complement: 28 crew

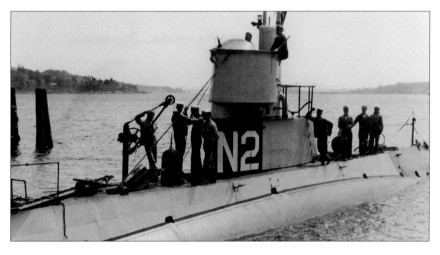

LEFT: **After war service patrolling the New England coast of America, *N2* served as a training ship for the Submarine School and in 1921 became a test platform for experimental Navy weapons, such as a radio controlled torpedo.**

N class

Displacement: 342 tonnes/336.6 tons (surfaced); 407 tonnes/400.6 tons (submerged)
Length: 44.85m/147ft 2in
Beam: 4.8m/15ft 9in
Armament: 4 x 457mm/18in tubes, 8 x torpedoes
Propulsion: 357.9kW/480hp diesel; 208.8kW/280hp electric
Speed: 13 knots (surfaced); 11 knots (dived)
Complement: 25 crew

N class

These boats were at the other end of the spectrum compared to *M1*, being relatively small and intended largely for harbour defence and even inland waterway patrols. *N3* became one of the first submarines to navigate the St Lawrence River and the Great Lakes and visited Halifax, Quebec,

Montreal, and Port Dalhousie before arriving at Toledo on June 25, 1921.

At most stopping points, she went on public display and took visitors aboard. Rushed into being towards the end of World War I to meet production targets, none saw any challenging duties in the few remaining months of the conflict.

Thereafter the N-class boats were used extensively as training platforms, given the absence of any serious threats in the intended role. Like the M class, they too had a short life. Seven of the class were built, but virtually all were decommissioned by the mid-1920s.

O class

After the small harbour protectors came the O-class boats, 500 tonnes/492 tons or more in surface displacement. These were laid down before America's involvement in World War I in sufficient numbers to provide a failsafe position should the worst happen – as, indeed, it did. It was in many ways rather ironic that the O boats began rolling off the production lines, along with the even more advanced R class, providing some satisfaction for the public and the media clamouring for new ships and submarines. In the event, the boats of this class saw little or no war service – at least not in the way they were intended. On November 2, 1918, a number of the Os were included in a 20-boat contingent that set out for European waters to take on the U-boats, but the Armistice was signed before the ships reached the Azores, and they returned to the United States without firing a single torpedo in anger.

It was a remarkable fact that, while many boats were disposed of during the 1920s and early 30s for scrapping – some in connection with the international agreements to limit submarine construction — eight of the O class were mothballed. These were brought back

ABOVE: **The O-class side view.** RIGHT: **After 12 years' service in her duties for the US Navy, *O12* was converted for use on the Sir Hubert Wilkins Arctic Expedition of geophysical investigation, for which she was given the temporary name of *Nautilus*. After being returned to the Navy, she ended up in a Norwegian fjord, where she sank in 1931.**

into service following the Japanese attack on Pearl Harbor in 1941, to become the oldest boats in the US submarine fleet to participate in World War II. Most survived the war, remaining in service throughout, fulfilling operational and training purposes, with two still in business in 1946.

There was one casualty among them, occurring in the months prior to America entering World War II. Recommissioned in April 1941, *O9* left New London with others of her class on June 19 for trials off the Isles of Shoals, 24km/ 15 miles off Portsmouth, New Hampshire. The following day, after sister ships *O6* and *O10* had successful completed their trials, *O9* hit trouble during deep submergence tests and slipped well below her depth limit of 60.9m/200ft. She was crushed by the pressure of the

water and sank. Search operations were launched immediately by the sister ships and one of the newer submarines, *Triton*, along with the submarine rescue vessel, *Falcon*, but they found no trace.

After two days, divers eventually located her in 134m/440ft of water in the same area where *Squalus* had been lost in 1939. The depth meant they could only stay down for a brief time and salvage operations were considered too risky. All further efforts to raise her were cancelled and the crew of 33 was declared lost.

ABOVE: **The starboard diesel engine of the O class, which was upgraded as the building of the O boats progressed to the last of that configuration, *O16*, which had Busch Sulzer Brothers diesels to provide 745.7kW/1,000hp driving a single propeller.**

O class	🇺🇸
Displacement: 513 tonnes/504.9 tons (surfaced); 619 tonnes/609.2 tons (submerged)	
Length: 52.41m/171ft 11in	
Beam: 5.5m/18ft 1in	
Armament: 4 x 457mm/18in tubes, 8 x torpedoes, 1 x 76mm/3in (23 calibres) deck gun	
Propulsion: 656.2kW/880hp diesel; 551.8kW/740hp electric	
Speed: 14 knots (surfaced); 10.5 knots (dived)	
Complement: 29 crew	

R class

The R class had a very similar story to that of the O boats, whose relatively short working life in the 1920s was also reactivated for World War II. This class also came into being as World War I was ending, with no fewer than 27 having been laid down in 1917 for commissioning by the end of 1918. At that time, plans for the much larger new S class were also on the drawing board. By then the emergency was over, and with such a surfeit of submarines available to the United States as the much larger S class also came into being, many of the R boats were laid up by the mid-1920s, and all had been decommissioned by 1931 in the wake of international agreements on undersea warfare.

The R class was built by three different submarine yards to achieve prompt delivery in case the war dragged on, and there were some differences in the final build, in terms of compartments and even overall length and weight. The first years of service for the class leader *R1* and many of her sister boats were spent on patrol, training crews and developing submarine tactics before being laid up. She was brought back to life in 1940 and, after a refit, was transferred to Squadron 7 to hunt U-boats on a patrol line 402km/ 250 miles north-east of Bermuda, a task which continued through World War II. From 1944, she and several sister ships were tasked exclusively with anti-submarine work.

The rest of the R-class boats followed much the same pattern, and suffered only two losses. *R12*, which was recommissioned in October 1940, spent much of her time patrolling the region around the entrance to the Panama Canal, operating primarily from Guantanamo Bay. However, on

June 12, 1943 while conducting torpedo practice with Brazilian observers on board, the forward battery compartment flooded as she prepared to dive. She sank in less than half a minute taking the 42 officers, crew and visitors with her. None escaped.

The demise of *R1*, on the other hand, was down to a case of mistaken identity. She was among the boats transferred to the Royal Navy under a lend-lease programme in 1942 and reclassified as *P514*. Unfortunately, she was rammed by HMCS *Georgian* on June 21, 1942 in the western Atlantic. The Canadians thought she was a U-boat. She sank in minutes with all hands.

ABOVE: *R2*, like many of her class of 27 boats, took a long layoff from duty for much of the 1930s, having been decommissioned only to be brought back into service in the period immediately prior to World War II.

R class

Displacement: 560 tonnes/551.2 tons (surfaced); 669 tonnes/658.4 tons (submerged)
Length: 56.7m/186ft
Beam: 5.5m/18ft 1in
Armament: 4 x 533mm/21in tubes forward, 8 x torpedoes, 1 x 76mm/3in (50 calibres) deck gun
Propulsion: 894.8kW/1,200hhp diesel; 745.7kW/1,000hp electric
Speed: 13.5 knots (surfaced); 10.5 knots (dived)
Complement: 29 crew

S class

S boats were built in three types in the 1920s under the same general specifications but with varying designs. However, as an overall mass-production class, it was the largest class ever undertaken by the US Navy, in every respect. Fifty-one boats of this class were built and, becoming America's most successful submarine to date, they were operational in each of the following three decades. The first, S1 – known as the Holland type — saw the culmination of the Electric Boat Company's single-hull design for the US Navy. S2 was known as the Lake-type and S3 as the Government-type. All three versions undertook experimental duties of varying kinds in the decade of their manufacture, which greatly contributed to future US submarine developments. One of particular note fell to S1 in that she became the experimental platform for the US Navy's first submarine aircraft carrier. This would also be tried by other countries, notably Britain, Italy and Japan, but only the latter continued the experiments into wartime operational use of any magnitude.

S1 was given a cylindrical capsule mounted to the rear of the conning tower to house a collapsible Martin MS-1 seaplane, first built of wood and fabric and later in two metal types. On the surface, the aircraft would be rolled out, assembled and launched from the deck by partially submerging the submarine. The first trials that took the operations through all phases, from loading the disassembled aircraft into its pod through to reconstruction at sea, launching and eventual retrieval were conducted in July 1926 on the Thames River at New London.

S1 then went on to become a divisional flagship operating in the Panama Canal Zone and later took up duties based at Pearl Harbor and in other home ports. By then, a fairly active peacetime training cycle had been established across the board so all boats took up rotational postings around all areas of operation. These preparations did not stop the Japanese attack on the Pearl Harbor base, but did however prepare the S boats for a staunch and versatile involvement in World War II, from defensive and offensive positions.

Six of the S boats became casualties: S5 sank after an accidental intake of water soon after being commissioned, but miraculously all aboard escaped through a hole cut in the hull. S26 sank after a collision in the Gulf of Panama in December 1941, with the loss of 46 men; three survived. On September 25, 1925, S51 was rammed and sunk off Block

Island, New York, by a merchant steamer, with only three survivors. S28 was lost at sea with all hands in July 1944. S39 became a victim of accidental grounding in 1942 after heroic action against the Japanese, but the entire crew was evacuated to safety. S44 was the victim of heavy enemy bombardment while stranded through mechanical problems on the surface in October 1943. Only two of the crew survived. They spent the rest of the war in a Japanese slave labour camp.

S class	
Displacement: 840 tonnes/826.7 tons (surfaced); 1,045 tonnes/1,028.5 tons (submerged)	
Length: 66.75m/219ft	
Beam: 6.35m/20ft 10in	
Armament: 4 x 533mm/21in tubes, 12 x torpedoes, 1 x 102mm/4in (50 calibres) deck gun	
Propulsion: 1,342.2kW/1,800hp diesel; 1,118.6kW/1500hp electric	
Speed: 14.5 knots (surfaced); 11 knots (dived)	
Complement: 38 crew	

LEFT: The S-class profile, which remained virtually the same for all of its 51 boats.

LEFT: **By now, the US Navy had reverted to names rather than numbers, and *Skipjack* came in the Salmon class, a strong class that showed influences from the recent trials with larger submarines such as the V boats *Barracuda*, *Argonaut* and *Narwhal*.** ABOVE: **The *Skipjack* badge.**

Salmon class

In the 1930s, the classification of new submarines in the US Navy reverted to the name of the lead boat, in this case *Salmon*, commissioned in 1938. This class was one of the new generation of huge submarines that had begun rolling out of the US shipyards in the wake of experimental fleet and cruiser submarines of the late 1920s, such as *Argonaut*, *Narwhal* and *Nautilus*, originally commissioned under the V classification. Indeed, from the mid-1930s and beyond, a massive production schedule was imposed upon the shipbuilders as the US government

embarked upon a programme of submarine construction matched at that time only by the Japanese. *Salmon*, laid down in April 1936 by the Electric Boat Company at Groton, Connecticut, was commissioned 23 months later, and was joined over the coming months by five others in her class, names which became famous in the annals of US submarine history – *Seal*, *Skipjack*, *Snapper*, *Stingray* and *Sturgeon*.

After coastal trials from Nova Scotia to the West Indies, *Salmon* became flagship of Submarine Division 15, Squadron 6 of the Submarine Force,

US Fleet, at Portsmouth, operating along the Atlantic coast for a year. She then transferred to the west coast to bolster the submarine presence prior to transferring to the Asiatic station in Manila, along with submarine tender *Holland* and three other boats, to strengthen defences around the Philippines in response to growing tension with Japan. *Salmon* had been leading defensive patrols from Manila when the Japanese attacked Pearl Harbor on December 7, 1941, and, like US submarines everywhere, was placed on an immediate offensive alert and a few days later fired her first shots in anger, sending a spread of torpedoes against Japanese destroyers to scatter their attack.

As the opposition became fierce in the region, the submarine base was moved out of Manila to Exmouth Gulf, Australia, from where sorties into the Java Sea were launched. In March, *Salmon* moved to the US submarine base at Fremantle, Australia, from where patrols were being organized and established along the south coast of Java to intercept Japanese shipping. On May 3, she torpedoed and sank the 11,625-tonne/11,441-ton repair ship *Asahi*, and on the 28th, sank the 4,452-tonne/4,382-ton passenger-cargo vessel, *Ganges Maru*. These operations were merely the beginning of a busy wartime career operating from both Australia and Peal Harbour, for which she was awarded nine battle stars for Asiatic and Pacific operations.

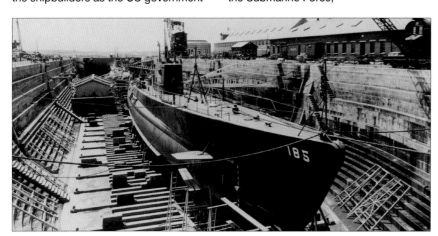

ABOVE: **A bow view of USS *Snapper* in dry dock in 1939. It was a fortuitous refit for what lay ahead, which in this boat's case amounted to 11 busy war patrols, for which she was awarded six battle stars.**

Salmon class

Displacement: 1,426 tonnes/1,403.5 tons (surfaced); 2,163 tonnes/2,128.8 tons (submerged)
Length: 93.8m/307ft 9in
Beam: 7.9m/25ft 11in
Armament: 8 x 533mm/21in tubes, 24 x torpedoes, 1 x 76mm/3in (50 calibres) deck gun, 2 x 12.7mm/0.50 calibre machine-guns, 2 x 7.62mm/0.30 calibre machine-guns.
Propulsion: 4,101.3kW/5,500hp diesel; 4 x electric motors developing 2,460.8kW/3,300hp
Speed: 21 knots (surfaced); 9 knots (dived)
Complement: 55 crew

LEFT: The launch of *Spearfish*, third of the ten-boat Sargo class, all of which were in for a busy war. Apart from aggressive patrolling, *Spearfish* was also engaged on dangerous reconnaissance work, winning ten battle stars. ABOVE: Sister ship *Swordfish*, launched in 1939. BELOW: The war is over in this photograph, which includes class leader *Sargo* with *Spearfish* and *Saury*. The mothballing process is underway with the preservative cocoons around the deck guns that would never again be fired in anger.

Sargo class

Ten boats from this class were commissioned progressively from February 1939 to become the first of the principal classes in the US Navy's submarine fleet amassed before and during World War II – a force which amounted to more than 400 boats in addition to another 100 from the classes listed previously. *Sargo* went straight to business with a war patrol off French Indochina and to the Dutch East Indies, delivering eight separate attacks on enemy shipping. However, her Mark 14 torpedoes malfunctioned, and her targets escaped. Later that year (1942), she temporarily took on the role of transport, offloading her remaining torpedoes and 76mm/3in ammunition to stow a million rounds of 7.62mm/0.30 calibre ammunition desperately needed by Allied forces in the Philippines, and thereafter took up station at Fremantle.

The welcome she received was somewhat unfortunate. As the first *Sargo* class in the region, she was mistaken for a Japanese vessel and attacked by an Allied aircraft. Fortunately, the damage was not excessive and she went on to participate fully in the war effort with ten patrols, receiving the Philippine

Presidential Unit Citation for her work in that area.

However, another blue-on-blue incident had a devastating effect on another in the *Sargo* class. *Sculpin* was scheduled to lead a co-ordinated group attack on enemy shipping located near the Eniwetok islands in the Pacific. During the raid, *Sculpin*, already at her depth limit, was blasted by 18 depth charges and with her pressure hull distorted, the boat leaking and diving plane gear damaged, Captain Fred Cromwell had no option but to surface. As her executive officers came on to the bridge, they were killed by shellfire, some of which went through the main induction. Cromwell could do nothing more, and ordered his submarine to be scuttled and all hands to abandon ship.

About 12 men "rode the ship down" according to an account in the *Dictionary of American Naval Fighting Ships*. Captain Fred Cromwell stayed aboard, determined to go down with his submarine, because he alone possessed secret intelligence of US Fleet movements and specific attack plans. He feared that he would be forced to reveal this information under Japanese torture or use of drugs, an action for

which he was posthumously awarded the Congressional Medal of Honour.

In all, 42 men were taken prisoner by the Japanese destroyer. The group was split up, 21 in the carrier *Chuyo* and 20 in another ship, bound for captivity. Now, an ironic twist of fate took hold: en route to Japan, *Chuyo* was torpedoed and sunk by another *Sargo*-class boat, *Sailfish*, on December 31, 1943.

Sargo class

Displacement: 1,427 tonnes/1,1404.5 tons (surfaced); 2,312 tonnes/2,275.5 tons (submerged)
Length: 94.5m/310ft
Beam: 8.25m/27ft
Armament: 8 x 533mm/21in tubes, 24 x torpedoes, 1 x 76mm/3in (50 calibres) deck gun, 2 x 12.7mm/0.50 calibre machine-guns, 2 x 7.72mm/0.30 calibre machine-guns
Propulsion: 4,101.3kW/5,500hp diesel; 2,043.2kW/2,740hp electric
Speed: 20 knots (surfaced); 7.75 knots (dived)
Complement: 55 crew

Gato class

Gato had a baptism of fire as one of the boats commissioned in December 1941 soon after the Japanese attack on Pearl Harbor. She was the first of 74 boats in this class, one of three main types that became the workhorses of the American effort in World War II. Developed towards the end of the 1930s, and employing the round-the-clock capacity of every major submarine builder in the United States, the new submarines were coming off the production lines at an incredible rate, a state of affairs that was to continue well into 1943.

Given that the surface fleet was being similarly enhanced, this represented an outstanding effort by the shipbuilders, who were producing brilliant boats that incorporated numerous

technological advances covering every aspect of submarine activity. These boats bristled with new and heavy deck armoury and carried a substantial stock of torpedoes to match their increasing endurance. The 1,500-tonne/1,476-ton (surfaced) Gato class could stay out on patrol for 74 days, and cruise 17,703km/11,000 miles surfaced at 10 knots, although the boats were capable of a top speed of 20 knots.

It was also a great credit to their designers, engineers and shipwrights that, unlike the many submarines produced up to that point in time, whose life expectancy was often quite limited, the Gato class led the way to longevity. Along with the other newer classes that followed, many boats were

ABOVE: **Larger still, in class and size, *Raton* is photographed here in post-war mode as a Radar Picket submarine, with a slightly different configuration, circa 1953–60.** LEFT: **The famous *Wahoo*, one of the US Submarine Force's most successful boats, whose exploits under Commander "Mush" Morton were legendary. During just six patrols she sank 27 ships, totalling 121,011 tonnes/ 119,100 tons, and damaged two more, making 25,300 tonnes/ 24,900 tons before her own luck ran out on October 11, 1943, when she was lost with all 79 hands.**

still in service in the 1970s, some of which were converted into the post-war classification of hunter-killers in the Guppy configuration.

Despite their increasing size, the versatility of submarines was also being extended to the full, especially in the areas of intelligence-gathering and combined operations with special forces. *Gato* herself, for example, did some fine work landing Australian commandos in Japanese-held territory while at the same time transporting evacuees to safety. In fact, the submarine survived 13 war patrols, her last a particularly dangerous mission, rescuing downed Army aviators after waves of air strikes off the eastern coast of Honshu. It was there that she received the signal "Cease Fire" on August 15, 1945, and then steamed into Tokyo Bay. She remained there for the signing of surrender documents on board USS *Missouri* on September 2, before setting off for home to receive the Presidential Unit Citation in recognition of daring exploits, and 13 battle stars for service in World War II.

In all, the Gato-class boats won more than 700 battle stars, although the cost was high, with the loss of 19 boats and more than 1,100 men to wartime action. The casualties included a particular, but not especially uncommon, misfortune that befell the last of the class, *Tullibee*, which occurred in 1943 while the boat was patrolling off the Philippines. She had fired a volley of torpedoes towards an enemy passenger ship and two destroyers, at least two of which were hit. Minutes later an explosion rocked the submarine and Gunner's Mate C.W. Kukyendall – on the bridge at the time – was knocked unconscious and thrown into the water. When he regained consciousness, the submarine was gone. One of her own torpedoes had apparently turned full circle and hit her. Kukyendall was the only survivor.

LEFT: **The patches for class leader USS *Dace* and USS *Gato*. Both boats survived the war with commendations for meritorious service.**

BELOW: **USS *Barb* had a busy after-life following her war service, first undergoing a Guppy conversion and later on being loaned to Italy in 1955, where she served under the name of *Enrico Tazzoli* until 1975.** BOTTOM: **A slightly cramped-looking control room in USS *Cero*, one of a large number of boats laid up in reserve after the war.**

Gato class

Displacement: 1,501 tonnes/1,477.3 tons (surfaced); 2,386 tonnes/2,348.3 tons (submerged)
Length: 95m/311ft 8in
Beam: 8.3m/27ft 3in
Armament: 10 x 533mm/21in tubes, 6 x forward, 4 x aft, 24 x torpedoes, 1 x 76mm/3in (50 calibres) deck gun, 2 x 12.7mm/0.50 calibre machine-guns, 2 x 7.63mm/0.30 calibre machine-guns
Propulsion: 4,026.8kW/5,400hp diesel; 2,043.2kW/2,740hp electric
Speed: 20.25 knots (surfaced); 8.75 knots (dived)
Complement: 60 crew

LEFT: **More big boats and a big history in the Balao class, this one being** *Pampanito*, **noted for her role in the American submarine service's own wolf-pack operations in the South China Sea, although she had to temporarily retire for repairs after a severe depth charge attack.**

Balao class

This was the largest class of submarines ever produced by the US Navy, in terms of numbers, with a total of 131 earmarked for production during World War II. Ten were subsequently cancelled towards the end of the production cycle, by which time the war's end was in sight. From first to last in production – *Balao* to *Tiru* – was a three-year span from the point in April 1942 when the class leader was laid down, to 1947 when the last was commissioned. *Balao*'s own war operations spanned a period from July 1943 until the end of August 1945. During this period, she completed ten war patrols and ended her war effort with a fine record, having sunk seven Japanese ships totalling 32,623 tonnes/32,108 tons, in addition to sinking 11,177 tonnes/11,000 tons of miscellaneous enemy small craft by gunfire.

As a whole, the Balao class, with the largest number of submarines afloat during the final 18 months of the war, undertook many successful patrols in all regions of the conflict. However, the cost was high. Nine boats and almost

600 men were lost to enemy action. Throughout the submarine stories, there were many examples of heroism and survival that provided dramatic true-life scenarios for numerous movies. One such event was recognized in 2004 with the erection of a plaque at the Damage Control Training Centre at Pearl Harbor, a story from November 1943 aboard Balao-class *Billfish* that led to extensive research in damage limitation. The submarine became riddled with leaks after being inundated with depth charges during an attack by the Japanese that incapacitated the boat's commander and senior officers.

As the attack continued, Lt Charles Rush, then 23, took charge and risked diving the boat to 51.8m/170ft below test depth for 12 hours. Meanwhile Chief Electrician's Mate John D. Rendernick gathered a team for emergency repairs to reduce the heavy flooding through the stern tubes by pumping grease into the worst leaking tube. He then used six men and a hydraulic jack to reposition the port main motor, which had been knocked

off its foundation. When the increasing heat reached the limit of the crew's tolerance, Rendernick told them to wrap wet towels around their heads. These actions and Rush's coolheaded command in the face of continuing explosions around the boat, saved it from destruction – and the lives of the entire crew. Crucially, he also turned his boat to regain a previous position to sit under an oil slick, thus fooling the Japanese destroyers above into thinking the boat had been destroyed.

After the war, many of the surviving Balao class underwent substantial remodelling, both internally and in the superstructure to keep them operational for years to come. *Balao* was among a number of boats sold to Turkey under a Security Assistance Program in 1970, and under the new name of *Burak Reis*, she remained on the Turkish naval register until 1996.

LEFT: **USS** *Blackfin*, **one of nine Balao submarines converted to the Guppy 1A configuration between 1947 and 1951. This was a less drastic remodelling than the costly Guppy II programme, an interim measure in the developing Cold War providing boats with streamlined sail and superstructure, new masts, snorkel and equipment, and greater underwater propulsion.**

Balao class

Displacement: 1,501 tonnes/1,477.3 tons (surfaced); 2,375 tonnes/2,337.5 tons (submerged)

Length: 95m/311ft 8in

Beam: 8.32m/27ft 4in

Armament: 10 x 533mm/21in tubes, 6 x forward, 4 x aft, 24 x torpedoes, 1 x 102mm/4in (50 calibres) deck gun, 1 x 40mm/1.57in gun, 2 x 12.7mm/0.50 calibre machine-guns

Propulsion: 4,026.8kW/5,400hp diesel; 2,043.2kW/2,740hp electric

Speed: 20.25 knots (surfaced); 8.75 knots (dived)

Complement: 66 crew

LEFT: **USS *Pickerel*, one of the Tench class which arrived too late for war service, was among 24 boats selected for the Guppy II conversion and later went into Guppy III mode.** ABOVE: **This is what *Pickerel* could do after that: surfacing at a 48-degree up angle, from a depth of 45.7m/150ft during tests off the coast of Hawaii, March 1, 1952.**

Tench class

The Tench boats came late to World War II, the first of the class not being laid down until July 1944, but she was speedily built and commissioned on October 6. Even though the build time was very swift indeed, only 31 of a planned 128 boats in this class were commissioned before the end of the war came into view and the remainder were cancelled. Those that did participate came at time when the Japanese were in desperate straits, and had long ago given up any semblance of adherence to the international agreements on the rights and safety of prisoners of war. Consequently, many of the US boats, and indeed surface vessels, were almost daily engaged in the recovery of downed air crews, attempting to snatch them to safety before they could be picked up by enemy ships and submarines.

Allied submarine tactics were by then also well developed, tried and practised, helped by the inclusion of the latest technological aids, particularly in the fields of communication and surveillance.

Another development that had successfully been employed by the US submarine command for many months was the utilization of the wolf-pack system of submarine deployment, used to great effect by the Germans. Thus, when *Tench* became the first of her class into battle, she did so in the company of *Balao*, *Sea Devil* and *Grouper* in what were by then described as "co-ordinated attack groups".

The patrol area to which they were assigned encompassed a region of the East China Sea south-west of Kyushu and extended north into the Yellow Sea. Their tasks ranged through rotational patrols, weather reporting, photographic reconnaissance and lifeguard duties. The latter could be extremely hazardous for a submarine, often requiring these massive boats to be manoeuvred close to the shoreline and in the shallows. If trouble came in overhead, there was no place to dive, as *Tench* discovered during her lifeguard stint in support of the 5th Fleet air raids on Nagasaki. Dyes were used to mark the position of downed pilots, and

spotter planes kept up a round-the-clock watch. When pilots were spotted, rescue submarines moved in with F6F Hellcat fighters providing cover overhead. On this occasion, the dye was no more than a reflection, and while *Tench* was searching, a flight of bombers appeared out of the sun, but due to the water depth the submarine could not dive. She was a sitting duck. However, the aircraft were friendly and *Tench* escaped unharmed. Further war patrols kept the submarine busy right up to the last, but that was by no means the end of *Tench*'s journey.

In 1950, she and others in her class were converted to Guppy 1A submarines, which involved considerable modifications in almost every department. Thus equipped, she was recommissioned and remained in service until the early 1970s, along with others who had undergone the same modifications.

Tench class

Displacement: 1,545 tonnes/1,520.6 tons (surfaced); 2,378 tonnes/2,340.4 tons (submerged)
Length: 95.02m/311ft 9in
Beam: 8.25m/27ft 1in
Armament: 10 x 533mm/21in tubes, 6 x forward, 4 x aft; 24 x torpedoes, 1 x 127mm/5in (25 calibres) deck gun, 1 x 40mm/1.57in gun, 1 x 20mm/0.79in gun, 2 x 12.7mm/0.50 calibre machine-guns
Propulsion: 4,026.8kW/5,400hp diesel; 2,043.2kW/2,740hp electric
Speed: 20.25 knots (surfaced); 8.75 knots (dived)
Complement: 66 crew

LEFT: **USS *Argonaut*, also of the wartime Tench class, was reassigned to Submarine Squadron 6 at Norfolk, Virginia. In 1947 she received some of the Guppy modernizations to become one of the first guided missile submarines armed with the new Regulus I missile.**

Holland

Britain's very first submarine, the *Holland* launched in 1901, can still be seen. She forms part of the collection at the Royal Navy Submarine Museum in Gosport, Hampshire. Bought for £35,000 and constructed under conditions of great secrecy, she was originally known as HM *Submarine Torpedo Boat No. 1*. Initially, Royal Navy engineers and shipbuilders Vickers had great difficult with the drawings, which had many discrepancies, and the British eventually went their own way and severed contact with Holland and the Electric Boat Company of America.

Unlike today's boats with their conning towers and periscopes, *Holland* looked more like a short fat cigar tube with a hatch or scuttle for the captain's head and shoulders, although an experimental periscope was designed and fitted to a later Holland. Built for the Royal Navy under licence, she was a copy of the US Navy's A-class boats.

Steering was by two vertically mounted rudders above and below the single screw and by a horizontal pair of rudders for when the boat was submerged. This design gave anti-submarine sceptics plenty of ammunition, and the boats were certainly no place for anyone with even a hint of claustrophobia. There were no interior bulkheads, very little ventilation and no real accommodation for sitting or sleeping. The fumes were appalling – a combined stench from the petrol engine and the buckets used for ablutions that could only be emptied when they surfaced.

Notoriously unstable, it took almost a year of trials and modifications to settle it down. When surfaced, the boats were difficult to control, and the captain and coxswain had great difficulty hanging on to masts and wheels while on deck, with water washing around their feet. Submerged, the boat seemed to have a constant "nose-down" attitude, which made it appear to be constantly diving. This unnerved the sailors at first, but underwater control and manoeuvrability were described as good.

ABOVE LEFT: **The Royal Navy customized the *Holland* designs they bought from the American Electric Boat Company; consequently, the British and US versions differed somewhat.** ABOVE: **Length and width remained the same, however, and room on top was still scarce.**

Exhaustive trials of *No. 1* lasted three years with the result that *No. 2* became the first submarine to be commissioned into the Royal Navy on August 1, 1903, quickly followed by four more entering service by the end of that year. Despite the experimental environment and their fragility, they saw a decade of service, and many a complacent warship captain was shocked to hear the clang of a practice torpedo hitting his ship's sides. Although only equipped with a single 356mm/14in tube, they were armed with either three long or five short torpedoes. *Holland 1* sank while taking part in manoeuvres off the Nab Lightship in March 1904. All her crew were rescued.

LEFT: **A pair of Holland boats undergoing a clean, probably prior to their display to the public, who were interested in the curious new craft.**

Holland	
Displacement: 114.8 tonnes/113 tons (surfaced); 124 tonnes/122 tons (submerged)	
Length: 19.5m/64ft	
Beam: 3.58m/11ft 9in	
Armament: 1 x 533mm/21in tube (bow); 3 x long or 5 x short torpedoes	
Propulsion: 119.3kW/160hp petrol; 55.9kW/75hp electric	
Speed: 7.5 knots (surfaced); 5 knots (dived)	
Complement: 8 crew	

A class

Developed from the Holland class, the A-class submarines were 50 per cent longer, but still put to sea with the primitive technology of their predecessors. *A1* was originally intended to be the sixth Holland class. However, with a raft of design improvements on the drawing board it was decided this boat would include the majority of them in an enlarged hull, which was increased by 12.2m/40ft. It was then decided to increase the number of torpedo tubes to two from *A2* onwards and this resulted in a further increase in size by almost 0.6m/2ft and was to become the standard for the rest of the class.

However, the improved design and engine power brought little improvement in terms of performance, with the engine speed changing little from the original Hollands. On the surface, speed was slightly quicker, but submerged things were virtually unchanged. *A5* was the first Group 2 boat and was fitted with a

410kW/550bhp 16-cylinder engine, replacing the 12-cylinder unit, but again this was a disappointment.

Speed increased by only half a knot and the engine was much less reliable. On the surface, this class was still powered by petrol engines, and the dangers soon became apparent. In February 1905, five crewmen on *A5* were killed in an explosion caused by a build-up of petrol fumes after refuelling. *A13* was fitted with an experimental heavy-oil-powered MAN engine built under licence by Vickers – what we call a diesel engine today. Although it used a much safer fuel, it was a much heavier engine, and consequently the boat had to carry a reduced amount of fuel.

It was not until the introduction of the D class that the improved diesel engines replaced the dangerous petrol-powered machinery. However, there were several changes that did work and improve safety – the conning tower being one.

It featured two hatches, one leading on to the bridge and a lower one sealing the conning tower from the control room. This prevented water entering the boat from larger waves and enabled it to put to sea in rougher weather. As well as giving better protection to the captain and coxswain when sailing on the surface, it also gave them a better view. *A11* featured an even larger conning tower, and although the lengthened hull gave a better passage than the Hollands while surfaced, overall it was still poor.

As experience was gained it was also found that – using care – the boats could be dived while under way, but with only rudders at the rear, control was difficult. *A7* was therefore fitted with a pair of hydroplanes on her conning tower.

RIGHT: *A2* was the first boat to be upgraded and slightly elongated to take an additional torpedo tube, and the two tubes fitted side by side.

A class

Displacement: 189 tonnes/186 tons (surfaced); 208 tonnes/204.7 tons (submerged)
Length: 32.1m/105ft 4in
Beam: 3.9m/12ft 10in
Armament: 2 x 432mm/17in tubes (bow); 3 x torpedoes
Propulsion: 447.4kW/600hp petrol; 111.9kW/150hp electric
Speed: 11.5 knots (surfaced); 6 knots (dived)
Complement: 11 crew

B class

The B-class boats were the first Royal Navy submarines to have a casing that gave extra protection to the hull and improved buoyancy on the surface. Additionally, they were also the first British submarines to be fitted with a second pair of hydroplanes near the bow in addition to those astern, enabling them to dive more easily when under way. Although surface speed was better than the A class, submerged it remained similar. With the B class came a giant leap forward for the Royal Navy, with the boats ranging further and further from home waters. To patrol in the Mediterranean, they would be towed there by surface ships before deploying. In spite of these long deployments, soon to be in a war environment, there were still no dividing bulkheads, accommodation space or improved ventilation.

Still rather limited in endurance and meant for defensive purposes, the two 432mm/17in torpedo tubes in this class were angled downwards in the belief that torpedoes would be discharged while the submarine rose to the surface. Two reload torpedoes were carried.

Just before Christmas 1914, it was a B-class boat in which Lt Norman Douglas Holbrook became the first submarine commander to be awarded the Victoria Cross, for a daring operation that resulted in the sinking of a Turkish battleship. Holbrook dived *B11* under five rows of mines and attacked the *Messudieh*, returning the same way, and braved attacks by gunfire and torpedo boats. The boat had been

ABOVE: *B4* was among the first boats to be taken out of coastal waters and towed to the Mediterranean, opening up vast possibilities for the future.

submerged for nine hours. As well as Holbrook's VC, all the crew were decorated for gallantry, each man receiving either a DSO or DSM.

One B-class boat was lost with all hands when run down by a surface ship off Dover, and another was sunk by Austrian aircraft. Other boats became inoperable because of a lack of spares and were modified and used as patrol boats instead of submarines, with their conning towers removed and replaced by wheelhouses.

They were also armed with a 12pdr gun. Eleven of these craft were built, and when the war ended only *B3* was operational, largely because she had mainly been used for trials and training.

ABOVE: *B5* demonstrates the relatively unpractised and therefore often hazardous task of taking on torpedoes at sea, which was necessary during operational manoeuvres, especially when far from home. Given that the class carried only two reloads for the two bow tubes, it was a regular occurrence during wartime.

B class

Displacement: 291.59 tonnes/287 tons (surfaced); 321.06 tonnes/316 tons (submerged)
Length: 43.34m/142ft 2in
Beam: 3.88m/12ft 9in
Armament: 2 x 432mm/17in tubes (bow); 4 x torpedoes
Propulsion: 447.4kW/600hp Vickers petrol engine; 149.1kW/200ehp electric
Speed: 12 knots (surfaced); 6.5 knots (dived)
Complement: 15 crew

LEFT: On July 6, 1918, a squadron of German seaplanes returning from a daylight raid on Lowestoft caught Harwich-based *C25* on the surface and used her for target practice. Her captain and six crew were killed outright, but the remaining crew, some badly wounded, managed to close up and dive the boat, and eventually reached the safety of their home base. BELOW: An interior view of the C class.

C class

Thirty eight C-class boats were built in total, all but six of these by Vickers and for the first time HM Dockyard at Chatham provided submarines for the Royal Navy by building this last half dozen. They also represented the last of the Holland design, and the last to be powered wholly by petrol engines. Given their limited endurance, the C-class boats made a remarkable contribution to the defence of the UK during World War I. All played a gallant and extremely dangerous role, operating mainly in the coastal regions in the North Sea, with many gallantry decorations won by the crews, although losses were also heavy. Safety was also being taken into account, with four of the boats equipped with airlocks and helmets, which were intended to give crew time to breathe extra air before trying to escape through the torpedo hatch.

As the submarine war became more intense, casualties among submariners began to mount and the C boats were to become involved in a daring plan to hit marauding U-boats, which were finding British North Sea trawlers easy pickings. Decoy trawlers would sail into the fishing fleets towing a submerged C boat until a U-boat had been lured into the trap, at which point the submarine was released. *C27* was involved in one such operation, being towed by the decoy trawler *Princess Louise* off Aberdeen, there to attack and sink *U23*. Another successful pairing was that of *C24* and the trawler *Taranaki* to sink *U40*. But then disaster struck. *C33* vanished, presumed victim of a mine while operating with the trawler *Malta*, and *C29* was lost after her towing trawler *Ariadne* strayed into a minefield in the Humber estuary.

Elsewhere, *C7* successfully attacked and sank *U63* and *U68* in 1917, and *C15* disposed of *U65* in what had developed into the dramatic cut and thrust submarine warfare in the North Sea and English Channel. Other British losses included *C31* and *C34*. Four C-class boats were also deployed to the Baltic Flotilla, tasked with attacking German shipping. In 1917, *C26*, *C27*, *C32* and *C35* were loaded on to barges at Archangel and transported to the Baltic using the Siberian Railway. C boats were also included in the taskforce used to block the U-boat base at Bruges, trapping many of the U-boats inside. Two old boats – *C1* and *C3* – were provided for the mission, with the bow of *C3* being filled with explosives and used to block the entrance channel at Zeebrugge.

LEFT: A typical view of the C-class boats, this one being *C22*, which had an active but uneventful life compared with some of her 37 sister boats. She was among the 24 in the class scrapped at the turn of the 1920s.

C class

Displacement: 291.59 tonnes/287 tons (surfaced); 321.06 tonnes/316 tons (submerged)
Length: 43.28 m/142ft
Beam: 4.11m/13ft 6in
Armament: 2 x 457mm/18in tubes (bow); 4 x torpedoes
Propulsion: 447.4kW/600hp petrol; 223.7kW/300ehp electric
Speed: 12 knots (surfaced); 8 knots (dived)
Complement: 16 crew

D class

This class saw the arrival of the first diesel-powered submarines of the Royal Navy and the first for which the Admiralty produced the basic design. Twin screws and saddle tanks were introduced along with an enhanced conning tower providing better visibility, and, from *D4* onwards, they were also the first boats equipped with a gun – albeit a paltry 12pdr.

Intended as an effective patrol submarine with overseas potential, the eight D-class boats were meant to undertake patrols in excess of 3,200km/1,988 miles. With better visibility came better manoeuvrability, and the placement of the main water ballast tanks outside the hull in a saddle tank configuration increased space internally. *D4* had its gun in a housing that could be retracted into the conning tower, and it was also fitted with a stern-firing torpedo and a new wireless system that enabled the crew to transmit as well as receive. Mounting the bow torpedo tubes vertically also led to a more streamlined shape. Six of the boats were built by

Vickers at Barrow, and the other two at Chatham Dockyard.

At the outbreak of World War I the D boats were stationed along the east coast of Britain, and their role was to support the Grand Fleet and to destroy German warships. *D5* became the first one to fire a torpedo in anger, but the setting used was that for peacetime training and it ran too deep and missed the target. In November 1914 *D3*, *D5*

ABOVE: **A photograph that puts things into perspective – a D-class boat a few hundred feet from a British battleship. It is easy to see why, in those pioneering days, a submarine could be sunk by the wash of a ship.**

and *E10* were sent to intercept German cruisers bombarding the Norfolk coast, but *D5* was lost after striking a mine.

Shortly afterwards, *D2* was also lost after being hit by a German warship. In 1918, *D3* was sunk accidentally in the English Channel after being bombed by a French airship. *D6* was sunk by a German U-boat off Ireland in 1918, leaving *D7* as the only boat of the class to conduct a successful attack, sinking a U-boat off the north of Ireland in September 1917. Only three boats – *D4*, *D7* and *D8* – survived the war, and they were used for training purposes before being paid off.

ABOVE: **Launched in May 1910, *D2* became an early victim of World War I when, on November 25, 1914, she was hit and sunk by gunfire from a German patrol vessel in the Ems estuary, The Netherlands.** LEFT: **A profile of the D class.**

D class

Displacement: 490.73 tonnes/483 tons (surfaced); 604.52 tonnes/595 tons (submerged)
Length: 50.16m/164ft 7in
Beam: 6.22m/20ft 5in
Armament: 3 x 457mm/18in tubes, (2 x bow, 1 x stern); 6 x torpedoes
Propulsion: 2 x 447.4kW/600bhp Vickers diesel engines; 206.6kW/277ehp electric motors
Speed: 14 knots (surfaced); 9 knots (dived)
Complement: 25 crew

LEFT: *E6*, whose class of 56 submarines had a heroic war, ran out of luck on December 26, 1915, while leaving port for her patrol duty. Nearing a sunken light vessel, she was signalled by a patrolling torpedo boat to keep clear. *E6* continued on her course and within minutes struck a mine and disappeared.
BELOW: The torpedo tubes of an E-class boat.

E class

The E-class boats were the teeth of the Royal Navy's submarine fleet, carrying out many daring operations throughout World War I and fulfilling both the conventional submarine role and being adapted to work as mine-layers. One was even adapted to carry aircraft in an attempt to counter the threat to London from German airships. Fifty seven of these brilliantly versatile craft were built and 28 were lost. Larger engines were fitted in an attempt to give the boats extra power, and this resulted in an increase in hull size. While a small increase in performance was achieved, the larger hull enabled more fuel and weapons to be carried.

However, with the increase in size came a problem with their manoeuvrability, and it became necessary to position the boat closer to its target in order to fire torpedoes. This gave the enemy an advantage in counter-attack. At one stage, consideration was given to getting rid of the bow torpedo tubes and firing them broadside. Torpedo tubes were introduced in the beam and again the hull had to be increased to accommodate the tubes and loading space.

E class were also the first boats to have watertight bulkheads, which meant compartments could be sealed in emergencies. Previous British submarines had comprised one single compartment. With the bulkheads came other complications in construction, but the boat builders quickly realized the safety benefits and willingly incorporated them in future designs.

Crew comfort was also becoming part of the equation because of the length of time the men were spending aboard. Although it normally took anything from 20 to 30 months to build a submarine, the pressure of war soon began to reduce build-time to around a year, with Vickers completing *E19* in just eight months. This boat went on to become the first Royal Navy submarine to sink a merchant ship, in 1915 in the Baltic, and increased its tally to eight sinkings, including a German light cruiser. *E1* was the first to torpedo a German battleship – attacking the battlecruiser *Moltke* in the Gulf of Riga in August 1915. The boats of the British Baltic submarine flotilla were so successful in their campaign against enemy shipping that the Germans withdrew all major warships from the area.

Six E-class boats were also modified to act as minelayers, with the mines located in chutes in their saddle tanks. An E-class boat – *E3* – also became the first British submarine to be lost in action, when she was attacked by a U-boat in October 1914. Her wreckage was not located until 1997. As well as operating in home waters and the Baltic, the boats carried the war to the enemy in the Dardanelles, braving minefields to carry out their attacks. *E11* sank shipping off Constantinople and sank a Turkish battleship, the *Hayreddin Barbarossa*. Such was the effect of the E boats and the gallantry of their crews that three E boat captains won the Victoria Cross.

E22 was modified to carry a pair of Sopwith Schneider seaplanes on her deck, and trials began with the aim of launching the aircraft in the North Sea to intercept Zeppelin airships attacking London and other cities. However, the aircraft were too frail to operate in anything other than very calm conditions and the trials were abandoned. Twenty-nine E-class boats survived the war and were finally scrapped between 1921 and 1923. The six minelayers laid almost 2,500 mines.

E class

Displacement: 665.48 tonnes/655 tons (surfaced); 808.73 tonnes/796 tons (submerged)
Length: 53.65m/176ft
Beam: 6.86m/29ft 1in
Armament: 4 x 457mm/18in tubes, (1 x bow, 2 x beam, 1 x stern); 8 x torpedoes; 1 gun of various calibres was carried from 1915
Propulsion: 2 x 596.6kW/800bhp Vickers diesel engines; 2 x 313.2kW/420ehp electric motors
Speed: 15 knots (surfaced); 9 knots (dived)
Complement: 30crew

V class (Early)

Four of the V-class boats were built by Vickers to compete with other experimental boats being constructed at other shipyards. They represented Vickers designers' interpretation of a coastal-type boat designed to meet the requirements of the 1912 Submarine Committee on future submarine development. The innovation was in the double hull section in the middle part of the boat, the result of a number of experimental hulls being tested in a tank.

Vickers built their own diesel engines for the V boats, although the battery was considered small for a boat of its size, and was in two of the class only a third larger than A-class batteries. The estimated cost of the four V-class boats was £75,790 each, and was clearly not the answer to the need for an ocean-going boat that was becoming ever more apparent in December 1913, as Germany pressed ahead with their U-boats. In the meantime, the V boats went into service,

but their performance was disappointing, and they lasted no longer than 1919, when they were paid off.

V class (Early)	
Displacement: 397.26 tonnes/391 tons (surfaced); 464.31 tonnes/457 tons (submerged)	
Length: 44.95m/147ft 6in	
Beam: 4.95m/16ft 3in	
Armament: 2 x 457mm/18in tubes (bow), 4 x torpedoes; 1 x 12pdr gun	
Propulsion: 2 x 335.6kW/450bhp Vickers diesel engines; 2 x 141.7kW/190ehp electric motors	
Speed: 14 knots (surfaced); 9 knots (dived)	
Complement: 20 crew	

F class (Early)

The F class were to be compared with other experimental boats, based on the V class and had similar performance. Although said to be less stable, *F1* and *F3* were equipped with Vickers diesel engines, with a MAN

diesel engine installed in the third boat for comparison.

They were also fitted with an additional stern-mounted torpedo tube. The three were built between 1913 and 1917 and, at one time, there were plans

for five of them to be built. This was scrapped once war broke out. They were used for local defence patrols and later sent to Portsmouth and Campbeltown to be used for training before being paid off in 1919.

F class (Early)	
Displacement: 368.8 tonnes/363 tons surfaced); 448.06 tonnes/441 tons (submerged)	
Length: 46.02 m/151ft	
Beam: 4.88m/16ft	
Armament: 3 x 457mm/18in tubes (2 x bow, 1 x stern), 6 x torpedoes	
Propulsion: 2 x 335.6kW/450bhp Vickers diesel engines; 2 x 149.1kW/200ehp electric motors	
Speed: 14.5knots (surfaced); 8.75 knots (dived)	
Complement: 19 crew	

LEFT: The *G13* immediately became part of the Royal Navy's 10th Flotilla, based in the Tees, in a class which was the first to be armed with 533mm/21in torpedoes, with which *G13* sank the German *UC43* off Muggle Flugga light house on March 10, 1918. BELOW: The G-class profile, based on an Italian double-hull design.

G class

The G-class boats, of which 13 were built, were supposed to become the British answer to ocean-going submarines to match the U-boats, but didn't quite make it. The design features added to the continuing improvements in overall accommodation, allowing more and better equipment to be installed; however, they cost £125,000 apiece. The crew were better off, with improved living conditions that even included an electric oven. The two eight-cylinder diesels generated a worthwhile 1,193kW/1,600bhp, providing a surface speed of 14 knots, but undoubtedly the biggest improvement

brought about by early war experience was the upgrade in armaments, which saw the beginning of larger torpedoes as standard. The specification was changed to provide two 457mm/18in bow tubes, two 457mm/18in beam tubes and one 533mm/21in stern tube.

The class also carried one 76mm/3in Quick Firing High Angle (QF HA) gun, which was fitted just forward of the bridge, and a portable 2pdr fixed to a pedestal at the after end of the bridge. In operations the boat is also known for diving to what was described as an exceptional depth of 51.8m/170ft, when

being chased in error by three British destroyers.

During World War I, *G7*, *G8* and *G11* were lost on active service through unknown causes, and in September 1917, HMS *Petard* sank *G9* in error off the Norwegian coast after the submarine had attacked the ship – also in error. Of the boats that survived, four were taken out of service at the end of the war, and the remaining six were withdrawn from service in January 1921. They had proved something of a disappointment to many, given that their performance was little better than that of the E class, even with the incorporation of the double-hull concept.

LEFT: **The control compartment of the G-class boats demonstrated the rapid pace of improvements aboard the new submarines coming on stream, as beam and length were increasing with each new design.**

G class

Displacement: 710.18 tonnes/699 tons (surfaced); 982.47 tonnes/967.9 tons (submerged)
Length: 57.02m/187ft
Beam: 6.86m/22ft 6in
Armament: 4 x 457mm/18in tubes (2 x bow, 2 x beam); 8 x torpedoes; 1 x 533mm/21in tube (stern); 3 x torpedoes; 1 x 76mm/3in gun
Propulsion: 2 x 596.6kW/800bhp Vickers diesel engines; 2 x 313.2kW/420ehp electric motors
Speed: 15 knots (surfaced); 9 knots (dived)
Complement: 30 crew

LEFT: **The stylish-looking H class, rushed into service for World War I, was of an American design, with some being built in Britain and Canada. They proved a handy boat with the fastest dive, down in thirty seconds.**
ABOVE: *H23* photographed in the Kiel Canal.

H class

As World War I continued to put pressure on British industry to feed the war machine, the country's shipyards were unable to satisfy the Admiralty's demands for more submarines. The Admiralty despatched a delegation to the United States, and 20 single-hulled craft were ordered from the Electric Boat Company.

The boats were to be shipped to the UK for assembly as America had not yet entered the war, but this idea was to fall foul of the US government's neutrality laws. It was then decided to build the first ten at Vickers Canada, with another ten being built by the Electric Boat Company. These, however, were interned at Boston by officials, still fiercely guarding America's neutrality while at the same time selling boatloads of vital supplies to Germany.

Eventually they were released to the Royal Navy, but by then the Canadians had shown the way by sending their boats across the Atlantic – the first such voyage by a submarine – and were in service in 1915. The first four, escorted by a warship, went straight on deployment in the Mediterranean, and the other six sailed to Britain escorted by a cruiser and support freighters.

With their up-to-date accommodation and facilities, these boats were very popular with their crews, and several of them were still serving in various navies in World War II. So successful was the H class that a further batch was ordered. They were to be built by Vickers at Barrow and were to be armed with the bigger 533mm/21in torpedo and fitted with a more powerful radio. Most of the components were shipped from America. A further 22 boats were ordered from various British shipbuilders in 1917, and most were delivered in 1918–19.

This completed a total fleet of 54 H boats in three groups, which until that point in time was only exceeded by the E class, although a number were not completed in time for action, and of those, eight American-built boats were ceded to the Canadian and Chilean Navy, the latter still running them in 1953 before they were scrapped.

LEFT: *H31* **was not completed in time for World War I, but was immediately in action in World War II and sank a U-boat on July 18, 1940. In December, she was involved in operations against the German battleship** *Scharnhorst* **near Brest, from which she failed to return, assumed mined.**

H class

Displacement: 369.82 tonnes/364 tons (surfaced); 440.94 tonnes/434 tons (submerged)
Length: 45.79m/150ft 3in
Beam: 4.80m/15ft 9in
Armament: 4 x 457mm/18in torpedo tubes (bow); 8 x torpedoes
Propulsion: 313.2kW/420hp diesel; 231.2kW/310ehp electric
Speed: 13 knots (surfaced); 10 knots (dived)
Complement: 22 crew

J class

The J-class submarine came into being because the Admiralty wanted a craft capable of sailing with the surface ships of the Grand Fleet at a speed of 21 knots on the surface. It was not to be achieved. Because of the extra power needed, the boat's length was increased by more than 50 per cent over the E class that it was intended to replace. An extra shaft and third diesel engine would be needed to try to increase the power. However, all this achieved was a bigger and heavier hull with an increase in speed of just four knots, bringing it up to 19 knots on the surface.

Once this became apparent the Admiralty turned their attention to the even larger K class, which was also under construction, and the J-class boats were reclassified as overseas boats. Eight J-class boats had been ordered in January 1915, but by April two had been cancelled. Another boat had been ordered with a modified design but, again, there was no great improvement in performance.

J7 had a different layout to others of the class, with the control room positioned between the two engine rooms and the conning tower built slightly further back, giving better access space for the bow torpedo tubes.

They operated from their base in Blyth with the Grand Fleet, but because of their insufficient performance saw little action. However, *J1* attacked four German warships with a salvo of torpedoes, seriously damaging the battleships *Kronprinz* and *Grosser Kurfurst*. At the end of World War I the six remaining J-class boats were transferred to the Royal Australian Navy.

TOP: **Most of the J-class boats were in action by mid-1916. *J1* had a spectacular initiation under Lt Commander Laurence when, sighting four battleships off Horns Reef, he fired four torpedoes and hit two enemy dreadnoughts.** ABOVE: **A profile of a J boat.** LEFT: ***J6* came to an unhappy end due to friendly fire, having been mistaken for *U6* and sunk by gunfire from the Q ship *Cymric* off Blyth on October 15, 1918. Fifteen survivors were picked up, but 19 other crewmen were killed.**

J class

Displacement: 1,223.26 tonnes/1,204 tons (surfaced); 1,849.12 tonnes/1,820 tons (submerged)
Length: 83.74m/274ft 9in
Beam: 7.16m/23ft 6in
Armament: 6 x 457mm/18in torpedo tubes (4 x bow, 2 x beam); 12 x torpedoes; 1 x 76mm/3in gun,1 x 12pdr gun, and depth charges
Propulsion: 3 x 894.8 kW/1,200bhp Vickers diesel engines; 3 x 335.6kW/450ehp electric motors
Speed: 19 knots (surfaced); 9.6 knots (dived)
Complement: 44 crew

Nautilus

This was the first Royal Navy submarine to be given a name, and in retrospect can be seen as a stepping stone to larger submarines. Designed with a double hull and increase in length, Nautilus' sea-keeping qualities, particularly in bad weather, were a great improvement on other submarines. Laid down in March 1913, she had an overall length of almost 79.2m/260ft, and was twice the size of any existing submarine. She was also the most expensive boat hitherto built by the Royal Navy, with costs escalating to almost £250,000.

Even so, there were a number of disappointing factors, especially in her speed, which did not meet the 17 knots on the surface called for in the design specifications. Her weaponry comprised two 457mm/18in bow torpedo tubes, four 457mm/18in beam tubes and two 457mm/18in stern tubes, with a combined load of 16 torpedoes carried. A 76mm/ 3in High-Angle gun was fitted on the superstructure just forward of the bridge, and this was raised and lowered on a vertical ram.

In the event, Nautilus never saw any active service and was used largely as a depot ship and for training purposes. However, there is no doubt that she provided a link in the British shipbuilding industry between the smaller boats and the great developments that followed in the quest for larger submarines.

The Admiralty was spurred on to seek better performances than 17 knots, and although engine performance was generally improving, as engines almost doubled in power during the building of these experimental boats, many difficulties and teething problems lay ahead. As for Nautilus, she was paid off in 1919 and sent to the scrap yard three years later.

ABOVE: **Nautilus, a large experimental boat built during World War I and described by the Royal Navy as an "exceedingly interesting" project, was ultimately a failure. She ended her days charging batteries for other submarines.**

Nautilus

Displacement: 1,464.06 tonnes/1,441 tons (surfaced); 2,058.42 tonnes/2,026 tons (submerged)
Length: 78.73m/258ft 4in
Beam: 7.92m/26ft
Armament: 8 x 457mm/18in tubes (2x bow, 4 x beam, 2 x stern), 16 x torpedoes; 1 x 76mm/3in deck gun
Propulsion: 2 x 1379.5kW/1,850bhp Vickers diesel engines; 2 x 372.8kW/500ehp electric motors
Speed: 17 knots (surfaced); 9 knots (dived)
Complement: 42 crew

LEFT: **The first of two boats named Swordfish. This one, built in 1916 (the other came with the 1930s S class), was an experimental steam turbine-powered submarine designed for long-range work, a development from the J class and the predecessor of the steam-powered K class.**

Swordfish

Swordfish was built as part of the Admiralty's ongoing attempt to have submarines which could keep up with the Grand Fleet on the surface at a speed of 21 knots, which was to be achieved by installing a remarkable steam-powered propulsion system, supposedly making her much safer. However, it became very hot inside.

During her trials it was discovered that despite having a mount which meant the gun could be stowed, an exposed gun created less water resistance than had been estimated in theory. The biggest disappointment was that the speed was hardly improved upon, and she had poor manoeuvrability, a dangerous failing

Swordfish

Displacement: 946.91 tonnes/932 tons (surfaced); 1,493.52 tonnes/1,470 tons (submerged)
Length: 70.48m/231ft 3in
Beam: 6.93m/22ft 9in
Armament: 2 x 533mm/21in tubes (bow), 4 x torpedoes; 4 x 457mm/18in tubes (beam), 8 x torpedoes; 2 x 76mm/3in guns
Propulsion: 2 x 1,491.4kW/2,000shp steam turbines; 2 x 1,044kW/1,400ehp electric motors
Speed: 18 knots (surfaced); 10 knots (dived)
Complement: 42 crew

when operating in company with the Grand Fleet. Eventually Swordfish was converted into a surface patrol boat and fitted with two 12pdr guns.

LEFT: *K26* was a new and improved version of the K class completed in 1923, but no others were built. She was noted for completing a successful journey to the Far East via Malta, through the Red Sea to Colombo, Singapore and back.

BELOW: The gunnery tasks on the K class become something of a nightmare, given the length of the boat, with ammunition stored in the bow and stern, thus requiring a long-distance haul by manpower.

K class

The obsession in certain quarters of the Admiralty for a fleet submarine that could operate with the Grand Fleet led to the K class. Designed to travel at 24 knots, it was also a reaction to a rumour around 1914 that the Germans had secretly developed a boat capable of 22 knots. With the current crop of petrol and diesel engines incapable of delivering the power required to drive a boat at that speed, steam power was chosen. As a production class, these were the largest and fastest submarines in the world with firepower to match, and such was the prestige surrounding them that ambitious officers cherished command of one of these boats – until the reality of sailing them hit home.

Initially they were armed with six torpedo tubes in the bow, four in the beam and three guns – but two of the bow tubes soon had to be removed to improve stability, followed by one of the guns. Even with a speed comparable to that of a destroyer, their manoeuvrability was a problem. Their turning circle was more like that of a dreadnought. They

were also slow to submerge and once under water difficult to control. Gunnery, too, was a problem as the guns were slow to bring to bear because of poor control and the ammunition being stored in the bow or the stern requiring a lot of men to get the shells to the guns.

Diving could take anything from three to five minutes because of the number of hatches, vents and other equipment which needed to be closed before the 28 ballast tanks could be blown – and this was another operation fraught with danger, to ensure the boat did not end up in a nosedive or submerge with a list. Forty valves had to be operated in a carefully-controlled manner.

It was also discovered that because of the speed at which the boats travelled on the surface with the Grand Fleet, the door shutters of the torpedo tubes were often unable to survive the high water pressure, which left the tubes fouled and inoperable. The crews who operated these boats became increasingly alarmed about their safety because of what they regarded as the vessels' poor seaworthiness.

Their forebodings were to prove correct as 16 major accidents and eight disasters hit the K-class fleet, costing lives and boats. On only one occasion did a K-class boat fire its torpedoes at the enemy when engaging a U-boat, and even then it missed.

K class

Displacement: 2,011.68 tonnes/1,980 tons (surfaced); 2,600.96 tonnes/2,560 tons (submerged)
Length: 103.32m/339ft
Beam: 8.07m/26ft 6in
Armament: 10 x 457mm/18in tubes, (4 x bow, 4 x beam, 2 x casing – later removed); 18 x torpedoes; 2 x 101mm/4in guns, 1 x 76mm/3in anti-aircraft gun
Propulsion: 1,193.1kW/1,600hp diesel; 4 x 536.9kW/720ehp electric motors
Speed: 24 knots (surfaced); 9 knots (dived)
Complement: 59 crew

L class

Unlike the K-class boats, the first batch of eight L class was developed from the successful E class, had increased speed, better range, and improved armament. They were equipped with six 457mm/18in torpedo tubes, four forward and two beam firing. A second batch of 26 L-class boats was then ordered, but only 18 of them were actually built. These were armed with four 533mm/21in torpedo tubes in the bow, which also necessitated lengthening of the boat. Six were then converted to minelayers, losing their beam tubes and replacing them with vertical chutes capable of launching 16 mines that were located in the saddle tanks.

A further 25 were then ordered, although only seven were delivered.

On these craft, the number of bow tubes was increased to six and the beam tubes were done away with altogether. Nearly all were fitted with a 101mm/4in gun, and the last batch had a rear-firing gun located in an enlarged conning tower. In May 1926, during the General Strike, L12 was one of several submarines used as an emergency electricity generator moored at the Royal Victoria and Albert Docks.

Popular with their crews, one of them – L8 – became known as "The Boat That Would Not Sink". Having survived two collisions in 1918, one of them with another L craft, she was towed into the Channel as a target in 1929 after being paid off when trials of new 119mm/4.7in ammunition were being carried out. After being hit several times, she

TOP: **The first of the L class were among the last to be commissioned in World War I, but they were a popular utility boat that continued on into the 1930s, although most were disposed of by the outbreak of war.** ABOVE: **The profile of** L23, **launched in 1919.**

remained afloat and was towed back to Portsmouth for further inspection before being finally scrapped. Although obsolete by the outbreak of World War II, L boats initially served operationally before being transferred to the training role and then taken to Canada to give anti-submarine training to convoy escorts. The last operational boat of this class, L23, was finally paid off in October 1945, and foundered off Nova Scotia while being towed to the breakers yard.

LEFT: **The firepower varied on the L class, and although they were designed to carry two 76.2mm/3in D/HA guns, most were only fitted with one.**

L class	
Displacement: 905.26 tonnes/891 tons (surfaced); 1,091.18 tonnes/1,074 tons (submerged)	
Length: 70.43m/231ft	
Beam: 7.15m/23ft 6in	
Armament: 6 x 457mm/18in tubes (4 x bow, 4 x beam),10 x torpedoes; 1 x 76mm/3in gun later replaced by a 101mm/4in gun	
Propulsion: 2 x 894.8kW/1,200bhp Vickers diesel engines; 4 x 298.3kW/400ehp electric motors	
Speed: 16.5 knots (surfaced); 10 knots (dived)	
Complement: 35 crew	

LEFT: *M2*, originally built with a 305mm/12in gun, was converted to carry aircraft by having a hangar installed in the empty space. A gantry was fitted to lift a Parnell Peto spotter plane. But disaster struck when the hangar doors were left open, and the submarine sank, with the loss of 60 men. ABOVE: The profile of the M class with the gun fitted.

M class

Admiral Sir John "Jackie" Fisher, the man who conceived the Dreadnought class of battleships, came up with the idea of a dreadnought submarine. He had little faith in the torpedoes of the day, believing they were incapable of stopping, let alone sinking, a warship.

These submarines would have a 305mm/12in gun forward of the conning tower similar to those fitted to the Majestic battleships. A smaller 76mm/3in gun would also be fitted as an anti-aircraft weapon. The main gun weighed 123.95 tonnes/122 tons, and 40 rounds – weighing a further 29.5 tonnes/29 tons –

were stowed. Then there was the gun crew – 11 specialist gunnery ratings plus 16 in the ammunition party for the main gun, plus another six for the anti-aircraft gun. One unexpected bonus was that all the additional weight made the boat very stable.

The gun mount had a non-watertight housing, and the mechanism for loading the shell and charge were inside a watertight tower. The gun had a range of 29,900m/32,699yds, and the boat had to surface to load and fire. Accuracy would be approximate because of the movement of the boat on the sea and the lack of an artillery spotter.

Approaching a target – whether afloat or on the enemy coast – the boat would pop up and down from periscope depth until it got into position. Then it could surface and fire between 30 and 40 seconds before disappearing back to periscope depth in a further 50 seconds. Although Admiral Fisher came up with the proposal in 1915, none of the three M-class boats was to fire its armament in anger. *M1* did not go to sea until 1919 and was joined by *M2* the following year. Although the gun was waterproofed at the muzzle end, it was not made watertight at the breech. Water in the barrel when firing was to prove disastrous, and at least four barrels were burst because of it.

The Washington Disarmament Treaty of 1920 meant that no submarine could have a gun larger than 203mm/8in, so *M2* and *M3* had their guns removed, with *M2* being converted to an aircraft carrier with a hangar constructed where the gun mount had been. She carried a single Parnell Peto aircraft specially designed for the project. She became the first submarine to have a watertight hangar which could be sealed when she was submerged. The boat was able to surface and launch its aircraft in around 12 minutes. However, in January 1932, one of the hatch doors was left open and she sank off Portland Bill, with the loss of her entire crew.

RIGHT: The attractive looking *M1*, leader of the class of three converted K boats was rammed and sunk by a Swedish collier in the English Channel in November 1925, with the loss of 69 crew.

M class

Displacement: 1,635.76 tonnes/1,610 tons (surfaced); 1,977.13 tonnes/1,946 tons (submerged)
Length: 90.14m/295ft 9in
Beam: 7.49m/25ft 7in
Armament: 4 x 483mm/19in tubes (bow), 10 x torpedoes; 1 x 305mm/12in gun, 1 x 76mm/3in anti-aircraft gun
Propulsion: 2 x 894.8kW/1,200bhp Vickers diesel engines; 4 x 596.6kW/800ehp electric motors
Speed: 15 knots (surfaced); 9 knots (dived)
Complement: 64 crew

LEFT: **With a streamlined shape, the first R-class boats were built for speed underwater, and this was achieved. However, there were setbacks in other areas of production, and although ten were built at considerable expense, all were scrapped within eight years.**

R class (Early)

Displacement: 421.64 tonnes/415 tons (surfaced); 513.08 tonnes/505 tons (submerged)
Length: 49.91m/163ft 9in
Beam: 4.61m/15ft 1in
Armament: 6 x 457mm/18in tubes (bow), 12 x torpedoes
Propulsion: 1 x 179kW/240bhp American diesel engine; 2 x 894.8kW/1,200bhp electric motors
Speed: 10 knots (surfaced); 15 knots (dived)
Complement: 22 crew

R class (Early)

These boats were the first anti-submarine submarines, or what today are called hunter-killers. Entering service with the Royal Navy in 1917 they were designed to be quicker submerged than when surfaced. This they achieved with a speed of 15 knots that was not to be bettered until the latter stages of World War II, more than a quarter of a century later. The R class had six 457mm/18in torpedo tubes in the bow,

and although it had originally been intended to mount a 101mm/4in gun, this was omitted in order to keep the weight down. The superstructure was as light as possible and ballast tanks were internal to keep the shape streamlined.

This boat also had problems. Although fitted with two powerful 895kW/1,200bhp electric motors, which enabled it to reach 15 knots when submerged, the 179kW/240bhp diesel engine was not strong

enough to charge the 220 batteries, and because of this lack of power, it was a difficult craft to steer on the surface. In addition to the periscope, the boats had five primitive hydrophones to assist with detecting enemy submarines.

The boats only ever mounted one attack on a German U-boat, and the torpedo failed to explode. Of the 12 ordered, 10 were built and all were paid off by 1925.

LEFT: **A profile of the twin-turreted *X1* cruiser submarine with six torpedo tubes – a brilliant-looking boat that promised great potential, but was a disappointment in the end.**

X1

Displacement: 2,824.48 tonnes/2,779.9 tons (surfaced); 3,657.6 tonnes/3,599.8 tons (submerged)
Length: 106.68m/350ft
Beam: 9.07m/29ft 9in
Armament: 6 x 533mm/21in tubes (bow); 12 x torpedoes; 2 x twin 132mm/5.25in guns
Propulsion: 2 x 2,237.1kW/3,000bhp MAN diesel engines; 2 x 969.4kW/1,300ehp electric motors and 1 x 894.8kW/1,200bhp diesel generator
Speed: 19 knots (surfaced); 9 knots (dived)
Complement: 109 crew

X1 class

Only one X1-class boat was ever built – the biggest submarine in the Royal Navy until the nuclear boats came into service decades later. Although conceived by the Royal Navy Submarine Committee in 1915 as a cruiser submarine armed with big guns as well as torpedoes, she was not laid down until November 1921. Dyed-in-the-wool naval planners still wanted submarines operating as part of the Grand Fleet, but submarine warfare experts wanted her to be able to operate in an independent role – a large, fast boat operating at extended ranges. At 2,824 tonnes/2,779 tons on the surface, she was certainly that. After World War I the navy had time

and opportunity to carefully examine captured German submarines, including their cruiser submarines. She would also be the first new boat since the war.

X1 was completed in September 1925, joined the Navy the following spring and was the largest submarine in the world at that time. She was sent on a return trip to Gibraltar but problems arose with her diesel engines, and she was sent back to the RN Dockyard at Chatham for repairs.

The following January she passed all her tests and was assigned to the Mediterranean Fleet, but within a year she again had engine trouble, this time in Malta. There were other niggles, too.

Officers claimed that she handled well and that most of her problems were because of crew errors. *X1* was laid up in reserve in 1933 and scrapped three years later – the only Royal Navy submarine built after World War I that did not survive until World War II.

O class

These were long-range submarines based on the L class and designed to operate in Far Eastern waters as concerns grew about Japanese intentions after failure to renew the Anglo–Japanese Alliance in 1922. The first one became *Oberon*, and although 2 knots slower than the L class, the hull was 12m/39ft 4in longer and they could carry double the number of torpedoes. Their range was also nearly double that of their predecessor. In addition, their wireless range was better and diving depth was deeper. The 101mm/4in gun mounted on the front of the conning tower was later modified to be fitted on a revolving mount. *Oberon* was also the first boat to be fitted with the ASDIC submarine detection system, which evolved into today's sonar.

An O-class boat, *Oxley*, became the first Royal Navy submarine to be lost in World War II when another submarine, *Triton*, mistakenly torpedoed her off the Norwegian coast in 1939. It was only when two survivors were plucked from the water that the true horror unfolded. *Triton* had been signalling *Oxley*, but when no recognition signal was received, assumed her to be an enemy U-boat and torpedoed her. With the recovery of the crewmen, they discovered *Oxley* had been returning the signals but her signal lamp was faulty. A full-scale cover-up was ordered, and it was not until the 1950s that the true account of what happened was released. At the time,

ABOVE: *Otway*, *Oberon* and *Oxley*, a trio of O-class boats built in two groups from the late 1920s, including two that joined the Australian Royal Navy but which returned for wartime duties. LEFT: Chile later bought and modified O-class boats, and renamed them as O'Brien class.

a cover story was put out that she had suffered an accidental explosion.

Oberon and *Otway* both went on operations in World War II, but were later transferred to a training role. A second batch of six O-class boats were fitted with a more powerful diesel engine that gave them a higher surface speed, and their hydroplanes were moved from the bottom of the pressure hull to the top and hinged so they could be turned in when not in use. Although this increased dive time, it eradicated a lot of the

damage they suffered when the boat was submerged for long periods of time.

As the Germans tightened their stranglehold on the strategic Mediterranean island of Malta by sea and air, causing havoc among the convoys trying to supply the beleaguered garrison, the O-class boats – the first to be given names instead of numbers – joined other large submarines to run the gauntlet underwater by ferrying in vital supplies of ammunition, aviation fuel, torpedoes, food and fresh water.

LEFT: *Oberon*, the class leader commissioned in 1927, was rather troublesome, suffering breakdowns that forced her into reserve status until she was brought out for war duty and then scrapped. She gave her name to the Oberon class of the 1960s.

O class

Displacement: 1,513.84 tonnes/1,489.9 tons (surfaced); 1,922.27 tonnes/1,891.9 tons (submerged)
Length: 82.19m/269ft 8in
Beam: 8.53m/28ft
Armament: 8 x 533mm/21in tubes (6 x bow, 2 x stern), 16 x torpedoes; 1 x 101mm/4in gun
Propulsion: 2 x 1,006.7kW/1,350bhp Admiralty diesel engines; 2 x 484.7kW/650ehp electric motors
Speed: 13.5 knots (surfaced); 7.5 knots (dived)
Complement: 53 crew

LEFT: *Pandora* was engaged in running supplies to Malta and was unloading when an enemy bombing raid began. Her crew courageously carried on only to receive two direct hits from bombs, and she sank on April 1, 1942. BELOW: HMS *Perseus* was mined off Cephallonia, leaving a sole survivor from the crew of 51 to tell the tale.

Parthian class

Like the O class before them, boats of the Parthian class were prone to leaking fuel from their saddle tanks when submerged, which then left a giveaway smear across the ocean's surface. The leaks were caused by the pressure on the riveted tanks. One of the boats, *Poseidon*, was lost after colliding with a Chinese coaster in the Yellow Sea in June 1931, but 35 of the 57-man crew managed to survive by taking part in the first big escape from a submarine using the Davis Submarine Escape Apparatus.

During the siege of Malta in 1941–42, Parthian-class boats *Pandora* and *Parthian* along with other submarines were used as supply craft. A section of their batteries was removed and their spare torpedoes left behind to create additional space for stores for the garrison to be carried. Petrol and other fuels were also ferried in, and fresh water was stored in the ballast tanks.

One of the most remarkable escape and survival stories of World War II involved *Perseus*, which struck an Italian mine in the Ionian Sea. Leading Stoker John Capes and four other survivors were trapped in the submarine at a depth of 52m/171ft. Their only means of escape was the Davis Apparatus. After downing a bottle of rum for courage, they began their escape attempt, but only Capes made it to the surface alive. Exhausted, he managed to struggle a further 8–10km/5–6 miles to the island of Cephalonia, where he was found by locals who looked after him before handing him over to the Resistance. It took 18 months for him to reach home, and he was awarded the British Empire Medal. There were sceptics who did not accept his account

of his escape. It was not until 1998 that the wreck of the *Perseus* was located with all the evidence, including the empty rum bottle. Capes went on to become a Chief Petty Officer, but, sadly, he died ten years before the wreck was found and his story verified.

One of the most deadly of the Parthian-class boats was *Proteus*, which had spent the pre-war years in the Far East. Deployed to the Mediterranean with other large submarines to help Malta, she was eventually sent back to Britain in 1943, but not before she had damaged or sunk 11 Italian transports.

LEFT: *Parthian* led the P class to China and then to the Mediterranean when war broke out. She is known to have sunk two Italian submarines, the Vichy French submarine *Souffleur* and other Italian vessels before she was herself posted lost, presumed mined in 1943.

Parthian class

Displacement: 1,796.29 tonnes/1,767.9 tons (surfaced); 2,067.56 tonnes/2,034.9 tons (submerged)
Length: 88.13m/289ft 2in
Beam: 9.12m/29ft 11in
Armament: 8 x 533mm/21in tubes (6 x bow, 2 x stern), 14 x torpedoes; 1 x 101mm/4in gun
Propulsion: 2 x 1,730kW/2,320bhp Admiralty diesel engines; 2 x 492.1kW/660ehp electric motors
Speed: 18 knots (surfaced); 8.5 knots (dived)
Complement: crew

LEFT: **HMS** *Scorcher* **was a late arrival in the large class of more than 60 S-class boats. Classic workhorses of World War II, although many were not commissioned until the latter stages, some, like** *Scorcher*, **remained in service for 20 years or more.** BELOW: **A profile of Group III S-class boat,** *Storm*.

S class

The S boats carried out some of the most daring and dangerous and, at times, most celebrated operations of World War II. With an increased capability in speed, range and depth, they were quicker to dive and were also the first boats to have escape hatches located both fore and aft, something which was to save the lives of many submariners as the war grew in intensity and they operated in some very hostile environments.

Slightly smaller than some other classes, they were able to operate in shallower and more confined waters. The first four boats joined the fleet in 1932–33 and were equipped with a 76mm/3in gun positioned in a forward extension of the conning tower that was stowed before diving. A second batch of eight boats was ordered with the gun mounted on the casing, which meant the conning tower could be reduced in height, although a small extension to the front served as an ammunition bunker. The next tranche of these craft began production at the outbreak of the war, and production continued throughout, with variations to lines and equipment as innovations were discovered. Eventually, instead of being riveted or part-riveted, the hulls were all welded. Air-warning radio direction finders, ASDIC, external stern tubes and more powerful anti-aircraft guns were introduced.

In addition to the German threat, these submarines suffered so-called "friendly fire" attacks from RAF aircraft, other submarines and, occasionally, Royal Navy ships. A lot of the British torpedoes were also found to be faulty, a problem shared by the German U-boat packs. An S-class submarine, *Sturgeon*, carried out the first successful Royal Navy submarine attack of the war when she sank the anti-submarine trawler *V209* off Heligoland in November 1939. In addition, *Salmon* carried out the first successful attack on a U-boat, sinking *U36* three weeks later. Just over a week later, she attacked a formation of German warships, hitting the light cruisers *Leipzig* and *Nurnberg*. *Spearfish* attacked and damaged the German pocket battleship *Lützow*, leaving her helpless with her propellers and steering gear out of action. *Lützow* had to be towed to port and was out of action for a year. However, the success was not one-sided and many brave men were lost with their boats after clashes with U-boats, aircraft and surface craft. Others perished when their boats struck mines.

Seraph was certainly the most famous of these boats, particularly after the war, with two films made about her exploits: the first, *The Man Who Never Was*, and the second, *The Ship With Two Captains*. The boats were also used to gather intelligence about possible landing sites for various operations to liberate Europe from the Germans.

RIGHT: **A quartet of S-class boats,** *Shark*, *Sunfish*, *Snapper* **and** *Sealion*, **of whom sadly only the latter survived the war.**

S class Group 1

Displacement: 650.24 tonnes/640 tons (surfaced); 941.83 tonnes/927 tons (submerged)
Length: 61.72m/202ft 6in
Beam: 7.31m/24ft
Armament: 6 x 533mm/21in tubes, 12 x torpedoes; 1 x 76mm/3in gun
Propulsion: 2 x 1,156kW/1,550hp diesel, 2 x 969kW/1,300 electric
Speed: 13.5 knots (surfaced); 10 knots (dived)
Complement: 38 crew

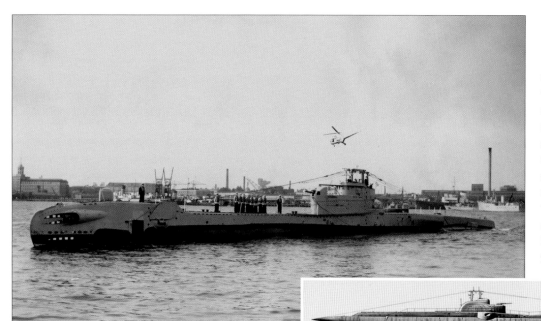

LEFT: "T" for "tremendous". A brilliant class of British boats, the T class came in abundance, saw great war service and continued on for 20 years or more. *Tally Ho*, for example, became the first T-class boat to cross the Atlantic on snorkel. BELOW: Profile of a T-class boat of the 1942 vintage.

T class

The T class were the first British submarines to have their fuel tanks inside the hull, which eradicated the problems caused by leaking fuel leaving a trail across the sea's surface. Intended to replace the O, P and R classes and 406 tonnes/400 tons smaller, they were superior in nearly every respect to those they were succeeding. They had better armament and two more torpedo tubes, and their all-welded hull meant that the boats were much stronger and able to dive deeper to escape attack and counter-attack. The London Naval Treaty of 1935 had placed restrictions on Britain's submarine ambitions, so these craft had to be constructed within the rules laid down.

There was a slight loss of speed, for example, as the size of the submarine was limited by the treaty, so larger engines could not be fitted. A variety of engines were used to try to improve performance, but with the outbreak of war only Admiralty or Vickers diesels were fitted. One batch of this class even featured 11 torpedo tubes plus a 20mm/0.79in anti-aircraft gun and 7.7mm/0.303 machine-guns.

One of the T class, *Thetis*, was at the centre of one of the most tragic episodes in Royal Navy submarine history when she sank while on trials in Liverpool Bay in 1939 with more than 100 people aboard, including shipyard workers, office staff and others there to celebrate the chance to sail in a submarine. Another T-class boat, *Tetrarch*, attacked a large merchantman in the North Sea, whereupon she was the subject of a very hostile counter-attack by the escorts. Forced to dive deep, she reached 120m/394ft and stayed there for 43 hours.

Triton attacked a German convoy taking part in the occupation of Norway, with a salvo of six torpedoes hitting the *Friedenau*, *Wigbert* and *V1507*, killing 900 German troops who were being sent to occupy the country. *Thistle* attacked U-boat *U4* in the North Sea in April 1940 unsuccessfully – but a few days later *U4* caught *Thistle* on the surface and sank her with the loss of all hands. T boats were heavily involved in the Mediterranean and in the Far East, scoring some spectacular results against the Japanese fleet, particularly *Trenchant* which fired a salvo of all eight of her

LEFT: Wartime T-class boats carried a 102mm/4in guns, and later in the war, three machine-guns were added.

ABOVE: **A typical T boat patch.** RIGHT: **An impressive whole boat view of HMS *Thorough*, the first Royal Navy submarine to circumnavigate the globe, when she travelled to Australia through the Mediterranean and the Suez Canal and returned via the Panama Canal.**

bow torpedoes at the Japanese heavy cruiser *Ashigara*. Five struck home, blowing away the bows and setting the ship ablaze before she sank.

Truant was the only Royal Navy submarine to sink enemy ships in three different theatres – Home, Mediterranean and Far East – sinking almost 81,284 tonnes/80,000 tons of enemy shipping. Before that, she was returning from a refit in America when she spotted a Norwegian ship acting suspiciously. *Truant's* captain discovered that the ship had already been boarded and was under the command of a German prize crew. As well as this, there were captured British survivors from the SS *Braxby* on board. The British crew were taken aboard *Truant*, along with the captain and his wife, the latter of whom became the first woman to sail in a submarine.

In February 1945, *Tantalus* completed the longest wartime patrol, during which she travelled 18,507km/11,500 miles in 55 days. One of the most bizarre stories surrounding a T-class boat came when *Totem* visited Canada and was in turn visited by members of the Cowichan Indian tribe, who presented the boat with a small totem pole. The sailors were told the totem pole had magic properties provided by the carvings of the thunderbird, grizzly bear, killer whale and Fire God, and while the totem remained on board no harm would come to Totem. The boat was transferred to the Israeli Navy and renamed *Dakar* in 1964 and the carved totem placed on display in the Royal Naval Museum in Gosport. In January 1968, *Dakar* was lost in the Mediterranean. In 1957, *Thorough* became the first submarine to circumnavigate the world.

LEFT: **Thermopylae was among the last of the T boats to be built, thus benefiting from the extensive modifications that were progressively applied to the class, especially in electronics and crew spaces.**

T class

Displacement: 1,326.90 tonnes/1,306 tons (surfaced); 1,597.15 tonnes/1572 tons (submerged)
Length: 84m/275ft 7in
Beam: 8.1m/26ft 7in
Armament: 10 x 457mm/21in tubes (8 x bow, 2 x beam – 5 of them external),16 x torpedoes; 1 x 101mm/4in gun
Propulsion: 2 x 1,864kW/2,500hp diesel, 2 x 1,081kW/1,450 electric
Speed: 16.25 knots (surfaced); 9.25 knots (dived)
Complement: 55 crew

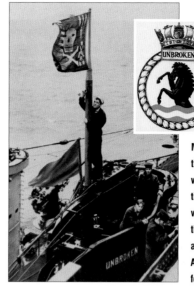

U class

FAR LEFT: **The British U-class boats were heroes of World War II. They saw extensive action and became the scourge of the Italian Navy in the Mediterranean.** LEFT: **Naturally, the raising of the Jolly Roger was a common sight at the time, as seen here by** *Unbroken*, **which torpedoed and damaged the Italian cruisers** *Bolzano* **and** *Muzio Attendolo* **on August 13, 1942.** INSET: **A patch for** *Unbroken*.

Originally designed as unarmed target submarines between the two world wars, the Admiralty quickly changed its mind as alarm bells began to sound across Europe, and it was decided to give them torpedo tubes so they could be used for training crews meant to man the much larger T-class boats. Only three of these boats had been completed by the outbreak of World War II, but their design was so simple it was easy to increase production. Moreover, their small size was considered an advantage for operating in difficult coastal waters, and they proved to be highly successful.

At the outset, the boats had six torpedo tubes with two in an external bulbous bow, but this shape caused wake problems, reduced visibility at periscope depth and was changed by removing the extra two tubes in later models. With fuel and ballast within the pressure hull and diesel-electric power, the shaft was driven at all times by the electric motors, with the diesel engine used on the surface to power the generator that, in turn, topped up the batteries and fed the motor.

The first to be commissioned was *Undine*, which was also the first to be lost when she attacked three German minesweepers in the Heligoland Bight. Her salvo missed, but the torpedo trail gave the enemy a fix on her position, and they counter-attacked. *Undine* dived and, after thinking it safe to return to periscope depth, she did so only to be hit by an explosion that wrecked the hydroplanes. Out of control, the crew had little option but to abandon ship, scuttling the boat with an explosive charge as they left.

U-class boats made a significant contribution to the war effort, particularly *Upholder*, commanded by Lt Cdr Malcolm David Wanklyn, VC, DSO, who sank or damaged 22 enemy ships totalling well over 101,605 tonnes/ 100,000 tons.

Another remarkable boat, *Unbroken*, used her last four torpedoes to attack an Italian heavy cruiser and a light cruiser which had been bombarding Allied convoys trying to get supplies to Malta. Attacking from close range, she put both ships out of action for the remainder of the war. The escorting Italian destroyers reacted with fury, unleashing a barrage of more than 100 depth charges to try to hit *Upholder*, who survived the onslaught and quietly slipped away to Malta.

Unbroken was eventually loaned to the Russian Navy, and several other U-class boats were loaned to other Allied navies. As soon as the war in Europe ended, the U class lost their operational role and reverted to being used as training craft.

LEFT: **The loading of torpedoes and armaments into** *Ursula* **prior to another patrol, possibly when she hit the Italian liner** *Vulcania*, **being used for troop transport in September 1941.**

U class

Displacement: 636 tonnes/626 tons (surfaced); 739.65 tonnes/728 tons (submerged)
Length: 58.21m/191ft
Beam: 4.88m/16ft
Armament: 6 x 533mm/21in tubes (bow – 2 x external), 10 torpedoes; 1 x 76mm/3in gun
Propulsion: 2 x 298.3kW/400bhp Davy Paxman diesel engines; 2 x 307.2kW/412ehp General Electric motors
Speed: 12.5 knots (surfaced); 10 knots (dived)
Complement: 30 crew

LEFT: **It was a great tragedy that *Porpoise* became the last British submarine to be sunk in hostile action in World War II, after laying mines in the vicinity of Penang, leaving a tell-tale trail of oil sighted by a Japanese spotter plane.**

Porpoise class

Porpoise class

Displacement: 1,792.22 tonnes/1,763.9 tons (surfaced); 2,068.58 tonnes/2,035.9 tons (submerged)
Length: 87.78m/288ft
Beam: 9.12m/29ft 11in
Armament: 6 x 533mm/21in tubes, 12 x torpedoes; 50 x mines (although more could be carried in place of torpedoes); 1 x 101mm/4in gun
Propulsion: 2 x 1,230.4kW/1,650bhp Admiralty diesel engines; 2 x 607.7kW/815ehp electric motors
Speed: 15 knots (surfaced); 8 knots (dived)
Complement: 59 crew

These boats, the Royal Navy's submarine minelayers, went about their business in perilous coastal waters which often left them vulnerable to danger from land, sea, air and their own deadly cargo. Of the six built, four were lost and one captured. Founded on the experience gained with *M3*, the boats featured a chain conveyor and rail system atop the pressurized hull that could carry 50 Mk XVI mines. Because of the extra space intended for mine-carrying, the Porpoise boats were pressed into service to carry vital supplies to the beleaguered island of Malta in 1941–42, with fuel, ammunition and other material occupying the space reserved for the mines.

With the development of a special submarine mine which could be launched using the 533mm/21in torpedo tubes, other Porpoise boats were cancelled. *Rorqual* laid minefields in both the North Sea and Mediterranean, and *Seal*, spotted laying a minefield, was attacked by a German aircraft which also alerted anti-submarine craft. However, before they could reach her *Seal* struck a mine and sank, becoming embedded in the mud on the sea floor. After a struggle she freed herself, but as soon as she returned to the surface, she was attacked, forcing the crew to surrender.

By the end of hostilities, the Porpoise-class minelayers had laid more than 2,500 mines, with only *Rorqual* surviving to the end of the war.

LEFT: ***X25*, one of the last of the midget submarines to be built in Britain, after some challenging operations and an exceedingly creditable history.**

X-craft

X-craft

Displacement: 30.48 tonnes/30 tons (surfaced); 33.02 tonnes/32.5 tons (submerged)
Length: 13.26m/43ft 6in
Beam: 2.44m/8ft
Armament: 2 x containers with 1,620kg/3,571.5lb of explosives; Limpet mines
Propulsion: 1 x 31.3kW/42bhp Perkins diesel engine; 1 x 18.6kW/25ehp electric motor
Speed: 6.5 knots (surfaced); 4.5 knots (dived)
Complement: 3–4 crew

Initially, when Winston Churchill was First Lord of the Admiralty, he and the Admiralty looked down their noses at the concept of midget submarines. They were dangerous and the sort of power a weaker nation would employ – certainly not the Royal Navy! However, come World War II and the German threat to both British shipping and the country itself, particularly from the massive German warships operating with seeming impunity from the fjords of occupied Norway, the Admirals began hailing midget submarines as the solution.

Built, developed and trialled under conditions of great secrecy, the midget submarines were crewed by a special breed of men, many of whom were to lose their lives in the service of their country as they struck at German capital ships and installations in seemingly impregnable locations.

After World War II, many films and books were made about the gallant men of the X-craft. Not only did they face the dangers of enemy fire, but they also had to brave minefields, anti-submarine nets, acoustic alarms and other perils just to reach their target before dropping their explosives and trying to find their way out again to rendezvous with their escorts.

For their gallantry in wartime, X-craft crews won 4 Victoria Crosses, 11 DSOs, 17 DSCs, 12 DSMs, 6 CGMs, 4 BEMs, 3 CBEs, 1 OBE, 10 MBEs and 27 Mentions in Despatches.

LEFT: *U14* was commissioned in 1912 with the altered specifications introduced with *U13*, but while serving as part of the I Flotilla, she was damaged by gunfire from the armed trawler *Oceanic II* and sank off Peterhead, with one member of crew killed and 27 rescued. BELOW: *U9*, noted for reloading torpedoes while submerged, for the first time in history, and later for sinking three British cruisers, *Aboukir*, *Hogue* and *Cressy* within an hour.

U1 (Early)

German shipbuilders were producing submarines for the Russian Navy a full two years before the first of what would prove to be a long and successful progression of U-boats made her appearance. *U1* was launched from the Germaniaweft yard in August 1906, and commissioned primarily for trials and evaluation by the Imperial German Navy. Already larger than the British and American counterparts of the A and B classes, *U1* did not, however, impress her own Naval chiefs. They complained that her displacement rendered her unfit for operations any distance from the coast, and modifications began immediately. Even so, *U1* was the precursor to 375 U-boats of three principal classes ranging through 29 different types available for World War I. These new offerings also came with the distinct advantage of a heavy oil motor that precluded the internal problems experienced by petrol-driven engines. However, the downside of this

development was that the boat billowed smoke and sparks from a rear-mounted upper-deck exhaust system, emissions that were more on a par with a steamer. Thus, any opposition would have no problem in tracking her on the surface.

This was soon to be modified with a development that dramatically changed surface propulsion forever, with the introduction of diesel engines for the bulk of the U-boats built by Germany. *U1* did impress in other areas, however, and notable among her early trials was a 1,087km/587-nautical-mile endurance test from Wilhelmshaven that took her around Denmark and back to Kiel in exceedingly dire conditions. Based upon these findings, Germany initiated a rapid programme of development and innovation, and by 1911, U-boats had progressed from 42.4m/139ft to 57.3m/188ft in length with subsequent upgrades in both speed, endurance and firepower, increasing her torpedo payload from one to four tubes, two bow and two stern. Further types in this series emerged with additional design improvements through to *U18*.

The fortune of war, however, did not favour these early submarines of the Imperial Navy. Four days after the United Kingdom declared war on the German Empire on August 4, 1914, ten boats, *U5*, *U7*, *U8*, *U9*, *U13*, *U14*, *U15*, *U16*, *U17* and *U18* were despatched to launch an audacious attack on the British Grand Fleet at Scapa Flow. Two boats, *U5* and *U9*, had to return to port with engine trouble, *U13* was lost without trace, and *U15* went down with all hands after being rammed by the British cruiser HMS *Birmingham* in the North Sea on August 9,

LEFT: **Loading torpedoes on the World War I training boat *U25*, which survived the war to be surrendered and broken up at Canning Town in 1922.**

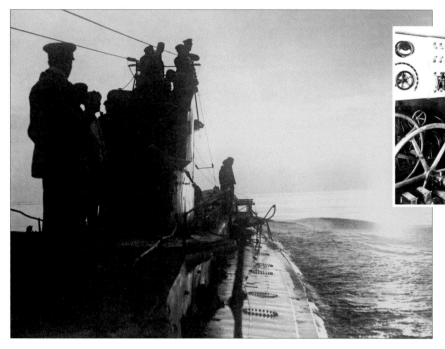

LEFT: **A classic silhouette of** *U35*, **one of the most successful boats of World War I, which, during 17 patrols with the II Flotilla in August 1915, is credited with sinking 224 ships for a total of 548,402 tonnes/539,741 tons, and survived the conflict, to be surrendered and broken up at Blyth.** ABOVE: **An internal view of the engine room.**

1914. This unpromising start was soon to be repealed. On July 16, 1914, the ageing *U9*, commanded by Otto Weddigen, became famous in the German submarine fraternity by performing a torpedo reload while submerged, for the first time in history. Weddigen began drilling his crews in fast reloads by moving members of his crew forward then aft while the ballast was regulated. On September 22, he used this technique to sink three British cruisers in an hour. It was an unique achievement in that after the first strike, the other British ships sailed to assist the stricken vessel thinking that it had hit a mine, unaware of *U9*'s presence. The succession of strikes occurred at 07:20 hours (*Aboukir*), 07:55 hours

(*Hogue*) and 08:20 hours (*Cressy*), each one with a single shot, and claiming a total of 1,400 lives. A few days later, *U9* torpedoed another British cruiser, *Hawke*, and in doing so, this one submarine had killed more British sailors than were lost by Lord Nelson in all his battles put together.

As for *U1*, although no wartime patrols are recorded, she survived the conflict and was decommissioned in the post-war surrender of German U-boats to the Allies. She was thereafter sliced in two and retained for posterity in the *Deutsches Museum* in Munich. The improvements achieved in the designs in the first 18 boats prior to the introduction of diesel propulsion can be seen by comparing the specifications below.

ABOVE: **A U-boat flotilla (left to right):** *U13* **was lost with all hands in 1914;** *U5* **survived the war after 22 patrols;** *U11* **was a training boat;** *U3* **was a training boat which surrendered in 1918 but sank on the way to the UK; and** *U16* **sank ten ships during the war, then sank on the way to surrendering.**

U1

Displacement: 234 tonnes/230.3 tons (surfaced);
278 tonnes/273.6 tons (submerged)
Length: 42.39m/139ft
Beam: 3.75m/12ft 4in
Armament: 1 x 450mm/17.7in tube (bow),
3 x torpedoes
Propulsion: 298.3kW/400hp heavy oil;
298.3kW/400hp electric
Speed: 10.8 knots (surfaced); 8.7 knots (dived)
Complement: 12 crew (22, then 28 on larger
types)

U18

Displacement: 555 tonnes/546.2 tons (surfaced);
680 tonnes/669.3 tons (submerged)
Length: 62.35m/204ft 7in
Beam: 6m/19ft 8in
Armament: 6 x 450mm/17.7in tubes (2 x bow,
2 x stern); 1 x 10.5cm/4.13in deck gun

RIGHT: **Impressively sleek for the era and suitably menacing, an array of early German submarines, from left to right in the front row, *U22*, *U20*, *U19* and *U21* pictured at Keil harbour, part of Germany's High Seas Fleet of 20 boats at the beginning of World War I. They were subsequently deployed as a defensive screen in the North Sea.** ABOVE: **Profile of *U21*, the first U-boat to sink a British warship, the cruiser HMS *Pathfinder*.**

U19: diesel

Innovations in U-boat construction continued at a rapid pace with the first four U-boats designed specifically for the ocean-going hunter role, entering service from 1913 with the leader boat of this type, *U19*.

Her commissioning brought another landmark in submarine development in that she was the first to be manufactured with a diesel engine, so-called after the German engineer who invented it. Even so, by 1914 Germany had only 24 boats in service, four others under repair or seconded to a training role and another 17 under construction, representing one of the smallest fleets among the major powers.

However, it had become clear that coming late to submarine warfare had enabled the Germans to learn from the costly lessons experienced by other navies, at least in design if not immediately in operational tactics. This benefit was beginning to show in the development of their first oceanic boats whose clear aim would be to attack merchant ships in wartime.

New targets had been set for endurance and surface speed, and it became evident, not least in the use and placement of deck guns, that these were to become an important element in surface operations against merchant shipping. Some boats of the new class were equipped with top-mounted guns that folded neatly away after operations, thus allowing greater speed.

It was also a noticeable tactic in the first ship attacks that torpedoes were only used on high profile targets. One such target appeared in the periscope vision of *U21* commander Otto Hersing off the Scottish coast on September 5, 1914. He opened fire to become the first submarine to release a torpedo in anger in World War I. The victim was the British light cruiser, *Pathfinder*.

Hersing went on to become one of the most successful U-boat commanders, sinking or disabling almost 40 ships in 21 patrols over the next three years, a run that included Allied battleships while assigned to assist the Turks during the Gallipoli crisis.

More famously, a sister ship in this class, *U20*, torpedoed the Cunard liner *Lusitania* on May 7, 1915, with the loss of nearly 1,200 passengers and crew.

RIGHT: **Given the prolific success record of *U35*, the submarine was also leading the league table of torpedoes fired. This series of U-boats carried only six torpedoes, so it required a constant re-supply, often at sea.**

U19	
Displacement: 546.25 tonnes/537.6 tons (surfaced); 669.25 tonnes/658.7 tons (submerged)	
Length: 62.35m/204ft 7in	
Beam: 6.10m/20ft	
Armament: 6 x 457mm/18in tubes; 1x 10.5cm/4.13in deck gun	
Propulsion: 1,305kW/1,750hp diesel; 894.8kW/1,200hp electric	
Speed: 15.4 knots (surfaced); 9.5 knots (dived)	
Complement: 35 crew	

U81

By 1914, Germany's U-boat fleet had numerically reached *U38* but as the war progressed, production doubled and then trebled, along with numerous changes in type, layout and variations of armament. However, the key to German submarine expansion was the drive for longer-range boats, introduced in numerous types built in small classes, which consequently allowed the introduction of new features and capabilities. By 1916, the series of 46 Mittel-type boats that began with *U81* was well underway, providing ever-increasing endurance and firepower, which enabled the expansion of operations outward from European waters into the Atlantic and ultimately in threatening posturing towards the east coast of America.

The capabilities of these boats were geared towards long patrols, packed to the gills with torpedoes. The 813-tonne/800-ton U81 series carried ten torpedoes and a substantial deck armoury to a range of up to 12,070km/7,500 miles, while their successors in the U90 and U100 series could take up to 16 torpedoes, although their endurance was significantly lower.

Given the possibilities for causing huge damage to the British, the Germans declared unrestricted warfare on February 29, 1916, under which enemy armed vessels could be attacked anywhere and merchant ships in the war zone could be attacked without warning.

This was curtailed only after strong protests from the Americans following the sinking of passenger vessels and the death of American citizens.

The retraction once again forestalled American entry into the war, but it had little effect on the mounting U-boat toll as the German submarine fleet continued to expand both numerically and in capability. *U81*, for example, sank 31 ships – excluding enemy warships – of

ABOVE: **An interesting view of *U117*, a minelayer of the UE2 class of which nine boats were commissioned. Although not operational until March 1918, she sank 24 Allied vessels** (warships excluded). **She was surrendered to the Americans and was used for exhibitions.**
ABOVE LEFT: **A profile of Type U139, a cruiser merchant class of which three were built.**

91,444 tonnes/90,000 tons on just four patrols, between October 1916 and May 1917, before she herself was sunk by the British boat *E24* off the west coast of Ireland, while *U90* took down 35 ships in the last year of the war.

ABOVE: **The mechanics of the ocean minelayer *U117*, capable of carrying 42 mines, as well as 14 torpedoes, thus providing not only greater firepower but also endurance at sea.**

U81

Displacement: 795 tonnes/782.4 tons (surfaced); 934 tonnes/919.2 tons (submerged)
Length: 70.06m/229ft 10in
Beam: 6.30m/20ft 8in
Armament: 6 x 508mm/20in tubes (4 x bow, 2 x stern), 16 x torpedoes; 1 x 8.8cm/3.46in and 1 x 10.5cm/4.13in deck guns
Propulsion: 1,789.7kW/2,400hp diesel; 894.8kW/1,200hp electric
Speed: 16.8 knots (surfaced); 9.4 knots (dived)
Complement: 39 crew

LEFT: **Class leader** *UB1*. **Built primarily for coastal work, although they did not come into production until the start of the war, they certainly made up for lost time in terms of patrols completed. A total of more than 100 patrols was not uncommon, although the casualty rate was high.**
BELOW: **A profile of a UB-class boat.**

UB classes I, II and III

While remarkable advances were being achieved by Germany in the construction of larger, long-range boats, there was a yawning gap in the coverage of areas where endurance and range were less critical. With a build time of up to 18 months for ocean-going U-boats, in the interests of sheer expediency, a smaller boat was required to undertake missions closer to home. A solution was quickly instigated under which two new classes of smaller submarines were designed, the UB and UC classes, the former to operate principally in the North Sea and coastal regions and the latter designed specifically as minelayers.

The great advantage of this policy was the dramatic cut in the build time. Initially, the UBIs at 125-tonne/123-ton surface displacement were just a quarter of the size of the newest U-boats and could be built in a fifth of the time by having prefabricated sections constructed in Germany and assembled in Belgium. The overall construction time was cut to 80 days for the first of the UB boats, with the first entering

service in the late spring of 1915, thereafter to be built in large numbers through three classes to accommodate ongoing improvements and higher specifications. The fact was the UBI series was underpowered, with a 44.7kW/60hp diesel engine turning a single screw.

They were slow and difficult to handle, and 17 of the UBI range were built before progressive improvements in almost every area were initiated. UBII was better and was extensively used, but still suffered from the limitation of

LEFT: **The familiar cigar shape of *UB64*, commissioned in 1917 in the UBIII series. It operated in the 5th and 2nd Flotilla respectively and claimed 30 ships sunk (excluding warships) during eight patrols in her 13-month lifespan, prior to being surrendered.**

being underpowered. This was evident from the fact that of the 30 built, only seven survived the war. Of those, *UB29* became famous for two reasons: in March 1916, she torpedoed and sank a French cross-channel steamer, *Sussex*. An international furore ensued when it was learned that among the 80 civilians who died were 25 Americans, although even that did not persuade the US to enter the war. In December the same year, *UB29* became the first boat to be sunk by a depth charge during action in the English Channel.

The final model in this class, UBIII, was a larger improvement on the previous two versions in every respect, but given the risk of the heavily mined areas in which they operated, the mortality was only slightly improved. Even so, of the 95 commissioned, 41 were lost or damaged, more than half of which were mined during coastal patrols.

TOP RIGHT: **A member of the UBIII class, possibly *U127*, which later disappeared, probably mined south of Fair Isle, with the loss of all 34 crew.** ABOVE: **The crew of an unidentified UB-class boat pay considerable interest in a passing *Mittel*-class boat.** BOTTOM: **A meeting at sea – *UB11*, a training boat, pulls alongside *U35*.**

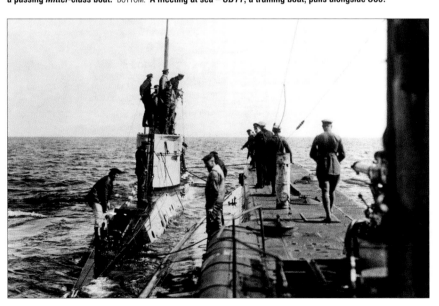

UBI class

Displacement: 125 tonnes/123 tons (surfaced); 140 tonnes/137.8 tons (submerged)
Length: 28.10m/92ft 2in
Beam: 3.15m/10ft 4in
Armament: 2 x 508mm/20in tubes (bow), 4 x torpedoes
Propulsion: 44.7kW/60hp diesel; 89.4kW/120hp electric
Speed: 6.5 knots (surfaced); 5.5 knots (dived)
Complement: 14 crew

UBII class

Displacement: 258 tonnes/253.9 tons (surfaced); 287 tonnes/282.5 tons (submerged)
Length: 36.10m/118ft 5in
Beam: 5.80m/19ft
Armament: 4 x 508mm/20in tubes (bow); 1 x 8cm/3.15in deck gun
Propulsion: 179kW/240hp diesel; 164.1kW/220hp electric
Speed: 9.5 knots (surfaced); 5.8 knots (dived)
Complement: 23 crew

UBIII class

Displacement: 508 tonnes/500 tons (surfaced); 650 tonnes/639.7 tons (submerged)
Length: 53.30m/174ft 10in
Beam: 5.80m/19ft
Armament: 3 x 508mm/20in tubes (2 x bow, 1 x stern), 16 x torpedoes; 1 x 8cm/3.15in deck gun
Propulsion: 179kW/240hp diesel; 164.1kW/220hp electric
Speed: 13.5 knots (surfaced); 7.8 knots (dived)
Complement: 34 crew

LEFT: The *UCI* coastal minelayers, which progressed through three classes, with modifications at each stage and for which 105 boats in total were either commissioned or being built when the war ended. The tally of Allied ships sunk through the mines that they laid was a horrendous total. ABOVE: A profile of a UC-class boat.

UC class (Minelayers)

Built with similar urgency to the UB boats, this class was a mining specialist destined largely for coastal work. The same problems also occurred with the UC boats in that the first in production were substantially underpowered, with the result that only 15 of the first series, UCI, were completed before UCII boats went into production in June 1915, with an order for round-the-clock manufacture in five shipyards.

A staggering 63 boats of the improved version were commissioned between June 1916 and January 1917 and with hurried training largely carried out on the older boats, the UCIIs took the brunt of the effort in this vital arena. From a German perspective, the UC crews made a courageous contribution.

Minelaying activities around the British Isles and the Mediterranean proved to be one of the most hazardous of all the diverse operations of German submariners. Of the 15 boats in the first class, only one survived to be surrendered in 1918. At least five fell victim to either their own mines or others laid by their own side.

In class II, the toll was equally horrific. Of the 63 UCIIs built, only 15 survived to complete the act of surrender after the Armistice was signed. This fate befell most of the UCIII version, which was introduced with a more powerful motor, but production came too late for the German war effort, and many were still under construction when the war ended.

LEFT: A mine taken from the coastal minelayer *UC5*, after the boat was grounded on the infamous Shipwash Shoal in the North Sea. She was scuttled, but the charges failed to explode and she fell into Allied hands.

UCII

Displacement: 410 tonnes/403.5 tons (surfaced); 485 tonnes/477.3 tons (submerged)
Length: 39.47m/129ft 6in
Beam: 5.40m/17ft 9in
Armament: 3 x 508mm/20in tubes (2 x bow, 1 x stern), 16 x torpedoes; 1 x 8.8cm/3.46in deck gun; 18 x mines
Propulsion: 372.8kW/500hp diesel; 313.2kW/420hp electric
Speed: 11.6 knots (surfaced); 7 knots (dived)
Complement: 14 crew

U151 class

The story of the appearance of a septet of giant and lethal U-cruisers that began to cause havoc among Allied shipping in late 1917 had its beginnings in what was a strangely peaceful mode in June 1916. It was in that month that Britain, and the Americans for that matter, were surprised by the arrival on the other side of the Atlantic of what was heralded as a civilian submarine, a 1,524-tonne/1,500-ton unarmed cargo-carrying boat christened *Deutschland*. The idea was that huge boats would transport cargoes across to the United States and return with much needed raw materials that were in short supply as a result of the British blockade of Germany.

The Americans were happy to accept such arrangements, and *Deutschland* completed the crossing safely and steamed untroubled into Baltimore, Maryland, in July, and unloaded her cargo. She returned unhindered in August, packed with much-needed supplies.

Encouraged, the Germans sent her on a second trip to New London, Connecticut. However, this voyage was less profitable, as the Americans were beginning to get agitated over Germany's application of unrestricted warfare. Consequently, the cargo-carrying mode was abandoned, and *Deutschland* and the rest of her class (*U151–U157*) were promptly converted into attack boats, each manned by 56 submariners and a prize crew of 21.

Outfitted during the summer of 1917, they were rushed into service to become much-feared raiders, literally cruising around the Atlantic for several months at a time. They each carried a relatively light load of 16 torpedoes, given the time they were on patrol, and relied heavily on deck artillery – 15cm/5.9in and 8.8cm/3.46in guns – for surface attacks. They were pointedly put under the command of some of Germany's most experienced and famous U-boat skippers.

Even so, these giants of the deep were difficult to manoeuvre and a nightmare for crews during heavy weather, when they rolled and tossed in a gruesome, uncomfortable manner. In spite of this, the boats scored considerable successes. *Deutschland*, recommissioned as *U155*, stayed out for 105 days on her first patrol, covering almost 16,093km/10,000 miles, sank 19 ships and shelled targets ashore on the Azores. *U151* was notably active along the coastline of America during

TOP: *U151* was the lead boat in a class of armed merchant cruisers that bore her name, of which seven – including the famous *Deutschland* – were designed and built as large commercial submarines carrying materials to and from locations otherwise denied to German surface ships because of Allied submarine operations. All seven boats were converted to cruisers after the United States entered the war in 1917. ABOVE: A glimpse inside *Deutschland*, or *U155*, as she later became known.

an eventful 13 week cruise, laying mines and sinking 23 ships. Overall, the six cruisers sank 174 ships for a total of 366,793 tonnes/361,000 tons.

LEFT: The engine room of one of the U-cruisers/merchant boats built early in 1916 and which created much interest when surrendered to the Allies at the end of the war.

U151 class

Displacement: 1,488 tonnes/1,464.5 tons (surfaced); 1,845 tonnes/1,815.9 tons (submerged)
Length: 64.9m/212ft 11in
Beam: 8.93m/29ft 4in
Armament: 2 x 508mm/20in tubes (bow); 20 x torpedoes; 2 x 15cm/5.9in guns
Propulsion: 2 x 298.3kW/400hp diesel engines; 298.3kW/400hp electric motors
Speed: 12.4 knots (surfaced); 5.2 knots (dived)
Complement: 56 crew, plus 21 prize crew

LEFT: *U1*, pristine leader of a brand new breed of U-boats built under the Nazi emblem and commencing with the IIA class. Commissioned in 1935, she lasted only six months into the war before she was lost with all 24 hands, probably to a mine in the North Sea.
BELOW: **A bird's-eye view of the tower for surface operations.**

U classes (1939) Types IIA, B, C and D

The Treaty of Versailles at the end of World War I saw the U-boat force decimated as the Allied nations took possession of the best of the surrendered submarines to plunder the technology, and destroyed the rest. Germany was also barred from building or possessing any submarines in the tiny navy she was allowed to retain. Even so, the vast storehouse of scientific and engineering acquired during those years could not simply be wiped away. Indeed, when the time came, it would form the backbone of the resurrection of what would become the greatest submarine force the world had seen, bar none.

In the meantime, German submarine crews secretly trained in Russia and Spain and within their own country under the guise of anti-submarine warfare exercises, which were allowed. Nor was Germany prevented from continuing

research into submarine development, and by the early 1930s, observers were reporting that a considerable team of scientists and engineers were employed on numerous projects that would prepare the way for the revival of the nation's submarine fleet. Indeed, it was a vital aspect of Hitler's plans when he announced that Germany would no longer be bound by the Versailles Treaty and began to re-arm.

With no navy to speak of, submarines immediately became a crucial element in the Nazi re-armament, and all the pre-planning that had taken place in earlier years now blossomed into reality at an incredible pace. Shipyards across the nation swung into operation, building rapidly during 1934–35, with the first U-boat commissioned on June 29, 1935. This was the date that marked the arrival of the new *U1*, the lead boat of the

Type IIA, whose eventful fate was to be lost with all hands, probably due to hitting a mine, in the North Sea on April 6, 1940. Five more boats came in the first wave of the new U-boats, before they were upgraded in size through three additional types, with 20 boats in IIB, 8 in IIC and 16 of IID. In the final reckoning, quite a number of this type survived World War II; however, the fate of a greater number was settled by mines and British ships in the North Sea.

LEFT: **The distinctive emblem, displayed here on the tower of *U9*, originally lead boat of the 1st Flotilla, from which position she sank seven Allied merchantmen and two warships before she herself went down in the Black Sea under a hail of bombs from a Soviet aircraft.**

U1, Type IIA

Displacement: 240 tonnes/236.2 tons (surfaced); 374.9 tonnes/369 tons (submerged)
Length: 40.90m/134ft 2in
Beam: 3.83m/12ft 7in
Armament: 3 x tubes (2 x bow, 1 x stern), 5 x torpedoes
Propulsion: 522kW/700hp diesel; 233.7kW/300hp electric
Speed: 13 knots (surfaced); 6.9 knots (dived)
Complement: 22–24 crew

U-VIIA, B and C

This is the boat that through its three versions became the principal enemy of the Allies for much of the war, especially when operating in wolfpacks. The ocean-going 670-tonne/659-ton Type VIIA, which arrived with *U27* in 1936, was developed from the Finnish Vetehinen design. An improved version came on stream in 1939. These were very efficient machines, agile and popular with their crews. The second version could carry 11 torpedoes or 22 mines, as well as a very effective 8.8cm/3.46in deck gun.

By 1940, the Type VIIC, which became one of the great assets of the German fleet, had overtaken this with more than 600 being built from 1941, beginning with *U69*. Her range was limited to around 10,461km/6,500 miles, but the collapse of France in June 1940 gave the Nazis access to the Atlantic ports, thus providing a haven for 12 U-boat flotillas subsequently to be based in Brest, La Rochelle, La Pallice, St Nazaire, Lorient and Bordeaux, providing access to British waters and the open Atlantic.

A number of the final batch of the VIICs were fitted with the snorkel and another, *U96*, became famous as the U-boat featured in the film *Das Boot*, although the boat was actually sunk by American bombers in Wilhelmshaven in 1945.

The material for the movie resulted from an excursion by Lothar-Günther Buchheim, who was ordered aboard as a war correspondent and artist for propaganda purposes. He took more than 5,000 photographs that survived the war, and his experiences resulted in a best-selling novel.

TOP: **One of Germany's VIIA boats, a new fast attack boat design of which ten were built in the late 1930s. Further improvements in range and firepower were added to the Type VIIB and Type VIIC.** ABOVE: *U251*, **one of the Type VIIC boats that were produced in great numbers from 1941 and became the workhorses of the German U-boat fleet.** BELOW LEFT: **The Type VIIB was given greater fuel-carrying capacity by the addition of external saddle tanks, thus providing a considerable increase in range.**

U-VIIC

Displacement: 755 tonnes/743.1 tons (surfaced); 857 tonnes/843.5 tons (submerged)
Length: 67.10m/220ft 2in
Beam: 6.20m/20ft 4in
Armament: 5 x 533mm/21in tubes (4 x bow, 1 x stern), 14 x torpedoes or 26 mines; 8.8cm/3.46in deck gun
Propulsion: 2,386.2kW/3,200hp diesel; 559.3kW/750hp electric
Speed: 17.8 knots (surfaced); 7.5 knots (dived)
Complement: 44–50 crew

U-IX

Another major development emanating from the 1935–36 period was the introduction of Type IX, an ocean-going submarine with a range of 19,312km/12,000 miles that could travel, when the time came, well into American waters. With 23 torpedoes on board, these boats carried formidable firepower. They were produced in three versions, and the second subtype, IXB, became the most successful type in U-boat history, with some boats accounting for more than 101,605 tonnes/100,000 tons of shipping. The total losses attributed to IXB amounted to 282 ships, displacing 1,551,006 tonnes/1,526,510 tons.

It was also an IXB boat, *U123*, that led the attack in US waters in early 1942 known as Operation Drumbeat, in which five boats sank nine ships in raids along the east coast of America. The marauding boats remained in the area for almost a month and were kept supplied with fuel by a U-boat tanker circling off the coast near Bermuda, an innovation that in this instance extended their patrol for an incredible eight weeks.

But even as these huge campaigns and wolf-pack operations reached their peak in 1943 – a period known among the U-boat men as "The Happy Time" – new scientific developments and sophisticated anti-submarine tactics by the British were already beginning to deliver the required results. This was especially effective in curtailing the operations of IX types, because they

ABOVE: **Under attack: a Type IX, designed as a long-range ocean-going boat, with five external torpedo containers and space for ten additional torpedoes. As mine-layers, they could carry 44 TMA or 66 TMB mines.** INSET: **A profile of *U123*, Type IXB, the most successful of the IX types, with each boat averaging over 101,605 tonnes/100,000 tons of shipping sunk.**

took far longer to replace. With mortality rates rising among U-boats of all types, production had to be stepped up to almost impossible levels to keep pace with losses.

Two areas where the British were scoring the most significant results were in the greater protection of convoys, which involved not only surface ships and submarines, but also aircraft equipped with the latest tracking devices. One of the most dramatic examples occurred in May 1943, when a wolf-pack of 12 U-boats attacked a convoy and lost three quarters of their number. The realization began to dawn that the days of such stunning victories against the convoys were coming to an end and, at the very least, would require a significant overhaul of tactics.

One of the Kriegsmarine's attempts to resolve the problem was the order that the IX boats should be fitted with more anti-aircraft guns to attack incoming aircraft, but the RAF simply introduced their own avoidance tactics of staying out of range until the U-boat was about to dive, thus stowing the guns, and then came in for the attack. The switch in

LEFT: **To counter the Allied radar threat, the Germans perfected a snorkel, enabling a submarine to run its diesel engines and recharge its batteries while operating just below the surface.**

operational tactics by the British brought some stunning results, notably in April and July 1943, when 109 U-boats were lost. Coinciding with declining success at sea, U-boat shipyards and pens were now being successfully and regularly bombed by the Allies. It was a major turning point in the fortunes of the German U-boat campaign, and one that resulted in Hitler's intervention, demanding new and better boats and defences. After all, according to his theory, the war should already have been won. As it was, only one IX boat survived the war.

U-IX

Displacement: 1,034.40 tonnes/1,018.1 tons (surfaced); 1,160 tonnes/1,141.7 tons (submerged)
Length: 76.50m/251ft
Beam: 6.70m/22ft
Armament: 6 x 533mm/21in tubes (4 x bow, 2 x stern), 22 x torpedoes or 44 mines; 10.5cm/4.13in (45 calibres) deck gun
Propulsion: 3,281.1kW/4,400hp diesel; 745.7kW/1,000hp electric
Speed: 18.5 knots (surfaced); 7.5 knots (dived)
Complement: 48–56 crew

U-Flak boats

This most deadly of contraptions emerged in the spring of 1943, when Germany realized that losses of their submarines in the fiery hell of the Bay of Biscay to Allied aircraft was reaching hugely damaging proportions. The boats were being picked off at an alarming rate as they travelled in and out of the U-boat bases of St. Nazaire, Lorient, Brest and Bordeaux. The region had become commonly known as the Valley of Death among U-boat submariners, and the statistics pinpointing their losses in that area show why they were getting exceedingly worried. More than ten per cent of the entire U-boat losses, or 28 boats, had been sustained in the Bay of Biscay in one year alone, and by the end of the war that total had risen to 72.

After much discussion, the Kriegsmarine came up with what they hoped would be a solution, converting a number of their superb VIIC boats into what amounted to floating flak platforms that could deliver massive firepower against incoming aircraft. Seven boats in all were earmarked for conversion, although only three were completed before the project was called off. They were fitted with two rapid-fire four-barrelled cannon, one placed forward of the conning tower with a shield to protect the

gun crew and another located behind the bridge.

A further upgrade was to add two heavy machine guns mounted on the bridge. With the additional personnel required for manning the guns and as ammunition handlers, the crew was increased in number from 48 to 69.

Towards the end of May, *U441*, operating under her new name of *U-Flak1*, moved out of Brest to take up her position. Within two days of operations, however, the British realized what was happening and an RAF Sunderland flying boat came over and sent a volley of depth charges that badly damaged the flak boat. Unfortunately, the Sunderland also crashed moments later. *U-Flak1* made an undignified retreat to base but, undaunted, she was hastily repaired and returned to her station in July only to come under

almost immediate attack in a pincer movement by three Beaumont aircraft of 248 Squadron, RAF. The boat was again heavily blasted topside, killing ten crew and wounding another 13. The commander had to risk diving with damage to escape total obliteration.

She made it safely back to Brest, but the Kriegsmarine did not give up and ordered three more of the converted flak boats to take up position as the losses in the bay continued to mount. By the middle of August, *U256*, *U271* and *U953* were sent out, but only completed one more patrol before the whole flak-boat concept was abandoned. Instead, the VIIC submarines were fitted with new anti-aircraft guns, and all the flak boats were restored to their former state.

RIGHT: **A U-boat under attack from the air, ever more common as the RAF extended its anti-submarine operations.**

U-Flak1

Displacement: 755 tonnes/743 tons (surfaced); 857 tonnes/843.5 tons (submerged)
Length: 67.10m/220ft 2in
Beam: 6.20m/20ft 4in
Armament: 2 x 2.2cm/0.87in 38/43U four-barrelled cannon; 1 x 3.7cm/1.46in automatic-firing cannon, 2 x MG 42 machine-guns, 8.8cm/3.46in rockets
Propulsion: 2,386.3kW/3,200hp diesel; 559.3kW/750hp electric
Speed: 17.8 knots (surfaced); 7.5 knots (dived)
Complement: 69 crew

LEFT: A sad end for a brilliant boat which was a generation ahead of its time. This is one of the many scuttled or sunk at the time of Germany's surrender and is apparently being recovered. In the years ahead, they were taken apart by the Allies, and the technology purloined.

XXI

Ironically, Germany already possessed and was developing technology that might well have won them the war at sea, and certainly the Battle of the Atlantic had it been introduced earlier. New engines were being built, such as the Walther propulsion system that attracted so much attention among the Allies. However, the new star of the show would undoubtedly have been the brand new XXI, a deep-diving combat submarine that had enormous potential, as demonstrated after the war when it became the model for the first nuclear boats. The principal advantages were the super-streamlining of the hull, the snorkel and the huge battery capacity for underwater speed and endurance.

In fact some of the technology had been available since the mid-1930s. The Dutch had already produced snorkel-equipped boats, which fell into both British and German hands after the Blitzkrieg. At the time, neither navy saw any value in them. The thinking among Germany's submarine hierarchy was that U-boats performed better and were safer on the surface

after dark, and in the first few years of the war this belief was confirmed. As noted above, the greater use of aircraft combined with radar, in which the British were well ahead in anti-submarine warfare, totally altered this conception. There is no doubt the Germans underestimated the British ASW capability, and in the event, daytime surface running became suicidal.

The solution might have been resolved by Dr Helmut Walther's propulsion system that would create the "true submarine" capable using hydrogen peroxide to power a boat that could operate submerged for a greater period of time, but the project had been shelved through cost and shortage of materials. However, he did resurrect the snorkel idea for modern application, and boats were converted in 1943–44. This permitted them to operate slightly submerged to take in fresh air for the diesels and remove engine exhaust. From there, the snorkel was to be used for a totally new boat, the XXI, with extra batteries in place of Walther's original idea of hydrogen peroxide. Now the Germans had the technology to meet the British counter-measures. It would arrive in the shape of the revolutionary new boat, the XXI ocean-going submarine, and the smaller XXIII coastal version.

The XXI would have electric power three times greater than the VIIC, the recharging process was also considerably shorter, and safer, and a new hydraulic torpedo reload system meant that six tubes could be loaded in the time it took to reload one in the VIIC. Furthermore, the facilities for the crew – always a bugbear among submariners – were excellent, with modern amenities such as individual showers and freezers for food storage.

LEFT: The sleek lines of the tower of an XXI submarine form the background of this scene of formal welcome for a VIP.

With its streamlined hull and exciting new features for greater submerged speed and overall efficiency, the boat was heralded as the most important development in submarine warfare, as indeed it was. In 1943 when the tide was definitely turning against the U-boats, Hitler demanded the immediate introduction of the XXI. More than 100 were ordered along with 30 XXIIIs.

Dönitz promised the first would be commissioned within six months. It didn't happen, on account of the increased Allied bombing raids over the shipyards, coupled with chronic shortages of raw materials. The Führer's anger was only placated when his trusted architect Albert Speer agreed to take personal control of the project, but by then the Allies were closing in on all fronts and Germany's war at sea was almost played out. Even so, work on the XXI continued to the last. The first one to undergo trials, *U2511*, went to sea just one week before Germany surrendered and performed in an excellent manner. Others lay in the shipyards, ready and waiting for the Allies to share the spoils – and to contemplate their good fortune that the XXI did not arrive earlier.

TOP: **Another boat before its time, a Type XVII with the Walther turbine. This was an experimental research boat, one of which was transported to the United States, the technology dissected and the boat then used for trials by the US Navy.** ABOVE: **A profile of XXI.** BELOW: **A profile of the Type XXIII, *U2326*, which subsequently became the British submarine *N35*. She sank after a collision in Toulon harbour in 1946.**

ABOVE: **Commissioned as *U2367* in March 1945, this Type XXIII sank before seeing service, after a collision near Schleimünde. She was raised in 1956 and incorporated into the German Federal Navy under the name of *U-Hecht* with pennant number S171, and remained in service for a further 20 years.**

XXI

Displacement: 1,595 tonnes/1,569.8 tons (surfaced); 1,789 tonnes/1,760.7 tons (submerged)
Length: 76.50m/251ft
Beam: 8.0m/26ft 3in
Armament: 6 x 533mm/21in tubes (bow), 23 x torpedoes 12 mines; no deck gun
Propulsion: 2,982.8kW/4,000hp diesel; 3281.1kW/4,400hp electric
Speed: 15.6 knots (surfaced); 17.5 knots (dived)
Complement: 60 crew

KD classes

The Japanese story in terms of submarines prior to 1945 is one of superlatives and extremes, and thus represents a fascinating array of technology. They produced some of the fastest, largest, longest, widest, heaviest and smallest boats, as well as excelling in aircraft-carrying, long-distance and huge armament, often not exceeded until the arrival of the post-war nuclear fleets. In so many areas their fleets, geared to the vastness of the Pacific Ocean, appeared to have the advantage over any of the other major powers.

Yet, for all that, in the final analysis the Japanese submarine campaign of World War II was widely regarded as an abject failure that even some of their most senior commanders recognized as such. Given the diversity of their fleet and the

ABOVE: **The Japanese Type KD1, built in the inter-war years and based on the surrendered German *U139*, it was used as the prototype for larger I boats (KD2–KD7 types) that came in its wake. A large double-hulled submarine, it was intended to operate with the battle fleet.** BELOW LEFT: **The torpedo tubes of the giant KD3A class.**

spectacular opening of their campaign with the raid on Pearl Harbor supported by 30 submarines, intelligence analysts in the West feared the worst as the Nippon shipyards powered ahead with everything from midget to multi-bomber-carrying boats, and from medium attack boats to giant cruisers. There was also a heavy concentration on endurance, enabling more than 60 of their ocean-going types to travel up to 32,187km/ 20,000 miles or 100 days at sea – a statistic unmatched by any other submarine fleet.

Another remarkable achievement was that of the 56 submarines exceeding 3,048 tonnes/3,000 tons operating in World War II, only four were not Japanese. Yet, tactically they often mystified their opponents, and appeared to be acting in a reconnaissance role to find Allied naval task forces in preparation for the big battles, rather than using their firepower in the hit-and-run role or as wolf-packs, which the British and the Germans in particular mastered so effectively with much smaller boats. Size did matter, and the sheer bulk of these giant craft often proved to be their downfall. They were slow to manoeuvre, sluggish to dive and thus became far easier targets.

The final score card told its own story and indicated the role to which their submarines at large were directed. Japanese submarines were credited with sinking a mere 184 merchant ships throughout the war, compared with the 2,800 claimed by the U-boats. Their losses meanwhile were catastrophic, losing almost three-quarters of her entire fleet, a figure matched only by the U-boats as both those nations faced an onslaught resulting from developments in anti-submarine warfare by the British and Americans. It was also a matter of some satisfaction to the Americans that none of the 30 Japanese submarines identified as having participated in the attack on Pearl Harbor actually survived the war.

The KD classes were among the workhorses of the fleet and had an interesting birth – with a prototype built in 1925, based upon *U139*, which came into the possession of the Japanese after World War I. The KD type progressed through various modifications to the KD7 class over a span of 16 years to 1942. By then a milestone was achieved when the KD6 class produced boats capable of the fastest surface speed of any submarine at the time.

The KD type was moderately successful although there was an early loss of *I70*, sunk by USS *Enterprise* off Oahu on December 10, 1941, in the American strike-back following Pearl Harbor. Overall, the KD classes suffered heavy casualties, with the KD7 class losing all ten boats within a year of coming into service.

TOP: *I176* was one of ten Japanese Type KD7 boats produced by 1942 as attack submarines. They had an outstanding endurance of 75 days and differed significantly from earlier types in that all tubes were sited forward. All were lost by 1944. ABOVE: The Type KD4 which were actually smaller than their predecessors of the KD3 class but were said to be unusually agile for Japanese boats and well liked by their crews. BELOW: The stylish KD6A, with the highest surface speed of any submarines upon their arrival in the 1930s, although this record was beaten by later Japanese boats. In spite of their speed, the whole class was wiped out by enemy action.

LEFT: The KD3A were massive submarines whose design was later revised to enable them to carry a second aircraft. The range of these boats was incredible, but because they were so large, they were easily spotted, slow to dive, easy to track and easy to hit. Consequently losses were also extraordinarily high.

KD7 class

Displacement: 1,804 tonnes/1,775.5 tons (surfaced); 2,560.88 tonnes/2,530.4 tons (submerged)
Length: 105.5m/346ft 2in
Beam: 4.57m/15ft
Armament: 6 x 533mm/21in tubes (bow), 12 x torpedoes
Propulsion: 2 x diesel engines, 5,965.6kW/ 8,000hp; 1,342.3kW/1,800hp electric
Speed: 23 knots (surfaced); 8 knots (dived)
Complement: 86 crew

Type A

Only three boats in this class were built, however they are very worthy of mention as a further development of the KD design, but once again much larger even than their forebear, *J3*. The A boats were among the largest built during the war, weighing almost 3,048 tonnes/3,000 tons surfaced and over 4,064 tonnes/4,000 tons submerged.

They were intended as flagship boats with communications systems that allowed them to have command and control of a submarine group, a more formal arrangement of the wolf-pack system.

The A1 design was also used to carry an aircraft, with the hangar pod opening forward of the conning tower, and for easy loading on to the catapult that would shoot the seaplane into the air while at the same time taking advantage of the forward movement of the ship at the point that the aircraft was launched. This development of submarines as aircraft carriers continued through the war, with some spectacular results.

A variation followed with the introduction of the A2 type in 1944 and two larger Modified A2s that carried two seaplane bombers. Once again, however,

A1	

Displacement: 2,872.9 tonnes/2,827.5 tons (surfaced); 4,083.5 tonnes/4,019 tons (submerged)
Length: 113.62m/372ft 9in
Beam: 9.54m/31ft 4in
Armament: 6 x 533mm/21in tubes (bow), 18 x torpedoes; 1 x 14cm/5.5in (50 calibre) deck gun; 1 x seaplane
Propulsion: 2 x diesel engines, 9,246.7kW/ 12,400hp; 1,789.7kW/2,400hp electric
Speed: 23.5 knots (surfaced); 8 knots (dived)
Complement: 114 crew

a complicated diving routine and inert manoeuvrability made these boats an easy target, and none of the class survived more than a couple of years.

LEFT: *I30*, one of the 20 boats of the B class, the largest and busiest group of the Japanese submarine force. Although they were efficient machines, only one survived the war. They were fast and had a forward catapult launch arrangement for their seaplane for a rapid take-off. *I30* was an early victim of Allied mines off Singapore in October 1942.

B1	

Displacement: 2,543 tonnes/2,502.8 tons (surfaced); 3,596 tonnes/3,539.2 tons (submerged)
Length: 108.66m/356ft 6in
Beam: 9.2m/30ft 2in
Armament: 6 x 533mm/21in tubes (forward), 17 torpedoes; 1 x 14cm/5.5in (50 calibre) deck gun; 1 x seaplane
Propulsion: 2 x diesel engines, 9,246.7kW/ 12,400hp; 1,491.4kW/2,000hp electric
Speed: 23.5 knots (surfaced); 8 knots (dived)
Complement: 95 crew

Type B

A busy general-purpose group and numerically one of the largest of the Japanese classes, the B1, B2 and B3 classes were also among the most successful, sinking almost a third of all the merchant ships claimed by Japan during the war, as well as a lion's share of warships. However, in time, they also suffered badly, with a 95 per cent loss rate.

Not quite a monster of the deep compared with others built around the same time, these boats were relatively fast, quicker to react and capable of an

impressive range of around 24,140km/ 15,000 miles at 16 knots. They also had a seaplane tucked away for catapult launching, but on this class the aircraft was aft-mounted. Later in the war, some of the aircraft were removed to provide space for more effective deck armaments, and in early 1945 two of the B3s – *I56* and *I58* – were converted to carry four Kaiten human torpedoes for special operations.

The B boats recorded a number of high profile successes. Of particular note was an action by *I19* in September

1942 when a salvo of six torpedoes sank two American warships and damaged another. She fired the salvo at the aircraft carrier USS *Wasp*. Two struck the giant ship forward and hit the fuel storage tanks, which exploded upon impact. The rest of the torpedoes sallied forth for a further 3,200m/3,500yd into the midst of another US carrier group, this time sinking a destroyer with one shot and causing sufficient damage to the battleship *North Carolina* for her to be withdrawn for major repairs.

The most infamous of the B boat attacks, however, came in early November 1942, when a number of US warships were limping away from the first naval battle of the Guadalcanal campaign. Among them was the light cruiser USS *Juneau* that had been torpedoed on her port side near the forward fire room. The shock wave from the explosion buckled the deck, shattered the fire control computers, and knocked out power. On November 12, however, the wounded American ships were being shadowed by the B type submarine *I26*. At 11:01 hours, the

submarine fired a three-torpedo salvo at the cruiser *San Francisco*. None hit that target, but one passed beyond and struck *Juneau* close to her previous damage. The magazine exploded and blew the cruiser in two. She sank within minutes, although 115 of *Juneau*'s crew survived the explosion. However, because of uncertainty about the number of Japanese ships in the area, rescue efforts did not begin for several days.

Exposure, exhaustion and shark attacks whittled down the survivors, and only ten men were subsequently rescued from the water eight days after

the sinking. The casualties included five members of one family, now written into US naval history as the Tragedy of the Sullivan Brothers. Many memorials have since honoured the brothers and caused the US Navy to review its policy of allowing family members to serve together at sea.

Thereafter, the fortunes of the B boats began to fade as the US Navy hunted them down. Between August and November 1943, 15 were sunk and others went in early 1944. By the end of the war, there was only one survivor of the B-type boats.

Type C

The Japanese built a large number of midget submarines between 1936–38, and the C boats, originating from the Type KD6 design, were among the classes capable of carrying them. They were active in that role from the outset, delivering five midgets to participate in the attack on Pearl Harbor. Only one of the midget-carrying boats actually entered the harbour, and that was promptly sunk after she had fired her two torpedoes, which missed their target.

Numerous attacks followed, and in many instances the success rate was less than encouraging for the Japanese Navy. At the end of May 1942, for example, *I16*, *I18* and *I20* spearheaded

ABOVE: *I16* was one the key players in the transportation of midget craft into attack zones, including Pearl Harbor, and was among the most successful of all the large Japanese submarines in conventional battle. With *I19*, she sank the carrier USS *Wasp* and the destroyer *O'Brien*. *I16* was herself lost in 1944.

an attack in which midgets were unloaded for an attack on a British base at Diego Suarez, Madagascar. Only two of the three midgets made it to the attack zone, and torpedoes from one of them hit both of their targets, damaging the battleship HMS *Ramillies* and sinking a tanker. However, in the return fire, both midgets were sunk, and the crews were killed as they attempted to escape to

shore. Later that month, five midgets were launched in an attack on Sydney Harbour but failed to score a hit, and all were lost. A similar result came when using midgets despatched from *I16*, *I20*, and *I24* on November 7, 1942, at Guadalcanal. The net result was all five midgets lost in return for damage to one US destroyer.

None of the midget-carrying C1 Type boats survived the war, most falling victim to US warships.

ABOVE: HMS *Ramillies* was damaged by torpedoes from midget submarines carried by the Japanese submarine *I16* during the bombardment by British warships of Diego Suarez, Madagascar, in May 1942.

C1 Type

Displacement: 2,513 tonnes/2,473.3 tons (surfaced); 3,540 tonnes/3,484.1 tons (submerged)
Length: 117.5m/385ft 6in
Beam: 9.44m/31ft
Armament: 8 x 533mm/21in tubes (forward), 20 x torpedoes; 1 x 14cm/5.5in (50 calibre) deck gun
Propulsion: 2 x diesel engines, 9,246.7kW/ 12,400hp; 1,491.4kW/2,000hp electric
Speed: 23.5 knots (surfaced); 8 knots (dived)
Complement: 102 crew

LEFT: *I3*, one of the J1 type built in the 1920s, was already tired by the time of their entry into the war, although the class had been fitted with German-supplied diesel engines which provided a higher degree of reliability but no great speed. Consequently, after early battles, they were converted into supply boats, but none survived the conflict. ABOVE: A profile of the J3 boat. Altogether more reliable, these were the largest submarines built by the Japanese prior to the war. Two boats, *I7* and *I8*, were intended as squadron flagships.

Type J

The J boats, produced through three classes – J1, J2 and J3 – had a heritage dating back to *U139*, and subsequently the prototype of the KD classes, with one big difference – they were much larger. Although the first were launched in the mid-1920s, they were still active in World War II, as can be noted by the naming/numbering system adopted in the same style as U-boats, and the J types were all early numbers. They also represented an early example of the Japanese penchant for monsters of *junsen*, or cruiser, boats that could turn their hand to a number of disciplines.

Even the earliest of the boats had substantial endurance of around 65–70 days and around 40,234km/ 25,000 miles, although they were inevitably very slow when dived. The diesel engines came from Germany, as did a number of technicians and scientists hired by the Japanese Navy

to bring their World War I expertise into their new breed of submarines.

Although deployed in a combat role at the start of World War II, the older boats were converted to cargo vessels and were especially used in the latter stages to ferry supplies to starving Japanese troops in far-flung theatres. Their guns were removed to provide accommodation for a barge used to shift their load to the hungry multitudes ashore.

The earliest of the boats, *I1*, became one such carrier but went into history for a totally different reason. While on a supply run to Guadalcanal, she was set upon by a pair of New Zealand frigates and sank less than a mile offshore. The escaping crew managed to scramble to safety with some of the boat's logs and codes, but left behind the past and future codes. However, the boat did not go under. Her bow was protruding above the water, and repeated attempts

by Japanese ships to blow her out of the water failed. The Americans arrived on the scene and managed to salvage a vast hoard of codes and charts, amounting to over 150,000 pages. It provided the intelligence for the American Navy to carry out a series of raids that sent more Japanese submarines to the bottom.

Only two of the last class, J3, were built, utilizing more of the design features of the latest KD types during construction in 1938. They were also the largest submarines completed by Japan before the war, and intended as squadron flagships.

Both carried a seaplane, which were known to have completed intelligence sorties over Pearl Harbor 11 days after the Japanese attack. The Americans sank the two submarines in 1944 and 1945 and indeed none of the J class survived the war.

LEFT: A ceremonial line-up: the J3-class boat *I8* enters German-occupied Brest harbour in 1943. She was later converted to carry the Kaiten human torpedoes, and was sunk off Okinawa in March 1945 by two US destroyers.

J3 class

Displacement: 2,484 tonnes/2,444.8 tons (surfaced); 3,526 tonnes/3470.3 tons (submerged)
Length: 109m/357ft 7in
Beam: 9m/29ft 6in
Armament: 6 x 533mm/21in tubes (bow), 21 x torpedoes; 1 x 14cm/5.5in (50 calibre) deck gun; 1 x seaplane
Propulsion: 2 x diesel engines, 8,351.8kW/ 11,200hp; 2,088kW/2,800hp electric
Speed: 23 knots (surfaced); 8 knots (dived)
Complement: 102 crew

Type Sen Taka

The Sen Taka I200-class submarine took its name from an abbreviation of the Japanese words for "submarine" and "fast", and it certainly lived up to that christening. It was the only World War II submarine that was easily a match for the German U-boat XXI and was superior to it in the three key areas of power, speed and weaponry.

The Sen Taka stood out among the Japanese boats, which had something of a reputation for slow manoeuvrability and diving. The two 2,051kW/2,750hp

BELOW: **A profile of the medium-sized Sen Taka I201 class, the only World War II boat comparable with the German ground-breaking Type XXI, with a streamlined double hull. She was faster submerged than on the surface, and had a snorkel fitted that allowed underwater recharging. Only three were built before Japan's surrender, and none saw service.**

engines and streamlined welded hulls provided around 17 knots on the surface, but even more impressive was the coupling with heavy-duty battery cells supplying an impressive 3,728kW/5,000hp electric motor capable of achieving 20 knots – double the speed achieved by contemporary American designs. They were equipped with a snorkel, which allowed for underwater diesel operation while recharging batteries.

Eight boats were laid down, but only three were completed before the end of the war, and the commissioning came too late to see any operational activity. The submarines were designed for mass production, which is why the incoming Americans made sure they kept the Sen Taka secrets to themselves. They took possession of two of the boats and were among the convoy of four Japanese

ABOVE: **One of the Sen Taka Sho type submarines, unusually small for the Japanese and designed for fast reaction in the defence of coastal regions. Two dozen boats of this type were planned, the later models with snorkels, but only ten were completed before the war's end, and none became operational.**

submarines, including two Sen Tokus, which were sailed to Hawaii for inspection by American engineers and designers. Once the inspection was complete, the boats were taken out to deep water near Oahu, torpedoed and sunk by the US submarine *Cabezon* on May 31, 1946, thwarting demands by the Russians to be allowed to examine the boats.

Sen Taka class

Displacement: 1,270 tonnes/1,249.9 tons (surfaced); 1,427 tonnes/1,404.5 tons (submerged)
Length: 79m/259ft 2in
Beam: 5.8m/19ft
Armament: 4 x 533mm/21in tubes (forward), 10 x torpedoes; 2 x 25mm/0.98in machine-guns
Propulsion: 2 x diesel engines, 2,050.7kW/ 2,750hp; 3,728.5kW/5,000hp electric
Speed: 16 knots (surfaced); 19 knots (dived)
Complement: 31 crew

Type Sen Toku

LEFT: **A giant, _I402_ was one of three Sen Toku boats that were more than 50 per cent larger than the biggest American submarine of that era and with almost twice the range. The three mono-winged aircraft carried by these boats could carry one aerial torpedo or a bomb.** ABOVE: **The open door of the Sen Toku aircraft pod.**

These huge submarines are really a postscript to World War II in that only three of a projected 16 were built before the war ended, and none saw any action. However, they must be noted for their sheer size, power and potential. At the time, they were the largest submarines ever built anywhere in the world, and more than half as big again as the largest American boat of that era, USS _Argonaut_. They were equipped with a snorkel and the latest radar and also had an incredible range of 59,546km/37,000 miles, almost twice that of the American giant, and were specifically designed to bomb the Panama Canal and west coast American cities. However, there were other major differences between the American and Japanese boats, mainly in the hidden added extra

that the Japanese had included that, given any further extension of the war, might well have had dire consequences.

As well as a formidable torpedo load, each of the submarines, numbered _I400_, _I401_ and _I402_, was equipped to carry three very efficient mono-winged bombers. They were the collapsible Aichi M6A1 Seiran floatplanes that could be stowed in a 36.6m/120ft hangar that would be opened forward to link to the catapult. They could be unpacked, armed and prepared for launch in 45 minutes. The aircraft payload was either one aerial torpedo or an 800kg/1,764lb bomb and claimed a range of up to 1,158km/625 nautical miles and a top speed of 475kph/295mph. The submarine carried enough stock for up to 20 flying missions.

Meanwhile, the submarines carried massive on-board anti-aircraft protection with 11 25mm/0.98in anti-aircraft cannon.

For all that, the Sen Toku came too late. They did not come into service until July 1945, and at the end of the month, the first two – _I400_ and _I401_ — set out on a mission to launch their aircraft in a joint attack with submarines carrying the Kaiten human torpedoes against an American naval anchorage off Ulithi, scheduled for the third week of August. Hostilities ended before they reached the target area, and the attack force returned to base to hoist the white flag.

Two of the boats were subsequently taken to the United States for a detailed examination and were subsequently scuttled in the Pacific a year later.

RIGHT: **Two Sen Toku boats, _I400_ and _I401_, were en route to launch their aircraft in kamikaze attacks on the American fleet anchorage at Ulithi on July 26, 1945, when hostilities ceased.**

Sen Toku class

Displacement: 5,140 tonnes/5,058.8 tons (surfaced); 6,456 tonnes/6354 tons (submerged)
Length: 121.92m/400ft
Beam: 11.9m/39ft
Armament: 8 x 533mm/21in tubes (forward), 20 x torpedoes; 1 x 14cm/5.5in (50 calibre) deck gun
Propulsion: 4 x diesel engines, 6,338.4kW/8,500hp; 1,491.4kW/2,000hp electric
Speed: 18.5 knots (surfaced); 6.5 knots (dived)
Complement: 145 crew

LEFT: **The great *Surcouf* was a one-off – the world's largest boat – and her mysterious sinking in World War II gave her an unsurpassed record for the largest loss of life in a single submarine accident.** BELOW: **A view of the boat in all her glory, with the twin gun turret – a powerful design feature.**

Surcouf

The single boat known as *Surcouf* was literally in a class of her own. Construction dated to 1929, when the French Navy won approval to build what was then the largest and most costly submarine the world had ever seen – and one to which the Japanese would soon pay homage by capping that title. *Surcouf* was commissioned in 1934, there to begin a controversial career and wartime escapades that might have been a plot for a James Bond thriller. She was designed and built as an underwater cruiser to fulfil France's avowed intention of keeping her coastline well defended.

For that mission, the boat carried a hangar for a floatplane, designed primarily for observation. The idea was that the submarine would cruise the coastline unseen, and in the event of being called into action, the giant would rise through the waves and become a warship. She also had the ability to blast the opposition out of the water with no fewer than ten torpedo tubes, and the floatplane was theoretically capable of directing fire for the boat's big guns, up to a range of 24km/15 miles.

There was also a 4.9m/16ft motorboat, and a cargo compartment below was fitted out to hold prisoners. She had a 90-day endurance, and a range of 18,520km/10,000 nautical miles. When the Germans invaded France in 1940, the submarine was in the process of being refitted at Brest, and was ordered to sail immediately even though she had only one engine in operation. Arrangements were made for her and other boats to cross the English Channel to Portsmouth, where, in due course,

her commander was called upon to surrender the boat to the British under the terms of Operation Catapult, launched to seize French ships and submarines to prevent them being used against Britain. He refused, and consequently British forces boarded her at Portsmouth, and placed the submarine under the control of the Free French. A fresh crew was mustered, and she began convoy patrol for a while but was then involved in allegations that she was spying for Vichy France, and the British sent two officers to join the boat to keep watch.

The following year, she was used to carry an admiral of the Free French to Canada, and subsequently took on the role of gunboat with other ships to liberate islands off the coast of Newfoundland, helping to remove the Vichy administration. This caused some difficulty with the United States, which had just concluded a deal with the Vichy Government to maintain neutrality in French possessions in the Western Hemisphere. She sailed again amid rumours she was off to liberate islands in the Caribbean. Others stories suggested she was carrying a cargo of French gold.

However, having called at Bermuda on February 12, 1942, the great *Surcouf* was mysteriously lost with all hands.

ABOVE: **The MB 410 and MB 411 were observation aircraft with a single central float and two small stabilizing floats. They were designed to be carried by *Surcouf* and were easily disassembled for stowage.**

Two theories were proposed, suggesting that she had either been attacked by American bombers, who mistook her for a U-boat, or that she had been accidentally rammed by an American freighter.

Surcouf

Displacement: 3,198 tonnes/3,147.5 tons (surfaced); 4,235 tonnes/4,168.1 tons (submerged)
Length: 110m/360ft 11in
Beam: 9.2m/30ft 2in
Armament: 6 x 550mm/21.7in tubes, 14 x torpedoes; 4 x 400mm/15.75in tubes, 8 x torpedoes; 2 x 203mm/8in twin turret guns, 2 x 37mm/1.46in anti-aircraft cannon, 2 x 13.2mm/0.52in anti-aircraft machine-guns; 1 x MB 411 float plane; 284.5 tonnes/280 tons cargo capacity
Propulsion: 5,667.3kW/7,600hp diesel; 2,982.8kW/4,000hp electric
Speed: 18.4 knots (surfaced); 10 knots (dived)
Complement: 118 crew

LEFT: **French submarine** *Glorieux* **from Series II of the Redoutable class, whose boats were launched between 1928 and 1937, was among the French boats that escaped the Nazi occupation at Toulon on November 27, 1942. She reached Oran to join the Allied cause, surviving the rest of the war before being sold for scrap in 1952.**
BELOW: *Sfax,* **on the other hand, remained faithful to Vichy France but was accidentally torpedoed and sunk by** *U37* **off Cape Juby, Morocco, in December 1940.**

Redoutable class

The French produced some extremely attractive submarines in the inter-war years, with sleek lines that sat well on the surface. However, the diversity of boats listed in a dozen classes, including what was then the world's largest submarine, made it difficult to read French policy. Indeed, there seemed to be no precise pattern of development, unlike British policy where an orderly progression was evident, in spite of the latter's financial constraints.

This was partially due to the carryover from World War I in which the 55 French submarines that participated quickly became obsolete. The aftermath saw disagreement between senior naval officers, government figures and international allies as to future requirements. Those who held sway were of the view that the French should concentrate on an armada of surface ships to protect the coastlines, and, where necessary, deliver gunboat diplomacy to their overseas interests in the Far East, Asia and Africa. In consequence, almost three-quarters of French submarines operational at the outbreak of World War II were of designs dating back to the 1920s. Numerically largest of all the classes – and the designated workhorse – was the Redoutable class, whose leader of that name was a 1,422 tonne/1,400-ton submarine known to be a slow diver in emergency situations.

In the event, the scenario confronting French submarines at the onset of World War II and during the early months of the conflict was like no other. There is hardly a story among the nation's 77 boats that prepared for the outbreak of World War II that can be told in the straightforward manner of service, action and fate, from which may be deduced the performance

of the boats. Consequently, unlike in World War I when French submarines joined Britain and Australia in the Dardanelles, their impact on the second war bore no comparison.

It was an unholy mess that resulted in great bitterness and the eventual loss of almost 50 per cent of the French submarine fleet, though not necessarily through operational activity at sea. Some boats fell victim to U-boats prior to the French surrender. Next, Winston Churchill announced that the British would sink or impound the French fleet unless the Navy put them out of commission, and eventually carried out that threat against those who did not conform. In a further development in November 1942, fleet commanders at the French naval base of Toulon scuttled their boats to avoid them falling into British or German hands. In the Redoutable class

LEFT: *Casabianca*, a heroic boat that escaped Nazi clutches at Toulon on November 27, 1942, joined the Allies at Algiers, and there performed sterling work in various intelligence roles, especially in delivering agents into hostile territory.
BELOW: Vichy submarine *Poncelet,* scuttled by her crew in December 1940. HMS *Milford* was blockading Gabon and forced *Poncelet* to the surface with depth charges and then shot off the boat's conning tower. The crew was saved.

BELOW: The profile of *Casabianca*, which was a standard *Redoutable*-class design.

of 17 boats, the situation was as follows: eight were scuttled, six were sunk by British destroyers in various locations, one on foreign service was arrested in the Far East and two rejoined the Allies.

There was a famous and mysterious exception to this tragedy. *Casabianca* under the command of Capitaine de Frégate Jean L'Hérminier was among those who took his boat towards the Allies in North Africa.

She was one of the third series of the Redoutable class of boats built and lost under individual type names such as Redoutable, Agosta and L'Espoire dating from 1924. Of the final overall total for the Redoutable series of 31 boats, two were lost before the war and another 23 sunk or scuttled. *Casabianca* had one of the most notable operational records

of any French submarine and was the only third series boat to survive the war, operating for the Free French under General de Gaulle's overall command. Commander L'Hérminier risked constant attack as his boat was employed on secret missions delivering agents and saboteurs into Nazi-held Europe and particularly in running supplies and weapons to Corsica for the French resistance. At the same time, he was fully operational as an attack submarine and achieved a number of successes against German shipping. *Casabianca* thus played a key role in the eventual capture of Corsica by the Allies.

RIGHT: *Conquerant*, a Series II Redoutable of the Agosta type, was launched in 1935 and sunk in November 1942 off Dakhla, Morocco, by two American Catalina aircraft.

Redoutable class

Displacement: 1,360 tonnes/1,338.5 tons (surfaced); 2,047 tonnes/2,014.7 tons (submerged)
Length: 92m/301ft 10in
Beam: 8.75m/28ft 8in
Armament: 9 x 550mm/21.7in bow tubes; 2 x 400mm/15.7in stern tubes; 1 x 99mm/3.9in deck gun; 1 x 37mm/1.46in anti-aircraft gun; 1 x 13mm/0.51in anti-aircraft gun
Propulsion: 4,474kW/6,000hp diesel; 1,491.4kW/2,000hp electric
Speed: 17 knots (surfaced); 10 knots (dived)
Complement: 63 crew

LEFT: The *Dekabrist* was produced by post-Tsarist Russia, but the shipbuilders of the Soviet Russia had to battle with out-dated technology.

Dekabrist class

Dekabrist

Displacement: 910 tonnes/895.6 tons (surfaced);
  1,190 tonnes/1,171.2 tons (submerged)
Length: 76.5m/251ft
Beam: 6.3m/20ft 8in
Armament: 8 x 533mm/21in tubes (6 x bow,
  2 x stern), 5 reloads; 1 x 45mm/1.77in
  anti-aircraft gun, 500 rounds
Propulsion: 820.3kW/1,100hp diesel;
  391.5kW/525hp electric
Speed: 15.5 knots (surfaced); 8 knots (dived)
Complement: 53 crew

Russia had fully embraced the concept of submarine warfare prior to World War I when the Tsar's Navy acquired almost 50 boats, including five American Hollands, eight from Simon Lake and others from Britain, Germany and France. They were based around the Baltic and the Black Sea as a defensive measure, but given the political turmoil within the country, her submarines had little impact on events of that era.

Towards the end of the 1920s, however, the new regime of the USSR once again sought external help in establishing a new submarine fleet, employing many German designers and engineers in their new production programme. The result was the Dekabrist class, which represented the new Soviet Union's first attempt at fully home-grown submarines.

The boats, said to be wholly Soviet creations, went into production in 1927 and were overseen by the Bureau of Submarine design, headed by engineer Boris Malinin, who designed the Bars class in 1916–17. They were the first Russian boats with watertight bulkheads and were designed for long-range attacks on enemy communications. They were constructed with riveted hulls of high-strength steel, with a 45mm/1.77in AA gun aft of the conning tower.

In fact, the Dekabrist class proved to be very useful boats for Soviet purposes – manoeuvrable and quick-diving – but eventually falling foul of poor maintenance routines in post-Tsarist Russia and subsequently in constant need of repair. Furthermore, the technology was a good 10 years behind that of the West, and the

boats required extensive modernization as World War II approached, when, in time, they would see service in the Baltic and Black Sea. Later in the war, the British loaned some technology, providing an ASDIC-129 sonar and a new torpedo launching system for one of the boats.

The Dekabrist class led the Soviet Union into serious submarine construction, and they next produced the Leninec class of six minelaying boats, laid down in 1928 and 1930 based on the same hull. In this class, which entered service in 1933, the two stern torpedo tubes were discarded in favour of tubes for 20 mines.

LEFT: Mini-submarines had been left behind by the major seafaring nations. Not so with the Soviets, who produced this small craft in vast numbers.

Malutka class

Malukta class

Displacement: 153 tonnes/150.6 tons (surfaced);
  187 tonnes/184 tons (submerged)
Length: 37.10m/121ft 9in
Beam: 4.15m/13ft 7in
Armament: 2 x 457mm/18in tubes, 2 x torpedoes
  (4 x tubes, 4 x torpedoes on later versions)
Propulsion: 507.1kW/680hp petrol;
  186.4kW/250hp electric
Speed: 13 knots (surfaced); 7.4 knots (dived)
Complement: 18 crew (30 for the XV version)

The class name Malutka, meaning "baby", was an apt description. Almost 100 were eventually built, and they were designed primarily as coastal submarines on a mass-production basis, intended largely to defend naval bases or, in times of war, to blockade enemy shipping routes and harbours. However, for the USSR, the Malutkas had a distinct

advantage in that they were also fully transportable by rail, thus enabling them to be carried towards any theatre of war across the vast Russian terrain to the nearest sea to begin their patrols – or, in some cases, the nearest lake. A number of the boats were said to have been transported to Lake Ladogo, near Leningrad, for operations. The M class

was built in four versions, each following on from the last with improvements, modifications and lengthening.

Scuka class

Displacement: 558 tonnes/549.2 tons (surfaced);
689 tonnes/678.1 tons (submerged)
Length: 57.50m/188ft 8in
Beam: 7.15m/23ft 6in
Armament: 6 x 533mm/21in tubes (4 x bow,
2 x stern), 12 x torpedoes; 2 x 45mm/1.77in
deck guns
Propulsion: 894.8kW/1,200hp petrol;
335.6kW/450hp electric
Speed: 12.5 knots (surfaced); 6.5 knots (dived)
Complement: 50 crew

Scuka class

This medium-sized submarine became one of the main workhorses of the Soviet fleet during World War II, passing through three versions, with 91 eventually operational. When originally planned, these boats represented the first major USSR programme of attack submarines designed to be "positioned against closed and defended enemy theatres of war" and, in due course, would be assigned for operations with four principal Soviet Navy fleets in the North, the Pacific, the Black Sea and the Baltic. It was in the latter two stations that they were eventually to suffer the heaviest casualties against the Nazis, where almost 70 per cent of their front-line boats were lost. World War II operational records also include confrontations with the Japanese in the Pacific, where their performance was outstanding.

Stalinec class

Displacement: 829 tonnes/815.9 tons (surfaced);
988 tonnes/972.4 tons (submerged)
Length: 77.80m/225ft 3in
Beam: 9.85m/32ft 4in
Armament: 6 x 533mm/21in tubes (4 x bow,
2 x stern), 12 x torpedoes; 2 x 45mm/1.77in
deck guns
Propulsion: 894.8kW/1,200hp petrol;
335.6kW/450hp electric
Speed: 12.5 knots (surfaced); 6.5 knots (dived)
Complement: 50 crew

Stalinec class

This boat was one that emerged in the 1930s as a result of direct co-operation between the USSR and Germany – a partnership that the latter nation subsequently came to regret. The boat emerged from a prototype originally built at Karhatena by a Dutch subsidiary using German designers for the Spanish Navy. When the Spanish subsequently cancelled the order, the Soviet Navy was invited to inspect the boat for possible inclusion in their fleet. An agreement was reached whereby plans and drawings for the boat would be purchased by the USSR. Later, a party of Soviet designers and engineers travelled to Bremen and Karhatena to discuss with the German engineers design changes to accommodate Soviet requirements. Thus, the S class was born, utilizing Soviet parts and machinery, built in five Soviet shipyards.

600 class

The build-up of Italian submarines began in earnest in 1925 under Mussolini and included a number of medium to large boats whose quality may well have been hampered by financial constraints in the aftermath of World War I. However, in the early 1930s, the Italians began a substantial programme of construction following an international disarmament conference in London in 1930 that set limits on the size – but not quantity – of boats built by the naval powers.

The conference was called amid international concern about the growth in submarine fleets, which had arisen since a 1921 conference that placed restrictions on the expansion of naval fleets but excluded submarines. Britain, the United States, Japan and France had already been demonstrating to the world some grandiose projects for international operations in the late 1920s. Thus, in 1930, defining limits were set for coastal and oceanic boats, 610 tonnes/600 tons for the former and 2,032 tonnes/2,000 tons for the latter. The Italian Navy took a somewhat pragmatic approach to the new regulations and responded by introducing what became known as the

600 class. This, in effect, set them on course to build a large number of boats of the coastal classification, which were well suited for their principal area of operations in the Mediterranean, under the generic name of the 600 class.

They were introduced progressively in five types, built to a master drawing with some deviations for each under the names Argonauta (after the first boat of the series), Sirena, Perla, Adua and Platino. The result was that by the time of Italy's entry into World War II, Mussolini was able to deploy a diverse range of modern submarines made up of 50 large, 89 medium, two cargo and assorted midget boats, to which further additions came during the war years.

The 600 class, built with remarkable speed by various shipyards across Italy, was at the heart of the nation's submarine force, and undoubtedly the most successful. Furthermore, the stream of boats emerging through this period was competitive and well managed. Unfortunately, the lead member of the group was not among those who participated. When Mussolini declared war on Britain on June 9,

ABOVE: *Argonauta*, one of the most successful Italian submarines, led the way in the pre-war 600 class, which consisted of a series of five types produced progressively under the names of Argonauta, Sirena, Perla, Adua and Platino. In all, 59 submarines were built by various shipyards, and these differed in their minor detail.

1940, the *Argonauta*, under the command of Lt Vittorino Cavicchia Scalamonti, was one of the 55 boats patrolling the Mediterranean.

Her station was to cover the British naval base of Alexandria and Suez where the Royal Navy was already engaged in anti-submarine activity. Eleven days into the patrol, she took a heavy bombardment of depth charges, and the damage included her periscope. She was forced to return to the Italian base at Tobruk, but there were no facilities for such repairs, and she was sent on to Taranto. Thereafter, nothing more was heard of her, and she was presumed lost with all hands.

LEFT: *Nichelio*, one of the Platino types in the 600 series. The 600-class boats were of a very decent and sleek design that evolved and improved through 59 units.

Argonauta Type

Displacement: 656 tonnes/645.6 tons (surfaced); 797 tonnes/784.4 tons (submerged)
Length: 61.5m/201ft 9in
Beam: 5.65m/18ft 6in
Armament: 6 x 533mm/21in tubes; 1 x 102mm/4in deck gun; 2 x 17.2mm/0.68in anti-aircraft guns
Propulsion: 932.1kW/1,250hp diesel; 596.6kW/800hp electric
Speed: 14.5 knots (surfaced); 8.2 knots (dived)
Complement: 36 crew

Marconi class

Among the new classes introduced by the Italian Navy in the 1935–40 period, Marconi boats had a good record in seaworthiness and ease of deployment, although later alterations when they were moved to Bordeaux in support of U-boat operations included enlargements that affected their buoyancy to what some naval specialists regarded as dangerously low levels. Even so, Regia Marina Italiana today maintains that they were "surely among the best vessels produced by Italy". One them, the *Leonardo Da Vinci*, was credited with the highest number of sinkings among Italian submarines, second only to U-boats. Infamously among them (from both points of view) was the sinking on March 14,1943, of the transatlantic liner *Empress*

of Canada with 3,000 British soldiers and 500 Italian prisoners of war aboard. The submarine managed to save only one, a doctor named Vittorio Del Vecchio.

The six submarines of the Marconi class operated in the Atlantic and Indian oceans for the majority of the war, sinking an aggregate total of 38 ships with a total of 219,697 tonnes/216,227 tons and damaging another 17 for a total of 118,558 tonnes/116,686 tons. None of them survived the war, five having been lost with all hands in the Atlantic. The sixth, *Torelli*, had an interesting journey towards her final demise. She was captured by the Japanese in Singapore after Italy's surrender in 1943 and was subsequently handed over to Germany's U-boat command, who renamed her

ABOVE: **The *Marcello* was the first one of a series of 11 boats of the successful Italian class of the same name, from which the Marconi design emanated. The six submarines of the Marconi class became renowned for "good seaworthiness and easiness of deployment, especially after the reduction in size of the conning tower displayed on the *Marcello*".**

U(IT)25. The boat operated with a German/Italian crew until Germany's own surrender, when she was hastily recovered by Japan, again operating with a mixed crew, including some Italians. The Americans subsequently sank her off the Japanese coast near Kobe.

Marconi class

Displacement: 1,172 tonnes/1,153.5 tons (surfaced); 1,465 tonnes/1,441.9 tons (submerged)
Length: 70.04m/229ft 9in
Beam: 6.82m/22ft 5in
Armament: 8 x 533mm/21in tubes; 4 x 13.2mm/0.52in anti-aircraft guns
Propulsion: 2 x diesel engines, 2,684.5kW/3,600hp; 2 x electric motors, 1,118.6kW/1,500hp
Speed: 18 knots (surfaced); 8 knots (dived)
Complement: 57 crew

ABOVE: **A profile of the *Leonardo da Vinci* from the Marconi class, credited with the highest number of sinkings among Italian submarines. This sink rate was comparable to U-boat performance and was a higher rate than most of the Allied submarine forces.**

Directory of Submarines

1945 to the Present Day

The defeat of Germany at the end of World War II provided Allied scientists and engineers with access to the Type XXI U-boat and a mass of other designs. In 1949, a report by US Naval Intelligence warned that Soviet exploitation of the U-boat technology presented the most potent post-war naval threat to the United States. The Soviets were of the same mind with regard to US intentions. No warship of the time could effectively detect and track a fast attack submarine like the German Type XXI.

In the US it was USS *Nautilus* that turned the tide when it went to sea propelled by a pressurized water nuclear plant in January 1955. The Soviets developed their own version, beginning a new quest among the two major powers to equip their submarine service with high-speed, nuclear-powered attack submarines. This was soon to be followed by the giant boomers, the ballistic missile carriers that could roam the seas undetected for months. Britain and France and then a handful of other nations launched their own nuclear-armed squadrons, while lesser navies equipped themselves with very effective diesel-electric boats. Today, however, nuclear-powered does not necessarily mean nuclear-armed. India, China, France, and Brazil either operate, or have under development, nuclear-powered fast attack boats which are becoming, as technology improves, harder to find and track.

LEFT: **By 1983, polar bears were used to nuclear submarines poking their sails through the ice.**

LEFT: **USS** *Seawolf*, at the beginning of an historic journey in which she would remain submerged for two months, demonstrating that a nuclear-powered submarine could operate completely without support or the need to surface for the length of an average war patrol, a first step towards rapid progression among the major powers.

Seawolf SSN (Early)

Although *Nautilus* was America's first nuclear-powered submarine, *Seawolf* also had the distinction of being the first SSN in this new era. Although, like *Nautilus*, she was fully armed from the outset, *Seawolf* was essentially an experimental platform whose every detail from performance to crew conditions was to be monitored and analysed so that any discoveries could be dealt with. The build-time was obviously far greater than the production-line efforts of the war years. She was laid down on September 7, 1953, and finally commissioned in March 1957.

Intensive training programmes occupied the crew for almost all of the first year of operations before *Seawolf* went public, steaming across the Atlantic to take part in NATO exercises at a time when the Cold War was already in the deep freeze zone. A number of nuclear firsts were claimed by the Americans during these early stages. Much was made of the fact that *Seawolf* submerged on August 7, 1958, and did not surface

again until October 6, having covered 13,780 nautical miles, thus "demonstrating to the world the ability of the nuclear-powered submarine to remain independent of the earth's atmosphere for the period of a normal war patrol".

Thereafter she went through a routine of both independent and fleet operations, including a period of service with what the US Navy described as the world's first nuclear task force, consisting of submarines and surface ships equipped with guided missiles.

Seawolf was the only submarine built with a liquid metal nuclear reactor. While the liquid metal (sodium) provided for a more efficient power plant, it also caused several hazards for the ship and crew, including fire potential and highly corrosive effects. After two years of operation, *Seawolf* was converted to a pressurized water reactor because of these concerns.

Her first overhaul and conversion came in 1967, and the following year she was grounded off Maine while

ABOVE: **President Dwight Eisenhower, the wartime general, pictured inside** *Seawolf***, had a special liking for submarines and now "pushed the boat out" to speed up the development of the nuclear era.**

conducting sound and weapons systems tests and had to be towed off. No other major incidents were recorded in her 30-year life span, ending her days in the role of what the US Navy described as a "special projects platform", having long ago been overtaken by the vast panoply of nuclear developments that were to come. She was decommissioned in 1987 and stricken from the naval register. She was then stored for ten years before finally being dismantled in the US Navy's Nuclear-Powered Surface Ship and Submarine Recycling Programme.

RIGHT: **The portraiture of nuclear submarines has become a fascination for many observers, especially as the whole boat is never visible when on the move. The amount of foam around the boat is the only way of judging its speed and size.**

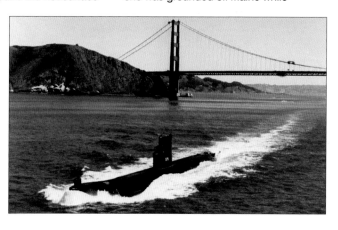

Seawolf SSN

Displacement: 3,209 tonnes/3,260.5 tons (surfaced); 4,045 tonnes/4,109.9 tons (submerged)
Length: 103m/337ft 11in
Beam: 8.5m/27ft 11in
Armament: 6 x 533mm/21in tubes, 8 x torpedoes
Propulsion: SG2 liquid metal nuclear reactor (later converted)
Speed: 23 knots (surfaced); 19 knots (dived)
Complement: 101 crew

Triton SSN

At her commissioning, *Triton* obviously set out to write herself into the history books from the very outset. Having put out to sea on what the US Navy describe as the "shakedown cruise", her maiden voyage on February 15, 1960, she set off submerged for the South Atlantic. She arrived in the middle Atlantic off St Peter and St Paul Rocks on February 24 to commence a history-making voyage. She had remained submerged since leaving the east coast of America, and carried on south towards Cape Horn. She rounded the tip of South America, travelling west into the Pacific, on past the Philippines and the Indonesian archipelago into the Indian Ocean, round the Cape of Good Hope, arriving back off the St Peter and St Paul Rocks on April 10. She had completed the first submerged circumnavigation of the earth in 60 days and 21 hours, although she did break the surface once to transfer a sick sailor to a surface ship off Montevideo on March 5.

If any proof was still needed, the voyage confirmed to the world the great advances that had been achieved in both speed and submerged endurance through nuclear power, not to mention the political dimension in this highly sensitive period. In fact, it was through such developments that the USSR and the United States – as the two key players in the nuclear race – now began the process of playing leapfrog, with each attempting to outdo the other at every turn. Nor was it simply a case of technical achievement. During the voyage, the submarine collected untold oceanographic data, which was not only important at the time but which pointed to the need for further and continual exploration for the future safety of the underwater armadas.

The achievement was recognized with a Presidential Citation for the crew and the award of the Legion of Merit for her commander, Captain Beach. It was no coincidence that international security analysts reported a rising threat as the

USSR piled resources into building up their own submarine fleet to "meet and beat" the Americans head on. Consequently, the US Navy made it clear that they needed more nuclear-powered attack submarines with anti-submarine warfare capability. Until that point in time, *Triton* had been a SSNR, which denoted she was part of the US radar picket patrol on the outer rims of the US coastal defences. In 1962, she was converted into an attack submarine to meet the navy's shortfall in numbers and served in that role until 1967. By then, however, new and more modern nuclear boats were arriving and in the pipeline. The escalating costs prompted a thorough review of US naval requirements, and indeed it was quite apparent that a hefty cull of older members of the submarine fleet was required.

Battle planners concluded that it would be utterly useless in modern submarine warfare scenarios to put forward some of the ageing boats in the US fleet. Consequently, *Triton*, along with 60 other vessels, was taken out of service.

TOP: **USS *Triton* began life as one of the nuclear vessels destined to patrol and protect the outer rim of the nation's coastline. However, she was converted into attack mode during the Cold War, as more submarines were required for what became something of an obsession on both sides – that of the potential for submarine-based warfare.** ABOVE LEFT: ***Triton's* hull cylinder, an indication of the massive scale of engineering now involved in submarine manufacture.** ABOVE RIGHT: ***Triton's* internal fit, spectacular at the time but merely a beginning.** INSET: **The patch tradition continues.**

Triton SSN

Displacement: 5,686 tonnes/5,596.2 tons (surfaced); 7,650 tonnes/7,529.2 tons (submerged)
Length: 136m/446ft 2in
Beam: 11.27m/37ft
Armament: 6 x 533mm/21in tubes (4 x forward, 2 x aft)
Propulsion: 2 x S4G nuclear reactors
Speed: 30 knots (surfaced); 27 knots (dived)
Complement: 159 crew

LEFT: **Size certainly mattered, as evidenced by the first major nuclear class of boats anywhere in the world, with its 14 members. USS *Barb* was the fourth, commissioned in 1963 and remaining in business for 26 years.**
ABOVE: **Taking shape, the evolving profile of the nuclear boats.**

Thresher/Permit-class SSN

The dual name for this class resulted from a disaster that was to befall the *Thresher*, and consequently the mantle passed to *Permit*. *Thresher* was a purpose-built nuclear attack boat to lead in what the Federation of American Scientists describe as "the world's first modern, quiet, deep-diving fast attack submarine". The design integrated such advanced features as a hydro-dynamically shaped hull, a large bow-mounted sonar array, advanced sound-silencing features, and an integrated control/attack centre with the proven S5W reactor plant. In short, the Thresher/Permit boats represented a major advance over previous submarine designs, and established the pattern of all successive American attack submarine classes. They were, for example, the first to have hulls constructed of High Yield-80 (HY-80) steel alloy, which allowed operations at substantially greater depths than previous submarines. They were the first submarines to have a large bow-mounted sonar, requiring the installation of

torpedo tubes amidships. They were larger than the previous Skipjack class, but with the lighter hull, they were able to use the same nuclear power plant without sacrificing speed. They were designed for prolonged periods submerged, and that certainly proved to be the case. In fact, they were limited only by the amount of food that the boats could carry, and were capable of sustained operation at high speed. The lead boat of the class, *Thresher*, spent the early part of her evaluation year of 1962 testing and participating in the Nuclear Submarine Exercise Programme (Nusubex). This was designed specifically to improve the tactical capabilities of nuclear submarines and anti-submarine warfare training, which was judged to be in need of constant review and overhaul in the face of increasing USSR capability.

She was engaged in operations off Charleston under the observation of the Naval Anti-Submarine Warfare Council before moving on to Florida for further trials. While

RIGHT: **The sheer scale of engineering now becomes apparent with the first pictorial evidence of the beam width. This photograph shows USS *Plunger* with intrepid submariners atop, beginning a 27-year journey that would be mainly devoted to the perfection of anti-submarine warfare techniques.**

manoeuvring into a berth at Port Canaveral, the submarine was accidentally struck by a tug, damaging one of her ballast tanks. The Electric Boat Company, at Groton, Connecticut, carried out repairs, and *Thresher* then went back to sea for deep-diving exercises. In addition to her 16 officers and 96 enlisted men, 17 civilian technicians remained aboard to record her performance in the company of a surface submarine rescue vessel *Skylark*, which was in constant communication with her during the trials.

Fifteen minutes after reaching her assigned test depth, the submarine communicated with *Skylark* by underwater telephone to report the boat was in trouble, but before the full story could be relayed, the transmission became garbled. Then, the listeners on the surface heard what they would describe as a noise like "air rushing into an air tank" and then nothing. The line went dead. As all hope of re-establishing communications vanished, a rescue group was hurriedly assembled and the submarine rescue ship *ASR-43* recovered items of clothing and debris, which indicated that *Thresher* has suffered a catastrophic failure. This was confirmed by photographs that showed that the submarine had broken up in 2,560m/1,400 fathoms of water, taking all on board to their deaths some 354km/220 miles east of Boston. *Thresher* was officially declared lost in April 1963.

The subsequent investigation into the disaster identified that the primary cause of the sinking was the failure of a seawater pipe in the aft engine spaces, which in turn caused a total loss of electrical power. In dire straits, the crew failed to operate the valves manually, which could have saved the submarine before they were overcome. With no power, the boat simply drifted down to the crush depth, where her structural integrity failed, resulting in a terrible death for the remaining crew members. The US Navy was stunned by the loss and vowed never to let such a tragedy happen again.

Consequently, the SubSafe Programme was developed from the lessons learned. This includes more rigorous manufacturing standards and operating procedures, and the relocation of safety equipment. SubSafe guarantees that every submarine in the US Fleet and every pressure-related part is certified as being 100 per cent safe for use on a submarine, and it ensures that the integrity of the material used on the ship can operate at design test depth. It was believed that this would provide for a situation in which disaster threatened the ship and its crew.

Other controls were also set in place as a result of the SubSafe programme, to ensure that when an emergency arose aboard a submarine, all vital equipment which sailors would need quick access to was clearly marked and accessible, even in gloomy conditions. Further, an operator should only be one second away from flipping the emergency main ballast tanks to vent, so the boat can rise to the surface. Further recommendations of a special Presidential Deep Submergence Review Group resulted in the creation of the Deep Submergence Rescue System, which was developed in the mid-1960s, and which initiated the development of the modern rescue vehicles *Mystic* (DSRV 1) and *Avalon* (DSRV 2) of the US Deep Submergence Unit.

ABOVE: **USS *Tinosa*, eighth boat launched in the Thresher class, spent the 28 years of her life on assignments and patrols throughout the world, undergoing two major overhauls, during one of which she received submarine safety improvements designed in the wake of the loss of USS *Thresher* in 1963.**

BELOW LEFT: **A declassified photograph of a test and evaluation firing of a SUBROC missile in 1963, USS *Permit* (SSN-594) becoming the first submarine to fire one.**

BELOW RIGHT: **USS *Dace*, from which 16 crew members were taken off at Roosevelt Roads Naval Station in critical condition from heat stroke after a cooling water pump seized up and the temperature in one part of the boat reached 85°C/185°F. The boat was on her way to dry dock for an overhaul at the time.**

Permit

Displacement: 3,484 tonnes/3,429 tons (surfaced); 4,133 tonnes/4,067.7 tons (submerged)
Length: 84.9m/278ft 7in
Beam: 9.7m/31ft 10in
Armament: 4 x 533mm/21in tubes (forward), Mk 48 torpedoes, Harpoon missiles, Mk 57 deep water mines, Mk 60 CAPTOR mines
Propulsion: S5W nuclear reactor
Speed: 22 knots (surfaced); 20 knots (dived)
Complement: 143 crew

FAR LEFT: **An historic event in the development of submarine warfare, the construction of USS** *George Washington,* **America's first ballistic missile carrier, which was hurriedly created and put into service by cutting the SSN** *Scorpion* **in two and inserting the missile compartment.** ABOVE: **The** *George Washington* **underway. She did not need to refuel for four years from commissioning, having then completed an incredible 160,934km/100,000 miles.** INSET: **The badge of the first SSBN of the United States Navy.**

George Washington SSBN

George Washington was the first ever ballistic missile carrier in the United States Navy, but she was not a purpose-built SSBN. In a previous life, she was the SSN *Scorpion* and had been reborn by being cut in two and having a 39.6m/130ft missile compartment inserted to accommodate the arrival of the much-vaunted Polaris ballistic missiles. According to the Federation of American Scientists (FAS), she became "the submarine that most influenced world events in the 20th century. With its entry into service in December 1959 the United States instantly gained the most powerful deterrent force imaginable – a stealth platform with enormous nuclear firepower."

She re-emerged from the Electric Boat Company yards in June 1960 as the lead boat in a new class bearing her name, and sailed to Cape Canaveral, Florida, to be equipped with two solid-propellant missiles for trials. She then went to the US Atlantic Missile Test Range with officials of the Polaris Submarine programme and on July 20, 1960, completed the historic event of launching the first Polaris missile from a submerged submarine, although it was unarmed. The launch was confirmed at 12:39 hours in a message sent by *George Washington*'s commanding officer to President Eisenhower: "Polaris – from out of the deep to target. Perfect."

A further missile was launched from the submerged submarine an hour later, travelling 1,770km/1,100 miles down the firing range to hit the target area. Two weeks later she duplicated the test firing before finally travelling to Charleston to take on board her full load of 16 Polaris missiles and as already noted in these pages, was thus equipped with a greater power than all the bombs dropped by all sides in World War II. The submarine completed her first patrol after 66 days of submerged running on January 21, and there began her lifelong series of patrols as part of America's nuclear deterrent programme, operations which today remain classified. The voyage over the next four years covered 160,934km/100,000 miles before she put in for a refuel, and of course that was just a beginning.

It is also noteworthy that the third member of the George Washington class, *Theodore Roosevelt*, was also something of a hybrid when she was rushed into service in 1961. Components initially assembled for the Skipjack-class nuclear attack submarine *Scamp* were diverted and used to speed up her construction.

Five days after commissioning, the submarine set off, bound for the east coast, and en route set another precedent by become the first fleet ballistic missile submarine to transit the Panama Canal.

ABOVE: **Same boat, different staff in the missile control room of the** *George Washington*, **who were thankfully never called upon to press the button in 25 years of dramatic service.**

Four days later, she arrived at Cape Canaveral to test-fire her first Polaris A1 missile before heading off to the American base at Holy Loch, Scotland, to begin the first of many years of patrolling. It was during her second tour of duty that the submarine ran aground off the western coast of Scotland while returning from her 21st patrol from the Holy Loch base. She was hauled into dry dock for temporary repairs before returning to the United States.

George Washington SSBN

Displacement: 5,512 tonnes/5,424.9 tons (surfaced); 6,424 tonnes/6,322.5 tons (submerged)
Length: 116.43m/382ft
Beam: 10m/32ft 10in
Armament: 16 Polaris missiles
Propulsion: S5W nuclear reactor
Speed: 20 knots (surfaced); 24 knots (dived)
Complement: 120 crew

Ethan Allen SSBN/SSN

*E*than Allen led her class into production, thus becoming the sixth SSBN submarine in the American fleet, and on May 6, 1962, she also took her place in history by test-firing the only nuclear-armed Polaris missile ever launched. The A1 missile was fired from the Ethan Allen while submerged in the Pacific, and the nuclear warhead was detonated over the South Pacific at the end of the programmed flight.

It was the only complete proof test of a US strategic missile, prior to an international ban on atmospheric testing. Later, this class became the first to be equipped with the A2 series missiles, and subsequently the A3 version in the 1970s. All five of the Ethan Allen boats were eventually reclassified as attack submarines under the Strategic Arms Limitation Treaty (SALT).

After almost two decades of service as SSBNs, their missile sections were decommissioned in 1981 in compliance

with the SALT I treaty. The missile fire control systems were removed, and cement blocks were placed in the missile tubes to assume the role of SSNs, although a number of the SSBNs from this and other classes were retained merely for training purposes or anti-submarine warfare duties. Sam Houston of the Lafayette class was also converted again for use during the 1980s as a transport and landing vehicle for US Special forces and remained as such for some years. Most, however, were gradually called in for decommissioning and subsequent entry into the recycling programme in the 1990s.

LAST DAY OF POSTAL SERVICE

TOP LEFT: **Class leader Ethan Allen also found her place in history for two reasons, firstly for firing a Polaris missile and then almost 20 years later, in being stripped of her nuclear armament completely as part of the scaling down of the nuclear arms race under the SALT I agreement.**
TOP RIGHT: **In the same class, the Thomas A. Edison was similarly converted to an attack submarine through the procedure of having cement blocks placed in the missile tubes.** ABOVE: **A Last Day cover to mark the retirement of Thomas Jefferson, which was converted in 1981 and ended her service completely on January 24, 1985.**

Ethan Allen SSBN

Displacement: 6,790 tonnes/6,682.8 tons (surfaced); 7,873 tonnes/7,748.7 tons (submerged)
Length: 125m/410ft 1in
Beam: 10m/32ft 10in
Armament: 16 Polaris missiles; 4 x 533mm/21in tubes
Propulsion: S5W nuclear reactor
Speed: 22 knots (surfaced); 25 knots (dived)
Complement: 110 crew

ABOVE: **Considering the mass of superstructure below, the Ethan Allen class kept a relatively low profile on the surface, as aptly demonstrated here by the second of the class, USS Sam Houston, which spent 20 years up close and personal against the USSR fleet before being reclassified as an SSN.** INSET: **The badge of the fourth and last member of the Ethan Allen Class, USS Thomas Jefferson.**

Lafayette-class SSBN

The 19 boats of the Lafayette class added a further dimension to the expanding US ballistic missile capability and were known as fleet ballistic missile carriers. They were commissioned with some speed over an 18-month period from early 1963, and the leader of the class, *Lafayette*, was operational from January 4, 1964, destined for her first deterrent patrol operating out of Rota, Spain. Over the course of the next three years, she carried out 15 such patrols, a typical workload for a member of the Polaris fleet, demonstrated by the fact that Lafayette's 15th actually marked the 400th patrol carried out by the Polaris-carrying fleet. The following year, she was called into Newport News Dry Dock Company for a refit, lasting almost a year, before returning to her deterrent operations.

Another boat of the same class, *James Monroe*, completed her overhaul around the same time and became the first submarine with Polaris A2s to be called in to be upgraded to the A3 capability. At that time, the ballistic boats were scheduled for refits after four years and a major overhaul after seven years, the latter taking the boat off line for around two years, a fact of life that could seriously limit the US Navy's ability to meet the SSBN patrols they were now expected to carry out. In 1974, they therefore introduced an SSBN Extended Refit Programme to provide additional preventive or corrective maintenance at

the mini-refit stage, thus enabling them to extend the major overhaul to ten years. Another of the Lafayette class, *James Madison*, was the first SSBN to undergo the extended refit, which was conducted at Holy Loch, Scotland in September 1974.

A further important development for the Lafayette class arrived in the same year when the Trident I ballistic missile programme was authorized, although the boats that would carry it – the new *Ohio*-class submarines – would not be available until 1979. Six of the Lafayettes were therefore selected for what was termed a "backfit" programme to take the Tridents. The class was therefore engaged in fleet SSBN deterrent operations over three decades, until decommissioning of the class began in the late 1980s and continued to 1994. One, *Sam Rayburn*, was taken out in 1985 to conform to the SALT II agreements and converted into a training ship with her missile tubes filled with concrete.

It is worth noting that the 12 boats of the Benjamin Franklin class that followed the Lafayettes were largely similar, except that they had new and quieter machinery and were thus considered a separate class. Two of them, *Kamehameha* and *James K. Polk*, were later converted to attack submarines exclusively for operations with SEAL special warfare forces, a role they performed for many years.

ABOVE LEFT: **The Lafayette-class *Woodrow Wilson* SSBN arrived at the Panama Canal on her maiden cruise in January 1964 to be met by violent anti-American demonstrations over an unconnected incident. The submarine was forced to transit the canal in a record 7 hours and 10 minutes while combat-ready Marines and soldiers guarded the locks.** ABOVE: **The USS *Sam Rayburn*, with her 16 Polaris missile tubes open, was converted into a training platform in 1986.**

ABOVE: **The USS *James Monroe* became the first submarine with Polaris A2 missiles to enter overhaul, and on January 9, 1968, she became the first to receive Polaris A3 capability.**

Lafayette-class SSBN

Displacement (standard version): 7,135 tonnes/ 7,022.3 tons (surfaced); 8,110 tonnes/ 7,981.9 tons (submerged)
Length: 129.6m/425ft 2in
Beam: 10.06m/33ft
Armament: 16 x missile tubes for Polaris or Poseidon; 4 x 533mm/21 torpedo tubes (forward); Mk4/16 anti-ship torpedo; Mk 37 anti-submarine torpedo; Mk 45 Astor nuclear torpedo; Mk 48 anti-submarine torpedo
Propulsion: S5W nuclear reactor; 2 x geared steam turbines, 11,185.5kW/15,000shp
Speed: 20 knots (surfaced); 25 knots (dived)
Complement: 143 crew

Sturgeon-class SSN

A major class of 39 submarines built specifically for anti-submarine warfare in the late 1960s and 70s, the Sturgeon boats became the highly flexible workhorses of the American fleet through some of the most tense and difficult times covering a span of more than 20 very active years. In using the same propulsion power pack as the smaller Thresher/Permit classes, the Sturgeons sacrificed speed for more efficient and versatile combat capabilities that, in fact, did not prove to be a handicap. Their versatility also took on another dimension when six of the boats were also modified to carry the SEAL Dry Deck Shelter (DDS) for "special operations", of which the class history is littered with references, without delving into great detail. Those that received this configuration were primarily used for the covert insertion of special forces from the DDS, a submersible launch hangar attached to the submarine's Weapon Shipping Hatch. This provided the most effective method of SEAL delivery because of its position on the ship.

The weaponry initially used by the Sturgeon boats was the Harpoon missile system and later the Tomahawk cruise missile, along with Mk 48 torpedoes with the tubes sited amidships to allow for the bow-mounted sonar. The class was also equipped with sail-mounted dive planes that rotated to a vertical position for breaking through the ice while surfacing in Arctic regions. The last ten of the class were also given an extended hull, with 3m/10ft added specifically to provide greater working and living space on long patrols.

The Federation of American Scientists noted in their summary of this class that, while the boats achieved little publicity during their heyday, this class of ship was "the platform of choice for many of the Cold War missions for which submarines are now famous". The Sturgeons were also subjected to a five-year study that resulted in their working life being extended from 20 years to 30 years, with a possible extension to 33 years on a case-by-case basis. In the event, many boats of this class were retired as the Cold War eased, to avoid expensive reactor refuelling.

TOP RIGHT: **An experience longed for and achieved by many submariners, as attack submarine USS *Pogy*, of the Sturgeon class of SSNs surfaces through 0.46m/18in of Arctic ice in November 1996. Perched high on the sail of the boat as lookout is Radioman Second Class Mark Sisson scanning the horizon for any inquisitive polar bears.** MIDDLE RIGHT: **With her smooth lines clearly evident, another of the Sturgeon-class boats, *Pintado*, was one of the most advanced submarines in the fleet when commissioned in 1971.** LEFT: **A starboard view of *Seahorse*, from the same class which was also able to boast of Arctic experience.**

Sturgeon-class SSN	
Displacement: 4,183 tonnes/4,116.9 tons (surfaced); 4,704 tonnes/4,629.7 tons (submerged)	
Length: 89m/292ft	
Beam: 9.75m/32ft	
Armament: 4x 533mm/21in tubes, Mk 48 torpedoes; Harpoon missiles; Mk 57 deep water mines; Mk 60 Captor mines	
Propulsion: S5W nuclear reactor, 2 x steam turbines, 11,185.5kW/15,000shp	
Speed: 20 knots (surfaced); 25 knots (dived)	
Complement: 110 crew	

LEFT: **The renowned** *Los Angeles,* **leader of the largest class of SSNs produced by the US Navy, a brilliant boat much loved by those who sailed in her. She was also historically important as the submarine whose target assignments included ASW against Soviet submarines assigned to sink US carriers, and ASUW against capital ships in the Soviet surface action groups.**

Los Angeles-class SSN

The Los Angeles class was numerically the largest post-war group built by the US Navy, with 62 boats commissioned between 1976 and 1996, costing $900,000 million apiece at 1990 prices. They had a projected lifespan of 30 years, and some of their makers predicted that the improved version introduced in 1988 could still be in full operational condition 40 to 45 years from their date of birth. They would be pleased to see that, remarkably, 26 remain in service at the time of writing, 45 years since the improved version appeared in service – these boats still make up over half of all the US Navy's fast attack submarines.

The range was designed and introduced specifically for anti-submarine warfare operations against Soviet submarines, which in turn were targeting US battlegroups. The early *Los Angeles* boats were primarily concerned therefore with Carrier Battlegroup protection. They were fast and exceedingly quiet, features that were improved even further as the class progressed through the 1980s and 90s. Initially, they were equipped with Harpoon anti-ship missiles and anti-ship Tomahawk cruise missiles. Later, as the Cold War faded, many were fitted with Tomahawk land attack missiles in support of the military in hotspots such as the Balkans and the Persian Gulf.

ABOVE: **An interesting perspective on size, with the Los Angeles-class boat** *Scranton* **surfacing in the North Arabian Sea while aircraft carrier** *George Washington* **cruises in the background.**

In the principal role for which they were designed, they were at the sharp end of the little-known Cold War beneath the waves in which US submarines and those of their British allies performed their duties with aplomb. This brought them into close contact with the opposition, with some scary shunts, bumps and close encounters given that the Russians were doing exactly the same thing, and both sides were conducting sweeps literally hundreds of miles ahead of their battle groups and strike boats.

To meet these requirements, the Los Angeles class boats were progressively updated and consequently were the most advanced attack submarines in the world. However, as time and conditions moved on, and the Cold War gradually receded, these boats were versatile enough to move along with the times and modern requirements. Unlike the SSBNs, great monoliths for which there was a shortage of alternative occupations, the fast attack submarines of the Los Angeles class possessed the stealth, speed and endurance to match the requirements of the modern political climate. These 110m/361ft boats became the epitome of the true submarine, driven by a brilliant power pack, highly accurate sensors, sophisticated weapons control systems and central computer monitoring.

They were built in three variants, first comprising the original Los Angeles class for the first 30 boats. The next 30 had an upgraded reactor core and 12 vertical tubes for Tomahawk cruise missiles. The last 23 came with an advanced BSY-1 sonar suite combat system and the ability to lay mines from their torpedo tubes. They were also adapted for under-ice operations by moving the diving planes from the sail structure to the bow, and the sail was strengthened for breaking through ice.

One great feature of the Los Angeles boats has been the constant upgrading of communications systems for use both within the boat and externally. The interior phones on the modern boats, for example, operate on sound-powered circuits without electrical power and were thoroughly reliable in battle situations. The possible need to stay submerged for long periods at a time also provided the impetus to ensure the crew were well catered for both in terms of atmospheric comfort and off-duty relaxation, and the configuration of these boats allowed a situation where work and rest were physically divided. Considerable thought had clearly gone into the boats' architecture, providing for two watertight compartments. All the living and rest-and-relaxation accommodation is housed forward, along with control centres, sonar and the computer suite. The after compartment houses the nuclear reactor and the ship's propulsion equipment.

A five-year study was carried out to evaluate potential life span of the class. It was discovered that after 30 years' service, a major overhaul would equip them for a further 10-year operating cycle. It was assessed that at 2001 prices, the additional overhaul would cost $400 million. Every option was considered given that Department of Defense studies at the time projected a need for 68 attack submarines by 2015 and 76 by 2025.

It is interesting to note the major difference between first and last in this class, from *Los Angeles* to *Cheyenne*, that of the Submarine Advanced Combat System AN/BSY-1, which was the very latest in technology and has been updated in service. It combines the Sonar and Fire Control Systems – the Combat Systems Department is divided into four distinct divisions: Torpedo, Fire Control, Sonar and Deck. The personnel in each of these divisions are responsible for ensuring that the Weapons System is always maintained in a condition of maximum readiness.

As the Federation of American Scientists (FAS) points out, the Sonar portion, utilizing advanced array systems, can detect, classify, and track multiple contacts at extreme ranges under adverse conditions. The Fire Control portion provides weapons orders, as well as targeting information to the ship's four torpedo and 12 vertical launch tubes.

The *Cheyenne* (first to launch Tomahawk missiles in Operation Iraqi Freedom) carries the latest variety of advanced submarine weaponry, including the Mk 48 Advanced Capability torpedo, the Harpoon anti-ship missile and the Tomahawk cruise missile. The Torpedo Division is manned by machinists, who stand their watch in the Torpedo Room.

LEFT: **Down the hatch – an aerial resupply operation aboard the Los Angeles-class boat, *Scranton*, deployed as part of the USS *Kearsarge* Expeditionary Strike Group participating in two major joint exercises, Caya Green, a bilateral US/Israel exercise, and Inspired Siren, with the Pakistani Navy in the summer of 2005.**
BELOW: **Balloons fly as the *Los Angeles*-class submarine *Newport News* slides down the launch-way at Newport News Shipbuilding and Drydock Co., Newport News, Virginia, on March 15, 1986.**

ABOVE: **The control room of USS *Toledo* has the appearance of an executive office suite.**
LEFT: **USS *Greeneville* dry-docked at the Pearl Harbor Naval Shipyard to perform necessary repairs following a collision at sea with the Japanese fishing vessel *Ehime Maru* off the coast of Honolulu, Hawaii.**

Los Angeles-class SSN

Displacement: 6,210 tonnes/6,111.9 tons (surfaced – variable depending on age); 6,750 tonnes/6,643.4 tons (submerged)
Length: 109.73m/360ft
Beam: 10m/32ft 10in
Armament: Harpoon and Tomahawk ASM/LAM missiles; 4 x 533mm/21in tubes (forward), Mk 48 torpedoes
Propulsion: S6G reactor; 1 x shaft, 26,099.5kW/35,000shp
Speed: 23 knots (surfaced); 30–32 knots (dived)
Complement: 129 crew

FAR LEFT: **The broad back of USS** *Pennsylvania*, **of the Ohio class.**

LEFT: **The first firing of a C-4 Trident I missile was staged at Cape Canaveral and later from a member of the Ohio-class ballistic fleet. Eight boats of the class were initially assigned to the Pacific, armed with Trident. The Ohio submarines were also fitted with 24 missile tubes as opposed to the 16 of earlier boomers.**

Ohio-class SSBN

In 1981 when the Ohio-class submarines were making their debut in what was planned as a long-running production schedule, few would have put money on an early end to the Cold War. Quite the reverse, and so the emphasis on strategic deterrence by way of a massively armed ballistic fleet remained unswerving and generally unopposed politically in spite of the enormous costs involved. Deterrence had been the sole reason to maintain a ballistic fleet since inception in 1960. Furthermore, because of the latter element, much work had been done in the meantime to keep the boats effective and at work for as long as possible in terms of life and as busy as possible in terms of the cycle of deployment.

The optimum level for SSBN operations was achieved in the late 1970s and maintained for the Ohio fleet: that they should be at sea at least 66 per cent of their life, and that included downtime for major overhaul periods of 12 months every nine years, although

modern design concepts allow the submarines to operate for 15 years between overhauls. At sea, a standard patrol would last 70 days, although this might be extended in exceptional circumstances, and indeed the Ohio class was designed for extended deterrent patrols. A 25-day period was then allowed for maintenance, reloading of munitions and supplies, and change of crew.

The Ohio class, first introduced in the 1980s, progressively replaced the older fleet ballistic missile submarines, whose working life was coming to an end, and they were fully up to date with the latest technology and internal comforts. The streamlining of the outer hull also allowed the boats to move with considerable stealth and to increase cruising speed when submerged. A rate of 25 knots was comfortably achieved at depths in excess of 243.8m/800ft.

The final member of the class, *Louisiana*, commissioned in 1997, completed the fleet of 18 Ohio boats. Ten were assigned to the Atlantic fleet,

initially equipped with the D-5 Trident II missile carrying eight independently targetable reentry vehicles. The remaining eight boats first went to work carrying the C-4 Trident I missile, but by 2008 these had all been converted to carry the D-5.

Whereas earlier ballistic boats carried 16 missiles, the Ohio class were capable of carrying 24 missiles bearing warheads that could all be launched within one minute and delivered to targets virtually anywhere on the world's surface, while at the same time able to operate at depths where it was possible to avoid detection.

When all 18 boats of Ohio are fully operational, they represent almost half of the total number US strategic warheads. As part of the Navy study on the longevity of boats, the Navy adjusted the lifespan of the class to 42 years, made up of two 20-year cycles separated by a two-year overhaul. The Ohio class is expected to be replaced from the early 2030s, gradually, by the Columbia class.

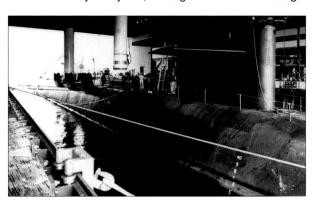

LEFT: **The loading of the most powerful weapons on earth into one of the Ohio-class submarines, whose larger hulls accommodate more weapons of larger size and greater range, as well as sophisticated computerized electronic equipment for improved weapons guidance and sonar performance.**

Ohio-class SSBN

Displacement: 16,500 tonnes/16,239.4 tons (surfaced); 18,453 tonnes/18,161.6 tons (submerged)
Length: 170.69m/560ft
Beam: 10.06m/33ft
Armament: 24 missile tubes for Trident I or II; 4 x 533mm/21in tubes, Mk 48 torpedoes
Propulsion: 1 x S8G nuclear reactor
Speed: 20 knots (surfaced); 25 knots (dived)
Complement: 157 crew

LEFT: **USS** *Virginia*, the attack submarine that reset the template for future strategic submarine design. This boat can act as a deployment platform for a wide range of missions and technologies: covert strikes by launching land attack missiles from vertical launchers and torpedo tubes, highly advanced ASW capabilities, Unmanned Undersea Vehicles, an Advanced SEAL Delivery System, plus 38 assorted weapons. BELOW: *Virginia* during her Alpha trials, which included a full range of speed and depth capability assessments, as well as checking all systems essential for the safe operation of the submarine.

Virginia-class SSN

The Virginia-class submarine was designed in the late 1990s as the first multi-mission, multi-purpose boat that will carry the US Navy's operations forward for most of the first half of the 21st century. The submarine was designed entirely by computer to provide maximum flexibility. The keynote features of the design were based on the requirements that the five boats of the Virginia class would be responsive to the changing needs, missions and threats of modern submarine warfare. The principal aim was that the V boats could be redirected to meet any need and updated by inserting new technologies using integrated electronic systems combined with Commercial-Off-The-Shelf (COTS) components. This, in turn, say the submarine's designers, will allow the state-of-the-art technology that is the boat's prime feature to be maintained

and updated throughout the life of the Virginia class, thus avoiding obsolescence. Other key features include:
• A sonar system with much greater signal processing power than any contemporary attack submarine.
• A sail designed for future installation of a "special mission-configurable mast" for enhanced flexibility and war-fighting performance.
• An integral Lock-Out/Lock-In chamber for special operations, combined with the hosting of Special Operations Forces equipped with underwater delivery vehicles.
• A substantial array of weapons encompassing the most advanced heavyweight torpedoes, mines, vertical-launch Tomahawk cruise missiles and Unmanned Undersea Vehicles for horizontal launch.

The US Navy maintains that the Virginia class will continue to surpass the performance of any current or projected threat submarine and will "maintain American undersea dominance well into the 21st century". Much of the thinking surrounding submarine development altered considerably with the end of the Cold War. Significantly, the fundamental focus in preparing the Virginia class for ASW conflict is to be achieved by combining the under-sea capability with the ability to attack littorals from the sea to influence events ashore. *Virginia*, the Navy maintains, is the boat that will achieve those ambitions.

LEFT: **Dressed and ready to go**, the Virginia class which has been the last word (for the moment) in advanced stealth multi-mission and SEAL delivery submarines but with an important break with the past: no periscope – simply two Photonics masts delivering images of the surrounding area on to large screens.

Virginia-class SSN

Displacement: Not known (surfaced); 6,567 tonnes/6,463.3 tons (submerged)
Length: 115m/377ft 4in
Beam: 10.36m/34ft
Armament: 4 x 533mm/21in tubes, Mk 48 ADCAP heavyweight torpedoes; 12 Vertical Launch System Tubes for Tomahawk cruise missiles, Advanced Mobile Mines, Unmanned Undersea Vehicles, Special Warfare Dry Deck Shelter, Advanced SEAL Delivery System
Propulsion: So far stated as 1 x S9G pressurized water reactor; Improved Performance Machinery Programme Phase III; 1 x secondary propulsion submerged motor; no power output data available
Speed: 20 knots (surfaced); 25 knots (dived)
Complement: 113 crew

Seawolf-class SSN

The Seawolf submarines, a fleet of 29 boats each costing billions of dollars, were to become the most expensive submarines ever built, and they would operate autonomously against enemy vessels should the occasion arise. In other words, their sole reason for being afloat was to destroy Soviet ballistic missile submarines before they could attack American targets, in the event of conflagration. When the Seawolf programme was being formulated in the mid-1980s, there was no greater concern among the Reagan administration than to secure total superiority over the USSR's seaborne nuclear capability. American defence analysts were convinced that in such a situation, the SSBNs were the most survivable parts of the Soviet nuclear arsenal, and they would have to be taken out.

ABOVE: **The ultimate in ASW, *Seawolf* can operate 75 per cent faster before being detected than any previous submarine and is said to be quieter at its tactical speed of 25 knots than a Los Angeles-class submarine at the pier-side and, according to the USN, is "capable of establishing and maintaining battlespace dominance".** BELOW LEFT: **The obligatory trip to see the polar bears, and vice versa.** BELOW: **Former US President Jimmy Carter visits to discuss the third and last boat in the Seawolf class, which carries his name.**

Consequently, the US government was prepared to write an open cheque to finance the building of what would be billed as the most advanced attack submarine the world had seen, the only one truly capable of destroying the Soviet SSBNs. Work pressed ahead but by the time the lead boat was in production, the Cold War was all but over. Approval for more two more Seawolf boats – to be named *Connecticut* and *Jimmy Carter* – was given by President George Bush, supported by Defence Secretary Dick Cheney, in 1992 at a cost of $2,765,900,000. They were to be the last. The cost of *Seawolf* forced the whole project into public debate, and thus it became the most controversial submarine programme in American history. When the Cold War ended, the Bush (Senior) administration cancelled the entire 29-ship order, except for the lead submarine.

However, the nuclear submarine community, led by Admiral Bruce DeMars, and influential shipyard lobbying forced the US Congress into a change of heart, and it was agreed that two additional boats would be built. With the reduction of the programme to a three-ship class, costs escalated astronomically, with the third boat in the series expected to cost in excess of $3 billion. The Clinton administration confirmed the cancellation of the remaining 26 on the grounds that there was no existing situation that could justify such vast expense against a threat that apparently no longer existed. Even so, the three that were approved were well worth having.

The sea trials of the first boat in 1996 proved that the great sales pitch that was given for them a decade earlier proved to be totally justified, and *Seawolf* was commissioned on July 19, 1997, at Electric Boat Shipyard. In fact, the US Navy claimed that trials had proved the aim that she should have the highest tactical speed of any US submarine. Stealth was the keynote, and proved by the novel additional of being able to put "combat swimmers" into denied areas.

Indeed, the whole concept of increasing the role of the submarine in special forces operations was also to the fore with the *Seawolf* project. A newly designed combat swimmer silo, along with the SEAL Dry Deck Shelter (DDS), would provide these additional facilities. The DDS for use with *Seawolf* is transportable by air and placed piggy-back on the submarine. It can accommodate and launch a swimmer delivery vehicle and combat swimmers. The swimmers' silo is an internal lock-out chamber that can deploy up to eight combat swimmers and their equipment at one time. Inside the boat, the tremendous innovations in virtually every aspect of seaworthiness make this another jewel in the crown of the US submarine service.

ABOVE LEFT: **The control room of *Seawolf*. This crew operates some of the most sophisticated electronics ever produced, providing enhanced indications and warning, surveillance and communications capability.** ABOVE: ***Seawolf* on her final trials.**

ROV Handling System

Advanced Communications Mast

New Hull Section

Auxiliary Manoeuvring Devices

Auxiliary Manoeuvring Devices

Reconfigurable Command Centre Suit

Ocean Interface with ROV

Reconfigurable Cargo Area

ABOVE: **When the third boat in the Seawolf class – USS *Jimmy Carter* – was being built, the US government approved an additional spend of $887 million for the development of advanced technology in naval special warfare, tactical surveillance and mine warfare operations.**

Seawolf-class SSN

Displacement: 7,432 tonnes/7,314.6 tons (surfaced); 8,992 tonnes/8,850 tons (submerged)
Length: 107.6m/353ft
Beam: 10.67m/35ft
Armament: 8 x 660mm/26in tubes, 50 Mk 48 ADCAP torpedoes or 100 mines, or 50 Tomahawk cruise missiles or 50 Harpoon anti-ship missiles
Propulsion: S6W nuclear reactor delivering 38,776.4kW/52,000shp
Speed: 25 knots (surfaced); 35 knots (maximum – dived)
Complement: 133 crew

Columbia-class SSBN

Developed to replace the United States Navy's Ohio class of Trident-armed ballistic missile submarines, the new Columbia-class submarines represent the very latest advancements in submarine technology and design. With an average price-tag per boat of around 5 billion US dollars, these 12 submarines have been developed to ensure the US Navy retains an effective and credible seaborne ballistic missile force that can operate unmolested by even the most advanced

ABOVE: Artist rendering of a Columbia-class ballistic missile submarine. The 12 submarines of the Columbia class will replace the Ohio-class submarines, which are reaching their maximum extended service life. BELOW: Cutaway view of a Columbia-class submarine, which has a crew of approximately 135 personnel, a relatively small crew compared to submarines of similar size, thanks to their advanced automation and computer systems. Crew members work in shifts to ensure that the submarine is always staffed and operational, with some personnel working 12-hour shifts and others working 6-hour shifts.

potential enemy anti-submarine warfare (ASW) threat. The new boats will have 16 missile launch tubes compared to the 24 of the Ohio class they will replace, starting in 2031. The boats will carry Trident II D5 missiles which can be launched from underwater over a range of more than 11,265km/7,000 miles. The Columbia fleet will represent around 70 percent of the US nuclear punch.

Building on decades of nuclear propulsion experience, the Columbia-class nuclear reactor heats water to drive steam turbines that will power electric motors to drive the boat propellers and onboard systems. This removes the need for noise-generating reduction gearing and mechanical drive systems typical of earlier US Navy nuclear-powered boats, and forms part of the vessels' stealthy design, which includes a hull that reduces drag and turbulence, together with the use of advanced sound-absorbing materials to dampen noise. Special coatings minimize their electromagnetic signature and radar cross-section and the boats' electronic emissions are carefully managed.

As ever, one of the key challenges facing modern submarines is the threat posed by increasingly innovative ASW technologies. To address this threat, the Columbia class submarines are equipped with advanced ASW countermeasures including torpedo decoys and advanced sonar systems. These systems work together to confuse and disrupt enemy sensors, making it more difficult or impossible for the enemy to detect and track the submarines. These countermeasures work together to make the vessels highly difficult to detect and track, even in the most challenging environments. The submarines are also equipped with advanced electronic warfare systems, which allow them to disrupt enemy communications and sensors. The boats are also equipped with high-resolution cameras and other imaging systems, which can be used to capture detailed images of the ocean floor and other features.

The class are also equipped with a range of advanced technologies, including next-generation sensors, advanced communications systems, and highly sophisticated fire control systems, enabling the crew to gather and process large amounts of data quickly, and respond to threats with pinpoint accuracy. In addition, the vessels are designed to be highly modular, allowing for easy upgrades and modifications as new technologies become available.

In addition to its nuclear weaponry, in terms of defensive and offensive armament, the class can deploy mines and are equipped with torpedo tubes to fire both heavyweight Mark 48 torpedoes and anti-ship missiles, as well as vertical launch tubes to launch subsonic Tomahawk cruise missiles and other long-range weapons to strike targets on land or at sea. The submarines can use modular Dry Deck Shelters (DDS), attached to their backs, to transport and deploy special operations personnel as well as small underwater vehicles, such as remotely operated vehicles (ROVs) and unmanned underwater vehicles (UUVs).

The 12 submarines, all to be named after US states, are expected to remain in service for at least 50 years.

LEFT: **An underwater launch of a Trident II D5 Trident from a Royal Navy submarine. The Columbia class has 16 missile launch tubes compared to the 24 of the Ohio class.**

Columbia-class SSBN

Displacement: 20,810 tonnes/21,140 tons (submerged)
Length: 171m/560ft
Beam: 13m/43ft
Armament: Up to 40 torpedoes, including Mark 48 torpedoes and submarine-launched mobile mines; Up to 16 Tomahawk cruise missiles for striking targets on land or at sea; Up to 16 Trident II D5 ballistic missiles with multiple independently targetable reentry vehicles (MIRVs)
Propulsion: Nuclear reactor, steam turbine, and electric propulsion system
Speed: Over 25 knots/46kmp/29mph
Complement: 135 crew

LEFT: **The Russian Kilo class entered service in the early 1980s. It was designed by the Rubin Central Maritime Design Bureau, St Petersburg. Subsequent developments led to the current production version and, most recently, Type 636.**
ABOVE: **The Kilo diesel electric boat has been a workhorse of the Russian fleet principally in anti-ship and anti-submarine operations. The class has also drawn an ongoing export trade from smaller nations.**

Kilo-class SSK

The Russian Kilo diesel-electric boats have been in constant use since the submarine first entered service in the early 1980s and more recently with the newer versions, the Type 877EKM and the Type 636. Further development of this class ensures that it will be around well into the 21st century with the introduction of the *Lada* (Project 677), which began sea trials in 2005. After some early setbacks and extensive design changes the first serial submarine of the class – B-858 Kronshtadt – was launched in 2018.

Designed for both anti-submarine and anti-ship warfare, Type 636 is considered to be one of the quietest of all the diesel submarines currently in production. The principal features in the boat's warfare capabilities are significant, and its designers at the St Petersburg shipyards claim she is capable of

detecting an enemy submarine at a range three to four times greater than it can be detected itself. That said, the role of the 636 is also highly practicable for general reconnaissance and patrol missions. With six watertight compartments separated by transverse bulkheads in a pressurized double-hull and a good reserve buoyancy, this class has a greater level of survivability if the submarine is holed. The 636 design is an improved development of the 877EKM Kilo class, with an extended hull.

The power of the diesel generators has been increased and the main propulsion shaft speed has been reduced to provide a substantial reduction in the acoustic signature. Conversely, the submarine's combat and command system is equipped with high-speed computers that can rapidly

process information from the surveillance equipment and determine submerged and surface targets and calculate firing parameters. Armaments include a launcher for eight surface-to-air missiles or alternatively, the vessels can be fitted with the Novator Club-S (SS-N-27) cruise missile system which delivers an anti-ship missile to a range of 220km/137 miles with a 450kg/992lb high-explosive warhead.

The computer-controlled torpedo system comes with an automated quick-loading device enabling the first salvo to be fired within two minutes and the second within five minutes. The six torpedo tubes are situated in the nose, all loaded, and with 12 reloads. Two of the tubes are designed for firing remote-controlled torpedoes that have a very high accuracy.

LEFT: **A considerably improved version of the Kilo design, which includes a much better noise insulation system and updated combat systems. Although production was eventually suspended for domestic purposes, several variants remained available for export.**

Type 636	

Displacement: 2,288 tonnes/2,251.9 tons (surfaced); 3,027 tonnes/2,979.2 tons (submerged)
Length: 73.76m/242ft
Beam: 9.9m/32ft 6in
Armament: 6 x 533mm/21in tubes, 18 x torpedoes; or 24 x mines; SA-N-8 Gimlet SAM
Propulsion: 2 x 1,118.6kW/1,500hp diesel engines; 1 x 4101.3kW/5,500hp electric motor
Speed: 10 knots (surfaced); 19 knots (dived)
Complement: 52 crew

LEFT: **The *Victor III* is a substantially upgraded version with improved noise levels and new sonar, sensor and command suites. This unusual image arose from the snagging of a frigate's towed array sonar, the cable for which can be seen looped around the submarine's stern fin.** ABOVE: **The *Victor II* cuts a sleek figure amid the foam, with rather a sporty look, but the reality was rather different, given that she was a merely a lengthened version of the *Victor I* to take a new ASW missile.**

Victor-classes I, II and III SSN

The Victor class is the NATO classification for the Soviet submarine developed under the name Project 671. It was among the earliest of the Russian boats to feature an advanced tear-drop hull design to achieve higher underwater speeds for the primary role of protecting Soviet surface fleets and to attack American SSBNs. The Victor first appeared in 1967, and 15 of the class were built with the capacity for 24 tube-launched weapons or 48 mines. They were later retrofitted to handle the TEST-68 wire-guided torpedo weapons. However, the boats were noisy, and the Victor II class was introduced in 1972 with the hull extended by 6m/20ft to accommodate sound insulation measures and space for additional weapons, including a new generation of heavy torpedoes that required power assistance to handle them in the torpedo room. The noise problem was not resolved, as the Russians discovered through the infamous Walker spy ring, which reported that the Americans could easily track the Victor II through its acoustic design. By then, seven of the Victor IIs had already been built, and work on any further boats was halted to await improvements in the design.

The final version, Victor III, was introduced in 1979, and over the next decade or so, a further 25 boats were built with the outer hull coated with anti-hydroacoustic materials to reduce the possibility of detection. Now generally quieter, they also had further internal alterations to accommodate a more up-to-date weapons stock, allowing for 24 tube-launched weapons or 36 mines on board. The outer hull of the Victor III was built partly from light alloys, and was distinguishable by a high stern fin fitted with a towed array dispenser – the first Soviet submarine to be fitted with a towed array.

LEFT: **A Victor III attack submarine with the towed array sonar clearly visible, here in company with a small Soviet ship (middle) and USS *Peterson* (back). This version, built between 1984 and 1992, was gradually withdrawn at the end of the 20th century and replaced by the Akula class. The remaining boats mostly served with the Northern Fleet.**

Victor III-class SSN

Displacement: 5,173 tonnes/5,091.3 tons (surfaced); 7,134 tonnes/7,021.3 tons (submerged)
Length: 106m/347ft 9in   **Beam:** 10.6m/34ft 9in
Armament: 2 x 650mm/25.6in tubes: 4 x 533mm/21in tubes, Type 53 and Type 65 torpedoes; SLCM-SS-N-21 Sampson; A/S: SS-N-15, SS-N-16 missiles
Propulsion: 2 x VM-4 reactors delivering 23,116.7kW/31,000shp
Speed: 18 knots (surfaced); 30 knots (dived)
Complement: 102 crew

LEFT: **The Yankees were the first class of Soviet submarines whose firepower was comparable to that of the Americans. As the Yankee versions progressed from I to III, they also became considerably quieter. Armed with 16 ballistic missiles apiece, they were the Soviet front-line boats, and at least three Yankees were continually positioned in a patrol box east of Bermuda.**
BELOW: **Yankee boats were heavily reduced to meet SALT I requirements, and many were converted to SSNs by having their ballistic missile compartments removed.**

Yankee-class 667A SSBN

The SSBN Project 667A was developed in 1962 as an improved version of a project that began four years earlier and which had suffered a number of problems, especially with the launch system. The result was a submarine unlike any other, in that the horizontal hydroplanes were arranged on the sail. It was designed with specific attention to the contours of the submarine to achieve minimal resistance under water. Similar attention was paid to the reduction of noise and a new type of propeller was designed for that purpose, as well as covering the pressure hull with sound-absorbing rubber and the external hull with an anti-hydroacoustic coating.

The submarine was initially equipped with the Soviet D-5 launch system for 16 R-27 missiles with a range of about 2,400km/1,491 miles, arranged in two rows in the fourth and fifth compartments of the ten-compartment boat. They could be launched from a depth of up to 50m/164ft and fired in four salvos each comprising four missiles at intervals of eight seconds per missile. The first four 667A Yankee submarines employed the Sigma navigation system, whereas the follow-on ships were equipped with the Tobol, the first Soviet navigational system that used a satellite navigation system that was shown to be especially reliable in the Arctic region, one of the main Soviet areas of operation. The first 667A Yankee submarine completed sea trials at the end of 1967, and it was introduced into the Northern Fleet between 1967 and 1974, with a total of 34 strategic submarines of the class being built. The early boats were all upgraded with the D-5U

launch systems and R-27U missiles in the late 1970s and early 80s, which provided a greater range, estimated at up to 3,000km/1,864 miles.

The Yankee class initially formed part of the important Northern Fleet as part of the 31st Division of Soviet strategic submarines based at Sayda. At the end of the 1960s, the 19th division of strategic submarines was also equipped with 667A submarines. Both divisions were a vital part of the Soviet strategic submarine coverage and consisted of 12 squadrons, which later became the 3rd Flotilla. In October 1986, considerable international concern was voiced when one of the Yankee boats, *K219*, suffered an explosion and a serious fire on board while operating to the east of Bermuda, in which four crew were killed. Attempts were made to put the boat

LEFT: A Yankee II conversion, one of the boats reconstructed for special duties which resulted in various new configurations when the ballistics equipment was removed. One, nicknamed the Yankee Sidecar, became a cruise missile carrier with 12 SS-NX-24 missiles as well as six tubes for Type 53 torpedoes, while another appeared in 1983 as a trial boat known as the Yankee Pod. BELOW: A depiction of an underwater release of missiles from a Yankee conversion. BOTTOM: Another conversion of a Yankee I, known as the Yankee Notch, an attack submarine that had six launch tubes for up to 20 missiles in addition to six torpedo tubes.

under tow, but eventually the task was aborted and she was scuttled into a depth of 5,500m/18,045ft. Subsequently a book and a television film appeared in the US about the incident and in the aftermath, the United States Navy categorically denied that any of their submarines was in collision with *K219*, or was in any way involved in the incident.

The ageing Yankee submarines were gradually removed from operational service between 1985 and 1994, and their missile compartments were taken out to comply with arms limitation agreements. Nevertheless, they had given good service, with two versions of the boat, 667A and 667AM, completing 590 patrols in most of the world's oceans. Several were also converted to perform special missions; most notable was the so-called Yankee Stretch, which was elongated to carry the new Soviet mini-submarines used for ocean research and intelligence. This was achieved by replacing the missile compartment with an extended hull so that the boat could serve as a mother ship for the very small special operations submarine AS-35 *Paltus*. The system was similar to that adopted by the Americans, utilizing the Dry Dock Shelter system for SEAL and other missions. These developments in both Russia and the United States, and to a lesser degree

the UK, reflected the need to meet new challenges in 21st century submarine operations. Another conversion, called the Yankee Pod, was equipped with radio equipment and a towed hydroacoustic station. Both of these versions were still active as the first decade of the 21st century came to a close.

Yankee-class 667A SSBN

Displacement: 7,760 tonnes/7,637.4 tons (surfaced); 9,600 tonnes/9,448.4 tons (submerged)
Length: 132m/433ft
Beam: 11.6m/38ft 1in
Armament: 4 x 533mm/21in tubes; 667A: D-5 launch system with 16 x R-27 missiles; 667AU: D-5U launch system with 16 x R-27U missiles
Propulsion: 2 x pressurized water reactors; 2 x steam turbines, 38,776.4kW/52,000hp each
Speed: 12 knots (surfaced); 25 knots (dived)
Complement: 130–140 crew

Echo-classes I and II SSN

Project 659 Echo was a boat on which old hands of the Russian Navy did not wish to serve. There was an inherent problem with the boats of this class in that it took at least 20 minutes for a trouble-free launching of the missiles, an operation which had to be conducted on the surface. Consequently, the boats were considered sitting ducks for the opposition. The five Echo I nuclear-powered cruise-missile submarines were designed to launch the land attack version SS-N-3c Shaddock missiles in erectable launch tubes mounted in pairs above the pressure hull on both sides of the sail. The Echo I boats were converted to attack submarines in the early 1970s. Some were decommissioned completely in the late 1980s, and others were taken out of service in the 1990s.

Twenty-nine Project 675 Echo II class were built from the mid-1960s, designed primarily to perform anti-ship duties at a time when the Americans had their carriers bristling with A3 Skywarrior aircraft capable of nuclear strikes against the Soviet Union. Echo II series boats

were later modified to enable them to launch the anti-shipping version of the Shaddock. These were primarily anti-carrier weapons, intended to respond to nuclear strikes against the Soviet Union by carrier-based aircraft. As such, their SS-N-3s came in both nuclear and conventional versions. A total of eight missiles were carried, two more than on the Echo I, and the hull was lengthened by 5m/16ft 5in to accommodate the extra pair of launchers.

To fire its missiles the submarine surfaced, deployed and activated tracking radar, and remained on the surface, linked to the high altitude cruise missile in flight via datalink, providing guidance commands based on the submarine radar's tracking data. The submarine itself was highly vulnerable to attack while on the surface operating its radar. A total of 29 Echo IIs were constructed between 1962 and 1968, of which a dozen were converted to carry the improved SS-N-12 by the mid-1980s. All had been decommissioned by the mid-1990s.

At least four Echo submarines suffered serious accidents. In August 1980 a fire in an Echo II off Japan killed at least nine crew members. On June 26, 1989, a fire erupted in the two reactor compartments on an Echo II submarine of the Northern Fleet. The reactor had to be shut down, and the submarine surfaced to return to Murmansk under auxiliary diesel power. Several crew members were injured, but none were killed in the incident.

Echo II-class SSN

Displacement: 4,710 tonnes/4,635.6 tons (surfaced); 5,905 tonnes/5,811.7 tons (submerged)
Length: 115m/377ft 4in
Beam: 9m/29ft 6in
Armament: 6 x 533mm/21in tubes (forward), 4 x 406mm/16in tubes (aft); 8 x SS-N-3 or 8 x SS-N-12 missiles
Propulsion: 2 x pressurized-water nuclear reactors delivering 22,371kw/30,000shp
Speed: 20 knots (surfaced); 23 knots (dived)
Complement: 92 crew

LEFT: **Echo II cruise-missile submarines were modified to carry a series of radars to launch anti-ship weapons, intended originally as a response to nuclear strikes against the Soviet Union by carrier-based aircraft.**

LEFT AND ABOVE: **The Alfa-class hunter-killer submarines were considered to be part of the Soviets' "demonstration of power", in which planned numbers and ability were exaggerated. They were very much experimental platforms to test innovations supposedly for a new generation of submarines, but although the Alfa boats were exceedingly fast and deep diving, they were also very noisy.**

Alfa-class SSN

Project 705 Alfa class was undoubtedly the fastest and deepest diving submarine of her age when she made her appearance in the late 1960s. Originally designed for the specific purpose of attacking American carrier battle groups, the first in this series was capable of 40 knots, a speed unmatched anywhere in the world for a 1,524-tonne/ 1,500-ton boat. This was largely achieved by the first-ever use of a titanium alloy, which meant the thickness and weight ratio of the hull to the power plant was substantially reduced against comparable boats of that era. The design of the submarine also included substantial automation.

The ability to travel at such speeds was increased further when the design

was revised in 1963. At that time, the displacement was also increased to around 2,337 tonnes/2,300 tons when the size of the crew was also doubled, and internal compartments increased from three to six. The outcome was a relatively small, fast submarine capable of 44 knots, an ability that caused great concern to American observers. It was wrongly assumed that the boat would lead the Soviet submarines in to a new era of development, although that proved not to be the case.

Even though she was eventually to be billed as a strong competitor to the US Los Angeles class, the claims were exaggerated. The submarine proved to be exceedingly noisy at the high speeds and turned out to be somewhat

unreliable and poorly armed. The lightweight hull was also suspect in the event of a torpedo attack. Even so, the Americans were sufficiently alarmed by the potential of a fast, deep-diving boat that they were provoked into a substantial investment in ASW weapons, especially in what has been described as a "dramatic improvement" in the Mk 46 and Mk 48 torpedoes.

Meanwhile, the Project 705 boats suffered a number of casualties as demands on them increased in the 1970s, and the programme was eventually ended in 1983. Four were lost due to reactor failures, one was retired in 1987, and four others were decommissioned in 1990–92. Even so, the Soviets felt they had served a useful strategic role.

ABOVE: **The Alfa-class submarine operated up close and personal against the American submarine force. This provoked a massive US investment in anti-submarine warfare.**

Alfa-class SSN

Displacement: 2,264–2,854 tonnes/2,228.2–2,828.9 tons (surfaced); 3,579–4,251 tonnes/3,522.5–4,183.9 tons (submerged)
Length: 79.5–81.4m/260ft 10in–267ft 1in
Beam: 9.5m/31ft 2in
Armament: 6 x 533mm/21in tubes (bow); 18 x 53-65K, SET-65 torpedoes or 20 x VA-111 torpedoes or 24 x mines; 21 x 81R (SS-N-15) missiles or 12 x Vodopad (SS-N-16)
Propulsion: 1 x liquid metal reactor; 2 x steam turbines, 29,828–35,048kW/40–47,000shp
Speed: 14 knots (surfaced); 43–45 knots (dived)
Complement: 31–45 crew

Delta-classes I, II, III and IV SSBN

A cruiser submarine continuing the Soviet penchant for largesse, the four versions of the Delta series became the mainstay of the Red ballistic fleet over the most vital period of the Cold War. Eighteen boats were built in the first series, the first completed in 1972. Based on the old Yankee class, they saw hefty service, with the last two being finally withdrawn in 2000. The Delta II boats added only an inertial navigational system before major advances were introduced in the Delta III SSBN class, which entered service in 1976.

ABOVE: **Big, bold and ugly: a Delta IV submarine, last of the nuclear missile-carrying boats placed together with Delta I, II and III under the NATO classification system, although the Russians' own classification put them as three different submarines, designed to attack cities, military and industrial installations.**

Fourteen of the boats were added to the Delta fleet over the next six years, with an anticipated lifespan of up to 25 years, and went straight into service, half with the Northern and the others with the Pacific fleets. The further improved Delta IVs, complete with sports complex and spa, brought another seven boats to the arena, all assigned to the Northern Fleet during their period of commissioning over a ten-year span, from 1982.

However, when the START-I treaty was signed in 1991, 25 older *Delta*-class, five *Typhoon*-class, and one *Yankee*-class ballistic missile submarines capable of launching over 400 missiles with over 1,700 warheads were due to be culled by 2005. It was an unlikely prospect given the large number of nuclear submarines around the world waiting patiently in line for the recycling experts to come along.

In 1999, the Russian Navy began a refit and overhaul programme for the remaining Deltas, which observers took to mean that there would be ongoing delays with the introduction

LEFT: **The *Delta III* carried a number of innovations: it was the first submarine that could launch any number of missiles in a single salvo, and it was the first that was capable of carrying ballistic missiles with multiple independently-targeted re-entry vehicles.**

LEFT AND ABOVE: **Although the *Delta IV* strategic missile submarine was classed in the West as a follow-on from the III-series whose design it resembles, the Soviets saw it as a separate development. Seven of the vessels were built between 1981 and 1992, with a propulsion system that provided speeds of 24 knots submerged.**

of the heralded replacement, the Borei class, six examples of which were in service in 2023.

The Delta name therefore remains a potent force in the 21st century and up to six examples of the *Delta III*/*DeltaIV*s remained in Russian navy service in 2023.

The IV boats are capable of launching the Novator SS-N-15 Starfish anti-ship missile or Mk 40 anti-ship torpedoes. Starfish is armed with a 200kT nuclear warhead and has a range of up to 45km/30 miles. The submarine has four 533mm/21in torpedo tubes capable of launching all types of torpedoes, including anti-submarine torpedoes.

The first of the Delta IV submarines was launched in January 1985 and was introduced into the Northern Fleet between 1985 and 1990, so there is still life left in the later members of the class still in service, although major overhauls would have to be performed every 7–8 years otherwise life expectancy willl be dramatically reduced.

LEFT: **An interesting starboard overhead view of the *Delta III* version. This is now the only way of viewing submarines of this class at sea, because every one of them is thought to have been taken out of service through a combination of arms limitation agreements and a lack of funding to keep them afloat.**

Delta IV-class SSBN

Displacement: 11,554 tonnes/11,371.5 tons (surfaced); 17,912 tonnes/17,629.1 tons (submerged – full load)
Length: 167m/547ft 11in **Beam:** 11.7m/38ft 5in
Armament: 4 x 533mm/21in tubes; 18 x Type 40 torpedoes or SS-N-15 Starfish ASW weapon with 200Kt depth charge; 16 x SS-N-23 Skiff SL ballistic missiles, 4–10 MIRVed 100kT warheads
Propulsion: 2PWR nuclear reactor
Speed: 14 knots (surfaced); 24 knots (dived)
Complement: 135 crew

LEFT: **At the time of its arrival in 1972, the Sierra class represented what Russian warfare analysts** *Warfare.RU* **described as the apex of Soviet attack submarine design. These boats were intended to be the primary Soviet attack weapon, "incorporating a variety of new sensors, silencing equipment, command systems and countermeasures".** ABOVE: **A profile of the Sierra design.** BELOW: **A starboard bow overhead view of the Sierra II.**

Sierra-class SSN

The Sierra series was introduced as a successor to the Alfa, again with the primary objective of attacking surface task forces, with a secondary commitment of launching cruise missiles against land-based objectives. Described in the Russian Arms Catalogue as the apex of Soviet attack submarine design when the class was developed in 1972, the Sierra boats became the first division of Soviet attack submarines of their time. Their eventual appearance in the early 1980s saw them generally accepted as being comparable in performance to early American Los Angeles-class vessels.

Noise levels, which had been a problem with the Alfa boats, were reduced by the addition of Cluster Guard anechoic tiles on the outer hull which, also like the Alfa, was constructed of titanium alloy for deep diving, while making the Sierra more difficult to detect. The double hull reduced possible damage to the inner

hull's six compartments, and there was also a crew escape chamber said to be capable of bringing up the entire crew from a depth of 1,500m/4,921ft. However, the cost of the titanium hulls made them expensive to produce, and consequently only limited numbers were built.

Even so, the boat performed well and a larger version, Sierra II, was introduced in the late 1980s. This boat was almost 6m/19ft 8in longer and contained an additional compartment, providing better accommodation for the crew, as well as a second crew escape chamber. Further silencing measures were also added, along with a new American-style spherical bow sonar. The expensive nature of the boat, however, was clearly causing concern in the Soviet naval hierarchy. As early as 1976, when the first submarines of the class were being built, it became evident that the titanium hulls were not suited to mass production.

As a result, construction was slower and in the end failed to meet the force requirements. In due course, production of the Sierra class was cancelled before completion of the required numbers, in favour of the less expensive Akula class. The last of the Sierra II boats were commissioned into Russia's Northern Fleet in the early 1990s and one or two of the four completed are believed to still be in service in 2023.

Sierra II-class SSN

Displacement: 7,479 tonnes/7,360.9 tons (surfaced); 8,956 tonnes/8,814.6 tons (submerged)
Length: 111m/364ft 2in
Beam: 14.2m/46ft 7in
Armament: 4 x 650mm/25.6in tubes; 4 x 533mm/21in tubes, 90kg/198lb HE Type 40 torpedoes; SS-N-15 Starfish anti-submarine weapon; SS-N-21 Sampson SLCM with 200kT nuclear warhead
Propulsion: 1 x OK-650 190mW/254,794hp pressurized-water nuclear reactor
Speed: 10 knots (surfaced); 32 knots (dived)
Complement: 59–61 crew

ABOVE: **A distinctive shape of the two-thirds submerged Sierra II boat, but not for long; only three were built before they were overtaken by the development of the Akula class.**

Akula-classes I and II SSN

This general purpose submarine, better known in the Soviet Union as the Bars (Snow Leopard) class, was constructed from low magnetic steel with a double hull noted for the substantial gap between the outer and inner hulls, thus reducing the threat of internal damage. The use of the hull was authorized in 1976, when the expensive titanium structures were ruled out for future use. Visually, the submarine was also different, with a distinctive high aft fin.

The first of eight boats was laid down in 1979 and in service by the mid-1980s. An improved version was introduced for the last three boats of Series I, and thereafter Series II took over in the 1990s, with 3m/9ft 10in added to the length, although that programme was curtailed after two boats were built, the last being commissioned in June 2000.

Throughout the building of the two designs, the Akula boats were constantly being upgraded and improved and eventually became one of the quietest Russian submarine classes, a vital improvement since the class was to function in various roles, principally as an attack boat against hostile battlegroups and against coastal installations.

The low acoustic signature was apparently achieved by, among other things, the installation of active noise cancellation techniques, some of which were unsurprisingly similar to Western commercial techniques, thus increasing the survivability potential while at the same time improving the sensitivity of the on-board sonar in detecting hostile weapons or boats. The weaponry was substantial, and included 12 Granat submarine-launched cruise missiles capable of carrying a 200kT warhead to a range of over 3,000km/1,864 miles.

ABOVE LEFT: **Project 971 submarines, known in the West as the Akula-class nuclear-powered attack submarines (SSN), were deployed to the Pacific region in multi-purpose roles, being capable of strikes against groups of hostile ships and against coastal installations. Akula I had already proved the class by the time of modifications planned for Akula II, which included lengthening to accommodate a quieter propulsion system. Improved Akula I and Akula II submarines were delivered to the Russian Navy between 1994 and 2001.** ABOVE: **The retractable masts viewed from bow to stern are the periscopes, radar antennae, radio and satellite communications and navigation masts.** INSET: **The badge of Akula K317 Pantera.**

Akula I class

Displacement: 7,381 tonnes/7,264.4 tons (surfaced); 8,956 tonnes/8,814.6 tons (submerged)

Length: 108m/354ft 4in

Beam: 14m/45ft 11in

Armament: 4 x 650mm/25.6in tubes; 4 x 533mm/21in tubes; 90kg/198lb HE Type 40 torpedoes; SS-N-15 Starfish anti-submarine weapon, SS-N-21 Sampson SLCM with 200kT nuclear warhead

Propulsion: 1 x pressurized-water reactor 190mW/254,794hp; 2 X 750hp emergency motors

Speed: 10 knots (surfaced); 28 knots (dived)

Complement: 62 crew

ABOVE: **The last Akula II submarine equipped with the best that the Russian shipbuilders could provide was commissioned into Russia's 24th Division, Northern Fleet, on December 4, 2001. President Putin described this as "an event of special national importance".**

Oscar II-class SSGN

This massive 14,225-tonne/14,000-ton boat that could dive to 304.8m/1,000ft was a brilliant construction with a blot on its copybook – the *Kursk* disaster. Again lining up in the Soviet armoury as a giant whose sole mission in life was to attack battlegroups of the North Atlantic Treaty Organization, the Oscar boats were at the epicentre of Soviet battle plans for two and a half decades. They came equipped with a strong stable of surface-to-surface weapons, with 24 missiles in two banks of 12. These were set in pairs on an incline of 40 degrees outside the 8.53m/28ft pressure hull. This in turn created a gap of 3.5m/11ft 6in between the inner and outer shell, resulting in a huge, unheard-of 18m/59ft beam that, in turn, made it possible to withstand moderate battle damage.

ABOVE: A portrait of Oscar II, or to give this one a name, *Veronesh*, first of the Oscar II SSGN, Type 9489A, whose eight sisters in this class included the ill-fated *Kursk*. As can be seen from this classic shot against the mountainous background, they were indeed massive submarines and were said to be slow to dive and tough to manoeuvre, though they are also credited with a submerged speed of about 30 knots, easily adequate to keep pace with their targets. BELOW LEFT: A close-up of the sail and missile hatch area of the Oscar II. At the stern, all have a tube on the rudder fin as in Delta IV, which is used for dispensing a thin line-towed sonar array.

It also came with numerous optional extras which were entirely fitting for a boat of this nature. They included a reinforced rounded cover of the sail to break through the Arctic ice cap. The two periscopes, radio-sextant and radar masts were sited in the retractable devices area, where there was a floating antenna buoy to receive radio messages, target designation data and satellite navigation signals at a great depth and under the ice. Although said to be slow divers and difficult to manoeuvre, down and in a straight line they could achieve in excess of 30 knots, which was more than sufficient to shadow their targets.

The firepower on board was 24 SS-N-19 Granat (which NATO codenamed Shipwreck) cruise missiles with a range of 550km/342 miles, with a 1,000kg/2,205lb warhead. Under the START treaty, however, high explosives replaced the nuclear warheads. The tubes opened in pairs with a single hatch covering each pair. The torpedo tubes, meanwhile, were capable of firing both torpedoes and shorter range anti-ship missiles. Consequently, a combination of 24 weapons was

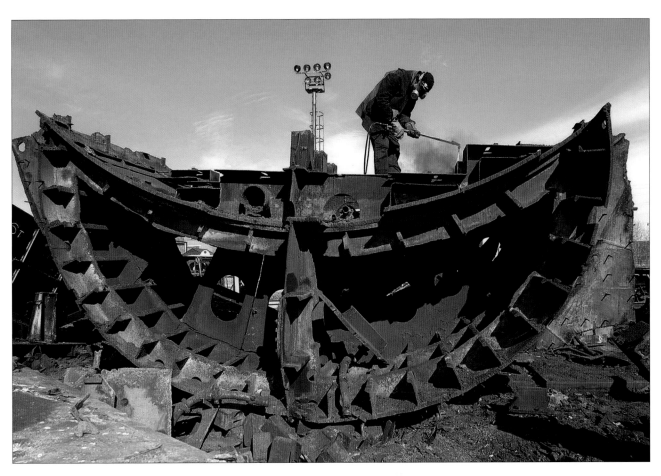

carried, as well as a Type 40 torpedo. It was a Type 65 high test peroxide 650mmm/25.6in torpedo that was found to have caused the sinking of the *Kursk* on August 12, 2000, with the loss of all 118 crew. The blast triggered a further explosion in the weapons compartment that caused the vessel to sink. The blast was caused by highly volatile torpedo propellant that leaked and came in contact with kerosene and metal. The Russians completed several new submarines of the third generation Oscar II, 11 of which were the larger Oscar II boats, built between 1985 and 2001.

ABOVE: **Despite the billions spent in dollars, pounds and roubles, it happens to them all in the end, and sometimes in an unsophisticated manner: this Oscar submarine is shown in a breaker's yard with its nuclear fuel and reactors detached and embalmed for safe disposal. The nuclear fuel is removed from the reactor and sent to a processing plant, while the nuclear reactor compartments are cut out, carefully sealed and taken to an approved disposal site.** INSET: **The badge of the Oscar II submarine** *Omsk.*

LEFT: **The exceptionally wide beam of the Oscar II version accommodates the surface-to-surface missile (SSM) tubes, which are in banks of 12 on either side and external to the 8.5m/27ft-diameter pressure hull. The tubes are inclined at a 40-degree angle, with one hatch covering each pair.**

Oscar II-class SSGN

Displacement: 13,680 tonnes/13,464 tons (surfaced); 18,010 tonnes/17,726 tons (submerged)
Length: 153.9m/504ft 11in
Beam: 18.19m/56ft 8in
Armament: 4 x 533mm/21in tubes; 4 x 650mm25.6in tubes, Type 45 torpedo; SSM – 24 x SS-N-19 Shipwreck; A/S: SS-N-15 fired from 533mm/21in tubes, SS-N-16 fired from 650mm/25.6in tubes
Propulsion: 2 x VM-5 190mW/254,794hp pressurized-water nuclear reactors (OK-650b); 2 x steam turbines, 67,113kW/90,000shp
Speed: 15 knots (surfaced); 28 knots (dived)
Complement: 107 crew

Typhoon-class SSBN

The Typhoon submarines were the largest ever built and truly a defining feature of the Cold War. The sheer size, capability and destructive power of these boats was awesome, as was the fact that they could stay submerged for months if need demanded it. They operated principally in the waters of the North Atlantic, with each boat capable of carrying 20 long-range ballistic missiles with up to 200 nuclear warheads that were once aimed specifically at cities of the United States. Indeed, one of the principal roles of this boat was that in the event of nuclear exchanges, the Typhoon would sit it out beneath the Arctic ocean to maintain a "survivable nuclear retaliatory strike capability" for the Soviet leadership. From the outset, the boats had been fully equipped for under-ice operations with a fin strengthened and contoured to break through an ice cap up to 3.7m/12ft thick. This, of course, was one of the reasons that American and British submarines were, over the years, to be found making highly publicized and well

ABOVE: **The Typhoon class was developed under Project 941 as the Russian Akula class – Akula meaning "shark", which was confusing in the West because Akula was the name NATO used to designate the Russian Project 971-class attack submarines. Typhoon submarines became one of the quietest sea vessels in operation at this time, being more silent and yet more manoeuvrable than their predecessors.**

photographed sorties to the Arctic, showing their own capacity for rising up through the ice.

The Typhoons were originally built at the Severodvinsk Shipyard on the White Sea near Archangel, and six were delivered to the Soviet Navy between 1981 and 1989 for service with the Northern Fleet. They were hugely expensive to run but even so, three remained in operation into the 21st century, with one converted to a training vessel. The rest were scrapped and recycled with assistance from the United States under the Co-operative Threat Reduction Programme. Britain

BELOW: **Inside the control room of a Typhoon-class submarine. Speed is 12 knots when surfaced and 25 knots when submerged, and the submarine is capable of spending 120 days at sea.**

BELOW: **The Typhoon carried intercontinental, three-stage solid propellant ballistic missiles, each missile consisting of ten independently targetable multiple re-entry vehicles, each with a 100kT nuclear warhead with a range of 8,300km/5,157 miles.**

an electronics suite that was unlike anything the Russians had previously produced in terms of its spaceship-style appearance. At the time of construction, there were also a number of interesting innovations, including an advanced stern fin with horizontal retractable hydroplane. The system also included two periscopes, radar, radio communications, navigation and direction finder masts. They were all housed within the sail guard.

The submarine's main arsenal was 20 RSM-52 intercontinental three-stage solid propellant ballistic missiles located in two rows of missile launch tubes in front of the sail between the main hulls. Each missile consisted of ten independently targetable re-entry vehicles (MIRVs), each with a 100kT nuclear warhead. The missiles had a range of 8,208km/5,100 miles, putting large portions of the Western Hemisphere into the attack zone without the submarine even leaving port.

The submarine's main machinery consists of two nuclear water reactors and two turbogear assemblies comprising a steam turbine and gearbox. One reactor and one turbogear assembly are fitted in each main hull. Each nuclear water reactor produced 190mW/254,794hp driving 37,285kW/50,000hp steam turbines and four 3,200kW/4,291hp turbogenerators. Two 800kW/1.073hp diesel generators served as standby propulsion units coupled to the shaft line. The two propellers are seven-blade, fixed-pitch shrouded. The built-in thrusters on the bow and stern are two telescopic turning screw rudders and are powered by a 750kW/1,005hp motor.

has also joined the disposal effort, and along with all nations who possess nuclear boats, there is now a worldwide strategy for processing these old nuclear reactors, and converting them into a state for recycling or long-term storage. There remains considerable international disquiet over the safety of the rotting hulls of nuclear-powered boats.

Even so, the Typhoon submarine was an incredible engineering feat, being a multi-hulled boat with five inner hulls within a superstructure of two parallel main hulls. Nineteen separate compartments within the boat included a strengthened module housing a vast control room and

RIGHT: **A Typhoon-class submarine showing the sail with its retractable masts. The design also includes features for travelling under ice and equipment for breaking through it. Maximum diving depth is 400m/1312ft.**

Typhoon-class SSBN

Displacement: 23,265 tonnes/22,897.6 tons (surfaced); 33,787 tonnes/33,253.4 tons (submerged)

Length: 172m/564ft 4in

Beam: 23m/75ft 6in

Armament: 4 x 711mm/28in tubes; 2 x 533mm/21in tubes; 22 x anti-ship missiles and torpedoes; 20 RSM-52 ballistic missiles and 20 launchers

Propulsion: 2 x mW190/254,794hp nuclear water reactors; 2 x steam turbines, 74,570kW/100,000shp

Speed: 20 knots (surfaced); 25 knots (dived)

Complement: 160 crew

Yasen/Graney class

The Russian Yasen-class submarine, also known as the Graney class, is a class of nuclear-powered guided missile attack submarines that was designed to replace the ageing Akula and Oscar-class submarines in Russian Navy service. The development of the Yasen class started in the 1980s, and the first submarine of the class, *Severodvinsk*, was finally commissioned in 2013 after a long delay due to budget cuts and long-running technical difficulties. Since then, four more have

been built, three are currently active and six are being built.

The Yasen class are among the most advanced attack submarines in the world, with several unique technical features

ABOVE: **K-560** *Severodvinsk*, **the first submarine of the Yasen class.** BELOW: **The Yasen class are among the most advanced attack submarines in the world, with several unique technical features that give them a powerful advantage over other submarines.**

ABOVE: **Sectionalized representation of a Yasen class boat.**

that give them a significant advantage over other submarines, such as the use of a titanium alloy in the pressure hull. This makes the boats lighter and more durable than other submarines of similar size and also allows the submarines to dive to deeper depths, giving them an advantage in underwater operations.

The submarines are equipped with a new generation of advanced sonar systems, including a spherical active/passive sonar system that allows the submarines to detect and track other submarines, surface ships, and underwater objects at long ranges. In addition, the submarines are equipped with a towed-array sonar system that provides additional coverage and depth of field. These advanced sonar systems make the Yasen-class submarine one of the quietest and most capable submarines in the world.

The class is equipped with a range of weapons, including anti-ship and anti-submarine missiles, torpedoes, and mines. The submarines can launch their weapons while submerged, which gives them a huge advantage over other submarines that must surface to launch their weapons. The submarines are also equipped with a new generation of cruise missiles, including the 3M-14 Kalibr and 3M-54 Klub missiles, which

have a range of up to 1,500km/932 miles and can carry nuclear or conventional warheads. The hull is constructed from low-magnetic steel.

The propulsion system uses a combination of nuclear and electric power. The boats are equipped with a fourth generation compact pressurized water reactor that generates electricity to power the submarine's electric motors, which drive the submarine's propulsion system. This includes a pump-jet propulsor that makes the submarines quieter and more manoeuvrable than other submarines with traditional propellers.

The Yasen-class submarines are primarily used for anti-ship and anti-submarine warfare, as well as for covert operations and intelligence gathering – these submarines are highly versatile and can operate in a wide range of environments, including shallow and deep waters. The Yasen-class boats are known to have been deployed in the Arctic region to protect Russia's strategic interests, and are also deployed in the Mediterranean and Pacific regions.

LEFT: **Ceremony of raising the flag of the Russian Navy on the lead submarine of the class,** *Severodvinsk,* **June 17, 2014.**

Yasen/Graney class

Displacement: 8,600 tonnes/8,4641 tons (surfaced) 13,800 tonnes/13,852 tons (submerged)
Length: 139.2m/457ft (Yasen)
Beam: 13m/43ft
Armament: VLS silos for 32 Oniks anti-ship cruise missiles/Kalibr multi-use SLCMs; 10 533mm/21in torpedo tubes for Futlyar heavyweight torpedoes
Propulsion: OK-650Kpm reactor driving two 200 MW turbines producing 43,000shp
Speed: 20 knots (surfaced), 35 knots (submerged, max)
Complement: 85 crew

A-class SSK

LEFT: **HMS** *Artful*, one of the A-class boats that were the backbone of the British submarine fleet in the immediate post-war years.

Work began in 1942 to produce a boat with superior speed, range and crew conditions, designed especially for use in the Far East. Based on the T class, but incorporating the lessons learned in war conditions, and even including air conditioning, the boats represented a leap forward. With fully welded hulls and a heavy armament of six forward-firing torpedoes and four firing aft, coupled with an air-warning radar which worked while the boat was submerged, they were a vast technological improvement. They also had the "Snort" breathing capability.

The Admiralty ordered 46 A-class boats with the first, *Amphion*, launched in August 1944. *Astute* was next and these were the only two delivered before hostilities ceased. At first they were unstable, but an extra buoyancy tank cured the problem. When Japan surrendered, 30 of the A-class boats were cancelled. But a new type of war – the Cold War – faced the world, and the 16 A-class boats were fully deployed in improving submarine warfare by undergoing strenuous trials and deployments. *Alliance* and *Ambush* were used to carry out exercises in endurance underwater as they stayed submerged for long periods. *Alliance* sailed submerged for 30 days, and in February 1948, *Ambush* sailed from Rothesay on a submerged patrol that was to last six weeks.

Other craft were submerged – unmanned – to see how deep they could go before the hull failed. *Andrew* sailed submerged for 4,023 km/2,500 miles from Bermuda to England in 15 days, the first

submerged trans-Atlantic passage. She was also the last Royal Navy submarine to be fitted with a permanent deck gun.

A-class SSK

Displacement: 1,497.16 tonnes/1,473.5 tons (surfaced); 1,645.92 tonnes/1,619.9 tons (submerged)
Length: 85.85m/281ft 8in
Beam: 6.78m/22ft 3in
Armament: 10 x 533mm/21in tubes (6 x bow – 2 x external, 4 x stern – 2 x external), 20 x torpedoes or 26 mines; 1 x 101mm/4in gun, 1 x 20mm/0.79in anti-aircraft gun
Propulsion: 2 x 3206.5kW/4,300bhp Admiralty or Vickers diesel engines; 2 x 932.1kW/1,250ehp English Electric electric motors
Speed: 18.5 knots (surfaced); 8 knots (dived)
Complement: 60 crew

Porpoise class (Late)

LEFT: **HMS** *Walrus*, of the Porpoise class, noted for its clean welded hulls and for being fast and silent underwater, undoubtedly among the best conventional boats in the world at the time.

Porpoise class (Late)

Displacement: 2,062.48 tonnes/2,029.9 tons (surfaced); 2,443.48 tonnes/2,404.9 tons (submerged)
Length: 89.99m/295ft 3in
Beam: 8.08m/26ft 6in
Armament: 8 x 533mm/21in tubes (6 bow, 2 stern), 30 x torpedoes
Propulsion: 2 x 1,230.4kW/1,650hp Admiralty Standard Range diesel engines; 2 x 3,728.5kW/5,000ehp electric motors
Speed: 12 knots (surfaced); 17 knots (dived)
Complement: 71 crew

If the A class was considered a leap forward, the Porpoise was a giant one. As the first post-World War II designed boat to enter service, it was capable of high underwater speed, very deep diving and was very quiet. It was fitted with very large batteries to store the power required, and with its advanced snort and replenishment systems could operate independently without support anywhere in the world for months – exactly what the old time submariners had dreamed of decades earlier.

Porpoise had both air and surface warning radar which could operate at periscope level and while on the surface, as well as an advanced snort system which allowed maximum charging even in rough seas. A bonus was that this provided adequate air conditioning for the boats to operate in Arctic or tropical environments and kept it dry internally.

Periods of six weeks underwater were also made possible because of its oxygen replenishment system and the

carbon dioxide eliminators. As well as being equipped to distil fresh water from seawater, they had enough space to carry substantial stores to enable them to operate far from home and far from support for long periods.

In general, they were excellent, seaworthy boats superbly manufactured. However, they were already out of date, at least in terms of Britain's ambitions towards being a nuclear power, and these diesel boats began to take a back seat.

LEFT AND BELOW LEFT:
HMS *Explorer* was an experimental boat, but initially had so many problems that her first captain was never able to take her to sea. The issues were eventually resolved, but the boat was scrapped.

Explorer class

Displacement: 1,117.6 tonnes/1,099.9 tons (surfaced); 1,216.15 tonnes/1,196.9 tons (submerged)
Length: 68.74m/225ft 6in
Beam: 4.76m/15ft 7in
Armament: Nil
Propulsion: 11,185.5kW/15,000shp Vickers Armstrong hydrogen peroxide plant; 2 x diesel engines; 2 x electric motors
Speed: 15 knots (surfaced); 25 knots (dived)
Complement: 41 crew

Explorer class

Designed to trial a new diesel-electric powerplant that incorporated hydrogen peroxide in its fuels, these were believed to be the fastest submarines in the world at the time. The main propulsion was provided by turbines powered with steam and carbon dioxide, which enabled the boat to produce full power while submerged, independent of any external air source. In addition, the *Explorer*-class boats were fitted with conventional diesel engines for use on the surface and battery-powered electric motors for underwater operations.

Only two boats in this class were built. With retractable fittings improving their already streamlined shape, they had excellent manoeuvrability combined with a high submerged speed. However the fuel was highly unstable, and there were several explosions. As the boats were purely experimental, they were unarmed, and their crews were accommodated in converted minesweepers for safety reasons. Capable of 25 knots submerged, they were very fast. But once the Americans succeeded in building a nuclear reactor for a submarine, the project with the Explorers was quickly terminated.

LEFT: **HMS *Orpheus* of the Oberon class was Britain's first major step into modern design, with improved detection equipment and the ability to fire homing torpedoes. Known for their reliability and quietness, many Oberons were sold to overseas buyers.**

Oberon class

Displacement: 2,062.48 tonnes/2,029.9 tons (surfaced); 2,448.56 tonnes/2,409.9 tons (submerged)
Length: 89.99m/295ft 3in
Beam: 8.08m/26ft 6in
Armament: 8 x 533mm/21in tubes, Mk 8 torpedo, Tigerfish torpedo; Sub-Harpoon anti-ship missiles
Propulsion: 2 x 2,237.1kW/3,000bhp Admiralty Standard Range diesels; 2 x 1,280kw/1,716.5hp electric motors
Speed: 12 knots (surfaced); 17 knots (dived)
Complement: 71 crew

Oberon class

Although almost identical to the Porpoise class, the Oberons were fitted with improved detection equipment and were equipped with homing torpedoes. In addition, for the first time in a Royal Navy submarine, plastic was used and glass fibre was incorporated on part of the bridge superstructure and casing. *Oberon*, the first of the class, was launched in 1959. In 1970, during trials in the Mediterranean with a submarine escape-team, a world record was established when the men "escaped" from *Osiris* while she was moving at a depth of 182.9m/600ft.

Only one *Oberon*-class boat – *Onyx* – saw active service when she was the only diesel submarine sent to the Falklands as part of Operation Corporate, and Historic Warships now preserve her at Birkenhead.

In the 1980s, the fitting of sonar and the capability to fire Tigerfish torpedoes and Harpoon anti-ship missiles enhanced the performance of Oberon boats, and the submarines had the ability to guide two torpedoes simultaneously. *Otus* also took part in a series of trials in a Norwegian fjord to determine at which depth submariners could safely expect to escape from a stricken submarine. Two sailors managed to "escape" from 182.9m/600ft yet again. A number of the boats were eventually leased and then sold to Canada.

Dreadnought SSN

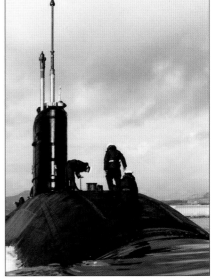

ABOVE LEFT: **_Dreadnought_ represented Britain's entry into the world of nuclear-powered submarines in 1962, completing her first dive in Ramsden Dock in January 1963, thus equipping the nation with one of the most potent attack submarines, albeit of an experimental nature, in the world at that time.**
ABOVE: **A close-up bow view of the _Dreadnought_ sail.**

B ritain's own nuclear reactor for submarines was still under development at the newly-formed naval section of the Atomic Research Station at Harwell when the decision was made to proceed with the building of Britain's first nuclear-powered submarine, *Dreadnought*. Consequently, with Cold War tensions rising by the day, American expertise was called upon in utilizing the new teardrop design of USS *Albacore* for the hull design, and the purchase of the nuclear reactor. She was laid down in June 1959, launched by the Queen on Trafalgar Day 1960 and commissioned in April 1963 in the role of hunter-killer.

It was the beginning of a long and successful British involvement in nuclear submarine production. *Dreadnought*, meanwhile, was soon displaying her mettle, when in 1967 she travelled from Rosyth to Singapore and back, travelling 7,467km/4,640 miles surfaced and 4,271km/2,654 miles submerged. In 1971, she became the first British submarine to surface through the ice at the North Pole.

Such events were, of course, soon to become commonplace, but at the time they were momentous and a great achievement by the crews, who had to adapt to a whole new way of life. With long periods submerged without a glimmer of daylight or fresh air, accommodation and facilities were of an unprecedented standard. Particular attention was paid to the decoration and furnishing of living quarters and recreational spaces, which include cinema equipment, a library and tape recordings to relieve the monotony associated with prolonged voyages.

Her early operations included the Royal Navy's first annual Group Deployment in 1977, designed to demonstrate to the world the fighting efficiency of British warships and submarines. In the same year, *Dreadnought* joined a secret task force to the South Atlantic with frigates *Alacrity* and *Phoebe* and auxiliaries *Resource* and *Olwen*, at a time when Argentina appeared to be taking an aggressive stance over her claim to possession of the Falkland Islands. The Argentine

military junta backed away, but the threat remained and within five years, *Dreadnought*'s sister submarines of the newer classes were called into action in those unforgiving waters.

As with the first nuclear boats of other nations, and the USSR in particular, *Dreadnought* was small and noisy compared with the later arrivals. Moreover, as the leader of what was, in effect, an experimental project, *Dreadnought* began to suffer from a number of technical problems. She was subsequently withdrawn from service under the 1981 Defence Review and moved to Rothsyth for her retirement.

LEFT: **The launch of _Dreadnought_ brought a new era of life at sea for the submariner, whose accommodation was of an unprecedented standard in terms of ablutions, living quarters and recreational areas, which included a cinema and library. This would help them as they faced the prospect of long voyages underwater.**

Dreadnought SSN

Displacement: 3,448 tonnes/3,393.5 tons (surfaced); 3,937 tonnes/3,874.8 tons (submerged)
Length: 81m/265ft 9in
Beam: 9.8m/32ft 2in
Armament: 6 x 533mm/21in tubes, 24 x torpedoes
Propulsion: Rolls-Royce-Westinghouse S5W nuclear reactor driving 2 x steam turbines, 11,185.5kW/15,000shp
Speed: 25 knots (surfaced); 30 knots (dived)
Complement: 113 crew

LEFT AND ABOVE: **A view of** *Warspite*, **of the Valiant class, similar in almost every respect to the** *Dreadnought.* **The Valiant boats were, however, significantly quieter than their predecessor and equipped with a diesel-electric generator that could be used for silent running in emergencies.**
INSET: **The badge of HMS** *Valiant*, **depicting a proud fighting cockerel.**

Valiant-class SSN

Valiant and sister ship *Warspite* led the all-British technology programme with a nuclear reactor developed at Dounreay, Scotland, by Rolls-Royce and the Atomic Energy Authority. Although *Dreadnought* was still under construction when *Valiant* was laid down in 1960, there was still sufficient time to take note of lessons learned, and consequently, noise levels rather than speed became the first priority with the new class ahead of *Valiant*'s commissioning in July 1966. She joined the Third Submarine Squadron at Faslane and, like *Dreadnought*, one of her early tasks was to undertake the run from the United Kingdom to Singapore. *Valiant* went one better than her predecessor on this mission, completing the 19,312km/12,000-mile journey in

28 days, during which she was submerged throughout. This was a record for any British vessel at the time, although it would soon be broken again and again.

In the 1970s, *Valiant* and her sister *Warspite* remained in constant service and set a number of endurance records for British boats, which to some extent was due to the delay in the arrival of further British SSNs when all resources were deployed on the construction of the nation's first Polaris-carrying SSBNs of the Resolution class. As a result, *Valiant* remained in service longer than any of the early British nuclear boats, recording a total of 1,068,148km/576,754 nautical miles and 53,840 hours (2,243 days) at sea during her career. Not unsurprisingly for such a workhorse, *Valiant* developed

engine problems in June 1994 while returning from America. One month later, she was sent into retirement and laid up at Devonport, where she was occasionally open for public inspection.

Warspite, commissioned in April 1967, was also in almost constant operational mode but in May 1976 suffered a fire which put her out of commission for two years for repairs and refitting. On her return to duty, she was part of the British Task force sent to the South Atlantic at the time of the Falklands War. She remained active for another nine years before she was taken out of service following the discovery of hairline cracks in the primary coolant circuit during a refit, and was laid up two years earlier than *Valiant*.

LEFT: **Leader of the class, HMS** *Valiant*, **after her much-vaunted launch following completion at the Vickers Barrow-in-Furness yards to begin 18 years of continuous and successful service. This inspired her use as the template for Britain's Resolution-class ballistic submarine and subsequent fleet submarines.**

Valiant-class SSN

Displacement: 4,232 tonnes/4,165.2 tons (surfaced); 4,800 tonnes/4,724.2 tons (submerged)
Length: 86.9m/285ft 1in
Beam: 10.1m/33ft 2in
Armament: 6 x 533mm/21in tubes (bow), 24 torpedoes
Propulsion: 1 x Rolls-Royce Pressurized Water Reactor (2 x English Electric steam turbines, 11,185.5kW/15,000hp); 1 x Paxman diesel-electric generator
Speed: 20 knots (surfaced); 28 knots (dived)
Complement: 116 crew

LEFT: **A giant of their own, but with American nuclear weapons, HMS *Resolution* heralded Britain's arrival in this exclusive club of ballistic boomers in which membership was expensive, beginning at £40 million for the first of the class and rising.** BELOW: **The American-supplied Polaris ballistic missile for the Resolution class underwent a British-designed life-extension programme called Chevaline, which reduced the number of warheads and added defensive countermeasures. It replaced Britain's own Blue Streak and Skybolt missiles, which were cancelled because of their cost.** BELOW LEFT: **The badge of *Resolution*.**

Resolution-class SSBN

The Resolution-class submarines were the first British strategic ballistic missile submarines to carry Polaris missiles. Five boats were originally planned, but the order was cut to four by the incoming Labour government in 1964. That their arrival marked the era of the submarine as a capital ship was recognized by naming the four boats after great British capital ships of the past, *Resolution*, *Repulse*, *Renown* and *Revenge*. Their arrival also marked an important milestone in Britain's overall capability as a nuclear power, two previous missile programmes having been aborted. The boats would each carry 16 US Polaris A3 missiles and consequently, the bow and stern were constructed separately to be assembled later with the American-designed missile compartment. The missiles measured 9.4m/31ft long and had a range of 4630km/2,500 nautical miles.

By then, the United States and the Soviet Union were already head to head in the era of using a submarine-based nuclear deterrent, where weapons could be hidden beneath the waves and launched from virtually anywhere in the world to reach virtually any position. At the same time, being nuclear powered, the submarines could and would roam the oceans unhindered for months on end without the need to surface.

Resolution was commissioned in 1967 and then pursued a year of training and sea trials before she took off for Cape Kennedy for the test firing of a Polaris missile. Five months later, in June 1968, *Resolution* commenced her first operational patrol, thereby embarking on a journey that was to last 28 years of Polaris patrols. At the time, the *Daily Telegraph* recorded in a leader article: "The *Resolution* in making her first dive of her patrol into the waters of a troubled world will be taking out on behalf of the nation the best insurance policy it has ever had".

LEFT: **Deliveries of supplies or personnel, or extractions of sick submariners unable to be treated at sea (as seen here), were often made by Sea King helicopters flown from a surface vessel. These helicopters were also extensively deployed on anti-submarine warfare operations by the Royal Navy, as well as in search-and-rescue and airborne early-warning missions.**

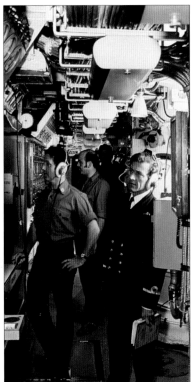

FAR LEFT: **The loading of the Polaris ballistic missiles into a Resolution-class submarine, thus enabling Britain to move a survivable nuclear system within range of enemy targets. Although the submarine was not capable of destroying hardened targets, it would have been effective against population centres, a targeting decision that would ultimately rest with the government.** LEFT: **A busy day at the office. For the most part, a smart dress code was adhered to in the control centres of the ballistic submarines, and indeed in all modern boats.**

The new boats had a similarity in size and appearance with the US Los Angeles class, although like all British submarines, the hydroplanes were located on the bow rather than the fin. At the beginning of their assigned patrols, the Polaris boats would leave Faslane, submerge and remain submerged on a course and location unknown to all but the highest ranking officers among the 156 men aboard. The Royal Navy operated a system similar to the both the Americans and the Russians whereby each submarine had two crews – known as Port and Starboard in Britain – with one on leave or training, while the other was at sea. Living conditions onboard were even better than on the new SSNs and they needed to be, given the length of time the crews would be on patrol.

In the early 1980s, the British government forged an agreement to take the new American Trident missile system, for which four new boats of the Vanguard class would be

needed. In the meantime, the existing Polaris system was upgraded with a new warhead codenamed Chevaline, and fitted to the four Resolution boats over a period of four years. This would keep the British nuclear capability afloat until the early 1990s, when the changeover was due to take place.

Revenge was paid off in May 1992, followed by *Resolution* six months later. *Renown* remained in service until 1995 and *Repulse* the following year, by which time the four Trident boats were operational.

The Resolutions left behind a remarkable record, having conducted an unbroken sequence of 229 patrols in which, fortunately, they were never called upon to fire in anger. Their record was marked by a monument to the Polaris submarines that recognized not only the contribution of the crews who took them on patrol, but also those on shore, and the control, command and maintenance teams, all of whose work was equally vital.

LEFT: **A view of the sail and missile compartment of *Resolution*, where 16 Polaris A3s were carried in two rows of eight. There was also an emergency diesel generator and six 533mm/21in torpedo tubes located at the bow, capable of firing Tigerfish wire-guided homing torpedoes.**

Resolution-class SSBN

Displacement: 7,381 tonnes/7,264.4 tons (surfaced); 8,267 tonnes/8,136.4 tons (submerged)
Length: 130m/426ft 6in
Beam: 10.1m/33ft 2in
Armament: 6 x 533mm/21in tubes (bow); 16 x A3 SLBM Polaris ballistic missiles
Propulsion: Rolls-Royce PRW1 nuclear reactor (2 x English Electric steam turbines producing 11,185.5kW/15,000shp); 1 x back-up diesel generator 2982.8kW/4,000bhp
Speed: 20 knots (surfaced); 25 knots (dived)
Complement: 156 crew

Churchill-class SSN

This class represented the resumption of work on the Valiant class, which had been suspended to place all British resources into the Resolution ballistic missile submarines. Now, three more boats, *Churchill* and *Courageous* at Vickers and *Conqueror* at Cammell Laird were built to begin what would become almost 60 years of combined service. The class leader was, of course, named after one of Britain's great heroes, who himself was a foremost advocate of submarine development when he was First Lord of the Admiralty prior to World War I. It was a fitting tribute since it was he who had insisted that submarines be named rather than carry a number.

With the benefit of Dreadnought and Valiant-class experience, the Churchills included a number of improvements, especially in weaponry. *Churchill* was selected to evaluate both the American Mk 48 torpedo and the Sub-Harpoon

anti-ship missile, although only the latter was selected for use and was fitted first to the sister ship *Courageous*. In terms of operational activity, the Churchills remained busy through their lifespan with *Conqueror*, under the command of Christopher Wreford-Brown (who was later awarded the DSO), famously sinking the Argentine ship *General Belgrano* during the Falklands conflict, an act which cost 368 seamen their lives.

Controversially *Conqueror*'s crew flew the Jolly Roger as she returned to Faslane, a customary act of Royal Navy submarines after a mission on which a "kill" has been achieved. Even so, she was the first nuclear-powered submarine to fire in anger, and remains the only one to engage and sink an enemy ship with torpedoes. *Conqueror* and *Churchill* remained in service until 1990. *Courageous*, which also served in the Falklands, was paid off in 1992.

LEFT: **The badge of HMS *Churchill*. She was taken out of service and laid up in the early 1990s for mothballing before finally being scrapped.**

LEFT: ***Conqueror* receiving her load of Tigerfish wire-guided homing torpedoes, although when she achieved the distinction of being the only nuclear-powered submarine to have sunk a surface warship in anger, the Argentine ship *General Belgrano*, she was using conventional Mk 8 torpedoes.**

Churchill-class SSN

Displacement: 4,133 tonnes/4,067.7 tons (surfaced); 4,822 tonnes/4,745.8 tons (submerged)
Length: 86.9m/285ft 1in
Beam: 10.10m/33ft 2in
Armament: 6 x 533mm/21in tubes (bow), 26 x torpedoes and/or mines
Propulsion: Rolls-Royce PWR nuclear reactor driving 2 x English Electric steam turbines, 11,185.5kW/15,000shp; 1 x Paxman diesel generator also fitted
Speed: 22 knots (surfaced); 28 knots (dived)
Complement: 103 crew

Swiftsure-class SSN

This class followed on from the Valiant and Churchill boats and with updates and improvements, including what was described as a cylindrical hull and improved sonar. The boats also showed an improvement on their predecessors in a number of operational areas in that they were quieter, faster to submerge and could dive to greater depths. The first boats came on the scene in the late 1970s, and indeed two of them – *Splendid* and *Spartan* – saw almost immediate action in the Falklands, operating at the time *Conqueror* was shadowing the *Belgrano*. At the same time, *Splendid* and *Spartan* were on the lookout for an Argentinian aircraft carrier which was reportedly heading towards the Falklands, but the vessel turned back prior to the *Belgrano* sinking, apparently through intelligence

that the British nuclear submarines were operating in the area.

The Swiftsure boats went on to have long careers, and were chosen to lead the Royal Navy into the conversion to Tomahawk cruise missiles. *Splendid* became the first Royal Navy submarine to be equipped with such a capability, having been retrofitted with the equipment in 1998. Her initial target practice was a small building in the United States 644km/400 miles inland, which she hit with perfection. *Splendid* then went on to become the first British submarine to fire a shot in anger since the Falklands and the first to launch an attack using cruise missiles when she joined the Americans in the bombing campaign against Serbian targets during the Kosovo crisis of 1999. Later, she and others were used extensively in cruise missile attacks on

land-based targets in Afghanistan and the Persian Gulf. Between 1987 and 1993 *Spartan*, *Splendid* and *Sceptre* were fitted with improved nuclear reactor cores, but the leader of the class, *Swiftsure,* was decommissioned in 1992 due to technical problems.

In 1997, the new Labour Government ordered a review of defence spending and, coupled with the need for a new SSN class within ten years, agreed to go ahead with the Astute programme if the overall number of attack boats was cut from 12 boats to 10 boats. This was to be achieved by the decommissioning of *Splendid* in 2004 and *Spartan* in 2006. The remaining Swiftsure class have all since been decommissioned, the last of them, *Sceptre*, in 2010.

LEFT: **HMS *Superb*, the last of the Swiftsure class, during the much-photographed event of bursting through the ice at the North Pole.**

Swiftsure-class SSN

Displacement: 4,445 tonnes/4,374.8 tons (surfaced); 4,900 tonnes/4,822.6 tons (submerged)
Length: 82.9m/272ft
Beam: 8.9m/29ft 2in
Armament: 5 x tubes capable of firing Spearfish torpedoes, RN Sub-Harpoon missiles, Tomahawk missiles
Propulsion: 1 PWR reactor; 2 x General Electric Steam Turbines, 11,185.5kW/15,000shp; 2 x Paxman diesels, 2982.8kW/4,000shp
Speed: 24 knots (surfaced); 30 knots (dived)
Complement: 116 crew

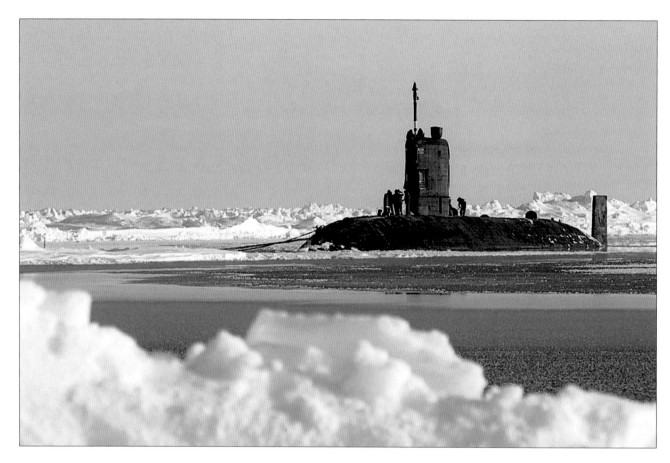

Trafalgar-class SSN

The T boats, as they became known after their World War II namesakes, represented the largest number in a single class of nuclear boats built by the Royal Navy. Seven boats were constructed and represented major improvements on the Swiftsure class, which was in turn a derivative of the Churchill class. The submarines *Trafalgar*, *Turbulent*, *Tireless*, *Torbay*, *Trenchant*, *Talent* and *Triumph* would ostensibly become the Royal Navy's most advanced nuclear fleet submarine until the introduction of the Astute class, which began in 2002.

The T boats, whose design literature came a full six years after that of the Swiftsures, arrived into commission over a ten-year period from 1983. They were heralded with publicity regarding their major improvements, which include a new reactor core and the Type 2020 sonar. Even so, internal layout was nearly identical to the *Swiftsure*, and they were only 2.5m/8ft 2in longer.

Once again the emphasis was on quietening processes, and instead of the seven-bladed propeller on the Swiftsures, Trafalgar-class submarines used pump-jet propulsion, which was a low-revolution propeller which is much quieter but much heavier than conventional propeller designs, although it was not available in time for the commissioning of the first boat,

ABOVE: **The famously named boats of the Trafalgar-class hunter-killers such as HMS *Tireless* used a high-pitch, low-revolution propeller which was much quieter than earlier designs. The hull was also covered in anechoic tiles designed to absorb sound. There were a number of other innovations, including a strengthened fin and retractable hydroplanes, allowing them to surface through thick ice. There was also a new record set in 1993, when *Triumph* sailed to Australia, covering a distance of 66,000km/41,000 miles while submerged and without any forward support. This represented the longest solo deployment by any nuclear submarine.** LEFT: **A typical control room of the Trafalgar class.** INSET: **The badge of the lead boat.**

LEFT AND BELOW: **Two views of the Trafalgar boats, showing the retractable sail attachments and missile areas. The Sub-Harpoon long-range anti-ship missile, with a range of 110kms/68.35 miles, became the principal anti-surface ship weapon in these submarines. They were also armed with homing torpedoes that can be used against other submarines or surface vessels.**

ABOVE: **An excellent port view providing an overall look at the Trafalgar class.**

BELOW LEFT: **The long endurance and sophisticated weapon systems of the**

Trafalgar. Despite these advances, there were problems that brought some boats in this class a good deal of publicity for the wrong reasons and resulted in them being laid up with reactor malfunction. This also resulted in checks being made on all members of the class. The first was *Tireless*, on which a coolant leak in the reactor caused her to interrupt a world cruise and limp into Gibraltar, where local inhabitants were none too happy.

Other boats were also laid up, some tested for what became known as The Tireless Fault. Several went through long refits in the early 2000s, keeping them operational well into the 21st century. The final boat in service, *Triumph*, is scheduled to be decommissioned in 2024.

Trafalgar boats made them formidable adversaries and of course required fully trained teams at every control centre and computer screen. Although there were three decks, the emphasis on technology meant that, while space was restricted, living conditions were comfortable.

Trafalgar-class SSN	
Displacement: 4,650 tonnes/4,576.6 tons (surfaced); 5,200 tonnes/5,117.9 tons (submerged)	
Length: 85.4m/280ft 2in	
Beam: 9.8m/32ft 2in	
Armament: 5 x tubes capable of firing Spearfish torpedoes, RN Sub-Harpoon missiles, Tomahawk missiles	
Propulsion: 1PWR nuclear reactor, 11,185.5kW/15,000shp	
Speed: 25 knots (surfaced); 30 knots (dived)	
Complement: 130 crew	

Vanguard-class SSBN

According to some naval analysts, the arrival of Britain's new SSBN *Vanguard* represented a masterclass in submarine building. Some 14 years after the start of the Trident project, the first submarine entered service on time, in December 1994. The remaining three – *Victorious*, *Vigilant* and *Vengeance* – repeated the performance at yearly intervals to form a squadron of purpose-built boats carrying the only remaining nuclear weapon system in the employ of the United Kingdom – the much-vaunted Trident D5.

At over 150m/492ft in length and 16,000 tonnes/15,747 tons displacement, they have almost twice the displacement of the Polaris carriers of the Resolution class. The 16-tube missile compartment is based on the design of the 24-tube system used in the American *Ohio*-class Trident submarines. Other than that, Vanguard is all British, designed and built by Vickers Shipbuilding and Engineering Limited at Barrow-in-Furness and, by a significant margin, the largest ever manufactured in the United Kingdom and the third largest vessel in the Royal Navy as a whole. In fact, a special manufacturing facility, the Devonshire Dock Hall, had to be purpose-built at Barrow for

TOP: **The Royal Navy was justly proud to take delivery of the Vanguard submarines, impressively deadly and as capable as any other submarines in the world.**
ABOVE: **Every picture tells a story. The Vanguard Trident ballistic missile carriers are Britain's largest ever submarines and in terms of design, style, accommodation and engineering, they are, without doubt, magnificent boats, notwithstanding that they carried the power to annihilate a large number of the world's population, perhaps in collaboration with their American counterparts, the Ohio-class submarines.** ABOVE RIGHT: **The *Vanguard* badge, which every member of the crews who alternately sail in her is proud to possess.**

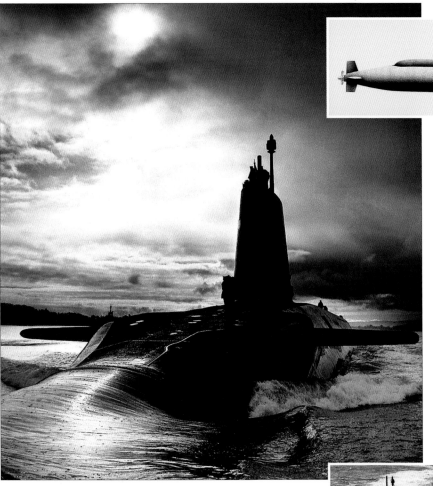

LEFT: **Shadows of the night.** *Vanguard* **arrived at Devonport Naval Base in 2002 for a two-year refit, which was completed in January 2005. Following sea trials, which included test launching of Trident II D5 ballistic missiles, the vessel returned to the fleet. HMS** *Victorious* **began its refit in January 2005.** ABOVE: **A profile of the** *Vanguard,* **which gives an idea of proportions.**

ABOVE: **A test firing of the Trident II missile, of which the** *Vanguard* **has the capacity to carry 16. Each missile can carry up to 12 warheads, giving a potential of 192 warheads in each boat. However, in line with arms limitation agreements, the British government has agreed that each of the D5 missiles carried by the Vanguard class would contain a maximum of four warheads, and that each vessel would therefore carry a maximum of 48 warheads.**

their construction. Even so, with greater automation, the crew of a Vanguard-class boat is smaller at 132 officers and men compared to a Polaris submarine's crew of 149.

The Vanguard-class boats include a number of improvements over previous British submarines, including a new design of nuclear propulsion system and a new tactical weapon system for self-defence purposes both before and after missile launch. Although each Vanguard-class submarine is capable of carrying 192 warheads, the boats will in fact deploy no more than 96, and possibly significantly fewer.

Since January 1995, British Trident submarines have taken on a secondary "sub-strategic" role in the international scheme of things since the Cold War ended, with a number of Trident missiles carrying only one nuclear warhead. The submarines in reserve may be armed with 11 missiles, each with eight warheads, four missiles with one warhead on each, plus an Active Inert Missile during trials.

Although the threat of a nuclear conflagration has subsided, some naval analysts consider that the £167 billion cost of acquiring the Trident fleet was money well spent, as is the annual operating costs, running at around £5.56 billion a year over an estimated 30-year in-service life. There is also a fair body of opinion, however, that disagrees. The class is scheduled to be replaced by Dreadnought-class submarines in the early 2030s.

ABOVE: **All above-water sensors on the Vanguard-class boats were combined into self-protection masts in the fin. The submarines were fitted with the CK51 search periscope and the CH91 attack periscope from Pilkington Optronics, which also included a television camera and thermal imager.**

Vanguard-class SSBN

Displacement: 15,130 tonnes/14,891 tons (surfaced); 16,000 tonnes/15,747.3 tons (submerged)
Length: 149.9m/491ft 10in
Beam: 12.8m/42ft
Armament: 4 x 533mm/21in tubes, 18 x Spearfish torpedoes; Trident D5 Weapons system
Propulsion: 1 x Rolls-Royce PWR-2, 20,507kW/27,500shp
Speed: 20 knots (surfaced); 25 knots (dived)
Complement: 132 crew

LEFT: **HMS *Ambush*, pictured during sea trials, 2012. The Astute attack submarine class was the result of a 1986 feasibility study by the Royal Navy. Already committed to billions of pounds on the Trident boats, the British government nonetheless agreed further massive expenditure on the new SSN class, which will comprise Britain's largest ever nuclear-powered attack submarines, the first of which, *Astute*, was launched in 2007.** ABOVE: **The first *Astute* under construction.** BELOW: **At the screens of the *Astute* combat management system.**

Astute-class SSN

With the Vanguard build underway, the Royal Navy's department of future requirements turned its attention to a replacement for the ageing Swiftsure attack submarines. A programme of studies costing an estimated £6 million was approved in 1991, which led to the issue of an invitation to tender for the design and build three submarines in the new Astute class. The process of design selection, affordability and a whole raft of other procedures had to be negotiated before a successful outcome was achieved six years later, when the prime contractor, GEC-Marconi (now BAE Systems), undertook to build the three boats, with an option for a further two.

The first of class, *Astute*, was laid down in January 2000, the centenary year of the Royal Navy's Submarine Service. Her arrival was anticipated with great interest and expectation, given that the design called for a truly multi-role submarine meeting today's requirements, with a growing emphasis towards possible rogue and terrorist seaborne activity as well as traditional forms of deployment. *Astute* is reckoned to match all requirements, and at almost 7,000 tonnes/ 6,889 tons will be the largest and most capable class of attack submarine, with Tomahawk cruise missiles as standard. She will also be armed with six torpedo tubes, able to fire

ABOVE AND BELOW: **Views of the new submarine on early test trials. The *Astute* is equipped with Tomahawk Block IV cruise missiles fired from 533mm/21in torpedo tubes. Guidance is by the Navstar Global Positioning System, and the Block IV deal includes a two-way satellite link that allows reprogramming of the missile in flight and transmission of Battle Damage Indication imagery.**

ABOVE: **Work in progress: the massive construction task confronting BAE Systems Astute Class Ltd, with the submarines being built at BAE Systems Marine Barrow shipyard. The next two Astute ships are to be named *Ambush* and *Artful*. The government ultimately committed to seven *Astute*-class submarines as the Trafalgar boats were progressively retired.**

advanced weapons, including the Spearfish guided torpedo, and, with a larger torpedo room than *Virginia*, she can carry up to 36 torpedoes.

Astute entered service in 2007. Two other boats of this class – *Ambush* and *Artful* – were launched in 2013 and 2016 respectively. *Audacious* is undergoing sea trials, with three more boats under construction. The project employs more than 5,000 people at the peak of production work.

Astute-class SSN

Displacement: 6,200 tonnes/6,102.1 tons (surfaced); 6,692 tonnes/6,586.3 tons (submerged)
Length: 91.7m/300ft 10in
Beam: 10.8m/35ft 5in
Armament: 6 x tubes for Spearfish torpedoes, Royal Navy Sub-Harpoon anti-ship missiles and Tomahawk land attack missiles; 38 weapon capacity
Propulsion: Unknown
Speed: Unknown (surfaced); 32 knots (dived)
Complement: 100 crew

Dreadnought-class SSBN

The Dreadnought class of ballistic missile submarines for the Royal Navy is now being built to replace the current Vanguard class, which are approaching the end of their service lives. Successor was the name for the programme of delivering these submarines for the Royal Navy until the first boat, HMS *Dreadnought*, was named in October 2016. The next three boats will be called *Valiant*, *Warspite* and *King George VI*.

The Dreadnoughts are expected to enter Royal Navy service in the early 2030s and will be equipped with a new generation of nuclear reactors more efficient and less wasteful than previous designs. The class will have an intended service life of around 35 to 40 years, an increase of up to 50 percent over the Vanguards.

The class will have a displacement of around 17,200 tonnes/16,928 tons, making them the largest submarines to ever serve in the Royal Navy. At 153.6m/504ft long, they are longer than the Royal Navy's current Vanguard-class submarines and about the length of three Olympic size swimming pools. They will have a crew complement of around 130 personnel, who will be housed in accommodation areas that are designed to be more comfortable and spacious than previous submarine classes.

Propulsion comes from a Rolls-Royce PWR3 nuclear reactor, which will enable them to, technically, remain submerged for their entire 25-year service life. They will also have a pump-jet propulsion system, which is designed to be quieter than traditional propellers. The boats will have a top speed of over 30 knots/56kmp/35mph submerged.

TOP: **Artist rendering of a Dreadnought boat. This class of submarines represents a significant advancement in submarine technology, with a range of advanced features and capabilities that will make them among the most capable submarines in the world.** LEFT: **The Dreadnought-class submarines will be equipped with advanced environmental control systems that will enable them to operate without producing any emissions. They will also be designed to minimize their environmental impact, with measures in place to reduce noise pollution and prevent oil spills.**

The submarines will be armed with the Trident II D5 nuclear missile system, which is capable of delivering multiple nuclear warheads to targets 11,265km/7,000 miles away. They will also be armed with torpedoes and missiles for self-defence.

The Dreadnoughts will be equipped with a range of advanced technology systems including an integrated platform management system that monitors and controls all of the submarine's systems, from propulsion to weapons to life support. Fly-by-wire technology and the glass-cockpit approach, developed for use in high performance military aircraft, will control key aspects of the Dreadnought class beneath the waves including heading, pitch, depth and buoyancy. The Vanguard class are a product of the 1980s, with movement controlled manually by "planesmen" operating aircraft-like control sticks. In the Dreadnought class, this fly-by-wire aircraft flight control technology will see computers replace the manual input from operators. This Active Vehicle Control Management (AVCM) system will oversee all major aspects of the Dreadnoughts' manoeuvring.

The submarines will be equipped with an advanced sonar system that can detect and track targets at long ranges. The submarines will also have a periscope system that allows the crew to observe their surroundings without exposing the submarine's hull to detection.

One of the key challenges in designing and building the Dreadnought-class submarines is managing their acoustic signature. This has been achieved through the use of advanced coating materials and design features that reduce the submarine's noise output.

The Dreadnought-class submarines are being built by BAE Systems in collaboration with other companies and organizations at a purpose-built facility in Barrow-in-Furness in north-west England.

ABOVE: **A Royal Navy Trident II launch. The Dreadnoughts will be armed with up to 12 Tridents, each of which has up to eight warheads.**

LEFT: **HMS *Victorious*, one of the Royal Navy's Vanguard-class submarines. The Vanguard class, designed in the 1980s and in service from the 1990s, will be replaced by the Dreadnoughts from the early 2030s.**

Dreadnought-class SSBN

Displacement: 17,200 tonnes/16,928 tons
Length: 153.6m/504ft
Beam: 12.8m/42ft
Draught: 12m/39ft 4in
Armament: 12 x ballistic missile tubes Lockheed Trident II D5 SLBMs carrying up to 8 warheads each; 4 533mm/21in torpedo tubes for Spearfish heavyweight torpedoes
Propulsion: Rolls-Royce PWR3 nuclear reactor, turbo-electric drive, pump-jet
Speed: Surfaced, classified
Speed: Dived, 30 knots
Complement: 130 crew

Rubis-Améthyste-class SSN

The French Navy operated six Rubis-Améthyste-class nuclear attack submarines from the naval base in Toulon, four of them originally commissioned as first generation nuclear attack boats in the 1980s. At the time of writing, four boats of the class remain in service with the *Escadrille de sous-marins nucléaires d'attaque*. In the 1980s, they were deployed in an anti-surface ship role in the Rubis class. However, a substantial modern upgrade for the first four boats in 1992 re-equipped them to carry both anti-surface and anti-submarine weaponry for what was called the *Améthyste* configuration. The two names were joined for the purpose of creating a useful class of attack boats without the expense of building new boats and enabling the older submarine to carry a mixed load of 14 missiles and torpedoes.

Indeed, there was already a great affection in the French Navy for *Rubis*, which was named after a distinguished World War II boat. The record of long patrols by the modern *Rubis* included operations with the Coalition Forces during the time of the first Gulf War, operating between September 1992 and July 1993. In July 1993, she undertook a major refit for the Améthyste missile upgrade. *Rubis* also took part in Operation Trident, the 1999 NATO bombing campaign over Yugoslavia.

Her role was to offer protection to the naval aviation group and later, with *Améthyste*, to keep the Serbian Navy out of the Koton Straits while gathering intelligence at the same time. In 2002, *Rubis* performed a similar role with Task Force 473 in the Indian Ocean, during Operation Hercules, the naval participation in the overthrow of the Taliban in Afghanistan. The others in the class are *Saphir*, *Emeraude* and *Casablanca*, commissioned with *Rubis* in the 1980s, and *Perle*, the 1990s sister of *Améthyste*.

TOP: *Rubis* is affectionately viewed in France for the link to her World War II namesake, although she was originally christened *Provence*. She was renamed *Rubis* in December 1980. *Rubis* was alleged to have entered the Pacific Ocean in 1985 in support of an operation that ended in the sinking of the Greenpeace ship *Rainbow Warrior*. ABOVE: An inside view of the weaponry, for which these submarines have the capacity to carry 14 Exocet missiles and torpedoes in a mixed load. The missiles are also launched from the torpedo tubes.

More of a general-purpose boat than exclusively an attack craft, the noise amelioration improvements of the Améthyste rebuild programme helped to prove its value to the French Navy in many ways. The development into littoral anti-submarine operations was only part of the new equation. Many additional features that came as a follow-on to the *Rubis* class specifically included a much quieter power system, to meet the requirements of the type of operations they were now to undertake. The boats were thus subsequently utilized in a variety of situations, and given a fairly wide brief that covers reconnaissance and intelligence gathering, as well as adopting the anti-shipping and power projection capabilities that the *Rubis* boats brought with them.

The improvements were noticeable in virtually every department, with a longer hull, far better accommodation, modern electronics suites and modern sonar. The major innovation in terms of weaponry was the introduction of the Exocet missile, which has proved to be a shudderingly effective ship killer. This was famously demonstrated against the Royal Navy by the Argentine naval aviation forces in the Falklands War in 1982 with devastating effect and great loss of life. The missile skims the surface of the sea in its approach to the target to avoid detection. It is armed with 165kg/364lb of high explosive and is guided by target range and bearing data downloaded into the Exocet's onboard computer.

Saphir and *Rubis* were decommissioned in 2019 and 2022 respectively and overall the *Rubis* class is being replaced in French Navy service by the Suffren-class submarines.

TOP: **A torpedo handler for the Rubis-Améthyste boats. Generally, up to 14 F17 Model 2 torpedoes may be carried, although the armaments compartment is versatile enough to take Exocet missiles in a combination of weapons.**
ABOVE: **Inside the control room of the Rubis-Améthyste boats, from where the armaments are fired.**

ABOVE: *Améthyste* **became a lead partner in the class title by virtue of the fact that she brought innovations to this series of boats when commissioned in 1992.**
RIGHT: **She was followed soon after by** *Perle*, **pictured here at the Golden Jubilee celebration of Queen Elizabeth II. The four earlier boats were then re-equipped to the same standard as the later submarines for both anti-surface and anti-submarine warfare.**

Rubis

Displacement: 2,362 tonnes/2,324.7 tons (surfaced); 2,558 tonnes/2,517.6 tons (submerged)
Length: 72.1m/236ft 7in
Beam: 7.6m/24ft 11in
Armament: 4 x 533mm/21in tubes, F17 Mod 2 torpedoes; 14 x Exocet SM39
Propulsion: Pressurized water K48 nuclear reactor, 48mW/64,369hp
Speed: 20 knots (surfaced); 26 knots (dived)
Complement: 70 crew

Améthyste

Displacement: 2,730 tonnes/2,686.9 tons (surfaced); 2,812 tonnes/2,767.6 tons (submerged)
Length: 73.6m/241ft 6in
Beam: 7.6m/24ft 11in
Armament: 4 x 533mm/21in tubes, F17 Mod 2 torpedoes; 14 x Exocet SM39
Propulsion: Nuclear reactor, 7,084.1kW/9,500shp
Speed: 22 knots (surfaced); 25 knots (dived)
Complement: 70 crew

LEFT: *L'Inflexible*, one of four French ballistic missile submarines whose origins dated to the 1960s–70s, but which remained in business through extensive upgrades and streamlining in the 1980s, including an improved reactor core and the back-fitting of the M4 missile. The massive cost of the overhaul, however, was deemed insufficient to keep them all operational until France's new generation of SSBNs arrived. ABOVE: The nuclear reactor core is lowered into the reactor room during the overhaul.

L'Inflexible-class SSBN

This class was previously known as *Le Redoutable* after France's first ballistic missile-carrying submarine. However, after 20 years of service, she was decommissioned in 1991 and the class was renamed L'Inflexible after the youngster of the class, but even she was retired in 2008. The class had certainly been a good servant of the French Navy, although its patrol programme over those years did not match the activity of the American and British SSBNs.

Indeed, while co-operating under the auspices of NATO, the French maintained singular independence in terms of operational strategy and always retained as the sole right of their Government the order for the launching and targeting of France's nuclear weapons. The reality was never likely to have brought about a situation in which France acted alone in any international nuclear exchange; the French submarine-launched nuclear weapons nevertheless remained under the trigger-finger of the French President, whereas the British, through their 1962 agreement with America, were bound to take response and targeting parameters from the US.

L'Inflexible and the four remaining submarines of this class underwent a two-year modernization refit and overhaul in the 1980s to allow continued commitment to France's Strategic Oceanic Force until their replacement boats of the *Le Triomphant* class began to be commissioned. Even so, they gave good service, and their hefty refit provided them with M4 missiles, a new missile launch system, new reactor cores, an updated sonar suite and some noise abatement measures. However, delays in the arrival of the new SSBNs meant that two of the L'Inflexible boats stayed in business for much longer than was originally intended by the French Navy.

Consequently, the class remained active well into the 21st century, although three other boats, *Terrible*, *Foudroyant* and *Tonnant* also went into retirement in the late 1990s, leaving *Indomptable* and *L'Inflexible* to carry the flag until their own retirement in 2003 and 2008 respectively.

LEFT: **The loading of a French M4 intermediate-range submarine-launched ballistic missile that is similar to the US Polaris. These entered service in the French SSBN fleet on 1 May 1985 and were the first French MIRV-capable nuclear missiles, replaced in service by the improved M45 SLBM missile.**

L'Inflexible-class SSBN

Displacement: 9,000 tonnes/8,857.9 tons (surfaced); 9,842 tonnes/9,686.6 tons (submerged)
Length: 128m/419ft 11in
Beam: 10.5m/34ft 5in
Armament: 4 x 533mm/21in tubes; Exocet SM39 missiles, 16 x M4 SLBM
Propulsion: Nuclear reactor, 11,931kW/16,000shp
Speed: 20 knots (surfaced); 25 knots (dived)
Complement: 130 crew

Agosta-class 90B SSK

The Agosta-class submarine has proved a popular export model for the French, as well as with their own navy. From the stable of DCN of France, variations of the class have served with the French, Spanish and Pakistani navies. The 90B is an improved version of the original and equally popular 1970 boat, but featuring higher performance and a propulsion system that provided a submerged endurance three times longer than earlier versions. Another feature is a substantially increased level of automation, which in turn enabled a reduction in crew from 54 to 36.

The submarine had a choice of propulsion systems: a French diesel-electric combination providing 2,685kW/3,600hp and a 2,200kW/

2,950hp electric motor driving a single propeller is offered as standard. However, the latest versions of the Agosta class were equipped with the MESMA Air Independent Propulsion System (AIP), consisting of a turbine receiving high-pressure steam from a combustion chamber, burning a gaseous mixture of ethanol and liquid oxygen. While a diesel-electric submarine has to surface to periscope depth to recharge the batteries, thus risking detection, with the MESMA AIP system, a submarine can remain submerged three times longer. The Agosta 90B's length was extended by 9m/29ft 6in to accommodate the AIP system.

Additional upgrades put the new improved Agosta well ahead in terms of clectronic warfare, equipped with the Thales DR-3000U radar warning receiver, using a masthead antenna array with omni-directional and monopulse directional antennae and a separate periscope warning antenna. The weaponry was also updated to include a mixed load of up to 16 torpedoes and missiles. They carried the wire-guided ECAN F17 Mod 2 torpedo that delivered a 250kg/551lb warhead to a depth of 600m/1,968ft. The Exocet SM39 missile, with a target range of over 50km/31 miles, could also be launched via the torpedo tubes and has a 165kg/364lb high-explosive shaped-charge warhead.

LEFT: **The refloating procedure in the dry dock.**
ABOVE: **A full-on bow view of the popular 90B** *Agosta* **attack submarine produced by France for both domestic use and export, with a choice of propulsion systems, the boats having served with the Spanish and Pakistani navies. The 90B is a direct derivative of the successful 1970s version and contains a greater level of automation, resulting in the ship's crew being reduced from 54 to 36. There are four bow torpedo tubes and a capacity to carry a mixed load of up to 16 torpedoes and missiles.** BELOW LEFT: **Cutaway images showing a comparison of internal layouts.**

Agosta-class 90B SSK

Displacement: 1,486 tonnes/1,462.5 tons (surfaced); 1,732 tonnes/1,704.6 tons (submerged)
Length: 67m/219ft 10in
Beam: 5.4m/17ft 9in
Armament: 6 x 533mm/21in tubes, mixed parcel F17 Mod 2/ Exocet SM39 submarine-launched anti-ship missiles
Propulsion: Diesel-electric, 2684.5kW/3,600hp or Mesma AIP
Speed: 15 knots (surfaced); 17 knots (dived)
Complement: 36/41 crew

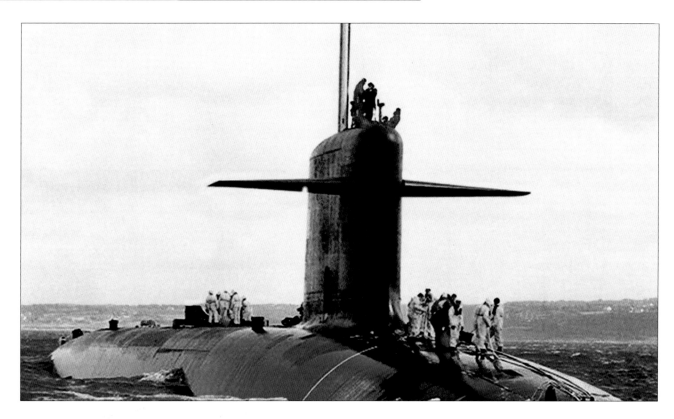

Le Triomphant-class SSBN

L e *Triomphant* became the new standard bearer of the French Navy's ballistic missile fleet in 1998, the first of four boats in this class to be delivered progressively through to 2008. This submarine was designed and built at *Direction des Constructions et Armes Navales* (DCN), Cherbourg shipyard, and the first-of-class entered service in 1997 with construction having started a decade earlier.

The boat initially carried 16 vertically launched M54 ballistic missiles each with a warhead of six multiple re-entry vehicles (MRVs). The explosive power of such weapons, indicated variously through this directory, can once again be demonstrated by the French figure: each MRV possessed the equivalent of 147,638 tonnes/145,306 tons of TNT –

ABOVE: **The pride of France, *Le Vigilant*, commissioned in 2004, was the third of four new submarines in the French *Le Triomphant* class, which became the French Navy's ballistic missile carriers succeeding the *Redoubtable/L'Inflexible* class. The first-of-class submarine, *Le Triomphant*, entered service in 1997.**

ten times greater than the atomic bomb dropped on Hiroshima in 1945.

The M45 missiles were replaced by M51 missiles, first deployed in 2010. The M51 carries six to ten independently targetable TN 75 150kt thermonuclear warheads. The missiles and their deadly payloads are designed to travel at speeds of up to Mach 25 over distances that are classified but estimated to be 8,000–10,000km/4,970–6213 miles. These formidable

LEFT: **Against the floodlit backdrop of its home base, *Le Vigilant* brings to the international scene France's own propulsion design, a nuclear turbo-electric system based on a Type K15 Pressure Water Reactor with an auxiliary diesel electric back-up. Le Triomphan*t*-class boats have a submerged speed in excess of 25 knots and a surface speed of 20 knots, a diving depth of more than 300m/984ft and an endurance in excess of 60 days.**

LEFT AND ABOVE: **The second of the French ballistic submarines, *Le Téméraire* commissioned in December 1999, followed by *Le Vigilant* in 2004, with the last member of the group, *Le Terrible*,**

submarines, replaced the six boats of the Redoutable/L'Inflexible class to provide the sea-based element of France's nuclear deterrent strike force, and are known in French as *Sous-Marin Nucléaire Lanceur D'Engins de Nouvell Génération* (Next Generation Device-Launching Nuclear Submarine, abbreviated as SNLE-NG.

It has been noticeable that France has continued to proceed with this, one of the most costly areas of naval defence, while other nations were substantially curtailing their expenditure. The second of the French boats, *Le Téméraire*, was commissioned in December 1999, *Le Vigilant* in November 2004, and the fourth, *Le Terrible* in September 2010. The submarine has four 533mm/21in torpedo tubes and has the capacity to carry a mixed loaf of F17/L5 torpedoes and Exocet SM39 anti-ship missiles. The class is also said, compared to the Redoubtable class, to generate around 1,000th of the detectable noise of earlier boats.

commissioned in 2010. These submarines initially carried 16 vertically launched M45 ballistic missiles supplied by EADS Space Transportation, based in Les Mureaux, France. The missile's propulsion system consisted of a three-stage solid-fuel rocket motor producing hypersonic speed and carried a thermo-nuclear warhead, developed by the *Commissariat à l'Energie Atomique*, with six Multiple Re-entry Vehicles, each of 150kT in the TN-71 warhead. The range was 6,000km/3,728 miles. In spite of the re-evaluation of nuclear requirements in recent times, the French introduced the more powerful M51 missile and retro-fitted all boats. It can carry a warhead with 10 MIRVS, and has an increased range of 8,000km/4,971 miles. BELOW: **A profile of a Le Triomphant-class submarine.**

ABOVE: **The leader of the class, *Le Triomphant*, at sea. Apart from her nuclear capability, the submarine and her sisters have four 533mm/21in torpedo tubes and the ability to carry a mixed load of F17/L5 torpedoes and Exocet missiles. The torpedo, armed with a 150kg/331lb warhead, is equipped with both active and passive homing and has a range of 9km/5.5m.**

Le Triomphant-class SSBN

Displacement: 12,440 tonnes/12,243.5 tons (surfaced); 14,108 tonnes/13,885.2 tons (submerged)

Length: 184m/603ft 8in

Beam: 12.5m/41ft

Armament: Nuclear: 4 x 533mm/21in tubes, 1F17/L5 torpedoes and Exocet missiles; 16 M51 SLBM missiles with 10 MIRV warheads

Propulsion: 1 x GWC PAR K15 nuclear reactor; 1x steam turbine, 30947kW/41,500shp

Speed: 22 knots (surfaced); 25 knots (dived)

Complement: 65 crew

Barracuda/Suffren-class SSN

The Barracuda class, also known as the Suffren class, is a new generation of nuclear-powered attack submarines (SSN) designed and built by the French shipbuilder, Naval Group, for the French Navy. The first of the class, *Suffren*, was launched in July 2019 and commissioned in November 2020, and a further five boats have been ordered, to replace the Rubis-class submarines in French service.

The development of the Barracuda-class submarines began in the late 1990s as part of France's military modernization programme, aimed at improving the capabilities of its naval forces. The design of the submarine was based on the requirements of the French Navy, which included enhanced stealth, improved detection and tracking capabilities, and increased endurance and range. A hybrid propulsion system includes a nuclear reactor and an electric motor enabling the submarine to stay submerged for extended periods of time and operate at high speeds without the need to surface for

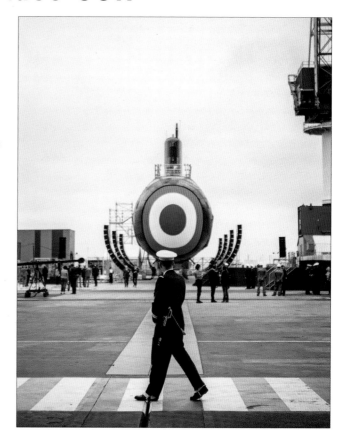

ABOVE: **A Barracuda boat under construction, 2016. The submarine's sonar suite includes a bow-mounted active/passive sonar system, flank-mounted passive sonar arrays, and a towed array sonar system. The submarine is also equipped with a range of sensors, including a high-resolution periscope and an optronic mast that provides 360-degree coverage.** RIGHT: **The Barracuda-class submarine *Suffren*, in a very patriotic finish for its official unveiling and launch in Cherbourg, France, July 12, 2019.**

refuelling. The submarine can operate on its nuclear power source for up to 20 years without needing to refuel.

Another key feature of the Barracuda-class submarines is their advanced acoustic signature reduction capabilities. The submarines are designed to be exceptionally quiet, reducing their detectability by enemy vessels and making them more difficult to track and target. The class also features an advanced combat management system and a suite of sensors, including sonars, to provide the crew with enhanced situational awareness and the ability to detect and track a variety of targets, from ships and submarines to underwater mines. The French Navy is considering adding hypersonic missiles to the submarines' arsenal, as well as new torpedo defence systems and improved sonar and sensor suites. The submarines may also be equipped with unmanned underwater vehicles (UUVs) for reconnaissance and surveillance missions.

The Barracuda boats are equipped with a variety of armament and weapon systems, including heavyweight torpedoes, anti-ship missiles, and the Naval Cruise Missile (NCM) developed by MBDA. This missile has a range of over 1,000km/621 miles and can carry a nuclear or conventional warhead. The submarine is also equipped with F21 heavyweight torpedoes with a range of over 50km/31 miles and can be used to engage surface ships or submarines. The torpedo launch system can also be used to launch naval mines, allowing the submarine to engage in mine-laying operations.

The Barracuda-class submarines are crewed by around 65 personnel, including officers, sailors, and technicians – the submarines are designed to be highly automated, with many systems and processes controlled by advanced computer systems and software.

The boats have been designed to be highly versatile, capable of performing a range of missions, from conducting intelligence gathering and reconnaissance operations to engaging in anti-submarine warfare and strike missions. The submarines are expected to play a key role in the French Navy's future operations, both in terms of supporting NATO missions and responding to regional security threats.

Suffren, the lead vessel of the class, became fully operational in June 2022. The second boat of the class, *Duguay-Trouin*, began sea trials on 26 March 2023.

ABOVE: **The Barracuda-class submarines have a relatively small crew of around 60 personnel and are equipped with modern living quarters, a galley and mess area, medical facility and gym. The submarine is designed to provide a high level of comfort and safety for the crew, even during long deployments.** BELOW: **The submarine's hull is made of steel and titanium, making it more durable and resistant to corrosion. The submarine also has a low acoustic signature, making it harder to detect by enemy sonar systems.**

Barracuda/*Suffren*-class

Displacement: 4,765 tonnes/4,690 tons (surfaced)
Displacement: 5,300 tonnes/5,216 tons (submerged)
Length: 99.5m/326ft 5in
Beam: 8.8m/28ft 10in
Armament: 4 x 533mm/21in tubes for; MdCN cruise missiles; Exocet SM39 Mod2 missiles; A3SM (MICA) missiles for air defence; F21 Artemis heavy torpedoes; FG29 mines
Propulsion: K15 nuclear reactor, 2 Turbo-generator groups: 2 emergency diesel generators, 1 electrically driven pump-jet
Speed: 25 knots/46km/29mph (surfaced)
Complement: 60 crew

Han-class Type 091 SSN

The Type 091 (NATO reporting name *Han*) attack submarine produced by China was the first nuclear submarine operated by the People's Liberation Army Navy (PLAN) Submarine Force. The first was commissioned in 1974 while the last of the class was launched in 1990, and despite being considered outmoded by the early 2000s, three of the five boats built were believed to still be in service in some form in the early 2020s.

While more modern designs were awaited, the 091 served China well, although, as with their SSBN experience, the Chinese had to surmount a series of technical problems to bring this class into production. Five submarines of this class were built during the 1970s and 80s to provide the Chinese Navy with the experience of operating nuclear-powered submarines.

On the way, and again with some help and input from Soviet and French technicians, the class was upgraded and modernized, including from the third boat, a lengthening of the hull to accommodate an anti-ship missile system, and modifications were made to the nuclear reactor to reduce noise and achieve greater reliability. A new French-designed intercept sonar set and the obsolete Soviet ESM suite were also replaced with a new French design. A further refit in the 1990s provided three of the boats with wire-guided torpedoes (20 each) and the capability to launch YJ-82 missiles from their six 533mm/21in torpedo tubes, but by 2004 two were reported to be out of commission. The Type 091 were also capable of carrying 36 mines in their

TOP: *Changzheng 1* (Long March 1) was the first of the class and was decommissioned in 2000. After thorough denuclearization, the boat was preserved as a museum ship in Qingdao Naval Museum, China.
ABOVE: **Profile of a *Han* class boat.**

torpedo tube tubes. Anechoic tiles were also added to the boats to reduce the high noise levels.

These boats were stepping stones to build experience and force the development of improved indigenous technologies, but as they were apparently restricted to operating in comparatively local waters and would not have fared well against potential adversaries, the submarines, apart from navies. reports of poor radiation shielding, did not pose a significant threat to opposing

ABOVE: **People's Liberation Army Navy Type 91 SSN, No. 405, pictured in 1993.**

Type 091

Displacement: 4,423 tonnes/4,353.1 tons (surfaced); 5,413 tonnes/5,327.5 tons (submerged)
Length: 98m/321ft 6in or 106m/347ft 9in
Beam: 10m/ft in
Armament: 6 x 533mm/21in tubes; YJ-82 anti-ship missiles
Propulsion: Nuclear reactor; power output not known
Speed: 12 knots (surfaced); 25 knots (dived)
Complement: 65 crew

Type 092 SSBN

The first nuclear-powered ballistic missile submarine (SSBN) operated by the People's Liberation Army Navy Submarine Force was the Type 092, given the NATO reporting name *Xia* class. This one-off, derived from the Type 091 by being extended to allow room for twelve vertical missile tubes, was laid down in 1978, completed in 1981 and was technically on active patrols from 1987. Ongoing issues with the design kept the boat mainly in port but still apparently with the ability to launch its missiles from there. Numerous upgrades sought to keep the boat credible although observers believe the boat has never patrolled outside Chinese regional waters and think it would not have survived long against the latest boats of potential enemies that would seek to destroy it in times of war.

The boat was considered so noisy to underwater detection gear that its chances of surviving an attack in ocean waters would be minimal. The home-designed and -built Xia experienced persistent problems through virtually every phase – construction, commissioning and sea trials. It was also three years after commissioning before the first successful firing of its JL-1 missile was achieved. It should therefore be considered more of a technology testbed stepping-stone that enabled

the PLAN to embrace new technologies and cut its teeth on the building and operation of an SSBN.

Undaunted by problems and challenges with the Type 092, and with some help from Russia and France, China announced plans for a new SSBN, the Type 094.

TOP AND ABOVE: **The *Xia* SSBN boat was heralded as a great advance in the Chinese Navy's defence capabilities against any potential enemy equipped with nuclear surface forces, although the creation and running of, at the time, the nation's sole vessel was fraught with technical problems and delays for many years.**

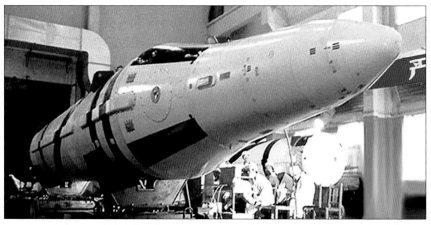

ABOVE: **The Xia class was initially armed with this Chinese-built JL-1, which was considered a major achievement. Experience with the Type 092 system helped shape the much improved JL-2 SLBM system in China's newer SSBN boats.**

Type 092 SSBN

Displacement: Not known (surfaced); 6,397 tonnes/6,296 tons (submerged)
Length: 120m/393ft 8in
Beam: 10m/32ft 10in
Armament: 6 x 533mm/21in tubes (bow), Set-65E torpedoes; 12 x Ju Lang-1 SLBM with 1 x single 250kT warhead and range of 1770km/1,100 miles
Propulsion: 1 x PWR nuclear reactor; 1 auxiliary diesel; power output not known
Speed: 20 knots (surfaced); 22 knots (dived)
Complement: 140 crew

Type 093/093A

The Type 093 nuclear-powered attack submarine, developed by China in the 1990s, continued the advancement of the nation's nuclear submarine design and build experience. Its appearance was seen as a significant development of China's naval capabilities.

The Type 093 (NATO codename *Shang*) was first introduced into PLAN service in the early 2000s. Advanced acoustic and electromagnetic shielding helps to reduce the boat's acoustic and magnetic signature, making it more difficult for enemy vessels to detect. The design's capabilities raised concerns among the United States and China's neighbours closely watching the increasing development of China's naval capabilities in the region. China

has however only built a small fleet of six boats over a number of years, suggesting the design has limitations that held it back from large-scale production. Nevertheless these boats that first entered service in 2006 are potent and are most likely deployed to protect China's ballistic missile submarines (SSBNs) against potential enemy threats.

In terms of armament, the Type 93 submarine is equipped with a variety of torpedoes and missiles, including the Yu-6 wire-guided torpedo and the YJ-82 anti-ship missile. It is also apparently capable of launching cruise missiles, which can strike targets on land from underwater.

Only two ships were commissioned in 2006 and 2007, then limited production

restarted in the 2010s with improved stealth, including anechoic small rubber tiles and an integrated towed sonar array housed in the top of the vertical rudder.

ABOVE: **The Type 093 can carry the submarine variant of the YJ-18B cruise missile, launched from vertical launch tubes, and possibly torpedo tubes, with an estimated range of 500km/310 miles and a terminal speed of twice the speed of sound. These vehicle-mounted versions give a clear impression of the size of these weapons.** BELOW LEFT: **The PLAN had, until the Type 093, relied on diesel-electric submarines with limited range and endurance – the Type 093 was a game-changer, offering increased range, endurance, and stealth capabilities.**

Type 093

Displacement: 6,100 tonnes/6,003 tons (submerged)
Length: 107m/351ft
Beam: 11m/36ft
Armament: 6 x 533mm/21.8in torpedo tubes, Yu-6 torpedoes, YJ-82 anti-ship cruise missiles
Propulsion: Nuclear reactor driving steam turbine
Speed: 30 knots (submerged)
Complement: 100 crew (approximately)

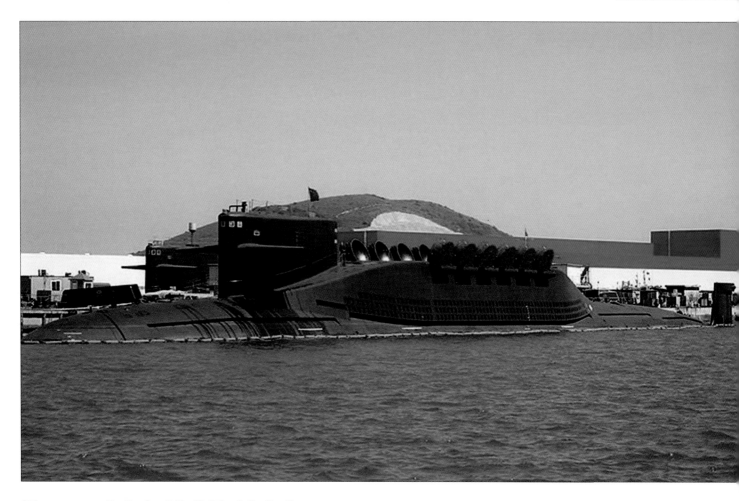

Type 094/095/096

The Type 094, also known as the *Jin* class, is the current class of ballistic missile submarines (SSBNs) operated by the Chinese People's Liberation Army Navy. The submarines are designed to provide China with a sea-based nuclear deterrent, allowing for a second-strike capability in case of a nuclear attack – the US Department of Defense states that the boats provide China with its "first credible sea-based nuclear deterrent."

Believed by observers to be based on the Type 093, the 094 was apparently first commissioned in 2007, was on active deterrent patrol from 2015, and six boats were in service by 2020.

The submarines were first armed with 12 JL-2 SLBMs in vertical launch tubes, each with one warhead and an effective range of 7,200km/4,500 miles. By late 2022, the fleet had been rearmed with JL-3 ICBMs with a greater range estimated at 10,000km/6,200 miles. With

a noise signature comparable to older boats, these submarines nevertheless possess incredible destructive capability.

China's Type 095 class of third-generation nuclear-powered attack submarines is under development for the PLAN. Few details are known of the boat's design but it is expected to

ABOVE: **A Type 094 with all of its 12 ICBM launch tube hatches open.** BELOW LEFT: **Type 94 profile.**

Type 094

Displacement: 11,000 tonnes/10,826 tons (submerged), (estimated)
Length: 137m/449ft 6in (estimated)
Beam: 11.8m/38ft 4in (estimated)
Armament: 12 launch tubes for JL-2/3 submarine-launched ballistic missile
Propulsion: One nuclear reactor, one shaft
Speed: Not known
Complement: 120–140 crew (estimated)

LEFT: **A JL-2 SLBM launched from a People's Liberation Army Navy Type 094 submarine, 2015.**
BELOW: **Ohio-class submarine, USS *Michigan*. The Chinese Type 094 is around 33.5m/110ft shorter than the established US Ohio class.**

have a substantially reduced acoustic signature compared to earlier boats and a hull type optimized to minimize noise and discoverability. Advances in China's nuclear reactor design will result in improved performance and reduced maintenance. Vertical launch system tubes are expected to feature, as are the very latest sensors and defensive systems. Observers believe the boats will be built in a new facility in China's Liaoning province, thereby removing the pinch point that limited the construction of earlier nuclear boats.

In parallel, development is underway for the Type 096, a new class of ballistic missile submarine (SSBN) for the PLAN Submarine Force – the new boat is expected to be armed with the JL-3 SLBM.

Type 035

The Chinese Type 035, known to NATO as the *Ming* class, is a diesel-electric attack submarine (SSK) that has been in service with the People's Liberation Army Navy (PLAN) in a variety of versions since the 1970s. The Type 35 submarine is designed for a wide range of missions, including anti-submarine warfare, anti-surface warfare, intelligence gathering, and reconnaissance.

Although the hull was based on the earlier Soviet Romeo class Type 033, the Type 035 was the first manifestation of China's ambition to develop an indigenous submarine-building industry. From just two boats completed by the mid 1970s, improved "A" models appeared in the 1980s. The most produced version, the Type 035G, saw 12 boats commissioned between 1990 and 1999, and was further improved with better sensors and noise reduction.

The Type 035G with hull number No. 361 suffered a major mechanical failure in April 2003 that resulted in the death of all 70 crew members. Confusingly, the latest version was the Type 035B, produced in the early 2000s, which could launch cruise missiles from its torpedo tubes – five boats were completed.

The Bangladesh Navy took delivery of two Type 035G in 2016 after refitting in China, a deal worth an estimated $203 million.

ABOVE: **Bangladesh Navy Type 035s were delivered in 2016.** BELOW LEFT: **The Type 035 is a greatly improved redesign of the original Type 035 that served in the PLAN submarine fleet from 1962 until 1984.**

Type 035

Displacement: 2,110 tonnes/2,076 tons (submerged)
Length: 76m/249ft 4in
Beam: in 7.6m/24ft 11in
Armament: 8 x 533/21in torpedo tubes, 6 in bow, 2 in stern, 14 torpedoes as well as mines or cruise missiles
Propulsion: Type E390ZC-1 diesel engine, 5,200 hp / 3,900 kW
Speed: 18 knots (submerged)
Complement: Unknown

Type 039/039A

The development of China's Type 039 (*Song* class) diesel-electric attack submarine in the 1990s was a significant milestone for China's naval capabilities and played an important role in modernizing China's submarine fleet. This was the first modern, conventional submarine design wholly developed within China and it was designed to

ABOVE: **The Type 039 was the first Chinese diesel-electric submarine to use the teardrop hull shape for improved submerged performance. This is the G variant without the stepped conning tower.** BELOW: **The upgraded Type 039A is capable of carrying out a wide range of missions, including anti-submarine warfare, anti-surface warfare, and intelligence gathering.**

provide a more capable platform for the Chinese navy's anti-surface and anti-submarine warfare operations than the older Type 035s could offer. Refinements to the design included improved sound levels and the main production version was the Type 039G, which can be most readily identified by the lack of stepped design for the conning tower which rises to the stern in the earlier version.

A bow-mounted sonar is used for both search and attack and the main weapon for the class is the Yu-4 passive homing torpedo, although anti-ship cruise missiles can probably also be deployed.

The improved 039A (*Yuan* class) was developed in the early 2000s as a successor to the class and features

a number of enhancements including: a new hull design with improved hydrodynamics; improved sonar systems including a flank array sonar and a towed array sonar; and advanced noise reduction technology. It is China's first AIP-powered submarine. It is believed to be deployed as an attack submarine with a secondary anti-ship cruise missile (ASCM) role.

The Type 39A is equipped with advanced torpedoes and anti-ship missiles, including the YJ-83 and YJ-18, which have longer ranges and greater accuracy than the weapons on the Type 39. Twenty boats are planned and the majority are already in active PLAN service.

Type 039A

Displacement: 3,600 tonnes/3,543 tons (submerged)
Length: 77.6m/254ft 7in
Beam: 8.4m/27ft 7in
Armament: 6 x 533mm torpedo tubes, 18 torpedoes or missiles (including land attack cruise missiles), naval mines
Propulsion: Diesel-electric, AIP system
Speed: 18 knots/ 33.3 kmh/20.7mph (surfaced)
Speed: 20 knots (dived)
Complement: 65–70 crew

Type 212A-class SSK

The Type 212A is equipped with a highly integrated command and weapons control system that interfaces with sensors, weapons and navigation systems. The design's conventional diesel propulsion is complemented by an additional air-independent propulsion (AIP) system through Siemens proton exchange membrane (PEM) compressed hydrogen fuel cells, the first submarine series thus equipped. These excellent submarines can operate at high speed on diesel power and when needed switch to the AIP system for silent slow cruising.

These submarines can stay submerged for up to three weeks generating little exhaust heat and the system is believed to be vibration-free and therefore effectively undetectable. In 2006, the German Navy's U-32 sailed from the Baltic to Rota, Spain, a distance of 2,800km/1,700m without surfacing or snorkelling. In 2013, during exercises in US waters, U-32 established a new 18-day submerged transit without snorkelling – a record for non-nuclear submarines.

Counter-measures for the Type 212A German and Italian versions of the submarines include an ultra-efficient electronic warfare system developed under a contract awarded to EADS Systems & Defence Electronics and Thales Defence. Counter-measures hardware includes the development of the TAU 2000 torpedo system, which has four launch containers, each with up to ten discharge tubes with a remarkable addition known as effectors – small underwater vehicles, similar in appearance to a torpedo. The effectors are jammers and decoys with hydrophones and acoustic emitters. Multiple effectors are deployed in order to counter torpedoes in re-attack mode.

LEFT: **The efficiently compartmentalized 212A is constructed in the manner of Airbus aircraft: different sections of the submarines are constructed at the two sites involved and then shipped to the respective other yard, so that both HDW and Thyssen Nordseewerke assemble two complete submarines each.**

Type 212A-class SSK

Displacement: 1,500 tonnes/1,476.3 tons (surfaced); 1,797 tonnes/1,768.6 tons (submerged)
Length: 57m/187ft
Beam: 7m/23ft
Armament: 6 x 533mm/21in tubes, 24 x stn Atlas Electronik DM2A4 torpedoes
Propulsion: 2 x MTU 16V 396 diesel generators; Permasyn electric motor, 600–900V battery, 3,164kW/4,243shp
Speed: 12 knots (surfaced); 20 knots (dived)
Complement: 32 crew

Type 206A-class SSK

Type 206A-class SSK

Displacement: 442 tonnes/435 tons (surfaced); 490 tonnes/482.3 tons (submerged)
Length: 48.6m/159ft 5in
Beam: 4.6m/15ft 1in
Armament: 8 x 533mm/21in tubes (bow), 12 AEG Seeschlenge Type 206 torpedoes
Propulsion: 2 x MTU 16V 396 diesel generators; Permasyn electric motor, 600–900V battery, 3,164kW/4,243shp
Speed: 10 knots (surfaced); 17 knots (dived)
Complement: 22 crew

Germany operated one of the smallest and, for its size, most successful and enduring attack boats anywhere in the world, with a surface displacement of just 457 tonnes/450 tons. The Type 206 first went into production in the early 1970s, when 17 were built, followed by 14 of the improved Type 206A.

A dozen of the first type went through a substantial upgrade in the early 1990s to bring them to "A" standard, and they continued to give excellent service in the primary role of anti-surface warfare, with capability for anti-submarine warfare, mine-laying and reconnaissance. Because of their size, they were especially suitable for operations in shallow water, with a tolerance of a mere 20m/65ft 7in in minimum depth.

As the new millennium approached, the German submarine flotilla still had 14 of the two types in operation. The area of operations was also extended around that time, extending from the Baltic Sea to the Atlantic Ocean and from the Norwegian Sea to the Mediterranean.

ABOVE LEFT: **The 206A proved to be a reliable workhorse of the 1980s and 90s.**

However, further decommissioning followed when two flotillas were merged and most of the rest of the boats were retired in 2010.

Colombia acquired four former Germany Navy submarines, two to be used for spares, and, after refitting in Germany, *Intrépido* (ex-U23) and *Indomable* (ex-U24) entered Colombian Navy active service in 2015.

Type 214 class

A further development on the Type 212 by HDW is the solely for export Type 214 submarine, which attracted attention from around the world. The Greek Navy ordered four, the first, *Papanikolis S120*, was delivered in 2004. Hellenic Shipyards, acquired by HDW in 2002, built *Pipinos S121*, *Matrozos S122* and *Katsonis S123* vessels at Skaramanga, and were commissioned between 2015

Type 214 class

Displacement: 1,700 tonnes/1,673.2 tons (surfaced); 1,859 tonnes/1,830 tons (submerged)
Length: 24m/78ft 9in
Beam: 6.30m/20ft 8in
Armament: 8 x 533mm/21in tubes, WASS Black Shark heavyweight torpedoes
Propulsion: 2 x MTU 16V 396 diesel generators; Permasyn electric motor, 600–900V battery, 3,164kW/4,243shp
Speed: 12 knots (surface); 15 knots (dived)
Complement: 30 crew

and 2016. South Korea also ordered nine Type 214s, which entered service between 2007 and 2020 – these were built by Hyundai Heavy Industries. Other customers incliude Portugal and Turkey.

The Type 214 has an improved pressure hull that gives an increased diving depth of over 400m/1,312ft 4in. Four of the eight torpedo tubes are also capable of firing missiles. Type 214 submarines for the Hellenic Navy are armed with the WASS Black Shark heavyweight torpedo, a dual purpose, wire-guided torpedo that is fitted with an Astra active/passive acoustic head and a multi-target guidance-and-control unit incorporating a counter-countermeasures system.

Performance of the propulsion system has been increased with two Siemens fuel cells that produce

ABOVE: **The German export market was clearly impressed by the hull of the 214, with its low-noise propeller, both of which decreased the submarine's acoustic signature.**

120kW/161hp per module and gives the submarine an underwater endurance of at least two weeks. A hull shape that has been further optimized for hydrodynamic and stealth characteristics and a low-noise propeller combines to decrease the submarine's acoustic signature. The submarine has an exceptional mission endurance of 12 weeks, of which three weeks may be spent submerged without snorkelling.

LEFT: **Norway is expecting its first submarine in 2029 and the two German boats will be delivered in 2031 and 2034 – these new submarines are expected to remain in service to at least the end of the 2060s.**
BELOW: **Like the Type 212A, the 212CD has a hydrogen fuel cell-based air independent propulsion (AIP) system, but has two diesel engines compared to just one fitted to the earlier design.**

Type 212CD

Derived from the successful Type 212 class, the much larger (17m/56ft longer) diesel-electric Type 212 CD attack submarine has been developed by ThyssenKrupp Marine Systems (TKMS) for the Norwegian and German navies. In 2017, the German and Norwegian Governments signed an agreement worth €5.5 million for the joint development, procurement, operation and maintenance of the new submarines. So far, the Deutsche Marine has ordered

BELOW: **The Type 212CD is derived from the proven and highly successful Type 212 class but is much larger (17m/56ft longer) and has a surfaced displacement of approximately 2,500 tonnes/2,460 tons, 670 tonnes/659 tons more than the 212A Germany Navy Type 212A U-34 shown underway.**

two boats while the Royal Norwegian Navy has committed to four.

The Type 212CD has a displacement of approximately 2,500 tonnes/2,460 tons when surfaced (670 tonnes/659 tons more than the model from which it is derived) and can reach a maximum speed of 20 knots when submerged. The submarine is equipped with an air-independent propulsion system, allowing it to remain submerged for longer periods of time without the need to surface and recharge batteries. The boat's AIP system uses hydrogen fuel-cell technology, which is more efficient, quieter and environmentally friendly than traditional diesel engines.

One of the key features of the Type 212CD is its unusual stealthy diamond-

shaped hull, designed to offer target echo strength (TES) reduction, while deflecting active sonar emissions from ASW vessels. The design features non-magnetic steel architecture, rendering the vessel undetectable to current and future magnetic anomaly detection (MAD) systems.

New command and control systems will enable the analysis of much larger amounts of data gathered by the boat's advanced sensor suite. Unlike the design on which it is based, the submarine does not have a traditional hull-penetrating periscope – instead it will have two optronic masts as well as a panoramic surveillance system, the Kongsberg SA9510S MKII Mine Avoidance and Navigation Sonar, as well as echo sounders for navigation.

The design has four 533mm/21in torpedo tubes for lightweight and heavyweight torpedoes, while the German version will also be armed with the IDAS medium-range air defence missile.

Type 212CD		
Displacement: 2,500 tonnes/2,460 tons (surfaced)		
Length: 73m/239ft 6in		
Beam: 10m/32ft 10in		
Draught: 7m/23ft		
Armament: 4 x 533mm/21in torpedo tubes, DM2A4 air defence missiles		
Propulsion: 2 MTU diesel and AIP propulsion		
Speed: 20 knots (submerged)		
Complement: Unknown		

Victoria-class SSK

Having had years of service from their fleet of British diesel-electric Oberon-class submarines during unrelenting anti-submarine warfare activities in the North Atlantic, the Royal Canadian Navy switched to another British boat for their new era of post-Cold War operations. They continued in the diesel mode with the purchase of four boats from the Royal Navy's Upholder class. These were built in the 1980s and 90s, but were withdrawn from UK service following a defence review in 1994.

The Canadians renamed the group as the Victoria class, and recommissioning work on the first, *Victoria*, was completed in December 2000. The remaining three were to be progressively taken into service by the end of 2004.

ABOVE: The Canadian *Corner Brook*, one of the highly regarded Victoria class, also known as the Type 2400, which are the renamed boats of the British Upholder class. These originally made their appearance in the late 1970s as a back-up to the UK nuclear attack submarines and are still regarded as among the best diesel-electric boats in the world. BELOW: A view of the Victoria class, which supports maritime law-enforcement, anti-narcotics and smuggling ops, as well as domestic and international operations.

However, the Canadians' delight on obtaining these boats was marred after work on the last of the four, HMCS *Chicoutimi*, was completed in September 2004. The vessel was handed over to the Canadian Navy at Faslane Naval Base, Scotland, in October 2004, but while sailing home to its base in Halifax,

Nova Scotia, a serious electrical fire broke out on the vessel, in which one Canadian crew member died and others were seriously affected by the heat and smoke.

The submarine was foundering when a Royal Navy Type 23 frigate, HMS *Montrose*, arrived to take the boat under tow back to Faslane. Subsequently, *Chicoutimi* was loaded on to a Norwegian sealift vessel in January 2005, bound for Halifax for repairs. In the meantime, the Canadians confined the Victoria class to port pending an inquiry. Some modifications were carried out and *Victoria* and *Windsor* were cleared for duty. The others would follow later.

Despite a difficult, decade-long period of introduction to service, the Canadian government states that these submarines "..form the core of the Royal Canadian Navy's underwater surveillance capabilities. Covert, well-armed, and capable of patrolling vast distances, these submarines provide support to maritime law-enforcement in investigating narcotics trafficking, smuggling, and polluting cases, as well as conducting domestic and international operations."

With no sign of a replacement, the Canadian government has commmitted to modernizing the Victoria class to ensure it remains in service into the late 2030s.

ABOVE: **HMCS *Victoria*, leader of the class, was assigned to operate in the Maritime Forces Pacific (MARPAC) fleet, which has a base at Esquimalt, near Victoria, in British Columbia. The hull is of a classic teardrop design, and the main sail houses a five-man lockout chamber.** BELOW: **An internal cutaway showing the compartmentalized layout of the Victoria submarines.**

LEFT: **An alternative view of *Corner Brook*, patrol-ready. She has an endurance of 54 days, and a cruising capability of 12 knots surfaced and 20 knots submerged. In snorting mode, at periscope depth, the range at an 8-knot snorting speed is 12,872km/ 8,000 miles.**

Victoria-class SSK

Displacement: 2,150 tonnes/2,116 tons (surfaced); 2,416 tonnes/2,377.8 tons (submerged)
Length: 70.3m/230ft 8in
Beam: 7.6m/24ft 11in
Armament: 6 x 533mm/21in tubes, 18 x Gould Mk 48 heavyweight torpedoes
Propulsion: 2 x Paxman Valenta 16SZ diesel engines, 2.7mW/3620.8hp each; 2 x 2.5mW/3352.6hp Alsthom alternators; Alsthom motor, 4mW/5364.1hp
Speed: 12 knots (surfaced); 20 knots (dived)
Complement: 48 crew

LEFT AND ABOVE: **The Yushio class were the mainstay of the Japanese fleet in the 1970s, first with the Type 575 and later with Type 576, a succession that has provided excellent vessels for the maintenance of that nation's highly efficient submarine force. These have been regularly updated and improved, including the ability to launch the Harpoon missile.**

Yushio-class SSK

From the late 1960s, the Japanese maintained a submarine force of around 16 boats, and this remained pretty much the norm through the rest of the century. In that time, they acknowledged and experimented with improving designs and technology but, perhaps not unnaturally, were not tempted by the nuclear-powered creations of other nations. As a result they have remained aligned to the diesel-electric ideal and have produced some fine boats in the process. One of the largest was the Yushio class, introduced in 1975 and of the teardrop design.

They were produced over a number of years, and numerous refinements and upgrades were added as the class progressed through the building of six boats. This was clearly demonstrated by the fact that the cost of the first boat was 23,724,000,000 Yen, while the final one cost 31,950,000,000 Yen.

Improvements included the ability to launch the Harpoon missile, and in later units the control navigation system was improved. Quietening measures included a novel solution of fitting a propeller of seven blades rather than five for the screw. Overall, the wide-ranging modernizations meant an increase of displacement of almost 406 tonnes/ 400 tons, compared with the earliest versions. The Yushio boats which came in to service through the 1970s and 80s remained in commission until towards the end of the century, when they were gradually transferred to training duties.

ABOVE: **Broaching, or breaking, the surface at some speed is a spectacular event, as demonstrated here by one of the Yushio boats.**

Yushio-class SSK

Displacement: 2,463 tonnes/2,424.1 tons (surfaced); 2, 830 tonnes/2,785.3 tons (submerged)
Length: 76m/249ft 4in
Beam: 9.9m/32ft 6in
Armament: 6 x HU-603 torpedo tubes; (dual use with Harpoon USM)
Propulsion: 2,535.4kW/3,400hp diesel; 5369kW/7,200hp electric
Speed: 12 knots (surfaced); 20 knots (dived)
Complement: 75 crew

LEFT: *Asashio*, the last ship of the Harushio class, was transferred to the training wing of the Japanese Navy with the designation of TSS rather than SS. This is in accordance with Japan's practice of providing boats for that purpose, which are equipped with the latest technology and therefore enable a high level of training for new recruits in a modern environment.

Harushio class

Displacement: 2,410 tonnes/2,371.9 tons (surfaced); 2,460 tonnes/2,421.1 tons (submerged)
Length: 77m/252ft 7in
Beam: 10m/32ft 10in
Armament: 6 x HU-603 torpedo tubes, Type 89 torpedo (dual use with Harpoon USM)
Propulsion: 2 x Kawasaki 12V25/25S diesel engines, 5,369kW/7,200hp
Speed: 12 knots (surfaced); 20 knots (dived)
Complement: 75 crew

Harushio class

An improved and slightly larger version of the *Yushio*, from which it was derived, the *Harushio* was easily recognizable by a projecting fin over the countermeasure intelligence sonar. The class, all retired by 2017, was built with a high-strength steel pressure-resistant boat hull for an increased operating depth thought to be in excess of 300m/984ft, although the Japanese Navy makes a point of keeping such details to itself. The rows of noughts on the budget figures again looks mind-boggling to those in the West without a calculator to hand. The budget for the Harushio boats was estimated at 38,673,000,000 Yen (equivalent to about $333 million), but construction expenses increased substantially, to 44,266,000,000 Yen (about $381 million).

The last of the six boats in this class, the *Asashio*, initiated a new practice introduced by the Japanese Maritime Self Defence Force. The *Asashio* was redesignated as a training boat and was specially modified for the role. This rather sensible move was to give the new recruits the experience of a modern boat, with modern techniques and equipment, rather than providing training experience in older ships where virtually every aspect of submarine life might well be so old as to be unrecognizable in a modern boat. Instead, the hierarchy decreed that where possible training should henceforth be carried out in boats with equipment as near as possible to newly built submarines.

LEFT: SS *Narushio* of the Oyashio class, a series that saw a departure from what has become the traditional teardrop hull form, opting instead for what is known as a "leaf coil" hull shape. A number of the class have already been the subjects of service-life extension work.

Oyashio-class SSK

Displacement: 2,706 tonnes/2,663.3 tons (surfaced); 2,986 tonnes/2,938.8 tons (submerged)
Length: 82m/269ft
Beam: 8.9m/29ft 2in
Armament: 6 x 533mm/21in tubes, (4 x bow, 2 x stern); 24 x stn Atlas Elektronik DM2A4 torpedoes
Propulsion: 2 x Kawasaki 12V25/25S diesel engines, 5369kW/7,200hp
Speed: 12 knots (surfaced); 20 knots (dived)
Complement: 68 crew

Oyashio-class SSK

The Oyashio class of eleven boats, the most powerful that Japan has built since the war, is something of a departure from previous submarine stock in that her naval designers in the Maritime Self Defence Force this time opted not for the classic teardrop hull but a form called the leaf coil type. It has a revolutionary form of hull, part single, part double, the whole having been produced from an unusual design approach, in which the arrangement of the sensors was considered first and the layout of the entire boat was built around that concept. Previously the sonar was mounted in the bow, but this new model designates the entire hull as the sensor, equipped with a sonar arrangement on the hull to provide improved detection efficiency.

A state-of-the-art combat intelligence processing system brings the boat's attack capability to one of high order. Further, the positioning of the torpedo tubes differs from conventional types, with the bow tube placement decided after the arrangement of the sensor. The acoustic stealth efficiency of the hull is improved by installing sound-absorbing rubber tiles. There is also a relatively small crew, compared with submarines of a similar size run by other countries. However, such technology does not come cheap — the Oyashio-class submarines cost over half a billion dollars each.

Collins-class SSK

Like Canada, Australia had relied on the British Oberons for many years, until finally they were forced to invest in new boats to replace their ageing workhorses. With a workload that alternates between coastal patrols and domestic surveillance work to long endurance operations in the Pacific, the Indian Ocean and the Antarctic, there were numerous design requirements to be considered. In the end, the Australian Government approved the purchase of six Collins-class Type 471 diesel-electric boats, designed by Swedish shipbuilders Kockums especially for the Royal Australian Navy.

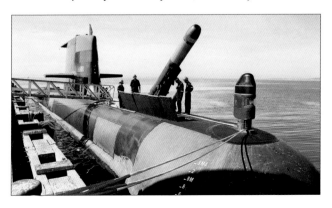

ABOVE: **Mostly home grown, the impressive Type 471 class, led by HMAS** *Collins*, **began the commissioning process in 1996, and delivery of six submarines was completed by 2003. Armaments include the Boeing Sub-Harpoon anti-ship missile.** BELOW LEFT: **HMAS** *Waller* **takes on its load, which now includes up to 22 Mk 48 Mod 4 heavyweight torpedoes.**

Construction was in part carried out in Sweden, although the bulk of the work was completed by the Australian Submarine Company of Adelaide. The first of class was commissioned in 1996 and the remainder were delivered by 2003. The lines were distinctive, with the single hull carrying a prominent sonar pod above the bows and a set of hydroplanes mounted halfway up the fin. However, in the years between the original design and final construction, certain elements of the boat were believed to have been overtaken by modern technology coming on stream at an ever more rapid pace, and there were problems that had to be attended to before they could become fully operational.

A Government inquiry initiated an upgrade programme to the weapon systems, sonar and noise reduction, and this was carried out in 2004. The boats are now subjected to a rigorous maintenance cycle that not only covers basic overhauls and

LEFT: **With a large crowd of shipyard workers looking on, a Collins boats is rolled out for the final fitting out process at the Australian Submarine Corporation in Adelaide.** ABOVE: **Under way and looking good.** BELOW: **HMAS** *Sheean*, **fifth of the Collins boats, commissioned in 2000.**

refits but also the inclusion of any new technology or significant improvements as part of the Collins Continuous Improvement Program.

The Collins fleet is based at Fleet Base West (HMAS Stirling) in Western Australia and their primary function is to patrol Australia's territorial waters and those of nations nearby. The boats gather intelligence using sophisticated electronic sensors and can also transport, deploy and extract special forces when required. The class has repeatedly distinguished itself in joint US Navy exercises.

The class will be replaced in Australian service by all-new nuclear-powered boats to be built in Australia with US and UK support as part of the AUKUS trilateral security pact between Australia, UK and US announced in 2021.

Collins-class SSK

Displacement: 3,002 tonnes/2,954.6 tons (surfaced); 3,300 tonnes/3,247.9 tons (submerged)
Length: 78m/255ft 11in
Beam: 8m/26ft 3in
Armament: 6 x 533mm/21in tubes for Harpoon missiles and Gould Mk 48 torpedoes – total of 22 carried or up to 44 mines in place of torpedoes
Propulsion: 3 x V18B/14 diesel engines, 1,475kW/1,978hp each
Speed: 10 knots (surfaced); 20 knots (dived)
Complement: 42 crew

Sauro-class SSK

For a time, the Sauro class of eight diesel-electric boats consituted the entire submarine fleet of the Italian Navy although, as noted above, the Italian and German governments reached agreement for the supply of two new Type 212As as successors. The Sauros were built in the shipyards of Fincantieri of Monfalcone and replaced the ageing Toti class, which was not only worn out, but had a bad reputation among the crews for cramped conditions. The Sauro dated back to 1967, when the first two were ordered, but financial constraints forced the Italian government to cancel and re-order in the 1970s. Even then, completion was delayed by defective batteries, which were subsequently replaced with Swedish units.

Once all of these problems had been resolved, the Sauros were delivered in four batches with modifications in size and updating as and when required. Subsequently eight submarines in three classes were built for the Italian submarine fleet over the following two decades, the last batch commissioned in 1993 under the name of the lead submarine *Primo Longobardo* having the advantage of more modern technology. In 2000 six of the eight boats began to go through the workshops again for further upgrades and refits to extend their life further, the Italian Ministry of Defence having ruled that they must remain in service for the foreseeable future, given the expenditure already committed on the two new Type 212As. The upgrades included combat data and control systems, silencing measures and ship control systems.

The addition of a new weapons system with wire-guided torpedoes completed the modernization to provide both anti-ship and anti-submarine capabilities.

TOP AND ABOVE: **Between the *Nazario Sauro*, leader of the class built in 1980, and the *Gianfranco Gazzana Prairoggia*, which slipped down the launch-way in 1995, numerous upgrades and improvements were applauded by submariners and analysts alike.**

The improvements were adjudged to be "remarkable" among the senior officers of the boats, with the addition of cutting-edge instruments. The upgrades to the six boats, combined with the two more modern versions, thus gave Italy an as-good-as-new fleet. At the time of writing, the most recently commissioned four of the class remain in service while the earlier four boats were decommissioned between 2002 and 2010.

LEFT: **The Sauro class benefits from an ongoing process of improvements including new combat data and control systems for the late-build examples of the Sauro class.**

Sauro-class SSK

Displacement: 1,452 tonnes/1,429 tons (surfaced); 1,635 tonnes/1,609 tons (submerged)
Length: 64.36m/211ft 2in
Beam: 6.83m/22ft 5in
Armament: 6 x 533mm/21in tubes, 12 x torpedoes
Propulsion: 3 x diesel engines, 3,184kW/4,270shp; 1 x electric motor, 2,394kW/3,210shp
Speed: 11 knots (surfaced); 20 knots (dived)
Complement: 55 crew

LEFT AND BELOW: **The
Salvatore Todaro,
based on the German
Type 212A but built
under licence in Italy,
was commissioned in
2005, and her sister
Sciré followed in
2007.**

Salvatore Todaro-class SSK

This Italian class of initially two diesel-electric boats, the first of which was commissioned in 2005, represents the full extent of the Italian Navy's spending on its submarine fleet for the foreseeable future, apart from the general maintenance and upgrading costs of its existing boats.

The new class took the name of the first built, *Salvatore Todaro*, and is based on the German Type 212A, and the boats are built under licence by the Italians at the Fincantieri shipbuilders at their Monfalcone yards. Although the overall specifications are similar, there are a number of significant differences in the final Italian version compared with that of the German builder. The Italians, for example, ordered a re-design of the interiors to allow for additional escape systems to be installed.

The German design allowed for individual escape mechanisms, whereas the Italians have installed a more efficient system allowing for collective rather than individual escape. Elsewhere, however, the state-of-the-art technology that has impressed so many remains unchanged from the original German manifesto. The boats are also considered ideal for the Italians' principal area of operations around the Mediterranean and Adriatic, both now requiring round-the-clock naval patrols in view of the amount of illegal traffic reaching Italian shores, in terms of criminal activity in drugs, contraband and people-smuggling.

LEFT: **A cutaway
illustration of the
Italian version of
the Type 212A.**

Salvatore Todaro-class SSK

Displacement: 1,610 tonnes/1,584.6 tons (surfaced); 1,830 tonnes/1,801.1 tons (submerged)
Length: 57m/187ft
Beam: 7m/23ft
Armament: 6 x 533mm/21in tubes, 24 x stn Atlas Electronik DM2A4 torpedoes
Propulsion: Diesel-electric AIP, 3,164kW/4,243shp
Speed: 12 knots (surfaced); 20 knots (dived)
Complement: 24 crew

Delfin-class SSK

The Spanish Navy has maintained a modest submarine force for over 30 years, effectively patrolling coastal waters. They are not and never have been really interested in the serious end of submarine warfare with all the responsibilities and finance that such an undertaking entails. However, they have participated fully with NATO in providing port facilities for the Atlantic patrols of American boats. For many years, theirs has been a more domestic requirement that falls within the general auspices of guarding shores. However, in recent times in which few European nations have escaped infiltration by terrorist cells, the Spanish along with others have been reconsidering their commitment to submarines.

For years, the Spanish Navy has relied on its good relationship with the French to provide submarines, and since the early 1970s has been running Delphin-class boats, which are a derivative of the French-designed

Daphne class, dating back to the 1950s but built under licence in Spain. Other nations with a more aggressive submarine defence policy than Spain's also equipped with these boats at the time because they were attack submarines, and at 1,000 tonnes, were substantial boats. Nevertheless, they had their limitations, not least because of the age of the actual design.

Over the years, they have been refitted and upgraded, but not to any exceptional degree, and it is a credit to the Spanish Navy that they have kept the flag flying with boats that some would now regard as old tubs – indeed the more elderly ones did look just like that towards the end of their service. They were fairly straightforward boats when originally designed, even down to the somewhat old-fashioned notion of aft-facing torpedo tubes for protection while escaping. However, that hardly mattered for the type of role for which the boats were employed by Spain.

ABOVE: **Four boats of the Delphin class, a derivative of the French Daphne, have given the Spanish Navy years of service, but they have reached the point where they are no longer viable in terms of upgrading.**

Even so, however lightly used, the sheer weight of miles covered over such a lifespan took its toll, and reinforced by the need for more effective units to face the dangers of the times, the Spanish Navy began phasing out the Delphins in the 1990s, with the last one decommissioned in 2007.

Delfin-class SSK

Displacement: 943 tonnes/928.1 tons (surfaced); 1,043 tonnes/1,026.5 tons (submerged)
Length: 57.9m/190ft
Beam: 6.7m/22ft
Armament: 4 x 533mm/21in tubes, 12 x torpedoes or mines
Propulsion: Diesel-electric, 1,491.4kW/2,000shp
Speed: 13 knots (surfaced); 14 knots (dived)
Complement: 56 crew

Galerna-class SSK

Displacement: 1,582 tonnes/1,557 tons (surfaced); 1,767 tonnes/1,739 tons (submerged)
Length: 67.7m/222ft 1in
Beam: 6.8m/22ft 4in
Armament: 6 x 533mm/21in tubes; mixed parcel of torpedoes and Exocet missiles
Propulsion: Diesel-electric AIP, 3430.2kW/ 4,600shp
Speed: 18 knots (surfaced); 22 knots (dived)
Complement: 54 crew

Galerna-class SSK

The four boats of this class also became stalwarts of the Spanish submarine fleet as they came into service from 1984. Although two of the class were decommissioned in 2012 and 2020, the remaining two, *Galerna* (S 71) and *Tramontona* (S 74) remain in service in 2023. The class originated from the French Agosta design but again were built under licence by the Spanish ENB Cartagena Company with substantially modified electric systems. These became the Galerna class that were required specifically for coastal patrols and therefore lacked some of the deepwater specifications of the *Agosta*. The Spanish versions do, however, carry an impressive array of weapons with a heavy leaning towards littoral operations.

Scorpène-class SSK

Scorpène-class SSK

Displacement: 1,460 tonnes/1,436.9 tons (surfaced); 1,565 tonnes/1,540.3 tons (submerged)
Length: 66.4m/217ft 10in
Beam: 6.2m/20ft 4in
Armament: 6 x 533mm/21in tubes (bow), 18 x torpedoes; SSM; SUBTICS combat system
Propulsion: Diesel-electric AIP, 2,833.7kW/ 3,800shp
Speed: 18 knots (surfaced); 20 knots (dived)
Complement: 33 crew

The effects of terrorist infiltration into national territories has become a number one security issue with regard to policing borders and coastlines, and submarines have an increasing role to play in such issues, both in their national deployment and international responsibilities. Spain was already considering its course of action long before experiencing a major terrorist atrocity, and one of the decisions the government took, upon the recommendation of the Spanish Navy, was to immediately bolster its submarine force and bring it into the 21st century.

Once again, the Spanish turned to the French when the decision was made to replace the old Delphins. The result was an agreement to purchase five of the new Scorpène class jointly developed by French state-owned shipbuilding firm DCNS (formerly DCN) and Spanish shipbuilder Navantia (formerly Bazan, then Izar). Spain however cancelled its order in favour of S-80s. Nevertheless, the class has been produced for Chile (2 boats), Malaysia (2 boats), India (6 boats) and Brazil (4 boats).

Subtypes are the CM-2000 conventional diesel-electric version, the AM-2000 air-independent propulsion (AIP) derivative, a downsized CA-2000 coastal submarine, and the larger S-BR for Brazil. A number of other nations continue to express interest in the class.

LEFT AND BELOW: **Unlike the Vastergotland class that they succeeded, Sweden's new Sodermanland-class submarines are constructed to undertake missions in warmer and more saline waters than the familiar seas around the Swedish coastline. In replacing the refrigeration system, analysts have assumed it is destined to join international peacekeeping missions in warmer climes now that the Soviet threat has diminished.**

Sodermanland-class SSK

The hunter-killer reputation of Swedish submarines has been impressive, given that they have the task of operating in regions that brought them up close and personal with the operations of the Soviet submarine force during some of the periods of great intensity in the Cold War. The Sodermanland class, named after a Baltic Sea port, was introduced as Sweden's prime attack vessel from its launch in the mid-1980s and commissioned in the early 1990s. By that time, international tensions had eased somewhat, but Sweden continued with its submarine construction programme, which would see the introduction of some fine new boats over the next decade that would carry them forward well into the 21st century.

The Sodermanland class was an upgraded and improved version of the slightly earlier Vastergotland class first introduced in 1988, and the two models would operate side by side, although in time they would all be outshone by the new Gotland.

In fact, the final two boats of the Vastergotland class became the Sodermanland class by virtue of their relaunch after having been refitted with some of the latest technology and a propulsion system designed for the new Gotland class. This was a substantial undertaking that required the two boats to be sliced in two immediately aft of the tower and lengthened with the insertion of the Stirling AIP propulsion compartment, which added another 12m/39ft 4in to the length of the boat.

The section was built and completely outfitted prior to installation as a complete unit, creating the *Sodermanland* in 2003 and the *Ostermanland* in 2004. The two boats were also equipped and designed for international peacekeeping duties and received conversion of their filtration systems and cooling apparatus to operate in warmer and less saline waters.

Meanwhile, the sister submarines of the Vastergotland class, although overtaken by the technology of the latest Swedish boats, remained a very capable weapons platform. They were retained for operations in the region for which they were originally designed: the cold, deep theatres of the North Atlantic, the Baltic and the North Sea.

LEFT: **The array of retractable antennae on the sail of the Sodermanland boats.**

Sodermanland

Displacement: 1,385 tonnes/1,363.1 tons (surfaced); 1, 446 tonnes/1,423.1 tons (submerged)
Length: 60.5m/198ft 6in
Beam: 6.1m/20ft
Armament: 6 x 533mm/21in tubes (bow); 3 x 406mm/16in tubes (aft); mixed package of Type 613 heavy torpedoes, Type 431/451 lightweight torpedoes and SSM
Propulsion: Stirling AIP, 1,342.3kW/1,800shp
Speed: 20 knots (surfaced); 24 knots (dived)
Complement: 30 crew

Gotland-class (Type A19) SSK

Sweden's Gotland-class of three diesel-electric submarines, commissioned in the late 1990s, have an excellent reputation and are noted for the fact that they are packed with first-class home-grown electronics and technology from the likes of Saab Industries, although the shipbuilder, Kockums, is actually part of the German HDW conglomerate.

The combined input of up-to-the-minute operational systems was doubtless one of the reasons why the US Navy selected the *Gotland* to take part in a modern "battle" scenario. In November 2004, the Swedish Government gave the go-ahead for the first of class and her crew to be leased to the Americans for a year to take part in naval exercises. *Gotland* arrived at the San Diego Naval Air Station in June 2005 to operate as part of the "enemy" force pitted against US submarines and surface vessels. It took

a number of photographs of the aircraft carrier USS *Ronald Reagan*, meaning that technically it could have sunk it.

The Gotland-class boats were equipped with a combat management system known as 9SCS Mark 3 from Saabtech Vectronics, an extended version of which is used in Swedish surface vessels. The fire control system can control a number of torpedoes in the water simultaneously. The submarines are fitted with four 533mm/21in tubes and two 400mm/15.75in tubes. Type 613 heavy-weight anti-surface ship torpedoes, fired from the larger tubes, come with wire guidance and passive homing, delivering a warhead of 240kg/529lb, while the smaller tubes fire the Saab Bofors Type 43 lightweight anti-submarine torpedo.

BELOW: **A cutaway illustration showing the internal layout of the *Gotland*.**

The Gotland boats also have the capacity to carry 48 mines externally fitted in a girdle arrangement. The Kockums V4-275R Stirling Air Independent Propulsion diesel engines provide an endurance of two weeks at a speed of 5 knots without snorting.

HSwMS *Gotland* and her sister ship HSwMS *Uppland* were first to receive mid-life upgrades and the MLU for HSwMS *Halland* was announced in 2022. The MLU included a series of platform and combat systems upgrades replicating the systems to be included on the new A26 submarines.

Gotland-class (Type A19) SSK

Displacement: 1,168 tonnes/1,149.6 tons (surfaced); 1,466 tonnes/1,442.8 tons (submerged)
Length: 61m/200ft 2in
Beam: 6m/19ft 8in
Armament: 4 x 533mm/21in tubes; 2 x 400mm/15.75in tubes; 16 x torpedoes; 48 x mines
Propulsion: 2 x MTU diesels; 2 x Kockums V4-275r air independent units
Speed: 11 knots (surfaced); 20 knots (dived)
Complement: 33 crew

Khalid-class SSK

The often tense political situation between Pakistan and India since the British pulled out in 1947 resulted in both sides arming themselves to the fullest extent, each with a counterweight to the other's armoury. Suppliers of such machinery seemed unconcerned as to their potential use, and both nations built up an effective naval force which included submarines.

In this case the supplier was DCN, makers of the popular Agosta class in service with several smaller navies around the world. Two boats were supplied in the late 1970s, apparently part of an order originally intended for South Africa but which was diverted to Pakistan instead. The boats received an extensive refit a decade later, with the addition of the famed Exocet missile, which represented a serious threat to the Indian Navy. More potent, however, was the agreement in the mid-1990s for

DCN to supply three of the new Agosta 90B-class boats to Pakistan, the first built at DCN's Cherbourg shipyard during the late 1990s for commissioning in time for the new century. The remaining two were to be assembled at the Pakistani Naval Dockyard at Karachi with the assistance of French engineers – both boats were in service by 2004. This proved to be a particularly useful agreement for the Pakistanis, both in regard to the government's ambitions to increase the nation's submarine capability as well as expanding its own industrial base in shipbuilding technology.

However, the latter objective hit a serious snag. Completion of the third submarine at Karachi was halted by a terrorist attack in 2002 in which more than 40 workers were killed or injured. Eleven French engineers were among the fatalities. The damage and subsequent delay meant that the third

ABOVE LEFT AND ABOVE: **In settling a deal with the French, the Pakistani Navy has acquired these classic SSKs of proven ability and whose weaponry consists of torpedoes, mines and the renowned anti-ship SM-39 Exocet missiles. The submarine is fitted with the most modern command and control systems and can dive below 300m/984ft.**

boat was not in service until 2006, and a programme of further modernization of earlier models was instigated.

In 2018 Turkish firm STM secured the contract for mid-life upgrades to the three submarines of class, the *Khalid* (S137), the *Saad* (S138), and *Hamza* (S139). The upgrades concerned the sonar suite, periscope systems, command and control systems, radar and electronic support systems, as well as modifications on the pressure hull.

ABOVE: **It is no wonder that it is with national pride the Pakistani Navy displays their latest acquisition, a boat they call the *Khalid*, which became the star of their submarine force and also the model for its shipbuilders to manufacture.**

Khalid-class SSK

Displacement: 1,486 tonnes/1,462.5 tons (surfaced); 1,732 tonnes/1,707.6 tons (submerged)
Length: 67m/219ft 10in
Beam: 5.4m/17ft 9in
Armament: 6 x 533mm/21in tubes, mixed parcel F17 Mod 2/Exocet SM39 submarine-launched anti-ship missiles
Propulsion: Diesel-electric, 2,684.5kW/3,600hp
Speed: 15 knots (surfaced); 17 knots (dived)
Complement: 36 crew

Sindhu-class SSK

Pakistani ambitions towards an effective submarine force were, of course, no match for their neighbours. Picking up from the naval tradition that the British brought to India, the newly-independent nation acquired substantial assets which became the foundations for what has kept it today among the world's top ten navies. Submarines were very much a part of that Indian force, especially in the purchase of ten diesel-powered Soviet Project 877 Kilo submarines, known in India as the EKM or Sindhu class.

They were built under a contract between the Russians and the Indian Ministry of Defence, with the last unit delivered to India in 2000, and all equipped with some well-proven electronics and modern weaponry. The final boat, for example, was fitted with the Klab ZM-54E (SS-N-27) anti-ship cruise missiles, with a range of 220km/ 137m. Of the ten boats, three have been decommissioned, and the rest have all been, or will be refitted, to extend their service life by a remarkable 35 years.

With a standard crew of 53 including 13 officers, the boats are today typically armed with Club-S cruise missiles, the Type 53-65 torpedoes, anti-submarine homing torpedoes or 24 mines in place of torpedoes.

Additionally, India bought four Type 209 diesel-electric submarines from Howaldtswerke Deutsche Werft (HDW) of Germany in the late 1980s and has then delved into the arena of nuclear-powered marine boats. In January 1988, her government reached an agreement with the Soviet Union to lease a nuclear-powered attack submarine of the 670A Skat series with eight Ametist (SS-N-7 Starbright) anti-ship missile launchers. In the Indian Navy, the submarine was re-christened *Chakra*, and was manned by a Russian crew to train Indian seamen. Upon expiration of the three-year leasing term in 1991, the submarine was returned to Russia and decommissioned from the Russian Navy.

However, India did not abandon the idea of a nuclear-powered fleet, and in 2004 laid down the lead boat in the Arihant class, an Indian-built nuclear powered ballistic missile submarine. Four of these powerful boats are planned – two have been commissioned – the 6,000 tonne/5,905 ton displacement INS *Arihant* (SSBN 80) and INS *Arighat* (SSBN81) – and another two of 7,000 tonne/6,889 ton displacement are under construction.

Sindhu-class SSK

Displacement: 2,180 tonnes/2,145.6 tons (surfaced); 2,400 tonnes/2,362.1 tons (submerged)
Length: 92m/301ft 10in
Beam: 8.6m/28ft 3in
Armament: 6 x 533mm/21in tubes (forward), 4 x 533mm/21in tubes (aft), 22 x torpedoes or 44 x mines; missile package
Propulsion: Diesel-electric; 2 x shafts, 3,952.2kW/5,300shp
Speed: 15.5 knots (surfaced); 19 knots (dived)
Complement: 75 crew

Walrus II class

The Royal Netherlands Navy has enjoyed a long love affair with submarines and so they should, given that their countryman Cornelius Drebbel played such a large part in bringing undersea boats into fruition. During World War I, they began the production of the K class built for service around the Dutch colonies, followed by the O (for *Onderzeeboot*) boats for coastal operations. There were a number of noteworthy developments, and especially significant was *O19*, regarded in many quarters as the first submarine class in the world to be equipped with a diesel "snort system" that was much copied later on. Post-war, the Dutch Royal Navy received the loan of a decommissioned member of the US *Balao*-class wartime submarines, *Icefish*. Following a refit to produce a Guppy configuration, she was rechristened *Walrus I* and saw many years of uninterrupted service. This was achieved under a post-war arrangement with the Americans called Mutual Defense Assistance in which a number of ageing US vessels were received

on loan by grateful European nations whose finances were tied up elsewhere, rebuilding the devastation of the war.

Upon her retirement, the name was continued with the introduction the Walrus II class, the diesel attack submarine that brought the Dutch Navy up to date with modern requirements in the 1980s, an event seriously delayed by a devastating fire in the first-of-class submarine during the latter stages of construction. Consequently, the lead boat had the embarrassment of being beaten into commissioning by the second of her class, *Zeeleeu II*. *Walrus II* was finally relaunched in April 1987, more than a decade after she was originally laid down. The Walrus II class replaced the ageing Dutch trio of the Zwardvis class, built between 1964 and 1972 and which gave good service over almost two decades.

In *Walrus II*, the Dutch had built a fast general-purpose boat, principally an attack submarine for operations in the Eastern Atlantic, the North Sea and the

ABOVE LEFT AND ABOVE: **Another relatively small but brilliant European submarine of strong pedigree is the Dutch Walrus II class, successor to the Zwaardvis. Although slightly larger, a high degree of automation has enabled a reduction in the crew from 67 to 49 men. They are popular submarines, especially with NATO who have used them extensively for operations, especially those involving special forces.** BELOW LEFT: **A profile and cutaway view of the *Walrus II*.**

Norwegian Sea, often under the auspices of NATO while participating in both exercises and active service roles. The Dutch – like the British – are dedicated users of their submarines in support of special forces operations and in intelligence-gathering in which the Walrus II class has excelled. Such is the value of the boats that two of the class will have their service life extended in the mid-2030s while a decision on a replacement is made.

Walrus II class

Displacement: 2,560 tonnes/2,519.6 tons (surfaced); 2,800 tonnes/2,755.8 tons (submerged)
Length: 67.7m/222ft 1in
Beam: 8.4m/27ft 7in
Armament: 6 x 533mm/21in tubes, 12 x torpedoes; mines
Propulsion: Diesel-electric, 4623.3kW/6,200shp
Speed: 18 knots (surfaced); 21 knots (dived)
Complement: 33 crew

Type 209-class SSK

This popular German-designed submarine that first appeared in the 1970s remains the mainstay of small submarine forces around the world. Of 61 examples completed mainly by Howaldtswerke Deutsche Werft (HDW) at Kiel, 58 remain in service around the word at the time of writing.

The Brazilian Navy, for example, won government approval to upgrade its submarine force in the late 1980s, initially taking delivery of the German-built Type 209 but with agreement from the supplier to continue indigenous manufacture in their own shipyards, all taking the name of the first-of-class submarine, *Tupi*. This was built in HDW shipyards in Germany and commissioned into the Brazilian Navy in 1989. Thereafter, three more boats of the class were built at the Arsenal de Marinha naval shipyard in Rio de Janeiro over the next ten years. The Brazilian Navy then contracted to buy a further boat

of the improved Type 204/1400 series. They came with the latest in electronics suites, including two Mod 76 periscopes supplied by Kollmorgen, the Calypso III I-band navigation radar from Thales, and the submarine's hull-mounted sonar, the CSU-83/1, from STN Atlas Electronik. Elsewhere in South America, and across the globe, Type 209 was appearing as the principal brand for a diverse range of nations and requirements.

Over two decades, orders were placed for boats with a variety of mission profiles for operations in the Atlantic, the Caribbean, the Indian Ocean and the Far East. Virtually every customer required their own design in terms of internal arrangements and equipment to meet the needs of the varying tasks, range, diving depth and climate. These requirements led to the Type 209 being produced in five series, and, by the 2020s, the following nations were equipped with

ABOVE LEFT AND ABOVE: **The theme of the general-purpose boat re-appears in various parts of the world, and is instrumental in recording the submarine acquisitions of the Brazilian Navy. It relies on the German 209, which has been exported to more than a dozen nations around the globe. In Brazil, it is known as the Tupi class.**

209s: Argentina (2 submarines, Type 209/1200), Peru (6, Type 209/1200, 209/1100), Colombia (2, Type 209/1200), Venezuela (2, Type 209/1300), Ecuador (2, Type 209/1300), Indonesia (4, Type 209/1300, 209/1400), Chile (2, Type 209/1400), India (4, Type 209/1500), Brazil (5, Type 209/1400), South Korea (9, Type 209/1200), Turkey (6, Type 209/1200, 4, Type 209/1400), and Greece (4, Type 209/1100, 4, Type 209/1200), Egypt, (4, Type 209/1400), South Africa (3, Type 209/1400), and Turkey 9 (14, Type 209/1200, Type 209/1400).

LEFT: **The Type 209 diesel-electric became one of the world's most popular submarines in the 1960s, and remains so into the 21st century. It is pictured here in Chile where, like in Brazil and several other South American nations, the navy has long relied on the German boats.**

Brazilian Tupi class (Type 109/1400)

Displacement: 1,462 tonnes/1,438.9 tons (surfaced); 1,560 tonnes/1,535.4 tons (submerged)
Length: 61m/200ft 2in
Beam: 6.2m/20ft 4in
Armament: 8 x 533mm/ 21in tubes, 14 x torpedoes/mines
Propulsion: Diesel-electric, 1789.7kW/2,400shp and 2610kW/3,500shp
Speed: 13 knots (surfaced); 22 knots (dived)
Complement: 33 crew

LEFT: **The Norwegian Ula-class boats are recognized as being among the most silent and manoeuvrable submarines in the world, which when combined with their relatively small size, makes them difficult to detect from surface vessels and ideal for operations in coastal areas and intelligence work.** ABOVE: **Systems operatives aboard the *Ula*.**

Ula-class SSK

For almost 40 years, Norway was precariously placed in the midst of Cold War activity as the Soviet Union transformed the Kola peninsula into a base for its formidable Northern Fleet, which at its height consisted of more than 150 nuclear-powered and nuclear-armed submarines and a similar number of surface vessels. Once described as the most complex and concentrated naval base in history, this vast array of boats needed to traverse the Norwegian Sea to reach the Atlantic Ocean.

Norway was therefore in a front-line position in the event of conflagration, and from the late 1970s a series of agreements involving allied support for reinforcing the defence of northern Norway were put in place and constantly reviewed along with a massive conglomeration of early-warning systems, both on land and at sea.

Radar stations in Norway, Iceland and Greenland continually oversaw the whole area while permanent listening devices for the purpose of monitoring the movement of the Soviet submarines were placed at strategic points under the Norwegian Sea, and NATO's Standing Force, Atlantic took responsibility for sea patrols. In the event of military action, allied reinforcements were on a permanent ready-to-move footing through Allied Command Europe under the Rapid Reinforcement Plan established in 1982.

So immense was the weight of submarine forces pitted against each other in this era of incredible tension that any serious involvement was simply beyond the capability of such a small nation. However, the Royal Norwegian Navy has maintained an efficient

submarine force which latterly consisted of six improved Kobben-class and six Ula-class submarines. Both classes were no more than patrol boats designed for littoral operations. The Royal Norwegian Navy, nevertheless, played a full part both in the efforts of self-protection and by involvement in the wider brief of supporting NATO operations and exercises.

The Norwegians, however, were always well aware of the reality that, in the event of war, their role could only be that of a lesser participant alongside their NATO allies, to which end the bulk of their training and operational activity was geared. Having said that, there is no denying that the Ula class was especially effective in intelligence gathering and had the ability to lay mines or attack the opposing forces if the event ever arose.

LEFT: **Norway played a vital role in NATO security exercises during the Cold War, and continues to. The class' life is being extended through to the end of the 2030s.**

Ula-class SSK

Displacement: 1,150 tonnes/1,131.8 tons (surfaced); 1,350 tonnes/1,328.7 tons (submerged)
Length: 59m/193ft 7in
Beam: 5.4m/17ft 9in
Armament: 4 x 533mm/21in tubes, 12 x torpedoes/mines
Propulsion: Diesel-electric, 1,416.8kW/1,900shp
Speed: 18 knots (surfaced); 23 knots (dived)
Complement: 21 crew

LEFT AND ABOVE: **The Taiwanese Hai Hu *Sea Tiger*
immaculately turned out, as are the crew lining
the deck, but behind this impressive façade is
a submarine service deeply concerned about
its future.** ABOVE: **Another of the Taiwanese boats,
Sea Dragon of the Dutch-built Hai Lung class.**

Hai Hu/Hai Lung class

The government of Taiwan has long been attempting to put together a viable submarine force to provide some protection from the ambitions of China to bring the nation back into the fold. In 2001, President George W. Bush said the United States was considering selling the Taiwanese eight diesel submarines for $4 billion, but internally there was much discussion about the implications with regard to China, which was clearly opposed to the idea. Sceptics pointed out that the United States hadn't built a conventional submarine for more than 40 years. In the event, the US quote was far higher than Taiwan had anticipated because America would have had the boats built in foreign shipyards. In addition, most of the world's major submarine-building nations, including Germany, the Netherlands, Sweden and Australia, have also ruled out providing

Taiwan with submarines or the use of their designs for fear of antagonizing Beijing.

In the summer of 2005, the attempts were continuing. Taiwan's Minister of National Defence, Lee Jye, re-affirmed his nation's intention to acquire more submarines, warning that "China's Navy is building a force with a long range war capability that will pose a serious threat to Taiwan by 2020".

The Hai Lung (Sea Dragon) class was manufactured in the Netherlands for the Republic of China, and the *Hai Lung* and *Hai Hu* were commissioned in 1988 and 1987 respectively. They were based on the Dutch Zwaardvis-class of submarines, which itself was based on the US Barbel class. Other boats were planned but Chinese pressure on the Dutch government led to the collapse of the deal. A later deal for four more

boats was also quashed after renewed Chinese pressure. The Hai Lung boats have undergone regular upgrades and are expected to remain in service into the early 2030s.

The other two submarines in the Republic of China's service are the SS-791 *Hai Shih* (sea lion), and SS-792 ROCS *Hai Pao* (seal) – incredibly, these are World War II-vintage designs and were transferred from the US in the 1970s. With US support, Taiwan has been developing its Indigenous Defense Submarine (IDS) Program to develop and domestically construct a class of diesel-electric attack submarines for the Republic of China Navy. Eight submarines are to be built with a mid-2020s entry into service for the first boat.

LEFT: **In dry dock for running repairs and upgrades, one of Taiwan's remaining Hai Lung submarines. Although these vessels put on a brave front in the head-to-head with the Chinese, they do require attention to the problems associated with old age.**

Hai Hu class

Displacement: 2,360 tonnes/2,322.7 tons (surfaced); 2,660 tonnes/2,618 tons (submerged)
Length: 66.9m/219ft 6in
Beam: 8.4m/27ft 7in
Armament: 6 x 533mm/21in tubes, 10 x torpedoes; surface-to-surface missiles
Propulsion: Diesel-electric, 3,803kW/5,100shp
Speed: 17 knots (surfaced); 20 knots (dived)
Complement: 67 crew

Glossary

AA Anti-Aircraft (deck guns).

abaft Toward the stern of a boat.

ACINT Acoustic Intelligence.

acoustic Torpedo that detects its target by means of sound, and uses that sound to steer along its path.

active sonar The type of sonar most commonly referred to in movies about submarines, in which the "ping" sound is emitted and targets are detected by echolocation. There are disadvantages to the system, since it may also give away the position and identity of the transmitting platform, rendering it vulnerable to attack. Furthermore, false targets may arise from the transmissions. *See also* passive sonar.

aft Rear or the rear extremity.

after trim Ballast tank used to adjust a submarine's weight and tilting movement.

AIO Action Information Organization. A station in all modern submarines that receives inputs from the sonars and other equipment to formulate a tactical picture around the submarine and ultimately to perform Target Motion Analysis of activity within an area up to 241km/150 miles from submarine.

AIP Air-Independent Propulsion.

Aphrodite German anti-radar device which gave out reflecting impulses.

ASDIC British Anti-Submarine Detection Investigation Committee, 1917, whose initials were used for the name given to a device that detected the presence of submerged submarines.

ASSW Anti-Surface Ship Warfare.

ASW Anti-Submarine Warfare; Anti-Submarine Work.

awash When a submarine is in a position whereby the sea is flowing over the superstructure.

ballast tanks Located between the pressure hull and the outer hull, and saddle tanks within the torpedo room. These are blown to provide positive buoyancy when the submarine is surfaced and completely flooded to give neutral buoyancy when submerged.

battle surface Surfacing manoeuvre to ensure the boat arrives flat, or nearly flat enabling quick deployment of gun crews.

BdU *Befehlshaber der Unterseeboote*, Commander-in-Chief for German submarines, Karl Dönitz, 1939–45.

beam Breadth of a boat at its widest part, usually amidships.

bearing Defining a course from a particular point.

boiler Original US slang name for a submarine (as well as pigboat or sewer pipe).

Bold A device used by U-boats to confuse ASDIC.

boomer Ballistic missile submarine.

bow Forward end of a vessel.

bow, stern planes Guiding fins that determine the submarine's angle of dive and permit the submarine to stay at any desired depth under water.

broach Breaking through the surface and rising out of the water. Also known as porpoising.

bulkhead Internal partitions of a submarine to compartmentalize the various functions within the submarine; many early boats were of single-compartment design, within which every activity was conducted, including the calls of nature. Later, as water-tight bulkheads were introduced, they became vital to a damaged submarine's survival.

casing Outer skin of light plating which encloses the ballast tanks and pressure hull.

cavitation Visible tracks on the surface caused by a submarine propeller, a long-standing problem even when submerged and easily detectable either by sound devices or aerial reconnaissance.

Chidori Japanese anti-submarine vessel; a type of torpedo boat.

commission Point at which a new submarine officially enters service.

COMSUBLANT Commander, Submarine Forces, US Atlantic Fleet.

COMSUBPAC Commander, Submarine Forces, US Pacific Fleet.

conning tower Heavily armoured horizontal hull over the control room

and below the bridge, which developed into the control centre of all operations.

control room Usually amidships, the compartment housing all diving and communications controls as well the ship's gyrocompass and radio room.

crash dive Emergency dive by a submarine.

displacement Weight displaced either when floating or submerged in water, the former lighter than the latter.

DISSUB Distressed submarine.

Dräger Tauchretter Underwater escape apparatus for U-boat crewmen.

draught Vertical extension of a hull below the waterline.

DSRV Deep Submergence Rescue Vehicle.

echo sounder Navigation or position-finding device to determine depth by measuring the time taken for a pulse of high-frequency sound to reach the sea bed or a submerged object and for the echo to return.

escape hatch Hatch positioned for an escape from a stricken submarine.

escape pod Many new submarines are now equipped with small pods which can be used to evacuate some of the crew.

fan A spread of torpedoes.

FAT Fedapparat Torpedo, developed by Germany for U-boat attacks on convoys, the torpedo travelling in a predetermined straight line then zigzagged.

fin The conning tower of the submarine, which contains the masts.

fire control The operation of directing action against the enemy.

Flak Anti-aircraft gun

flood down To fill tanks until the decks are awash.

Foxer A British noisemaker towed behind ships to fool German acoustic torpedoes.

GNAT The name given by the Allies to the German T5 acoustic torpedo.

GUPPY The Greater Underwater Propulsion Power Program was launched in the US in 1945 to combine captured German technology with American developments. Since GUPPP didn't sound quite right, the third P was dropped and a Y added, to be named after the fish. To coincide with this development, all US submarines were for the time being named after undersea life.

head A somewhat complicated toilet on board submarines

hunter-killer Attack submarine, or (in US) anti-submarine operation by surface ships and/or air units to hunt out and destroy submarines.

hydrophone An underwater sound detection device.

Kriegsmarine **(KM)** The German Navy 1935–45.

littoral ops Using modern digital technology, modern submarines approach a coastline in shallow water to make a significant contribution to the intelligence collection effort prior to any subsequent maritime or land action.

masts Modern submarine masts carry a plethora of technology that covers many functions, including periscopes, navigation, radar, communications and electronic detection masts.

MCM Mine Counter-Measure groups have become the renewed focus of most submarine forces around the world, as terrorist threats to coastal waters and estuaries escalate. The latest equipment, such as Sonar 2193 (S2193) and NAUTIS3, employs mine-hunting sonar, utilizing state-of-the-art techniques to meet the emerging possibilities of modern mines.

NSRS NATO Submarine Rescue System, currently a small team based in Abbey Wood, Bristol, UK, managing a single international co-operative procurement project. The UK is acting as Host Nation on behalf of three participant nations, France, Norway and the UK.

nuclear reactor A sealed unit that is the source of power and electrical requirements on board modern nuclear submarines, and has a lifespan that can outlive the boat itself.

passive sonar The covert nature and long-range capability of the passive systems (as opposed to active sonar) made this system more popular for much of the second half of the 20th century. They pick up sound radiated (usually involuntarily) by the target. In this case, only one-way transmission is involved, and the system centres around the hydrophone array (*see* Towed Array Sonar). However, the advent of much quieter submarines brought a renewed interest in active sonar.

periscope (or scope) A tube-like optical instrument containing an arrangement of prisms, mirrors and lenses that enabled vision of the sea above while the submarine was submerged.

Poseidon Russian deep submergence rescue vehicle.

pressure hull The inner hull and conning tower, built to withstand sea pressure at a stipulated depth.

rudder Rudders and planes used to steer the submarine and as an aid to the diving and surfacing process, along with the flooding or emptying of ballast tanks.

SACCS Submarine Automated Communications Control System.

SAR Search and Rescue, defined as the use of aircraft, ships and submarines with specialized rescue teams and equipment to search for and rescue personnel in distress, noted for a most comprehensive radio fit to support multi-agency communications.

SARR Submarine Automated Radio Room.

screws Propellers.

scuttle Deliberately sinking a vessel.

SLAB Submarine Locator Acoustic Beacon, an electronic device used by submarines in distress, for emitting a repetitive sonic pulse underwater.

SLBM Submarine-Launched Ballistic Missile.

SLMM Submarine-Launched Mobile Mine.

sonar Sound Navigation and Ranging device for locating objects underwater by emitting vibrations similar to sound and measuring the time taken for those vibrations to bounce back from anything in their path. Originally, the US equivalent to British ASDIC.

SS The initials denoting conventionally powered submarines.

SSB Conventionally powered submarine that carries nuclear-tipped ballistic missiles.

SSBN Nuclear-powered submarine that carries nuclear ballistic missiles as its primary weapons system.

SSG A conventionally powered submarine that carries guided missiles as its primary means of attack.

SSGN Nuclear-powered submarine that carries guided missiles.

SSIXS Submarine Satellite Information Exchange System Surveillance. This modern technology enhances the classic capability of the submarine in surveillance of opposition forces and to monitor their operations and movements while remaining undetected. This surveillance can include underwater photography, sometimes of surface warships, which will almost certainly be unaware of the submarine's presence.

SSK Non-nuclear hunter-killer submarine, specifically designed to hunt other submarines rather than surface ships.

SSN Nuclear-powered submarine, also known as a Fast Attack Submarine. Primary tasks involve supporting SSBN submarines, anti-submarine and anti-ship warfare, surveillance/intelligence gathering, task group operations, land attack and special operations.

TCM Torpedo Counter Measures, an ongoing aspect of submarine warfare, which in the UK consists of a multi-discipline team whose purpose is to provide a comprehensive Torpedo Defence capability for the Royal Navy to counter current and future threats. All British submarines are being fitted with a defensive countermeasures system.

TLAM Tomahawk Land Attack Missile, in this context a submarine-launched, long-range precision-strike weapon designed to hit strategic targets with the minimum of collateral damage, capable of travelling subsonically at low or high altitude to deliver a 454kg/1,000lb warhead over a range of around 1,609km/1,000 miles with pinpoint accuracy.

torpedo room Used for the firing of torpedoes, although in modern times will control an armoury of wire-guided torpedoes, anti-ship missiles and cruise missiles.

Towed Array Sonar Used to listen to the target sounds. These arrays are towed behind the submarine and may be greater than 500m/1640ft long, usually in the form of a flexible, neutrally buoyant pipe, with many low-frequency passive sonars along its length.

trim Balancing of a submarine's weight and equilibrium underwater.

trim down Reducing buoyancy until the boat is running virtually awash.

Y Gun US anti-submarine gun used to launch depth charges.

Acknowledgements

Research for the images used to illustrate this book was carried out by Ted Nevill of TRH Pictures – Cody Images, which supplied the majority of the pictures.

The publisher and Ted Nevill would like to thank all those who contributed to this research and to the supply of pictures:

Alamy
ArtTech
BAE SYSTEMS
Chrysalis Images
Jeremy Collins
DCN
General Dynamics Electric Boat
Howaldtswerke-Deutsche Werft
Italian Navy
James Fisher Defence
Kockums
Naval Photographic Club and
  Dr Duncan Veasey
Norwegian Ministry of Defence
Photographic Section, Naval Historical
  Center, Washington, DC, USA
Robert Hunt Library
Royal Navy Submarine Museum
David Saw
Still Pictures, National Archives
  & Records Administration,
  College Park, Maryland, USA
US Navy
Wikimedia Images

Key to flags

For the specification boxes, the flag that was current at the time of the vessel's commissioning and service is shown.

 Australia

 Brazil

 Canada

 China

 France

 Germany: World War I

 Germany: World War II

 Germany: post-World War II

 India

 Italy: up to 1946

 Italy: modern

 Japan

 The Netherlands

 Norway

 Pakistan

 Spain

 Sweden

 Taiwan

 UK

 USA

 USSR

Index

269

This edition is published by
Lorenz Books
an imprint of Anness Publishing Ltd
info@anness.com
www.annesspublishing.com

© Anness Publishing Ltd 2023

Publisher: Joanna Lorenz
Editorial Director: Helen Sudell
Editorial: Felicity Forster
Cover Design: Nigel Partridge
Designer: Design Principals
Production Controller: Ben Worley

A CIP catalogue record for this book is available from the British Library.

PUBLISHER'S NOTE
Although the information in this book is believed to be accurate and true at the time of going to press, neither the authors nor the publisher can accept any legal responsibility or liability for any errors or omissions that may have been made.

NOTE: The nationality of each submarine is identified in the specification box by the national flag that was in use at the time of the vessel's commissioning and service.

Front cover: HMS *Astute*
Page 1: French Navy *Rubis*
Page 2: USS *John Warner*
Page 3: German Navy *Type 212A*
Endpapers: Canadian *Victoria*-class *Corner Brook* (front); British HMS *Vanguard* (back)